'Standing up for Scotland'

In memory of Nigel Smith,
1941–2020

'Standing up for Scotland'

Nationalist Unionism and Scottish Party Politics, 1884–2014

DAVID TORRANCE

EDINBURGH
University Press

Edinburgh University Press is one of the leading university presses in the UK. We publish academic books and journals in our selected subject areas across the humanities and social sciences, combining cutting-edge scholarship with high editorial and production values to produce academic works of lasting importance. For more information visit our website: edinburghuniversitypress.com

Edinburgh University Press Ltd
The Tun – Holyrood Road, 12(2f) Jackson's Entry, Edinburgh EH8 8PJ

First published in hardback by Edinburgh University Press 2020

Typeset in 10/13 Giovanni by
IDSUK (DataConnection) Ltd, and
printed and bound by CPI Group (UK) Ltd,
Croydon, CR0 4YY

A CIP record for this book is available from the British Library

ISBN 978 1 4744 4781 2 (hardback)
ISBN 978 1 4744 4782 9 (paperback)
ISBN 978 1 4744 4783 6 (webready PDF)
ISBN 978 1 4744 4784 3 (epub)

CONTENTS

Acknowledgements / vi

ONE / Prelude / 1

TWO / Nationalist Unionism / 6

THREE / 'Every Scotsman Should Be a Scottish Nationalist' / 24

FOUR / 'Scottish Control of Scottish Affairs' / 48

FIVE / Scottish (Conservative and) Unionist Party: Rise and Fall / 71

SIX / The Liberals and 'Scottish Self-Government' / 96

SEVEN / The Scottish Labour Party and 'Crypto-Nationalism' / 121

EIGHT / The SNP and 'Five Continuing Unions' / 148

NINE / 'The Fair Claims of Wales' / 168

TEN / Northern Ireland and 'Ulster Nationalism' / 186

ELEVEN / Conclusion / 202

Endnotes / 220
Bibliography / 228
Index / 251

ACKNOWLEDGEMENTS

This is my first full-length academic publication, so I have accumulated a number of debts. Jen Daly at EUP agreed to consider publishing 'Standing up for Scotland' even before I had submitted my PhD, which was guided to completion by the good Drs Murray Leith and Duncan Sim at the University of the West of Scotland (only about 30 per cent of this book, however, is derived from that thesis). Murray also offered helpful comments on the 'Nationalist unionism' chapter, as did Professor Colin Kidd (St Andrews). Dr James Kennedy (Edinburgh) and Dr Willis Pickard gave helpful feedback on Chapter 6 (on the Scottish Liberals); Dr Ewan Gibbs (UWS) on Chapter 7 (Scottish Labour); Dr Peter Lynch (Stirling) on Chapter 8 (the SNP); Professor Richard Wyn Jones (Cardiff), Dr Sam Blaxland (Swansea) and Dr Adam Evans (House of Commons) on Chapter 9 (Wales); and Professor Graham Walker (Queen's University, Belfast) on Chapter 10 (Northern Ireland). I want to record my gratitude to them all.

Dr David Torrance
Walthamstow, September 2019

ONE

Prelude

On 16 January 1884, under the auspices of the Convention of Royal Burghs of Scotland,[1] hundreds of people made their way into Edinburgh's Free Church Assembly Hall to take part in a 'national' meeting regarding the governance of Scotland. At just after 1 p.m., the Marquis of Lothian arrived and was induced to take the chair. To his right sat Arthur James Balfour, and to his left Lord Balfour of Burleigh. Sitting close by as an observer was the young Earl of Dalhousie. Most were Conservatives, Dalhousie a Liberal.

Speaker after speaker lamented the handling of Scottish business at Westminster, while Lord Lothian summed up the views of many by stating that

> They recognised the great blessings which had accrued to Scotland and England from the Union, and they loyally abided by the terms of the Union – (cheers) – but they wanted to assure for themselves for the future – what their forefathers in signing the Treaty of Union had assured to them – that Scottish business should be managed independently, to a certain extent, of English business. (Cheers.) While they wanted more union, they objected to anything in the shape of absorption. (Cheers.)

The Earl of Aberdeen believed that if the meeting's proposals to improve 'the inner circle of Scottish government' were carried out, then 'the grand system of the British Empire would also be improved'. The Rev. Dr McGregor added that no 'sensible person' could wish to see Scotland 'denationalised'; its 'ancient' national institutions 'thrown overboard, even when there was no storm'. Provost Wilson of Greenock, meanwhile, was proud that 'national aspirations beat as strongly in the hearts of leading Conservatives as in the bosoms of the most fiery and rampant Radicals'.

Others were more cautious. The future Conservative Party leader, prime minister and foreign secretary, the languid A. J. Balfour, raised an objection he had heard expressed by 'true Scotsmen and patriots':

> They had said – Are you not by this movement emphasising the difference between England and Scotland, and initiating a movement which after all might end in something not unlike Home Rule. With the spirit of the objection he heartily agreed he should absolutely refuse, so far as he was concerned, to move a single step in a direction which should in any way sever the connection which had so long existed between the two countries for their mutual benefit.

Nevertheless, even Balfour conceded that Scotland 'had business which was distinct from English business – distinct by a different system of laws, of customs, and manners'. The Rev. Dr Walter C. Smith added later that it was 'not separation of any kind that they wanted', merely that Scottish affairs, hitherto 'largely neglected, should get due attention from Parliament' (CRBS 1884: 12–40). The only dissenting voice was that of the Earl of Wemyss, who could not attend but said in a letter that he believed reform was quite unnecessary. Those present in the Assembly Hall hissed as his words were read out. 'The meeting,' concluded *The Times*' account of the gathering, 'separated after giving three cheers for the Queen' (*The Times*, 17 January 1884).

But what was it the national meeting desired? A local legislature of the sort then being demanded by Irish Home Rulers? Not a bit of it. A resolution, overwhelmingly supported by delegates on that winter's day in 1884, stated that

> in the opinion of this meeting more satisfactory arrangements for the administration of Scottish affairs are imperatively required; that the increasing wealth and population of Scotland make its proper administration most important to the empire, while its marked national characteristics and institutions, and separate legal and educational systems, render it impossible to govern Scotland solely through the Home Office and other existing departments of State; and that, therefore, Government should create a separate and independent department for the conduct of distinctively Scottish affairs, responsible to Parliament and the country for its administration. That the department should be presided over by a Minister for Scotland of personal eminence and position in Parliament and the country. (*Scotsman*, 17 January 1884)

The language and arguments would have been recognisable 130 years later, yet the proposed solution – from the vantage point of 2014 – was modest:

a separate UK government department and minister with responsibility for Scottish affairs. There was no mention of full independence, rather reform within Britain and its empire under the Crown.[2]

Some of the arguments were what would later be called 'civic', the references to Scotland's distinct institutions and its separate legal and education systems, and others 'cultural', for example, Scotland's 'marked national characteristics'. As a commentator noted a few months after the gathering, the demand for a Scottish minister was 'many-sided', partly practical but also partly based on 'sentiment':

> They know that the features peculiar to the laws and system of local government under which they live are not merely arbitrary differences separating them from their southern brethren, but the natural expression of a distinct type of national character growing on a distinct historical soil. (*Scottish Review*, April 1884)

Kellas saw this as part of 'a wave of nationalism', the 'strongest since the Union', and notable for drawing support from peers, landowners, MPs, Scottish pressure groups, the Convention and even Free Church disestablishers (Kellas 1968: 125–6). Similarly, Coupland considered the campaign for a Scotch 'Secretaryship' part of the 'second nationalist movement', the 'first' having taken place in the 1850s (Coupland 1954: 290).[3] This, the National Association for the Vindication of Scottish Rights (NAVSR), drew inspiration from Ireland, where a separate executive (if not legislature) had survived the 1801 Union with Great Britain.[4] It therefore demanded restoration of a Secretary of State for Scotland, abolished after the 1745 uprising, while other 'grievances' related to the 'neglect' of Scottish interests at Westminster and 'a number of symbolic issues relating to heraldic insignia' (Tyrell 2010: 87).

Although the NAVSR quickly fizzled out, it successfully inserted 'administrative devolution' (as it would later become known) into the Scottish Tory agenda, the idea that Scotland – like Ireland – ought to have a distinct administration. By the early 1880s, however, the enduring spirit of this 'nationalist movement' also encompassed Liberals. The Marquis of Bute later celebrated the 'remarkable spirit of common devotion to the good of the common Fatherland which animated the meeting held in Edinburgh . . . where no voice of partizan division marred the patriotic unanimity of the assembly' (*Scottish Review*, October 1889).

This was, as Paterson later put it, a cross-party Scottish nationalism which was 'successful, practical and official'. 'It was a nationalism which did not demand a parliament for the simple reason that it believed that it could get what it wanted without a parliament – economic growth, free trade, liberty, cultural autonomy' (Paterson 1994: 61). Within what has been called the 'Overton window', the range of ideas tolerated by public discourse (Overton 2017), the 1884 demand for a Scottish minister and department struck some as romantic tomfoolery, others as a harmless concession, and a minority as the beginning of a slippery slope to secessionism and the collapse of empire.

The legislative response to the national meeting in Edinburgh was also a bipartisan affair. A few weeks following the meeting, a large delegation – which included the Scottish Liberal MP Duncan McLaren (who had also been involved in the NAVSR) – presented its recommendations to the prime minister in London, emphasising that 'on behalf of the Scottish people they were seeking not to interfere with the Union or look for home rule but to ensure better government' (Pickard 2011: 264).

With Gladstone's reluctant blessing, therefore, the Earl of Dalhousie introduced a Bill to create a 'Secretary for Scotland'. Moving its second reading on 8 May 1885, he recalled the spirit of that January meeting in hyperbolic terms:

> In the opinion of many whose judgments are much more worth having than mine, such a meeting has rarely, if ever, taken place in either Scotland or any other country of the world. There were representatives of every class, representatives of every section of the nation, representatives of every shade of opinion, political and religious. The discussion lasted for some three hours, and I think there were some 30 or 40 speeches; and, so far as I can recollect, there was not one single discordant note from beginning to end. (HL Debs 8 May 1885 Vol 287 cc1664–5)

When the Liberal government fell a few months later, the Secretary for Scotland Bill was taken up by a new Conservative administration headed by Lord Salisbury, who, with an eye on Scottish votes during the intervening election campaign, had declared himself friendly to its objectives. Asking the Duke of Richmond (who had privately opposed the Bill) to fill the new 'Scottish Office', Salisbury remarked that 'the whole object of the move is to redress the wounded dignities of the Scotch people – or a section of them – who think that enough is not made of Scotland' (Salisbury 1885).

So the pattern had been set: a nationalist demand from the periphery met with a concession from the centre, a concession predicated not only on the basis of good governance but also on the fact of Scottish nationhood. Over the next century and more, there would be an ongoing constitutional bidding war between all Scotland's main political parties – Liberal,

Conservative and Labour – something also reflected in party organisation, nomenclature and rhetoric. Not only was nationalist sentiment tolerated in Scotland, (Northern) Ireland and Wales, but at times it was officially encouraged – so long as it stopped short of the traditional nationalist claim to separate statehood. And there would be further concessions from the centre, something that continued even *after* devolution to Scotland and Wales became a reality in the late 1990s.

And although any memory of these events had faded by the close of the twentieth century, on 1 May 1999 the Scottish Parliament was officially opened by Queen Elizabeth, the very sort of 'Home Rule' Arthur Balfour had feared might be the consequence of then modest demands for a Scottish secretary. The devolved parliament was temporarily housed in what was now the General Assembly of the Church of Scotland; the same hall, as it happened, in which the 'national meeting' had convened back in 1884.

TWO

Nationalist Unionism

Unlike many 'modern' nations, the UK was formed over several centuries through various unions, each of which retained traces of earlier epochs. First was the union between England and Wales during the 1530s, then two unions (regal and parliamentary) which created 'Great Britain' out of England and Scotland in 1603 and 1707.[1] Finally, that 'united kingdom' of Great Britain joined with Ireland in 1801 to form the United Kingdom of Great Britain and Ireland, modified after 1922 to *Northern* Ireland, making the UK in its current form less than a century old.

Indeed, much of the terminology still familiar in the early twenty-first century is derived from the debate surrounding 'Home Rule' for Ireland in the late nineteenth and early twentieth centuries. 'Nationalists' supported Home Rule for Ireland, while 'Unionists' opposed it.[2] The latter term entered the political lexicon when, in 1886, the Liberal Party split, with its anti-Home Rule wing calling itself 'Liberal Unionists'. Yet this terminology, like a lot of political language, was reductive and masked important nuance.

Firstly, 'Home Rule' did not (initially) mean the formal secession of Ireland from the 1801 Union; rather it meant the 'devolution' of certain policy responsibilities to a new (or revived) legislature based in Dublin – not unlike the devolution later granted to Scotland and Wales. While Home Rulers recognised Ireland's claim to this devolution on nationalist grounds – i.e. Ireland's status as a distinct 'nation' – they sought to reform the UK rather than end it. Contemporary hyperbole also helped muddy the waters, for political and media opponents of Irish Home Rule often accused supporters of being 'separatists'.

On the other hand, 'Unionists' neither denied Ireland's nationhood nor the desirability of separate administrative arrangements and 'national' institutions – as in Scotland – they simply regarded the creation of an Irish parliament to be unnecessary and potentially detrimental to both the UK and its empire (for a thorough discussion, see Jackson 2003). Following the partition of Ireland in the early 1920s, however, to be a 'unionist' came to mean one of two things: either someone who supported the preservation of Northern Ireland as part of the UK, or a believer in the continuing (and earlier) Anglo-Scottish union.

By this point, a 'Home Rule' parliament had, ironically, been created in Northern Ireland, while Scotland enjoyed increasing administrative 'devolution'. But still the terminology from an earlier era persisted. 'Nationalists' in a Scottish context generally wanted legislative devolution (rather than independence) while unionists did not. In Northern Ireland, meanwhile, the situation was even more confusing, for its nationalists actually wanted union (or reunification) with the now-sovereign Irish Free State, while 'Ulster' unionists wanted to preserve their distinct culture and legislative autonomy.[3] Nationalists, therefore, were neither fully nationalist, nor unionists unequivocally unionist.

'A State of Unions'

'Unionism' as an ideology has generally had more attention from historians than political scientists.[4] Kidd, for example, posits that the idea of a 'greater Britain' originated in Scotland, citing John Mair, a Paris-educated Glaswegian, and his 1520 *Historia Majoris Britanniae* which, in Kidd's words, argued that an Anglo-Scottish union 'would achieve the same political benefits for Scotland as independence, as well as a range of social and economic goods' (Kidd 2013a).

Colley, meanwhile, asserted that 'Great Britain was an invented nation superimposed, if only for a while, onto much older alignments and loyalties', held together by a shared Protestantism, the threat of invasion from France and a common empire (Colley 2003: 5). Earlier, Rokkan and Urwin had classified this 'invented' British nation as a 'union state'. In other words, while

> administrative standardization prevails over most of the territory, the consequences of personal [dynastic] union entail the survival in some areas of pre-union rights and institutional infrastructures which preserve some degree of regional autonomy and serve as agencies of indigenous elite recruitment. (Rokkan and Urwin 1982: 181)

This was another way of saying that the UK encompassed two established churches, three legal systems, several different educational traditions and, by the early 1980s, three territorial government departments dealing with Scotland, Wales and Northern Ireland.

This 'union state', in other words, was a pluralist one. Later, Mitchell reworked this, arguing that by the early twenty-first century the UK was 'a state of unions' (Mitchell 2009: 15), having evolved as a result of the four unions described above, each of which had left an institutional legacy. Later still, Mitchell concluded that the UK might best be characterised as 'a state of evolving unions' (Mitchell 2018: 187), given the constitutional events of 2011–16.

One reason unionism has been so little examined was its dominance, at least until the late 1960s. Rose reckoned this hegemony had produced an 'unthinking Union' governed by 'unthinking Unionism' (Rose 1982: 222), while Kidd later paraphrased Billig in calling this 'banal unionism', an ideology 'so dominant that it does not need to be demonstrative' (Kidd 2008: 25fn). Others viewed unionism as a kind of 'official' nationalism, a term used by Seton-Watson to describe Tsarist and Soviet attempts to develop a pan-Russian identity (Seton-Watson 1977: 148).

Keating, meanwhile, differentiated between 'state' and 'regional' nationalisms, unionism being a form of 'state nationalism' which was generally challenged by the 'regional' variety. To this, Mitchell added a distinction between 'exclusive' state nationalism, which believed in assimilation and uniformity, and the 'inclusive' sort, which tolerated not only different identities but a variety of governing arrangements (Mitchell 1998: 118) – for example, the UK.

Only rarely was this 'official' nationalism discussed in theoretical terms. McLean and McMillan viewed post-1921 British unionism as 'primordial or instrumental' and 'instinctive but instrumental' in relation to both Northern Ireland and Scotland (McLean and McMillan 2005: 135, 155). Armstrong, meanwhile, identified 'three main forms' of unionism, the 'most powerful' of which was 'conservative unionism', which had 'tried to balance the two poles of the various hybrid-British identities by further extending the existing administrative devolution to the constituent parts of the UK – Scotland, Ireland and Wales' (Armstrong 2018: 33–4).

Although this form of unionism was chiefly associated with the Conservative Party, it also 'commanded significant support in both the later Liberal and Labour parties'. Armstrong's second form was 'liberal unionism', which was prepared to concede Home Rule and was initially associated with the Liberal Party before becoming 'the new conservative unionism'. Labour took this up from the Liberals, as did the Conservatives after 1999 (and, one could argue, in 1921 vis-à-vis Northern Ireland). The third form, meanwhile, was 'reactionary unionism', which Armstrong associated with the Conservative Right and the United Kingdom Independence Party, the latter being almost alone in remaining hostile to legislative devolution after 1999 (Armstrong 2018: 33–4).

Managing the 'Territorial Code'

Importantly, Scotland, Wales and (Northern) Ireland were viewed as central to the development of unionism. Phillips noted the extent to which various 'British' identities were 'continually remade' in the 'periphery' before passing to the mainstream of the 'core' (Phillips 2008: 8). Similarly, Ward concluded that unionism was 'not an imposition from the core but a product of the periphery' (Ward 2005: 186).[5]

This process, as well as the manner in which the UK as a 'state of unions' had come into existence, necessitated what Bulpitt called 'territorial management' by whichever party governed from London. As he noted, the 'unitary provisions' of the UK 'manufactured' between 1536 and 1800 'did not extend very far'. In Wales, the pre-union Council of Wales and the Marches had continued until 1689, as had the largely autonomous Courts of Great Sessions until 1830; in Ireland, Dublin Castle hosted a separate bureaucracy, viceroy and chief secretary; while Scotland had, after 1707, retained its distinct modes of law and local government and, perhaps most importantly, its own church, which in turn facilitated separate educational and poor-law systems (Bulpitt 1983: 95–6).

Until the second half of the nineteenth century, the English 'official mind' was against the construction of a highly integrated union and content to operate a system of 'indirect rule' in Wales, Scotland and Ireland, the 'Centre' focusing on 'High Politics' while 'hiving off' its peripheral responsibilities to the Welsh gentry, Scottish 'managers' such as Henry Dundas, and Dublin Castle (Bulpitt 1983: 97). This system of 'territorial politics', however, began a process of modernisation after 1870, not least because it was challenged by the campaign for Irish Home Rule and also by Scottish and Welsh demands for more effective 'national' administration (Bulpitt 1983: 119).

Before 1886, territorial management had been largely a Liberal affair, but following the Home Rule crisis of that year, Lord Salisbury, the Conservative leader, imposed his own 'territorial management code' on both his party and the UK. This had no truck with legislative devolution but allowed 'considerable operational autonomy' to local government, local parties and Dublin Castle, who were all free to pursue their own 'Low Politics' so long as it did not threaten parliamentary sovereignty (a central feature of Unionist ideology) and the centre's command of high politics, chiefly economic and imperial concerns (Bulpitt 1983: 127). Lord Salisbury's 'code' endured until the First World War, tacitly supported by Liberal governments.

The Irish settlement of 1921–2 had what Bulpitt called 'a profoundly conservative impact on territorial politics', removing the 'principal motor' behind Scottish and Welsh nationalism. After 1926, he posited the existence of a 'Dual Polity' in which Centre and Periphery 'had relatively little to do with each other' (Bulpitt 1983: 129–30, 160), most notably vis-à-vis North-ern Ireland, whose 'low politics' could not even be discussed at Westminster. Bulpitt rejected views of the UK as a unitary state or internal colonial society and instead defined 'territorial politics' as

> that arena of political activity concerned with the relations between the cen-tral political institutions in the capital city and those interests, communities, political organisations and governmental bodies outside the central insti-tutional complex, but within the accepted boundaries of the state, which possess, or are commonly perceived to possess, a significant geographical or local/regional character. (Bulpitt 1983: 52)

Thereafter, this Dual Polity, sustained by both the Conservatives and Labour, came under increasing attack from renewed agitation in (Northern) Ireland and 'new dissidents' in Scotland (the Scottish National Party) and Wales (Plaid Cymru). Between 1961 and 1968, this 'duality' declined, threatened to 'collapse' completely between 1968 and 1977, and experienced a 'partial reconstruction' between 1977 and 1979 (Bulpitt 1983: 171). During this period, the Centre became more interventionist in the Periphery, not only economically but through 'direct rule' in Northern Ireland and an attempt to devolve power to Scotland and Wales.

Margaret Thatcher's 'composite' territorial code after 1979 was charac-terised by Madgwick and Rose as 'very radical', forsaking the 'traditional reliance on intermediate collaborative elites' and 'seeking the reestablish-ment of central autonomy' (Madgwick and Rose 1982: 168). Although certainly mistrustful of the Scottish and Welsh Offices, this was an exag-geration, for Mrs Thatcher still tolerated 'Walkerism' in Wales and George Younger's emollient approach in Scotland – even the 'Poll Tax' was the ill-advised consequence of peripheral autonomy. In Northern Ireland, meanwhile, Conservative governments attempted power-sharing govern-ment and conceded an Irish dimension, which was hardly an attempt to re-establish 'central' control.

Bradbury (2006) argued that (New) Labour followed the Conserva-tives' centre-autonomy strategy in government after 1997, devising and managing the Scottish Parliament, National Assembly for Wales and Northern Ireland Assembly in much the same way as their predecessors had dealt with the old territorial departments. Until 2007, Labour control of the UK, Scottish and Welsh governments made this run smoothly, but once Bulpitt's not-so-new 'dissidents' entered devolved government, the Labour–Conservative 'code' came under challenge as never before. With the Centre's glass ceiling of parliamentary sovereignty already abandoned in 1997–9, it now compromised on common levels of welfare and taxation; by the time of the 2014 independence referendum, Convery (2014) believed the Conservatives would be compelled to create a new territorial code in response to yet another of Bulpitt's 'critical junctures'.

The Dual Polity had its critics (for a comprehensive discussion, see Bradbury and John 2010), and indeed it exaggerated not only the degree of peripheral autonomy between 1926 and 1961 but also the Centre's alleged lack of interest in 'low politics'. At the same time, Bulpitt provided one of the few theoretically and historically grounded overviews of the development of the UK as a territorial state while giving more weight than other analysts to 'overtly political matters, such as interests, parties, elite codes and conventions' (Bulpitt 1983: 50).

Bulpitt challenged future scholars to explore the empirical validity of his claims, a challenge this book hopes to meet. The territorial codes of the Liberal, Conservative and Labour parties not only overlapped but developed over time, contributing to the constitutional palimpsest that was an evolving 'state of unions'. But the unionism of the Centre and the nationalism of the Periphery were easy neither to separate nor even to describe.

'Unionist Nationalism'

A pathbreaking text in this regard was Graeme Morton's *Unionist Nationalism: Governing Urban Scotland, 1830–1860*, a response to those, such as Tom Nairn, who believed nationalism to have been absent from mid-nineteenth-century Scotland. Morton, therefore, analysed the expression of Scottish nationalism as a function of 'the nation/state axis, rather than of party politics in waiting'. In doing so, he drew a distinction between nationalism with a secessionist intent and another form that 'was strongly pro-Union' but also 'explicit in its demands for the better government of Scotland' (Morton 1999: 9–10).

Morton went on to argue that 'Scotland's mid-nineteenth-century nationalists believed their nation had entered the Union of 1707 as an equal, and that was how they demanded to be treated', and thus the 'icons of Scotland's *ethnie* were used to celebrate both Union with England and Scotland's independent nationhood' (Morton 1999: 190). Paterson had earlier provided his own interpretation:

> Unionism and nationalism were mutually dependent. To be a true unionist, it was necessary to be a nationalist, because otherwise Scotland would not be a partner in a Union but become dependent on England. Thus the

exploits of national heroes such as Robert the Bruce and William Wallace – whose leadership had liberated Scotland from English dominance at the beginning of the fourteenth century – were celebrated as a unionist achievement. (Paterson 1994: 60)

Morton and Paterson's argument was not new. In a generally overlooked volume from 1967, Hanham had observed that Scottish nationalism's 'main function' in the mid nineteenth century was to 'remind' the British nation that Scotland was 'a cultural and political entity' and to 'fight against the more blatant form of assimilation with England'. There was 'no direct challenge to the Union with England – merely a reminder that prosperity is not everything' (Hanham 1967: 177).

Naturally, Morton's assertion that his 'unionist-nationalism' was 'in no way inferior as an (abstract) nationalism' (Morton 1999: 9–10) was challenged by historians and political scientists. Glass accused him of conflating 'nationalism' with 'national identity', arguing that Scots had simply expressed pride in their 'involvement with the British state' and 'contribution to the British Empire' (Glass 2014: 6–9). Given the difficulty of separating the two, this was unconvincing. At a basic level, nationalism was simply the expression of national identity, the 'objectifiable ways in which ideas or feelings of Scottish difference are and have been articulated or displayed' (Pittock 2001: 1).

Others were more sympathetic. Tomlinson and Gibbs, for example, applied 'unionist-nationalism' to mid-twentieth-century economic thinking in Scotland (Tomlinson and Gibbs 2016: 585), while Kidd argued that Morton's term caught the 'multiple, subtle scents and tastes which existed beneath the powerful flavours which predominated in Scottish politics'. It captured the compelling truth that

> so much political debate, certainly on constitutional and territorial questions, involved politicians who were neither outright Anglicisers, nor outright separatists, but unionists who variously supported, say, a devolved assembly or administrative devolution or the repatriation of the Stone of Destiny, and nationalists who wished to gain greater traction, salience or autonomy for Scotland within larger supra-national political or economic entities such as the British empire, a looser Union of the Crowns, a social union, or the European Union. (Kidd 2019: 223)

We're All Nationalists (and Unionists) Now

Even before Morton provided 'a new sense of direction' with his description of 'unionist nationalism' (Tyrell 2010: 88), it had been widely acknowledged that the pursuit of independent statehood was not the *ne plus ultra* of nationalism. The first academic study of Scottish nationalism, Coupland's *Welsh and Scottish Nationalism* (1954), had looked beyond the 'sinister' implications of 'nationalism' associated with the Second World War to define it more broadly as 'no more than an active consciousness of nationality and a devotion to the national interest' (Coupland 1954: xvii).[6]

Similarly, by the early 1970s Kellas concluded that nationalism was of 'first-order importance' to the 'Scottish political system':

> It sustains the Scottish Office and the other institutions of the system, which could hardly exist without it. It colours the speeches of Scottish MPs in the House of Commons, and permeates the demands of interest groups. It makes Scotland a framework of reference for the mass media, education, and research. (Kellas 1989: 161)

Smith, meanwhile, noted that the SNP had only become 'separatist' in 1942, and therefore there existed a division between political nationalism (the desire for a Scottish Parliament) and administrative or cultural nationalism (such as that deployed by 'unionist' parties). Smith, however, observed that these 'autonomist movements' conformed to the 'basic pattern of nationalism':

> Whether the argument concerns oil or tourism, university locations or language rights, migration or regional powers, the ultimate premises are never in doubt. It is always collective autonomy, collective solidarity and collective identity which is being sought and found, in the hope of ethnic regeneration and fraternity which is embodied in the concept of 'nationhood'. (Smith 1979: 157)

Smith returned to this point in *National Identity*, observing that the 'notion that every nation must have its own state' was a common, 'but not a necessary, deduction from the core doctrine of nationalism', thus his definition of nationalism as 'an ideological movement for attaining and maintaining the autonomy, unity and identity for a population some of whose members believe it to constitute an actual or potential "nation"' (Smith 1991: 74).

Neil MacCormick, an SNP politician, legal academic and son of John MacCormick (who had left the SNP over its 'separatist' turn in 1942), reached a similar conclusion, defining what he called 'acceptable nationalism' as the

> members of a nation are as such in principle entitled to effective organs of political self-government within the world order of sovereign or post-sovereign states; but these need not provide for self-government in the form of a sovereign state. (MacCormick 1996: 566)

Bond went even further a few years later, arguing for a 'broader conception of Scottish national identity' which could even include those opposed to legislative devolution: 'Scottish nationalists, then, could equally be those who believe in Scotland's status as a nation and feel a strong sense of Scottishness, but do not necessarily support either of the two most obvious political manifestations of Scottish nationhood' (Bond 2000: 31, 33). This echoed Levy, who noted the 'sense in which all parties in Scotland and Wales can be considered to be "nationalist", irrespective of their label' (Levy 1994: 147), and Kellas, who observed 'nationalist political behaviour' well beyond the SNP, in 'other parties, in trade unions, and in cultural bodies'. As a result, SNP-centric studies usually understated the strength of nationalism, with non-nationalist parties often 'using nationalist appeals in order to pre-empt the nationalists' campaign' (Kellas 1998: 96–7, 218).

The same year, Mitchell noted that in contemporary debates

> unionism and nationalism are presented as if they are mutually exclusive ideologies; one asserting the 'sovereignty of Parliament' against another asserting the 'sovereignty of the Scottish people'. In fact, there are many variants of unionism and in one form it closely resembles Scottish nationalism. Indeed, unionism in any of its forms is a form of nationalism – a collective identity. The real issue is its composition. That remains contested. (Mitchell 1998: 137)

Hearn defined nationalism as 'the promotion of national interests and identity, whether in cultural or political terms, and the pursuit of greater political autonomy, no matter in what form' (Hearn 2000: 57), while several comparative studies of Scotland and Canada put this analysis in an international context. Henderson (2007) looked at the relationship between national identity and 'political culture' in Quebec and Scotland, while Thomson (2010) focused on what he called 'autonomism' in Newfoundland and Scotland, noting that the ambiguity of aims such as 'administrative devolution' or 'Home Rule' did 'not comply with orthodox theories of nationalism as an ideology that strives towards national and political borders being congruent and unambiguous' (Thomson 2010: 5–6).

Kennedy, who also compared 'liberal nationalism' in Scotland and Quebec, called it 'state-reforming nationalism', which did not seek to 'subvert the existing state' but rather to 'reform it in order to accommodate, culturally or politically, the aspirations of sub-state nationalists'. As a political project, he concluded, nationalism

> seeks an arrangement in which the status of the nation is politically and/ or culturally enhanced. This is a deliberately ambiguous definition, yet its

strength lies in its general applicability, it allows for greater understanding of the role that nationalism, in all its forms, has played, outside of the 'one nation, one state' formula. (Kennedy 2015: 16)

Others preferred to view nationalism on a spectrum. Keating, for example, acknowledged that nationalism in Scotland had 'never been the exclusive property of one party', although he believed the SNP represented 'its clearest expression' (Keating 2001: 219). Properly understood, Keating wrote later, the term 'unionism' already captured and implied a recognition of 'national diversity under unitary authority' (Keating 2009: 368). Hechter, meanwhile, defined it as 'collective action designed to render the boundaries of the nation congruent with those of its governance unit'. If a particular group, therefore, aimed for something less than complete sovereignty, then it was 'perforce less nationalist' (Hechter 2000: 7–8).

Another approach attempted to differentiate between 'patriotism' and 'nationalism'. This could be traced back to George Orwell, who in a 1945 essay viewed the former as 'defensive, both militarily and culturally', while nationalism was 'inseparable from the desire for power' (Orwell 1945). Day and Thompson, for example, preferred to reserve the term 'nationalism' for 'more overt expressions of ideas about national interests and national fortunes' (Day and Thompson 2004: 99), while Lukacs, *pace* Orwell, viewed patriotism as 'defensive' and nationalism as 'aggressive' (Lukacs 2005: 71–2).

Neil Davidson, meanwhile, drew a distinction between 'political nationalism' and what he called 'patriotic national consciousness' (Davidson 2000: 14–15). Ruth Davidson, leader of the Scottish Conservative Party between 2011 and 2019, referenced Orwell in a 2017 speech even though, two years earlier, she had acknowledged her party's 'own nationalism', one that recognised Scotland 'as a nation in its own right' but also sitting 'united as part of the nation-state of the UK' (Davidson 2015).

But this begged the obvious question of where 'national consciousness' or 'patriotism' ends and 'nationalism' begins. As Billig observed, the 'distinction would be convincing if there were clear, unambiguous criteria, beyond an ideological requirement to distinguish "us" from "them"' (Billig 1995: 55). As Pittock put it:

Nationalism is often, and misleadingly, contrasted with patriotism. The one is narrow and evil, the other natural and admirable. As long as it confines itself to St. Andrew's Day orations, patriotism is all right. When it takes the form of wanting to do something here and now about Scottish problems, patriotism, by some mysterious alchemy, becomes nationalism, which troubles the peace of the world. (Pittock 2001: 6)

In *Banal Nationalism*, Billig had made the useful differentiation between secessionist nationalism and the 'everyday' variety utilised by most modern nation states (and indeed nations within states). As he observed, the term 'nationalism' was generally 'associated with those who struggle to create new states or with extreme right-wing politics', leading 'those in established nations – at the centre of things' to see nationalism 'as the property of others, not of "us"'. But, at the same time, established nations continually 'flagged' or reminded everyone of their nationhood, providing 'a continual background for their political discourses, for cultural products, and even for the structuring of newspapers' (Billig 1995: 5–8).

But simply describing it as 'unionism' or 'nationalism' (even with caveats like 'state-reforming' or 'banal') feels inadequate, unintentionally perpetuating a polarised, mutually exclusive view of the two 'isms'. It has had many other labels: quasi-, crypto- or soft-nationalism, but this book will use the term 'nationalist unionism',[7] a sort of nationalism simultaneously autonomist and unionist, an 'official' Scottish nationalism operating *within* another, broader, 'official' British (and in its earlier stages, imperial) nationalism (or, indeed, unionism). As Kidd has observed, 'far from being the antithesis of Scottish nationalism', unionism was actually complementary and overlapping (Kidd 2008: 20).

Nationalism: Civic or Cultural?

But what sort of nationalism was 'nationalist unionism'? Most scholars have approached nationalism in Scotland from a 'modernist' perspective, which holds that nations – including Scotland – are relatively modern in origin, a product of industrialisation and mass communications. This does not, of course, deny the existence of Scotland and Scottishness *before* the modern era, just that Scottish national identity and nationalism are taken to have assumed their *current, recognisable form* during the nineteenth century.

Nairn, for example, believed nationalism to have been 'determined by certain features of the world political economy, in the era between the French and Industrial Revolutions and the present day' (Nairn 1981: 332); Hechter (1985) posited that 'uneven' economic development since the Industrial Revolution had created 'internal colonialism' in the UK and thus nationalism in Scotland and Wales, while Hobsbawm and Ranger pointed – more credibly – to what they called 'invented traditions', which automatically implied 'continuity with the past' (Hobsbawm and Ranger 1983: 1). Also influential was Anderson's definition of the 'nation' as 'an imagined community', imagined 'as both inherently limited and sovereign' (Anderson 1991: 6).

Scottish modernists have, furthermore, emphasised the post-1707 institutional 'autonomy' of civil society in Scotland – its distinct forms of law, education and religion – to argue that Scottish nationalism within that timeframe had been inclusive and 'civic' rather than 'cultural' or 'ethnic' in nature. This stresses a shared sense of territory, residence and public institutions rather than birth, language or ancestry; it is liberal rather than illiberal, concerned with policy solutions rather than historical events. McCrone drew on Webb (1978) and Brand (1978) in arguing that the 'cultural content' of Scottish nationalism was 'relatively weak', less ready 'to call up the ancient ghosts of the nation, its symbols and motifs, in its quest for independence' (McCrone 1989: 161). Rather it was, according to Keating, based on 'practical arguments about institutions, accountability and policy', making it 'one of the least romantic nationalist movements' (Keating 2001: 221).

Since the 1970s, this has been, to quote John Kenneth Galbraith, the 'conventional wisdom', that is, 'the ideas which are esteemed at any time for their acceptability' (Galbraith 1958). Importantly, the concept of 'civic' Scottish nationalism holds not just in the academic and journalistic sphere but also among political actors, mainly members of the Scottish National Party (SNP), although it could also be found in the Scottish Labour and Scottish Liberal Democrat parties during the 1980s and 1990s.

It is true that the nationalist arguments made between the late nineteenth and early twenty-first centuries – the focus of this book – display many civic characteristics: a concern with Scots Law, education and the Church of Scotland (and threats – perceived or real – to their distinctiveness), as well as an institutional focus in that a goal was often the creation of new 'national' institutions as well as the defence of existing ones: a Scottish Office, Scottish Secretary and, later, a Scottish Parliament. The historical and political science literature has, therefore, focused to a large degree on these 'civic' examples.

Although a distinction between two sorts of nationalism had been made before, the dichotomy of 'civic' or 'ethnic' most likely originated with the Canadian public intellectual Michael Ignatieff.[8] His 1993 book, *Blood & Belonging: Journeys into the New Nationalism*, drew a clear distinction between 'ethnic nationalism', 'that an individual's deepest attachments are inherited, not chosen', and 'civic nationalism', which 'envisages the nation as a community of equal, rights-bearing citizens, united in patriotic attachment to a shared set of political practices and values' (Ignatieff 1993: 3–5).

In a related documentary for BBC Scotland, *A Different Country*, Ignatieff concluded that Scottish nationalism (by which he meant the campaign for devolution as well as independence) was 'civic' in nature, although he also noted hearing 'casual, friendly anti-English statements' while in Scotland, with everybody saying they were 'more egalitarian, nicer, more democratic, less capitalist' than the English. He wondered if 'civic nationalism' was 'mutating into ethnic nationalism' (Ignatieff 1994). Orwell had made a similar observation in his 1945 essay, observing that the Celt was 'supposed to be spiritually superior to the Saxon, simpler, more creative, less vulgar, less snobbish' (Orwell 1945). Indeed, Scottish nationalism often made reference to a natural or innate national 'character', the 'central motif' of which is 'the *inherent* egalitarianism of the Scots' (McCrone 2001: 91; author's italics).

What Ignatieff (if not Orwell) had detected was the difficulty of fully separating 'civic' and 'ethnic' nationalism in a Scottish context, something also acknowledged by MacCormick a few years later. Mis-attributing the distinction to Gellner, he warned against 'seeing or defining the civic and the ethnic in straightforward either/or terms':

> They are more ideal types than exclusive alternatives, for of course civically identified communities develop cultural practices and institutions around them ... There can, then, be a kind of 'cultural nationalism' associated with civic nationalism, and yet tending towards the ethnic to the extent that racial or ethnic difference is postulated (usually or always as a kind of fiction or myth, I suppose) as the source of culture or of its special value. (MacCormick 1996: 554, 563)

At around the same time, Smith (a former student of Gellner) posed a key question to modernists: why were human beings so willing to ardently identify with an 'invented' nation and national identity and be, in some cases, willing to sacrifice their lives for it? (Smith 1996: 134). Indeed, there was little room in the modernist account for emotion, yet it seemed clear that 'the powerful commitments felt by so many people to their own national identities' could not 'be explained in conventional economic and political terms' (Smith 1998: 3).

Smith agreed with Anderson (1991) that nationalism was more akin to a religion than liberalism or socialism, the main reason 'modernist' and 'post-modernist' critiques 'seem so often to miss their mark' (Smith 1995: viii–ix). Instead, he emphasised the 'central role of myths, memories, symbols, and traditions' in nationalism (Smith 1998: preface), an approach he called 'ethno-symbolism'. This was intended as 'a useful supplement and corrective to the dominant modernist orthodoxy, but in no sense a theory' (Smith 2009: xi); Smith intended it to 'fill out' the modernist narrative rather than replace it (Smith 2009: 1).

As we have already seen, Morton referenced Smith in arguing that the 'icons of Scotland's *ethnie*' had been 'used to celebrate both Union with

England and Scotland's independent nationhood' (Morton 1999: 190). This sort of thing did not land well with Scottish modernists. McCrone, for example, probably had Morton and Smith in mind when he asserted that in Scotland, nationalism was derived from 'institutional autonomy' and 'not some vague set of historic emotions' manipulated by politicians (McCrone 2001: 195).

But there were several obvious weaknesses with this view of Scottish nationalism (either secessionist or autonomist), not only in the early twenty-first century but in the century or so that preceded it. Not only had historians identified – in Scotland *and* England – 'lively ethnocentric identities based on history, religion and conceptions of freedom . . . long before the nineteenth century' (Kidd 1993: 5; see also Hastings 1997),[9] but Scottish politicians from Lord Rosebery to Alex Salmond had stressed its 'ancient' provenance. Also overlooked was the importance of the flags, songs and poems identified by Smith as central to modern nationalism, not least the enduring myths of Wallace and Bruce, cultural 'raw material' deployed by unionists and nationalists alike between 1884 and 2014. This, too, did not fit easily into a 'civic' narrative.

And did Scottish national identity really rest upon institutions? As even Nairn came to argue, when asked to define their identity no Scot had ever responded 'with a short lecture on the beauties of the sheriff system' or 'the merits of the Scottish generalist education' (Nairn 1997: 206),[10] especially as the Church of Scotland (like most other Western religions) declined in importance and Scottish education was no longer 'the best in the world'. Furthermore, Scotland's institutions were not – as in most 'modern' nations – those of an independent country, but rather those carried over from the sovereign Scottish nation that had ceased to be in 1707. Besides, did the masses feel the same way as autonomous civil society? Several surveys suggested not, with majorities (or at least sizeable minorities) believing birth and parentage to be as integral to Scottishness as shared territory and institutions (see McCrone 2001; Leith and Soule 2012; Mitchell *et al.* 2012).

It took a while, therefore, for the conventional wisdom to be more directly challenged. Ichijo (2004), a student of Smith's, applied an ethno-symbolist critique to the SNP's use of history in fashioning its policy of 'independence in Europe', while a 2012 edition of *Nations and Nationalism* interrogated the modernist consensus more extensively. Mycock provided contemporary evidence that 'ethnic constructions of the Scottish nation and its people' continued to resonate (Mycock 2012: 54), although that did not mean it was 'hot', 'irrational and bigoted', just that there was 'a far more delicate interplay between what can be categorised as civic and open forms and non-civic and closed forms of Scottish nationalism' (Leith and Soule 2012: 13).

The central point was that while politicians, journalists and academics might affirm 'their commitment to civic and inclusive criteria of national identity', they did so 'within a discourse laden with atavistic tendencies, historical references and irrational collectivism'. Even 'stories' about education or legal tradition could not escape 'an emotive representation' (Leith and Soule 2012: 143). And while acknowledging the importance of history in the construction of an 'imagined community', Liinpää argued that 'what is of interest is the question of *which* myths are remembered and *who* is included in this perceived "common ancestry"' (Liinpää 2018: 14).

In other words, Scottish nationalism could include an ethnic component without being ethnically exclusive. As Ferguson put it, Scottish national identity and 'national feeling' had 'subsumed and absorbed many ethnic groups and spoken many languages' (Ferguson 1998: 316). But with so many nationalist arguments predicated upon the fact of (Scottish) nationhood, ethnicity, ventured Kearton, 'comes in through the back door of history', so that a 'predominantly forward-looking civic conception of community' could find itself 'anchored around a historically grounded ethnocultural core'. Paradoxically, the 'ethnic' core of Scottish national identity was 'used to project an inclusive, forward-looking vision of the nation', something Kearton called a form of 'civic-perennialism' (Kearton 2012: 25, 39–40).[11]

The importance of intellectuals in the development of nations and nationalisms has long been noted (see, for example, Hroch 2000), although the striking degree of consensus between certain Scottish academics, journalists and politicians has been little interrogated.[12] As Anderson said of Nairn, he treats 'his "Scotland" as an unproblematic, primordial given' (Anderson 1991: 89). Later, Davidson went further in arguing that Nairn was 'no longer merely a theorist of nationalism . . . but a nationalist theorist' (Davidson 1999). Hobsbawm famously declared that no 'serious historian' of nations and nationalism could be a 'committed political nationalist' for it required 'too much belief in what is patently not true' (Hobsbawm 1990),[13] while Kearton viewed the civic paradigm as another Scottish 'myth' (Kearton 2012).

As Pittock (2008) more modestly suggests, it could be that Scotland's academic and political leaders had failed to reconcile the romantic with the rational. The retrospective application of the 'civic nationalism' thesis certainly produced a degree of confusion in the literature. It makes little sense to argue, for example, that the campaign for a Scottish minister and department in 1884 did not constitute nationalism but later agitation for Home Rule did (Keating 1988), or that the Scottish Covenant Movement was not nationalist but the later campaign for a Scottish Parliament was (Mitchell 2000). As Ichijo has observed, if all political parties 'claim to work for Scotland as a nation', then it follows 'that they are all operating in a nationalist or nationalized discursive framework' (Ichijo 2012: 34), a point also made by Leith and Soule (2012).

Outline and Approach of This Book

This book started life as a PhD thesis looking at the 'nationalist unionism' of the Scottish Unionist Party between 1912 and 1965. Chapters 3–5, therefore, deal with the Scottish Conservative view and deployment of Scottish national consciousness, looking at, first, its 'ascendancy' between 1912 and 1939; second, its 'Scottish Control of Scottish Affairs' policy from 1940 until the 1951 general election; and third, its subsequent rise and fall between 1955 and the Scottish independence referendum of 2014. Chapter 6 then considers the Scottish Liberals from the same angle, as does Chapter 7 with the Scottish Labour Party. Chapter 8 takes a detour from the main thesis, looking instead at the Scottish National Party and its 'unionism' between 1934 and 2014, while Chapters 9 and 10 return to the script by charting nationalist unionism in other parts of the United Kingdom, Wales and Northern Ireland. Chapter 11 draws together the main themes and arguments in a conclusion.

In keeping with the original thesis, this book combines historical analysis with a theoretical approach. Given the clear blend of institutions, ethnicity, history and imagery deployed by the unionist parties under examination, this lends itself to the ethno-symbolist approach discussed earlier in this chapter, as well as Billig's 'banal nationalism' and the broader territorial analysis of Bulpitt. This book is concerned with high politics as well as low, but endorses Paterson's dictum that 'we should pay more attention to events than to constitutional theories – to what happened in practice, rather than to what the rules said should happen' (Paterson 1994: 179).

Although theory is important, here it is used analytically rather than dogmatically. Rather the focus throughout is on party discourse, either public or private, for as Calhoun argues, 'traditions are not simply inherited, they have to be reproduced: stories have to be told over and again, parts of traditions have to be adapted to new circumstances to keep them meaningful'. Nationalism, therefore, is 'a way of speaking that shapes our consciousness' (Calhoun 1997: 3, 50). And this way of speaking had a clear purpose, for 'politics is a *public* activity' and politicians 'need to win support for themselves, their parties, and their causes' (Williamson 1999: 14–15).

When it comes to primary sources, well-known archives as well as lesser-known collections have been consulted,[14] while some effort has been made to break out of the *Scotsman/Herald* duopoly in terms of contemporary media coverage; neither was ever a big-circulation newspaper, while the *Daily Record* and *Scottish Daily Express*, for example, were. The author has also made use of television and film archive material where possible – so often neglected by historians and political scientists in spite of its mass reach – as well as printed ephemera from his own collection of Scottish political material.

This book, however, does not argue that 'nationalist unionism' was the only – or even the most important – aspect of Scottish party politics between 1884 and 2014, merely that it constituted one strand among many. Nor is it overly concerned with electoral patterns, which can end up distracting from less obvious patterns: just because Scots did not vote SNP in sizeable numbers before the late 1960s did not mean they were lacking in 'nationalism', just as the same party's performance after 2007 did not mean 'unionism' (of whatever variety) was pushing up the daisies.

Just as civic and ethnic/cultural nationalism existed on a spectrum, so too did nationalism and unionism, with most discourse conducted 'in the vast yet variegated terrain which constitutes the middle ground between the extremes of anglicising unionism and Anglophobic nationalism' (Kidd 2008: 300). Much of that variegated terrain, however, remains underexplored. While Labour's relationship with nationalism has been the subject of several books and articles, the Scottish Liberals have been largely ignored (generally as well as nationalistically), as were the Scottish Conservatives until relatively recently (see Pentland 2015). Similarly, only in recent years have the nuances of SNP constitutional thinking been more thoroughly explored (see Brown Swan and McEwen, forthcoming).

As Cameron has argued, the 'polarity' between 'Yes' and 'No' encouraged by the 2014 independence referendum was not 'a particularly helpful way' of understanding Scottish political history: 'There have been different strands of unionism and nationalism and both themes, as well as others, have been present in all of the main political parties which have traversed the changing political landscape of Scotland since the 1880s' (Cameron 2016: 18). The same remained true, perhaps even more so, after 1999. Writing in 2017, the journalist Kenny Farquharson observed that if there had been 'one touchstone issue in Scottish politics for the past 20 years it has been this: who stands up for Scotland?'

> This is a very real political battleground. It matters, not least because the criteria by which voters come to a conclusion about whether someone is 'standing up for Scotland' are so subjective. Largely it is a matter of tone and impression rather than an intellectual assessment of policy positions. (*The Times*, 22 November 2017)

This book, therefore, aims to look at Scottish party politics between 1884 and 2014 from a different angle of vision, away from left versus right and eschewing the idea that 'nationalism' and 'unionism' are somehow mutually exclusive; to look, as per Morton, 'beyond Scottish nationalism as a party-political movement striving to match nation and state' (Morton 2008: 127).

All Scotland's political parties drew upon myths, symbols and historical heroes – indeed, often the same ones – in order to legitimise their goals, be it administrative or legislative devolution; all of them believed that 'the political and the national unit should be congruent', just that the 'political unit' need not be an independent state (Gellner 1983: 1; Kearton 2012: 24). As Miller observed, nationalist ideas 'may be appropriated and used in different ways by conservatives, liberals, and socialists, even within the political tradition of a single country' (Miller 1995: 4). Let us begin by looking at the Conservative and Unionist Party.

THREE

'Every Scotsman Should Be a Scottish Nationalist'

In May 1914, Sir George Younger, the Scottish Unionist Party's Westminster 'whip', sent Andrew Bonar Law, the Leader of the Opposition, a memorandum prepared 'by a small committee of the Scottish Unionist Association' (SUA) entitled 'Scottish Home Rule' (Younger 1914). 'Scottish National sentiment is a strong force in all ranks of Scottish life', it declared, something its authors believed might 'either be turned to good account or bad'. The 'Radicals' (i.e. Liberals) were attempting to channel it into 'narrow political Scottish nationalism' which wanted a Scottish Parliament, and therefore it fell to Unionists 'to turn it into good'.

So rather than a 'parochial parish-pump type of Scottish nationalism' (based 'largely on jealousy of others'), the SUA promoted the 'wider and better ideal of Imperial patriotism' to which Scots 'invariably show themselves ready to respond . . . when it is properly made'. The memo had three recommendations for Unionist candidates, to (a) 'show a full appreciation of the fine worth and patriotic importance of Scottish National sentiment when directed into legitimate channels', (b) 'to expose the fallacies of . . . Parliamentary severance of Scotland from the other parts of the United Kingdom' and, beyond this, (c) 'point to the important part which Scottish National patriotism has played and must still play in the wider patriotism of the whole British Empire'.

'Scottish National patriotism' included civic aspects – 'Scottish national institutions, its separate Courts and System of Law [and] Church' – and also cultural – 'Literature, and Music, to say nothing of the history and tradition of the Scottish Regiments'. Furthermore, the memo made some suggestions for improvements: 'some form of Imperial Council' to relieve the UK Parliament of its legislative backlog as well as 'delegation of certain matters of more exclusively local concern' from Westminster to local bodies in 'the several countries of the United Kingdom'. It also suggested overhauling the twenty-nine-year-old Scottish Office, adding 'at least two' under-secretaries, granting 'greater administrative powers' and gathering together various boards and departments 'in one building' situated in Edinburgh.

Finally, a detailed appendix filleted the Liberal MP Sir William Cowan's recent *Government of Scotland Bill*. This, it argued, 'sins against the doctrine of a larger patriotism and nationalism' by seeking to create but a 'glorified Town Council'. Many other objections would remain familiar a century later: the best people would not stand for election; it would not have enough to do; 'housing a Scots Parliament' would be expensive; taxes might have to go up; and the new parliament 'would have to borrow at a higher rate of interest'. In short, there was little to justify such 'a leap in the dark'. 'The game', concluded the memo of legislative autonomy, 'is not worth the candle' (SUA 1914a).

But as a briefing for parliamentary candidates this memo proved academic, for the general election expected in 1914 was postponed on account of the First World War. Nevertheless, the battle lines were broadly set. Scottish Unionists not only acknowledged the existence of Scottish 'national sentiment' but believed this nationalism could be harnessed in a positive, imperialist way. And when it came to reforming the 'machinery of government', they would consider everything short, as Sir George Younger characterised it in the House of Commons, of 'a Government at Edinburgh with an executive responsible to a Scottish Parliament'. 'At that', he added conclusively, 'we draw the line' (HC Deb 15 May 1914 Vol 62 c1549).

Importantly, this 'line' lay not, as it would a century later, between those ('Nationalists') who believed in full sovereign 'independence' for Scotland and others ('Unionists') who wanted it to remain a devolved part of the UK. In 1914, full independence sat outside the 'Overton window'; rather the debate ranged between support for 'administrative devolution'[1] or a devolved Scottish Parliament, with proponents of the former depicting supporters of the latter as 'separatists' or 'bad' nationalists, even though they also sought to maintain Scotland as part of the UK and broader British Empire, pushing them to what Billig called the 'periphery' of political discourse.

The thirteenth Unionist *Campaign Guide*, issued in advance of the election that never came, is a case in point. Denigrating the 'sentimental' argument for a Scottish Parliament which sought 'to foster Scottish patriotism at the expense of British patriotism', it encouraged Unionist candidates to 'strenuously oppose' any devolution scheme, although they were encouraged to support 'any reasonable project for introducing more decentralization and elasticity into administration' (SUA 1914b: 133–41).

None of these challenges or positions were new to Scottish Unionists in 1914, for their party 'had a variety of intellectual traditions on which it could draw' when it came to the Scottish dimension. Underappreciated, however, were its nationalist traditions – civic, historic, cultural and occasionally ethnic – but those would be central to Unionist success for the first half of the twentieth century, 'not only in their effective deployment of the language of Scottish nationality but also in their leadership of the reform of Scottish government and administration' (Pentland 2015: 256).

'The Edinburgh People'

In his letter to Bonar Law, Sir George Younger made a point of emphasising that the memo on Home Rule had 'not in any way been prepared or influenced' by the Scottish Unionist Whip's Office in Westminster, but was rather 'quite a spontaneous effort on the part of the Edinburgh people' (Younger 1914), the 'Edinburgh people' being those in charge of the autonomous Scottish Unionist Association, established two years earlier following a 'fusion' of the Scottish Conservative Party and Liberal Unionists in Scotland.

The two Unionist parties (Conservative and Liberal) had initially merged in England and Wales, but north of the border the Scottish parties were left to 'settle it for themselves' (Chamberlain 1936: 156). They chose to keep the SUA 'independent of London' but abandoned the term 'Conservative', which in a Scottish context was considered 'a label with a regrettable past and, as far as could be told, an unpromising future' (Fry 1991: 130). While in England 'the Conservatives absorbed the Unionists, in Scotland it was, at length, to be the other way round' (Fry 2013: 308). Indeed, it was a former Liberal Unionist who attempted perhaps the first definition of the new 'Unionism' as 'not only the union of Scotland, England and Ireland, but the union of all classes of the Empire, and also the union of all classes of the community in a homogenous whole' (*Scotsman*, 6 December 1912).

The new SUA, therefore, 'clearly had a Scottish national as well as unionist identity' (Lynch 1999: 16) and it is clear from SUA archives that its officials viewed themselves as a distinct party operating within a distinct political system; one report even made reference to 'the English Conference' taking place in Birmingham in October 1933 (SCUA 1934). In 1932, meanwhile, this organisational autonomy was further strengthened by the formation of a Scottish Unionist Members' Committee (SUMC) at Westminster, which was open to all Scottish MPs and thereafter met between five and twelve times a year. Norton regarded this as a 'national' rather than 'regional' committee of the Conservative Parliamentary Party (Norton 1994: 115), one which had a clear bearing on the policy agenda of the Scottish and UK parties as well as its nationalist-unionist agenda.

Also 'national' in character were a little-known aspect of the 1707 settlement, the 'sixteen peers of Scotland'. At that time, a Scottish peerage did not automatically carry a seat in the House of Lords, and at the Palace of Holyroodhouse whenever a general election was held, hereditary Scots peers would gather to 'elect' sixteen of their number to represent Scotland in the Upper House. Kellas noted 'a curious tinge of Scottish nationalism about some of them' (Kellas 1994: 672), for example, the third Marquis of Bute and the sixth Duke of Montrose, and indeed they were generally more enthusiastic about legislative devolution than their colleagues in the House of Commons. A Scottish Unionist fete in Lanark in 1927 even celebrated the Douglas family (the Earls of Home) as 'the mainstay of Scottish independence' (Jackson 2012: 250).

This 'tinge' of nationalism also existed beyond Parliament and party HQ. In 1927, the Scottish Conservative Club (a name considered 'distinctive and national') celebrated its fiftieth anniversary in Edinburgh (SCUA 1926), demonstrating that even the social dimension of Scottish Toryism had a long pedigree. The symbolism of Scottish nationhood also featured in the party's youth movement, the logo of the Junior Imperialist Union (JIU), formed shortly before the SUA, featuring, as the Unionist MP Sir Robert Horne noted approvingly, 'a Scottish Lion, and St. Andrew with his cross' (Horne 1933).

'Home Rule All Round'

In the decade following the formation of the SUA, there was renewed discussion of what Liberals called 'Home Rule all Round', that is 'devolved' government for Scotland and Wales as well as Ireland, or even a federal reconstitution of the UK. And despite the SUA's general opposition to 'bad' nationalism (legislative devolution), this discussion included many Scottish Unionists, the widespread desire to answer the Irish Question having 'created some ideological space within Unionism for a measure of Scottish home rule' (Kidd 2008: 18).

These debates, however, generally 'lacked passion or historical references' (Coupland 1954: 307), being regarded as a means to a constitutional end rather than desirable in their own right. At the same time, the First World War had 'reinforced the identification of some Scots with the United Kingdom and the Empire' (MacDonald and McFarland 1999: 55), with the politics of remembrance often intensely nationalistic. At commemorative ceremonies one Unionist MP, Sir Aylmer Hunter-Weston, gave his Scottishness 'free reign, reinforced by a stout Ayrshire patriotism', the latter drawing upon a local military prowess stretching back to William Wallace (McFarland 2014: 55). As Harvie put it, Scottish Unionists comprised 'the patriotic party of the "Anglo-Scottish" Empire' (Harvie 1992: 247).

Unionist literature at the 1918 general election even embraced 'a wide spectrum of approaches to Scottish self-government' (Arnott and Macdonald 2012: 47), while some Scottish Unionists fretted about the threat to Scottish nationhood from having been 'absorbed into a wider area' (Finlay 2004: 98). In 1919 a Speaker's Conference considered a comprehensive scheme of devolution, something the new Unionist MP Frederick Thomson supported 'whole-heartedly', observing that the British constitution was not 'fully unitary', having included 'an absolutely separate Scottish administration' since 1885 (HC Deb 4 June 1919 c2087).

By 1920, not only had a putative federal scheme been truncated and applied to 'northern' and 'southern' Ireland via the Government of Ireland Act, but the Speaker's Conference on devolution was nearing completion. During one debate, the Unionist MP James Kidd spoke of nationhood as 'merely a stage in the progress of a people. Some have not reached it, some have passed it . . . Scotland has passed the stage of nationhood. Her nationhood has been absorbed – in a wider area' (HC Deb 16 April 1920 c2045), an argument that anticipated much later debates about 'post-sovereignty' (MacCormick 1999). Similarly, Walter Elliot (Lanark) distinguished his own nationalism from the 'Chauvinist' variety that had recently 'swept Europe like a pestilence', the 'claim' for devolution being both 'entirely separate' and 'absolutely necessary' (HC Deb 16 April 1920 c2066), a very different take from that being expressed by Unionists just a few years earlier.

Thus by 1920 there existed a near consensus that a holistic approach to devolution for different parts of the UK was necessary, but shortly afterwards the Speaker's Conference ended in an impasse, split between Speaker Crowther's support for indirectly elected 'Grand Councils' and Murray Macdonald's alternative scheme for directly elected subordinate legislatures. Thereafter the 'cause of Scottish nationalism in Parliament fell back into the old pre-war slough of still-born Bills and sterile speeches' (Coupland 1954: 397), and with it died the Scottish Unionist Party's brief flirtation with legislative devolution.

A 'Sentiment of Nationality'

As well as providing the impetus for debates on 'Home Rule all Round', the Irish Question also compelled Scottish Unionists to define their nationalist unionism more clearly. In a wide-ranging essay, *Nationality and Home Rule*,

Arthur James Balfour, the former Scottish Secretary and Prime Minister, called this 'sentiment of nationality' 'patriotism' (i.e. 'good' nationalism), noting that it might 'embrace a great deal more than a man's country or a man's race', or indeed 'a great deal less'.

Using himself as a case study, Balfour observed that 'some combination of different patriotisms' was 'almost universal among thinking persons', his being affection 'for the communities which compose the British Empire, for the United Kingdom of which I am a citizen, and for Scotland, where I was born, where I live, and where my fathers lived before me'. This quotation neatly combined the three central elements of nationalist unionism – imperial, British and Scottish – simultaneously civic (the emphasis on communities and citizenship) and ethnic (Balfour's bloodline).

Echoing Renan's (1882) definition of nationhood, and anticipating Anderson's 'imagined community' (1991), Balfour posited that patriotic sentiment might 'crystallise' around

> a real or supposed community of race, of language, or religion, of institutions, of culture. It may be due to geographical conditions; or it may be the offspring of common memories, or of common hopes, or of common interests. Only of this we may be sure, that whatever its real origin or justification, it will endeavor to draw nourishment from all sources, and will be especially apt to justify its existence by a version of history which at the best is one-sided, at the worst it purely mythical.

Balfour intended this last point as a warning, of how easily 'good' nationalism could turn to 'bad', selectively interpreting history to serve its own ends. This served as a hook for the primary purpose of Balfour's essay, the situation in Ireland. 'If race and blood be the essential root of Nationalist theories as applied to the United Kingdom,' he wrote, 'the Scotland of history must perish, and Ulster must be divided from the rest of Ireland.' Therefore, Balfour optimistically predicted, 'Irish patriotism will as easily combine with British patriotism as Scottish patriotism combines now' (Balfour 1913: 9–23).

Sir Robert Rait, who became something of a court historian for Scottish Unionists, also did much to legitimise this view of Scottish 'patriotism'. He viewed the 1707 Union as the 'greatest and wisest measure ever passed by the Parliament of Scotland', while also questioning the assumption, 'less common now than it was fifty years ago, that national progress must always be measured by constitutional advance' (Rait 1914: 239, 243).

Rait was also close to the constitutionalist A. V. Dicey, and together they produced *Thoughts on the Union Between England and Scotland*, also written in the context of the Irish Question. They defined nationalism as 'the love of a special country by the inhabitants thereof as their homeland':

> They love this home, be it England, Scotland, or Wales, its religion, its institu-
> tions, its laws, its traditions, its history, its heroes, and above all its spirit, with
> a love resembling the affection which a man feels for his family, for his father,
> for his mother, for his brothers and sisters. The love, it is true, may originate
> in various causes, in community of race, of language, of religion, or of history,
> but whatever its origin, this attachment of a man to his own country is itself
> a matter of moral value. It is at once the cause and the result of patriotism.

This account did not deny that the Union of 1707 had 'deprived Scotsmen of something to which for centuries they had attached the highest value', i.e. determining 'her own course of action independently and in defiance of the wish of England'. But 'partnership made on fair terms' was, asserted Dicey and Rait, 'an essentially different thing from subjection or servitude', and thus the recognition in the early eighteenth century that 'the sacrifice of Scottish independence need not mean the loss of Scottish Nationalism' had been an indication of the 'most statesmanlike foresight'. Thus Scottish nationalism had been 'kept alive' by the retention of 'administrative government' and the Church of Scotland (Dicey and Rait 1920: 321–62).

Ironically, although Dicey possessed a 'far more sophisticated understanding of the territorial constitution' than many accounts allow, his legacy – a strong belief in unimpeachable parliamentary sovereignty – ended up stiffening Unionist resolve against 'autonomous bodies' (Mitchell 2009: 8). Yet his and Rait's nuanced definition of 'nationalist unionism' was influential, surfacing in Chiao's exhaustive survey (1926) of Scottish devolutionary discourse between the late nineteenth and early twentieth centuries. He drew a similar distinction between 'good' and 'bad' nationalism, 'local patriotism and local attachment' being 'quite natural and wholesome' (Chiao 1969: 221).

Having argued that 'Scottish nationalism' had been safeguarded by the Act of Union, it therefore followed that Unionists had to defend it from perceived threats. During the 1920s these took two forms, one internal (socialism) and the other external (Irish immigration), the latter highlighting an ethnic dimension to nationalist unionism.

'Alien Rule of the Most Disastrous Type'

Unionism in Scotland and Ireland made a useful contrast during the 1920s. What Jackson regarded as the 'great success' of the Scottish variety, 'its ability to define itself in the language of nationality', thereby encapsulating 'Scottish values and Scottish heritage', was not mirrored across the Irish Sea, where Unionism was associated with 'alien nationality, alien interests, an alien history, and alien religious convictions' (Jackson 2012: 221).

It is revealing that Dicey and Rait made no attempt to champion the preservation of 'Irish Nationalism' alongside the Scottish and English varieties, for by 1920 the Irish Question was about to be (partly) answered following decades of debate. And even before the Anglo-Irish Treaty created an 'Irish Free State', encompassing what had been known as 'southern Ireland', Unionist policy had 'switched rather suddenly from defence of the Union to defence of Ulster' (McLean and McMillan 2005: 121).

Given that the Scottish Unionist Association had been formed in 1912 partly as a response to renewed Liberal plans for Irish Home Rule (Burness 2003), the loss of most of Ireland troubled the party. The Unionist MP Sir Henry Craik feared it would 'arouse in Scotland' a similarly 'deadly fruit', while his colleague Walter Elliot warned that the 'fearful poison of nationalism' risked Scotland reverting 'to the tribalism from which she emerged successfully centuries ago' (HC Deb 26 May 1922 Vol 154 c1648).

In other words, 'good' nationalism risked giving way to 'bad'. Prior to the general election of November 1922, however, a substantial chapter on Scotland (prepared by several Unionist members of the Scottish Bar) in the party's *Campaign Guide* adopted a less alarmist position on 'Home Rule for Scotland'. Although it reheated all the usual arguments against (primarily economic), it did not completely rule it out. 'Scotland may demand a Scots legislature' at some point in the future, it stated, which would be acceptable as long as it did not 'detract from a full appreciation of the fine worth and importance of that wider and nobler Imperial Patriotism to which Scotsmen have never been indifferent' (NUA 1922: 917–30).

Another general election followed in December 1923, by which point the Scottish Unionist line had hardened. An SUA leaflet took care to point out that those opposed to Home Rule were 'just as alive to sentiment and practical needs' as those in favour, while noting that 'for all matters that directly reflect its national characteristics', Scotland already had 'a separate legal system and a separate administration'. 'Its art, its literature, its poetry, its music are its own,' it continued, 'it has its own national Regiments with their own dress and customs, and all these things, in so far as they represent an unchanging national characteristic, must and will remain separate' (SUA c. 1923: 3–8).

But this 'unchanging national characteristic' was considered to be under threat. The Unionist MP Sir Robert Horne said Scottish Home Rule would lead to a 'form of very insidious Irish domination in our politics' (Mitchell 1990: 41), while a 1923 SUA publication warned it would likely produce

'Alien Rule of the most disastrous type', with a Scottish Parliament led not by Scotsmen 'but a more ignorant type of Irish voter, Lithuanians, and other aliens, working in or about the mines and factories in the industrial areas of the West', a clear reference to immigrants both from the British Isles and the Baltic region. And it was 'to this block of representatives with this type of un-national support' that voters were 'being asked to transfer the guidance of Scottish affairs' (SUA c. 1923: 3–8).

As Jackson observed, Unionist ideology during this period 'continued to be inflected by religious bigotry' (Jackson 2012: 15), closely aligned with the Church of Scotland ('arguably the Unionist Party at prayer'), which in 1923 had published a controversial report entitled *The Menace of the Irish Race to our Scottish Nationality*. This accused Scotland's Roman Catholic population of subverting Presbyterian values and thus argued for an end to Irish immigration in order to achieve a 'racially pure' Scotland (Forrester 1999: 80–9). Although Sir John Gilmour, the Unionist Secretary for Scotland, had served as a deputy grand master of the Orange Order, he distanced himself from the Kirk's stance. As Cameron put it, the 'campaign against the Irish in Scotland cut little ice with the Unionist party, which generally eschewed religious politics' (Cameron 2010: 165).

But given Scottish Unionists had inherited what Seawright called the Liberal Party's 'once impeccable Presbyterian credentials' (Seawright 1996: 56), the Orange vote in the west of Scotland, to quote Kellas, still 'sustained the Conservative Party, which would have been relatively weak there had "class voting" alone prevailed' (Kellas 1994: 677). Nevertheless, the broader Conservative outlook was still 'based on a form of civic nationalism' which might on occasion have appeared ethnic, but was not ethnically exclusive (Cragoe 2006: 193). Rather, these accounts of the (British) nation focused on 'allegiance to common institutions, a shared history and a political culture which fosters common values' (Lynch 1999: 154).

'An Unrepentant Scottish Nationalist'

The main conduit for this 'civic' Tory nationalism were the leading Conservative (and Unionist) politicians of the 1920s and 1930s, and it certainly helped the party's tripartite Scottish/British/imperial patriotism that so many senior figures hailed from Scotland. When, in 1937, Sir Lewis Shedden retired following half a century as secretary of the Glasgow Unionist Association, it was noted with pride that he had served under '11 Prime Ministers – five of them Scotsmen, and two of them business men from our own midst in Glasgow' (SCUA 1937). The appointment of the Unionist MPs John Buchan and A. D. Cochrane as, respectively, the governors of Canada and Burma also emphasised that the 'opportunities' for Scots facilitated by the Union were global as well as domestic.

Stanley Baldwin, the Conservative Party leader and Prime Minister during this period, was, as Ward-Smith (2001) has argued, consistently presented to Scottish voters in multi-national and even ethnic terms. A contemporary biography of Baldwin by Adam Whyte, a Scottish member of staff at Conservative Central Office in London, referred to his mixed 'racial' origins, possessing English, Scottish and Welsh ancestry (Whyte 1926: 14). Indeed, Baldwin's Scottish speeches were full of such references, not least his 'profound admiration for the characteristics of the Scottish race', which he said embodied 'that indestructible love of your own people and your own soil'.

The Prime Minister was careful, however, to balance this ethnic nationalism with the civic variety, frequently praising distinct Scottish institutions such as its education system and highlighting the ways in which he believed Scots had contributed 'to that common stock that makes up the character of the British race'. The 1928 Glasgow University rectorial election even pitched Baldwin in a symbolic battle against a 'bad' nationalist, Robert Cunningham Grahame, who had recently helped launch the National Party of Scotland (NPS). Baldwin won by a margin of just sixty-six votes, but he had clearly been alive to the threat of defeat, at one point protesting that 'the things that make Scottish Nationalists anxious are matters in which they have my full sympathy'.

Elsewhere, Baldwin made much of his Jacobite credentials, his mother's family having fled the Highlands following the 1745 uprising, while extolling the virtues of Sir Walter Scott, whose works he had read as a child. He praised the manner in which Scott had 'deepened, enriched and ennobled' long-standing patriotism, his 'greatest service' having been 'the interpretation of Scotland to England'. Baldwin's nationalist unionism, therefore, was multi-faceted, encompassing the civic and ethnic strands that had been a persistent feature of Unionist party politics since before the First World War.

Baldwin also took care not to neglect the imperial dimension, repeatedly emphasising the role of individual Scots in the creation and development of the Canadian and New Zealand Dominions. Speaking to a Glasgow audience in 1928, Baldwin even asserted that 'Scottish Nationalism is one of the most prized fruits of the British Empire' (all references from Ward-Smith 2001: 61–82). As Kearton acknowledged, this approach 'backed up' the Unionist account of the Anglo-Scottish Union with 'myth, symbol and history', providing 'a powerful means of legitimising contemporary political aims by rooting them in a particularly Scottish idiom' (Kearton 2012: 23–50). Not only did

Baldwin champion 'good' Scottish nationalism, but he presented himself as its defender.

And it clearly had an effect, not only judging by the electoral success of Scottish Unionists during the 1920s, but in contemporary media coverage. The Unionist-supporting *Glasgow Herald* claimed that 'the Scottish element in [Baldwin's] ancestry is in itself sufficient to establish a bond of sympathy' with Scottish audiences, while it was the opinion of the *Weekly Scotsman* in 1933 that 'no politician of the present day stands higher in the favour of a Scottish audience than Mr Baldwin' (Ward-Smith 2001: 70).

Unionist Scottish Secretaries, meanwhile, were generally titled land-owners, businessmen and advocates. And nearly all were educated in whole or in part at English public schools and Oxbridge, something that was 'to emphasize the Unionist (British) character of the party, as well as its upper-class political leadership' (Kellas 1994: 684). The most prominent Scottish Unionist politician of the 1920s and 1930s, Sir John Gilmour Bt, was a case in point, and a nationalist unionist par excellence.

In 1926, Baldwin finally promoted Gilmour from 'Secretary for Scotland' to 'Secretary of State for Scotland'. The Scottish Unionist Association's thirteenth annual report recorded 'great and general satisfaction' at Sir John's new 'status and dignity' (SCUA 1926), while the Earl of Mar and Kellie made a point of presenting several portraits of pre-1745 Secretaries of State to the Whitehall home of the Scottish Office 'to mark the restoration of that Office in your person', a clear attempt to draw a line between early eighteenth- and twentieth-century Scottish administration (Mar and Kellie 1926).[2]

Gilmour's junior minister at the Scottish Office, Walter Elliot, was, if anything, even more of a nationalist unionist than his superior, although he has divided opinion. Harvie concluded, surprisingly, that he 'was no nationalist' (Harvie 1998: 95), although Kellas viewed Elliot and his Labour contemporary Tom Johnston, more accurately, as 'Scottish nationalists of a kind' (Kellas 1994: 685). In the House of Commons in April 1920 Elliot called himself 'an unrepentant Scottish Nationalist' (HC Deb 16 April 1920 Vol 127 c2058), while Ward has argued that 'Elliot's life within the Union reflected the mutually reinforcing nature of his Scottishness, Unionism and, to a lesser extent, imperialism' (Ward 2005: 154). Like Baldwin, Elliot weaponised history to legitimise his nationalist unionism, arguing that Scotland had entered the 1707 Union 'as an equal partner rather than as a conquered country' (Ward 2005: 26). He constantly drew dividing lines between Scottishness and Englishness, arguing in 1934 that Scots could never by instinct be 'as tolerant as the English, as fair as the English, as forbearing as the English' but rather made a 'special contribution' from their own 'special qualities – industry, fury, romance' (Coote 1965: 226).

Elliot was particularly alive to what Hanham called 'a burst of nationalist fervour' (Hanham 1969: 12) in the late 1920s, discussion of Home Rule having been relatively dormant since the early part of that decade. In May 1927, a Home Rule Bill promoted by the Labour MP James Barr had been debated in the House of Commons, while the following year the NPS was formed. Most likely in response, the Scottish Unionist Whip's Office issued an updated statement of Scottish policy in August 1928. This made specific reference to Barr's scheme, asserting that it went 'far beyond devolution' and would involve the 'separation of England and Scotland'. It then reiterated material from the 1924 *Campaign Guide* while observing that the Scottish Secretary had been restored to his 'rightful status' in 1926. Of legislative devolution more generally, it judged that 'few in Scotland have got beyond the sentimental phase of what they believe, honestly enough, to be a patriotic national aspiration' (SUWO 1928: 128–31).

Beyond the Home Rule debate, there was sustained 'political debate on the status, nature and mechanism of the Scottish Secretary's authority' (Levitt 1992: 13), not only Sir John Gilmour's status in Cabinet but the reorganisation of government machinery north of the border. This, as in the late nineteenth century, encompassed a myriad of Scottish 'boards' all housed in separate accommodation in Edinburgh. This Sir John regarded as inefficient, thus he introduced a Reorganisation of Offices (Scotland) Bill to abolish the Scottish Board of Health, Board of Agriculture for Scotland and Prison Commissioners, replacing them with the corresponding Scottish Office 'departments' of health, agriculture and prisons (Mitchell 2003).

It was not a universally popular move. In one way, noted Fry, the move 'represented a step away from autonomy' given that the board system, 'for all its faults, had allowed the Scots to conduct their business without excessive reference to Whitehall norms' (Fry 1991: 144). Indeed, opposition MPs attacked it on that basis, with the former Labour Scottish Secretary William Adamson even quoting a disgruntled Unionist who had complained to a newspaper about Scotland yet again being 'fixed upon for experiments', and that 'this continual flouting of Scottish national sentiment' was 'really very galling to patriotic Scottish Unionists' (HC Deb 23 March 1927 Vol 204 c473).

The Bill was also severely criticised by two Unionist MPs, Noel Skelton, whose father had served as vice-president of the Local Government Board for Scotland, and Fred Macquisten. The Labour MP James Brown hoped both would 'stand by and claim the rights of Scotland' by voting against the measure which, added Brown, 'practically denationalises Scotland' (thus anticipating an argument Scottish Unionists would use against a Labour government twenty years later). He even warned that 'the people of Scotland' would 'deal drastically' with Members who 'dared to take away the only remnant left of

Scottish nationality' (HC Deb 09 July 1928 Vol 219 c1981). Sir Henry Keith, another Unionist MP, would later claim the reforms violated the 1707 Treaty of Union (*Glasgow Herald*, 27 August 1928).

In response, Sir John Gilmour took care to defend himself in nationalist terms, protesting that if he felt 'for a single moment' he was 'taking an action which would denationalise my country' he would not be introducing the Bill, nor did it 'spring from a Cabinet desirous of inflicting injury upon Scotland'. Rather his aim was 'to strengthen and improve the administration in the sole interest of efficiency', although he took care to acknowledge that for as long as Scotland remained part of the UK then 'the real controlling power' would remain at Westminster (HC Deb 09 July 1928 Vol 219 c1982).

This was a restatement of Diceyan orthodoxy, a strong belief in Parliamentary sovereignty, whatever the administrative arrangements in Scotland. As Mitchell observed, while the Scottish Office 'embodied the UK's willingness to acknowledge Scottish distinctiveness', as 'part of Whitehall and accountable to Parliament at Westminster, it also represented the unity of the state' (Mitchell 2003: 1). Gilmour's subsequent proposals to consolidate a panoply of parish, town, district, county and education authorities in Scotland once again led to accusations by Labour and Liberal MPs that the Secretary of State was attacking 'historic' units of Scottish administration. Thus, the Scottish Unionist Party fought the 1929 general election on the defensive, conscious that some of Sir John Gilmour's reforms had left it vulnerable to charges of failing to defend Scotland's institutional 'autonomy'.

'Every Scotsman Should Be a Scottish Nationalist'

That election found the Scottish Unionist ascendancy briefly halted, while a split emerged between proponents of 'administrative' and 'legislative' devolution. Prominent in this respect was the advocate Andrew Dewar Gibb, who had contested seats at the 1924 and 1929 general elections. He regarded Scots Law as an important survivor from the pre-1707 period, a 'legal nationalism' (Grant 1976) shared by many Scottish Unionist MPs. Dewar Gibb was close, for example, to Thomas Cooper, later a Unionist MP, who viewed Scots Law as 'the mirror of Scotland's history and traditions and a typical product of the national character' (Cooper 1949: 65).

Thus legal nationalism overlapped with nationalist unionism, 'nationalist sentiments laid over a secret life of unionism' (Farmer 2001: 152), though not necessarily 'entailing support for nationalist politics' (Grant 1976: 77). In 1928, Dewar Gibb's proposed conference resolution on 'the increasing provincialization of Scotland' was rejected by the Scottish Unionist leadership, although John Buchan agreed with him that the party ought to support 'what is sane in the Nationalist movement' (Dewar Gibb 1928). He also lobbied Stanley Baldwin, urging him to recognise 'the new spirit alive in Scotland' with a 'definite Conservative policy for Scotland', including a Royal Commission. Such moves, he concluded, would benefit both Scotland and the Scottish Unionist Party (Dewar Gibb 1930a).

Dewar Gibb's book *Scotland in Eclipse*, meanwhile, caused controversy with its attack on Sir Harry Lauder for vulgarising the popular conception of Scotland. The *Glasgow Evening Times* described Gibb as 'a Conservative Nationalist', while the *Daily Telegraph* said the author saw 'nothing incompatible in a blending of stout Scots nationalism, on fresh, statutory, but resourceful lines, and British Conservatism' (Dewar Gibb 1930b). *Scotland in Eclipse* also argued that Scotland's place in the empire had been compromised by its subordinate status within the UK, a radical break with mainstream Scottish Unionist thought. In private correspondence, Dewar Gibb called this 'unionist-nationalism'.

In 1930, both Dewar Gibb and the polemical journalist George Malcolm Thomson joined the new Scottish (Self-Government) Party, intended as a counterpoint to the more left-wing National Party of Scotland and mainly comprising former Unionists. Dewar Gibb also believed Scotland to be suffering from an 'influx' of inferior Irishmen and women. This 'hibernophobia', as Kidd put it, thus 'surfaced in Scottish nationalist polemic', not least because several former Unionists played such 'an influential role in the partial reinvigoration of Scottish nationalist politics during the 1930s' (Kidd 2008: 20).

The national 'movement' also received a fillip shortly before the 1931 general election when the popular writer Compton Mackenzie beat the Scottish Unionist grandee (and former Chancellor) Sir Robert Horne to become Lord Rector of Glasgow University. This kept discussion of Home Rule firmly on the political agenda, so much so that at the beginning of 1932 Stanley Baldwin, now Lord President and de facto Prime Minister, given Tory dominance of the National Government, felt it necessary explicitly to rule out a Home Rule Bill and, in May, to decline to summon a round-table conference of Scottish representatives to discuss re-establishing a Scottish Parliament, there being no evidence 'that the creation of small units makes for the prosperity of the world' (HC Deb 4 May 1932 Vol 265 cc1107–8).

In the spring of 1932, meanwhile, the Scottish Unionist Whip's Office had been sufficiently alert to rising Home Rule sentiment to produce a pamphlet entitled, simply, *Scottish Nationalism*. This drew heavily upon previously published material from the 1920s, but was notable for referring to 'Independence' rather than 'Home Rule', just as 'Separatist' would shortly replace 'Nationalist' in Scottish Unionist discourse. It opened with Rait's brief account of the Union from his 1929 *History of Scotland*, going on to warn that a Scottish Parliament would lead to 'mutual jealousies and frictions between the Highlands and the Lowlands', not least because the latter would be called upon to subsidise the former, potentially reviving 'old feuds and old cleavages within the country'.

Rather it said the aim 'of those who wish well of Scotland' should be to avoid 'political isolation' by fostering 'all that is best in the Scottish character and traditions', or in other words 'good' nationalism, that specific blend of Scottish, British and imperial patriotism:

> The Union between Scotland and England is an historical event of unique kind. Under it, two independent nations united and, while maintaining their own individuality, have together successfully developed a worldwide Empire. Scotland, while engaged in this great partnership, has preserved, and will ever preserve, her traditions, her character, and distinctive institutions.

Scottish Nationalism concluded, however, with an open mind: 'The necessity for further devolution may become a practical question, and Scottish Unionists would not refuse to consider the matter carefully; but any scheme hitherto proposed contains more disadvantages than gains for Scotland' (SUWO 1932: 5–16).

Subsequent events, meanwhile, vindicated this pre-emptive propaganda strike, for in June 1932 a more serious split occurred, when the 'large and prosperous' Glasgow Cathcart Unionist Association 'suddenly severed its connection with the Tory Party and declared that it stood for Scottish Home Rule and Imperial Federation' (MacCormick 1955: 64). Led by a Glaswegian lawyer called Kevan McDowall, the resulting row rumbled on for months, having been given a high media profile by the relatively new tabloid newspaper, the *Daily Record and Mail.*

The 'Imperial Committee of the Unionist Association of Cathcart' even issued a manifesto, emblazoned with a Union Jack, saltire and lion rampant. It declared that measures of 'Dominion government' for Scotland, England and Wales were 'essential for the better government of these nations' and the empire, as well as 'to realise the Aspirations and preserve the Characteristics of the Scottish Nation'. But it repudiated the 'Separation, by isolated Home Rule, of Scotsmen from their Kith and Kin in the British Isles and the British Dominions beyond the Seas' and closed with a quotation from Burns (ICUAC 1932: 3). The Scottish Unionist Association's response, as Mitchell described it, was 'swift . . . well organised and decisive' (Mitchell 1990: 202), with three important meetings held later in the year designed to isolate the association and minimise the political fallout.

The new 'Scottish' *Daily Express*, published in Glasgow since 1928, also took an interest, its proprietor Lord Beaverbrook (a Canadian of Scottish descent) expressing his support for what he called a 'sound movement'. The *Express* also conducted the earliest (but not very scientific) mass survey of Scottish public opinion on the question of a Scottish Parliament, finding 112,984 in favour and only 4,596 against. The Cathcart secession clearly worried Scottish Unionist MPs, as did growing nationalist sentiment in general, not least because it was 'emanating from traditional middle-class quarters', something reinforced by the media, intellectuals and businessmen who noticed the economic disparities vis-à-vis England. The party, therefore, began to refashion their unionist ideology to 'acknowledge the legitimacy of nationalist sentiment' but 'without encouraging political separatism' (Finlay 1996: 114–16).

Newspapers during the summer of 1932 were full of half-baked schemes as this refashioning took place. Interviewed by the *Daily Record*, the Unionist MP Thomas Moore said he was 'in favour of a certain amount of devolution', which he suggested would involve having the Secretary of State resident in Edinburgh for three months of the year, alongside a representative of the king. Scottish Bills would also be considered in committee by Scottish MPs sitting in Edinburgh, 'where the Scottish atmosphere of criticism and interest could be gathered and appreciated more fully than is possible under present circumstances' (*Daily Record*, 21 July 1932).

In the *Scotsman* a month later, Sir Patrick Ford, another Unionist MP, made the usual distinction between 'good' and 'bad' nationalism, saying that 'a genuine revival of purely Scottish national sentiment is entirely welcome', yet a 'confusion of thought that identifies a specialized national sentiment with a factitious political separatism is surely to be deprecated'. A devolved Scottish Parliament would, in his view, constitute 'extreme separatism', although Scotland possessed 'grievances' both political and economic. Curiously, Sir Patrick believed the existing Scottish Office was the 'root of all our difficulties', being 'more and more the lapdog of the Treasury and the Government of the day, and less and less the watchdog of Scotland' (*Scotsman*, 17 August 1932).

A few months later, a whole day in the House of Commons was devoted to Scottish affairs, an unprecedented move in Parliamentary terms and an indication of how seriously the National Government took the political situation. It opened with a speech from Sir Robert Horne, the Scottish Unionist MP who had been defeated by Compton Mackenzie at Glasgow University a year earlier. He admitted frankly that the issue had been 'forced upon our attention by certain movements which have been taking place in Scotland', a phenomenon he linked directly to the economic situation.

Sir Robert said he intended to 'curb any tendency' he 'might have towards expression of patriotic sentiment' and instead give the House 'a quite cold matter-of-fact analysis of the position'. This drew on the usual strands of nationalist unionism, ethnic and civic, while, interestingly, Horne divided supporters of a Scottish Parliament into two camps, which he called 'the Nationalists and the Moderates', in other words those who believed the Act of Union to be a 'curse' and those who desired reform rather than repeal (HC Deb 24 November 1932 Vol 272 c243). This, however, suggested a more nuanced position that in fact existed, for as Mackenzie observed, Unionists 'were presented with the chance of answering the first group, which they could easily do, and thus avoiding argument with the second, while preserving an appearance of candid discussion' (Mackenzie 1947: 394–5).

Continuing with his speech, Sir Robert reiterated earlier Unionist warnings that Scottish Home Rule might lead to 'a form of very insidious Irish domination in our politics', while in a more civic frame of mind he proposed reforming Scottish private Bill procedure at Westminster, creating an additional under-secretary to assist the Secretary of State for Scotland and, more substantially, concentrating 'in Edinburgh . . . all the main work of the Departments which look after the business of Scotland', the status quo being 'unworthy of the dignity of Scotland'. He suggested the construction of a 'suitable edifice', perhaps on Edinburgh's Calton Hill. All of this, suggested Horne, would give the 'impression of Scotland's position in this Kingdom which it deserves' (HC Deb 24 November 1932 Vol 272 c252–3). Sir Robert's words were still being quoted in Scottish Unionist literature sixteen years later (see, for example, SUA 1948).

John Buchan, a 'romantic Scottish nationalist' (Kellas 1994: 685) and long-standing friend and associate of the historian Robert Rait, took a step beyond the official Unionist position in dismissing many of the arguments against Home Rule as 'foolish' and declaring that 'every Scotsman should be a Scottish Nationalist'. 'If it could he proved that a separate Scottish Parliament were desirable,' he added, 'Scotsmen should support it.' He also expressed fears that Scotland's best 'race stock' might be replaced 'by those who, whatever their merits, are not Scottish', while agreeing with Horne that a 'suitable edifice' in Edinburgh would represent the 'logical consequence of Scotland's constitutional position', simultaneously 'a nation in a true sense' but also one 'in the closest corporate alliance with her Southern neighbour'. Finally, Buchan contradicted himself by differentiating between 'an artificial nationalism' based upon 'barren separatism' and the 'sane nationalism' he believed 'necessary for all true peace and prosperity' (HC Deb 24 November 1932 Vol 272 c262–3).

Such contributions demonstrated that nationalist unionism was reasserting itself in response to a perceived shift in public opinion. Finlay viewed the events of 1932 as representing a turning point in Unionist strategy towards Scotland, ending the 'notion of the Union as an equal partnership between Scotland and England' and instead stressing the former's economic reliance on the latter, acknowledging and gratifying Scottish national sentiment 'without surrendering any political power from Westminster' (Finlay 1997: 103–4), 'arguably the most profound shift in Scottish political thinking of the twentieth century' (Finlay 2004: 113–14).

This is an overstatement, for Unionist strategy was actually quite consistent, most of its features departing little from what had been set out in the 1914 memo quoted at the beginning of this chapter. Finlay's account also ignored the fact that the economic backdrop *had* changed, with a recent financial 'return' (a revival of pre-1921 practice in relation to Ireland) showing Scotland to be a net beneficiary from the Treasury. There was also, as Cragoe argued, a degree of consistency between 'Conservative priorities . . . north and south of the border' (Cragoe 2006: 201), i.e. a mutually reinforcing 'civic' English, Scottish and British nationalism. Jackson believed it reflected a 'sincere expression of Scottish patriotism' compatible with 'the effective devolution of some Scottish business to Edinburgh' (Jackson 2012: 257).

Shoring this up was *A Scotsman's Heritage*, a sort of nationalist-unionist manifesto published in 1932, doubtless a response to more negative tracts from Dewar Gibb *et al.* In his contribution to the book, Walter Elliot dwelled at length on the wars of independence, while sanctifying the Church of Scotland as the 'characteristic gathering' of 'our people . . . a Covenant sealed in blood'. Furthermore, the 'political soul of Scotland', which he conceded was 'undoubtedly disembodied', did not in his view require a 'synthetic' Parliament in Edinburgh.

Other contributors highlighted the remainder of Scotland's 'holy trinity', Professor John Graham Kerr arguing that one of the 'great tasks' of education was to 'protect' and 'cherish' Scottish patriotism, training young people to revere 'the national flag as a sacred symbol' and the 'beneficient achievements of our race'. Finally, Lord Macmillan gave full expression to 'legal nationalism', praising the 'tenacity' of the Scottish 'race' for having retained, in spite of repeated attempts at assimilation, 'its own distinctive laws, its own legal procedure, and a judicial establishment entirely apart from that of England' (Atholl 1932: 58, 64, 87–8, 100).

Also helping communicate this more muscular nationalist unionism was the Scottish media. As Anderson (1991) has argued, newspapers contributed to the formation of national consciousness by treating their readers as a national 'community', and this was certainly true in inter-war Scotland for, as Brand put it, between 1931 and 1934 'it was difficult to avoid the home rule issue if one read a Scottish newspaper' (Brand 1978: 214). As McNair observed, although these newspapers believed wholeheartedly in the Union 'they spoke with a distinctively Scottish voice', subconsciously contributing 'to the growth of Scottish Nationalism' (McNair 2008: 237, 367–70).

The Scottish media also played an important part in what became known as the 'Scottish Renaissance', a response to a widespread feeling, articulated earlier by Buchan, that Scotland was 'gradually being emptied of its population, its spirit, its wealth, industry, art, intellect and innate character' (Muir 1935: 78). Later, this frustration was channelled into the formation of the Stair (1934) and Saltire (1936) Societies to study and promote, respectively, Scotland's legal and artistic heritage. Many Unionists – legal and cultural nationalists – were active in both.

Also formed in 1934 was the Scottish National Party (SNP), from a merger of the left-leaning National Party of Scotland and right-leaning Scottish (Self-Government) Party – indeed historians have made remarkably little of the SNP's origins in a Unionist split – but by this point the Home Rule sentiment that had spooked the Unionist hierarchy in 1932 appeared to have subsided. As Cragoe observed, with 'an apparently sound administrative structure in place, and a membership that, on paper at least, was numbered in the tens of thousands, the Tories encountered nationalism from a position of some strength in the 1930s' (Cragoe 2006: 202).

And while Dewar Gibb had found a new (if never entirely happy) home in the SNP, later serving as chairman between 1936 and 1940, other Unionists such as James A. A. Porteous continued to try to nudge the Scottish Unionist Party in a devolutionary direction. His lengthy 1935 book *The New Unionism* urged Scottish Unionists to acknowledge demands for 'a greater measure of national self-expression' by reaching a 'compromise with separatism where National and Imperial interests require that course'. There was 'plenty of room', concluded Porteous, 'for devolution in unity' (Porteous 1935: 25, 87–9).

Another notable rebel was James Graham, the sixth Duke of Montrose, whose squabbles with the Scottish Unionist hierarchy went back more than a decade. Proud that his ancestor Sir David de Graham had signed the Declaration of Arbroath and supported Robert the Bruce at Bannockburn in 1314, Montrose helped Dewar Gibb found the Scottish Party in 1930 and subsequently oversaw its merger with the NPS in 1934. Montrose's 1933 pamphlet, *Self-Government for Scotland*, claimed the Scottish Party was free from all 'hatred of England' and played down Unionist fears of Home Rule leading to 'Rome Rule'. The 'Irish element' in Scotland, argued Montrose, was only 10 per cent of the electorate so the tail could not 'wag the dog', while far from weakening the UK and the empire, legislative devolution would enable Scotland to 'play her part with pride as an Empire-builder enveloped in the robe of nationality' (Montrose 1933: 4–10).

In spite of these views, Montrose somehow retained the Conservative whip in the House of Lords, only joining the more enthusiastically pro-Home Rule Liberals in 1936. 'No lasting good in my opinion can result until we are granted decentralized government, with a Legislature in Scotland', he wrote to Lord Halifax, the Conservative leader in the Upper House. 'I have endeavoured for a long time to interest the Unionist Party in this question; but have met with nothing but opposition.' To Montrose, Unionist concessions were little more than a 'fig leaf' and the Secretary of State for Scotland a 'dictatorship' (Montrose 1952: 192–3).

But having seen off the (capital 'N') nationalist threat, by the mid-1930s the Scottish Unionist Party was in no mood to compromise with individual Unionists (James Porteous would also ultimately quit, becoming the SNP's economic adviser). Rather the party, once again in office following the 1935 general election, was preoccupied with delivering a key element of Sir Robert Horne's 1932 nationalist-unionist manifesto, more 'administrative devolution' and a suitable 'edifice' in the Scottish capital.

'An Agreeable Compromise with Home Rule'

There had always been a strong institutional dimension to nationalist unionism, stretching back to the mid nineteenth century and the National Association for the Vindication of Scottish Rights. Later, as Mackenzie observed, nineteenth-century 'self-government agitation had led to the granting of a Scottish Office as a placebo. That of the twentieth transferred the Office from Whitehall to Edinburgh' (Mackenzie 1947: 400).

Thereafter that 'placebo' was repeatedly prescribed, administrative devolution becoming the Scottish Unionists' 'preferred method of soothing nationalist grievances' (Kidd 2008: 18–19), the most 'civic' strand of nationalist unionism. Again, this had a provenance beyond Scotland. Since the age of Disraeli, Conservatives had presented themselves as defenders of national institutions – parliament, the church and the monarchy – while also creating new ones, not least the Scottish Office, so that by the 1930s Unionism was 'identified with key aspects of Scottish national institutions' (Hutchison 1998: 80).

Unionist politicians such as the Duchess of Atholl had long emphasised the differences between Scottish and English administration, while as the 1930s progressed the National Government increasingly treated Scotland as a separate and distinct economic unit, a so-called 'Special Area'. In 1936, the

SUA's Central Council noted approvingly that a Scottish Economic Committee, 'representative of Scottish business interests', had been appointed by the Scottish National Development Council with a remit 'to examine and advise regarding the possibilities of economic expansion in Scotland' (SCUA 1936).

The Scottish Office, however, possessed limited economic responsibilities, although efforts continued to relocate its Whitehall-based officials to Edinburgh. In February 1935, a Scottish Unionist Whip's Office publication noted that 96.2 per cent of civil servants were 'now resident in Scotland', in 'accordance with the desire to have Scottish administration in as close touch as possible with Scottish public opinion'. A new office for the Scottish Secretary had also been opened in Edinburgh (at Drumsheugh Gardens), 'entrusted with responsibility for many matters hitherto dealt with by the Scottish Office in London' (SUWO 1935: 15).

But something more ostentatious was also required. In 1936, a 'Committee on Scottish Administration' was constituted under the chairmanship of the former Scottish Secretary Sir John Gilmour in an attempt, as Mitchell put it, 'to recognise Scottish distinctiveness and simultaneously professionalise and consolidate the public service' (Mitchell 1989: 173). Gilmour must have regarded this as unfinished business, for this time his reforms were 'vigorously presented in Scottish patriotic terms' (Jackson 2012: 260).[3]

Sir John published his recommendations in the autumn of 1937. The Liberal/Nationalist Duke of Montrose dismissed it as little more than a 'game of musical chairs for the boys of the Scottish Office' (*Glasgow Herald*, 16 October 1937), while the SNP's response noted 'with satisfaction' that by implication the government now endorsed its view 'that the affairs of Scotland cannot be properly administered from a centre 400 miles away', although of course the 'logical conclusions' (i.e. a Scottish Parliament) had 'not been drawn' (Murray 1938: 123).

This was, of course, deliberate. Dewar Gibb later viewed it as a 'bold attempt, not wholly unsuccessful . . . to confuse the electorate as to the functions of legislature and executive' (Dewar Gibb 1950: 258), while Compton Mackenzie concluded that the decision to concentrate Scottish Office functions in Edinburgh rather than London was 'undoubtedly' due to the 'influence and devoted work' of various nationalist parties (*Picture Post*, 8 July 1939). That might have been true, but what Mackenzie called 'an agreeable compromise with Home Rule' (Mackenzie 1947: 400) did not, of course, benefit the SNP electorally.

Another aspect of administrative devolution was more symbolic. Just as Stormont, the custom-built home of the Northern Irish Parliament in Belfast, embodied the defiant statement of Ulster Unionism (itself a kind of nationalism, see Chapter 10), a new purpose-built home for the Scottish Office was intended to represent the Anglo-Scottish Union in bricks and mortar. The process, much like that associated with the Scottish Parliament building project six decades later, was lengthy and controversial. The contract was awarded to a Scottish architect, Thomas S. Tait, who aimed to create a 'Scottish Acropolis' (Walker 1989: 28). Its site, on Edinburgh's Calton Hill, was to be visible, elevated (on one side) and, like Stormont, imposing.

On 28 April 1937, the foundation stone was laid by the Duke of Gloucester (also the Earl of Ulster and Baron Culloden), the fourth son of the late King George V, and indeed royalty was also deployed by Unionists as their nationalist unionism grew more proactive. George and Mary had made a point of spending more time at Holyroodhouse, while after the abdication of King Edward VIII, the new sovereigns 'made it clear from the start that they knew they were King and Queen of more than one kingdom', something aided by the new queen being 'a Scotswoman of an ancient house' (Mackenzie 1947: 444–5). Indeed, Unionist MPs were often irritated by their southern colleagues' references to the 'King of England', William Paterson Templeton complaining that his 'Scottish soul rose in revolt against the expression' (HC Deb 23 November 1933 Vol 283 c385).

Walter Elliot, Scottish Secretary since 1936, encouraged more royal visits (as suggested by John Buchan in 1932) and reached into the past for inspiration, planning a grand ball at Holyrood Palace for George VI's coronation tour, an imitation of that hosted by Prince Charles Edward Stuart in 1745. More money was also found for Scottish museums and libraries (work started on a new home for the National Library of Scotland in 1938), with records removed during the reign of Edward I returned to Scotland (Finlay 1996: 119). The *pièce de résistance* was the Empire Exhibition in Glasgow, an event carefully choreographed to emphasise Scotland's distinctiveness within the British Empire. As the SUA's Central Council reported in 1938, its opening by King George VI had been 'an event of importance to Scotland', with the monarch attributing 'its origin and to a great extent its execution to the people of Scotland' (SCUA 1938).

The co-ordinating architect was again Thomas S. Tait, who conceived three major axes representing the affiliations of the Scottish nation: The Scottish Avenue, Kingsway (Britain) and the Dominions and Colonial Avenues (the empire), neatly mirroring the three main strands of nationalist unionism. Mackenzie noted 'more care' by the government in the 'use of national adjectives and of such signs as flags and coats of arms'. All these things, she added, were doubtless 'trifles in themselves', but they helped foster a more nationalist 'frame of mind' (Mackenzie 1947: 445).

Privately, however, Elliot acknowledged that no amount of symbolism was sufficient to 'dispose of the problems upon whose solution a general improvement in Scottish social and economic conditions depends'. As he added in a memo entitled 'The State of Scotland', it was 'the consciousness of their existence which is reflected, not in the small and unimportant Nationalist Party, but in the dissatisfaction and unease amongst moderate and reasonable people of every rank' (Finlay 2004: 165). Even the editor of the Unionist-supporting *Scotsman*, 'whose patriotism no one would call in question', was nevertheless 'troubled about the condition' of Scotland (Murray 1938: 52).

But, as in 1932, this crisis of confidence appears to have passed, and as a troubled decade drew to a close, the consolidated headquarters of the Scottish Office were nearing completion on Edinburgh's Calton Hill. Only in 1939 did it earn the name 'St Andrew's House' (following a radio appeal), but it was ostentatiously Scottish, its embellishments pointing 'to a more restrained, but intense national symbolism' (Glendinning 2004: 273). The Secretary of State's office was also panelled with walnut from a tree reputedly planted by Mary Queen of Scots (Walker 1989), a nod to Scotland's pre-Union past.

Above the entrance, meanwhile, were a series of figures symbolising the department's myriad responsibilities, including one holding a scroll entitled 'State Craft'. Indeed, the opening of St Andrew's House on the eve of the Second World War represented the culmination of a specifically Unionist form of statecraft, albeit one that contained a significant paradox. For Miller, the administrative settlement of 1939 meant that Scottish government had been reformed along 'coherent' but at the same time 'separatist' lines, 'of Scotland' rather than 'about Scotland', thus marking the end of the Scottish Office's role as 'a national unifier . . . and the start of its role as separatist within Britain' (Miller 1981: 9).

Mitchell agreed, noting that the newly constituted Scottish Office meant 'new public responsibilities and government duties' would thereafter 'be provided for on a Scottish basis' (Mitchell 2009: 19). Thus Unionists unwittingly encouraged a 'ratchet-like effect', meaning that as pre-Union institutions declined in influence, for example the Church of Scotland, the Scottish Office increasingly assumed a role as 'the chief manifestation of the union state' (Mitchell 2003: 209). Unionists, however, clearly believed they had successfully fixed, to paraphrase Parnell, the 'boundary' of the Scottish nation, and it was to be administrative and no further.

Conclusion

The period covered in this chapter straddles two distinct phases of the Conservative territorial code, 1914–26 and 1926–39, the latter being the first decade of the 'Dual Polity', in which the Centre (Westminster) apparently had little to do with the Scottish Periphery. The evidence above suggests a more nuanced dynamic than that described by Bulpitt. It is true that the Scottish Office consolidated and expanded its responsibilities between the late 1920s and the opening of St Andrew's House in 1939, but this pursuit of 'autonomy, unity and identity' (Smith 1991: 74) was driven by the London-based party, however much the 'Edinburgh people' had pointed the way in 1914.

UK party leaders such as Stanley Baldwin were also crucial to the success of the nationalist unionism that underpinned this political project. This was both civic and ethnic, with Scottish Unionists regularly adapting Scotland's 'myths, memories, symbols and values' to 'new circumstances', according them 'new meanings and new functions' (Smith 1986: 3–4). They also stressed the importance of the 'holy trinity', Scotland's Kirk, law and educational traditions. But there was also a darker strain, with persistent concerns in the 1920s and 1930s that migrants from Ireland were somehow weakening purely Scottish 'stock'.

This nationalist unionism was also banal, with what Scottish Unionists regarded as 'negative' nationalism (the campaign for legislative devolution) frequently pushed to the periphery and denigrated as extreme, anathema to a broader sense of British and imperial 'patriotism' embodied by the Conservatives. This, as we have seen, was alive to Scottish nationhood and sentiment, and was even prepared – in the troubled context of Ireland – to contemplate a Scottish Parliament, however much it railed against 'separatists'. But with the opening of St Andrew's House in 1939, there was a sense that Unionists were becoming victims of their own success, that they were ceding a little too much political and intellectual territory to their opponents.

FOUR

'Scottish Control of Scottish Affairs'

It was ironic that just as the doors opened at St Andrew's House in Edinburgh – the physical manifestation of newly self-confident inter-war nationalist unionism – Scotland and the UK faced an existential challenge from a very different sort of nationalism on the Continent. But just as in 1914–18, the Second World War was to have an impact on Scottish national identity while fundamentally redrawing the pre-war boundaries of UK party politics, and thus the ever-adaptable Scottish Unionist Party was once again compelled to respond.

During and after the war there was also a renewed challenge from within, not only from a better-organised Scottish National Party but also from the non-partisan Scottish Convention movement, which desired legislative autonomy within the United Kingdom. Both these forces would serve to make nationalist unionism even more ostentatious in its acknowledgement of the Scottish dimension, while further developing its political 'offer' within the confines of the Union.

Although the 'ethnic' nationalism that surfaced in the 1920s and 1930s in response to a perceived threat from Irish immigration receded, nationalist unionism still rested upon myths and symbols derived from Scotland's pre-Union history; these reminders of Scottish nationhood, meanwhile, were 'flagged' with greater frequency than before in party propaganda, speeches and election literature, a 'banal' nationalist unionism sitting alongside the British variety, particularly during and after the war.

The immediate post-war era also found Scottish Unionist strategy taking a more overt form during a process that culminated in the quasi-nationalist 'Scottish Control of Scottish Affairs' agenda. Although developed in concert with the unionist 'centre', this demonstrated a willingness to allow the Scottish 'periphery' a degree of autonomy when it came to containing growing pressure for legislative devolution. Conveniently, as will be shown, this dovetailed with a Britain-wide Conservative campaign against Labour's 'centralisation', thus 'local patriotism' was to be encouraged, not just in Scotland but also Wales and parts of England, the party's 'territorial code' at its height.

Putting 'the Interests of Scotland First'

The appointment of the English-born Ernest Brown (the Liberal MP for Leith) as Secretary of State for Scotland in May 1940 provoked something of a nationalist-unionist backlash. Robert Boothby wrote to Churchill after meeting his Scottish Unionist colleagues at the Carlton Club, recording 'their indignation at the appointment of an Englishman as Secretary of State'. 'They take the view, unanimously,' he added, 'that it is nothing short of a public insult to Scotland at the most critical moment in her proud history' (Boothby 1940).

And when, in May 1942, the House of Commons debated 'Scottish Affairs', many Members from both main parties 'expressed sentiments of [a] strongly Nationalist flavour' (MacCormick 1955: 110), the Unionist MP Alexander Erskine-Hill even commending a Labour Scottish Secretary, the ecumenical Thomas Johnston, for putting 'the interests of Scotland first' (HC Debs 12 May 1942 Vol 379 c1659). Privately, Walter Elliot confided to a friend that he was sometimes 'tempted to become a Home Ruler', a Scottish Parliament appearing to him likely 'owing to the growing divergence' between Scotland and England (Jackson 2012: 258). In 1944, he challenged (unsuccessfully) moves to 'transfer' control of National Insurance 'out of Scotland, where it is properly used, and where it can liaise completely with other parts of Scottish administration, into England' (HC Deb 14 November 1944 Vol 404 c1871).

Even so, nationalist unionism lacked its pre-war focus. Individual Unionist MPs such as Duncan McCallum in Argyll, meanwhile, ploughed their own furrows. Generally resentful of English MPs taking part in exclusively 'Scottish' Parliamentary debates, McCallum also championed Gaelic broadcasting, complaining in 1943 of the BBC's 'partial suppression' of Gaelic-language programmes (McCallum 1943). By 1945, McCallum was warning of rising nationalist sentiment in the Highlands and asked the Scottish Unionist Members Committee to establish 'the position of Scottish Unionists to Scottish Nationalism' (McCallum 1945).

In response to this request, P. J. ('Pat') Blair, a senior Scottish Unionist Association official in Edinburgh, distributed his *Scottish Nationalism* pamphlet from 1932, which he thought 'still applicable' despite being thirteen years old (Blair 1945a). The SUMC, meanwhile, concurred with McCallum and charged Blair with preparing a new pamphlet which 'would enable

Members to deal with Nationalist points when they arose' (SUMC 1945), a task that actually fell to the Unionist MP Sir Arthur Young.

As if to vindicate this activity, on 12 April 1945 Robert D. McIntyre became the first SNP MP following a by-election in Motherwell. Although the wartime truce largely explained the result, Unionists were conscious that McIntyre had attracted some Conservative votes (Somerville 2013: 4). On 28 May, Blair distributed copies of a new pamphlet, *The Answer to the Scottish Nationalists*, noting in a covering letter that there were, of course, 'various kinds of Scottish Nationalist', from those who desired 'complete separation' to others who wanted 'a measure of devolution'. He believed the main grievances were the failure to designate Prestwick as an international airport and construct a Forth Road Bridge, but he simply reaffirmed that Scottish Unionist MPs would ensure 'full weight' was given in Parliament to 'Scottish interests', and that any failure to achieve 'desirable advantages' could not be 'attributable to the existence of the Union' (Blair 1945b).

The pamphlet itself opened with lengthy quotations from the Unionists' court historian Robert S. Rait (who had died in 1936) and Sir Robert Horne's 1932 Commons speech, further reinforcing its dated quality by listing financial statistics from the early 1920s. It aimed to foster 'all that is best in the Scottish character and traditions' while furthering the economic development of the country, 'which is, and must be, bound up with that of England; rather than artificially to introduce from the past a political isolation necessarily resulting in weakness, jealousies and frictions'. And while there might be 'room for improvement' in the machinery of local and central government, democracy had to 'keep a watchful eye upon bureaucracy', with Scottish MPs balancing the 'claims of Scotland as a nation' against its political status 'as part of the island of Great Britain' (SUWO 1945: 5–19).

None of this was terribly convincing and certainly not as sensitively pitched as previous statements of party policy. Rather nationalist unionism seemed to be trapped in 1932, crude, defensive and uncertain of how to respond to the shifting dynamics of the post-war era. At the general election that followed, Unionist candidates railed against the idea of a Scottish Parliament, some even depicting it as un-Scottish, although the SUA correctly anticipated a relatively good result: while the UK Conservative vote fell to 39.8 per cent (from 47.7 in 1935), in Scotland the decline was less marked, falling from 42 to 40.3 per cent of votes cast. Nearly half of Unionist candidates, meanwhile, had 'discussed the problems of Scottish government' in their election literature (*Scotsman*, 10 April 1947).

A Gallup poll in 1945 put support for Scottish independence at just 8 per cent, with devolution at 53 and the status quo on 39 (Harvie 1992: 31). An *Edinburgh Evening News* poll in November 1945 found support for a Scottish

Parliament at 75 per cent, a finding later replicated by the *Daily Express* (76 per cent), including surprisingly high support among Unionist voters who had been canvassed (75 per cent; it was at 80 per cent among 'Socialists'). The Scottish Convention concluded, not unreasonably, that 'the Labour and Unionist Party leaders do not represent their own electors' (Scottish Convention 1946).

It certainly indicated that Home Rule sentiment – or rather support for the creation of a devolved Scottish Parliament within the UK – was salient but dispersed. Thus, 'menaced from opposite sides by the competing ideologies of socialism and nationalism' (Cragoe 2015), Scottish Unionists began to fashion what Harold Macmillan might have called a 'Middle Way' between those twin political threats, developing a renewed nationalist unionism for the late 1940s and early 1950s. As ever, the media was important, with the *Scotsman* depicting Unionist MPs as 'standing up for Scotland' and unusually 'busy in the assertion of Scottish rights and viewpoints' (*Scotsman*, 6 February 1947).

The SUMC even engaged directly with the Scottish Covenant Association (SCA), the aims of which were hardly extreme from a Unionist perspective: royalist, imperialist and resolutely non-ideological. The movement was also full of former Unionists such as the Duke of Montrose (honorary president), Professor Andrew Dewar Gibb (a commissioner) and James A. A. Porteous (economic adviser). An SCA delegation in May 1946 'received a warm reception from both sides of the political divide' (Somerville 2013: 29), although the official Unionist record of that meeting criticised their ideas as having been expressed in 'a woolly manner' (Clark-Hutchison 1946).

The backdrop was a debate over the Attlee government's Civil Aviation Bill, which along with other government measures contributed to cross-party concern about centralisation in London of responsibilities hitherto resting (to some degree) in Scotland. Proposals for a national health service and welfare state also spoke of uniformity and distant control, while Labour's policy of nationalisation would serve to elevate the terms 'Britain' and 'British' in the public consciousness, 'which may have instilled a stronger sense of British identity and Unionism amongst the Scottish people' (Somerville 2013: 84), as well as a more left-wing form of 'welfare unionism' (McLean and McMillan 2005).

'De-nationalisation'

In August 1946, the *Scotsman* carried a 'Statement of Conservative Policy' couched in nationalist-unionist language not seen for more than a decade. Laying claim to a long-standing policy of 'administrative decentralisation', it now believed that 'in the interest of the United Kingdom' this should be extended until 'all matters solely of Scottish concern' were 'administered in Scotland', a response to a Labour policy it believed had not only resulted in 'unnecessary delays and inefficiency', but in 'a great loss of Scottish prestige'. Unionists believed 'in variety' and not 'standardisation', wishing to foster in local government and education 'the spirit of Scottish sentiment and tradition' (*Scotsman*, 19 August 1946). This was also published and distributed as '20 REASONS for joining the Unionist Party'.

The Conservative Parliamentary Secretariat (CPS) also published the party's most comprehensive statement of Scottish policy since 1932. Stating that while the 'integrity' of the UK had to be maintained for economic reasons and 'to preserve the influence of Scotland in Imperial and World affairs', at the same time Parliament ought to give 'separate consideration to legislation affecting Scotland in all cases where Scottish tradition or Scottish needs differ from those of England'. Strikingly, rather than playing down 'growing resentment' over the government's 'indifference' regarding Prestwick Airport and a Forth Road Bridge, as it had during the war, it now made those grievances its own.

The CPS, however, ruled out a separate parliament in Edinburgh or legislative powers for the Scottish Grand Committee; thus by a process of elimination it settled upon an administrative response, a consistent feature of nationalist unionism since the nineteenth century. If, therefore, agreement could be reached between the SUMC and the Shadow Cabinet regarding powers such as broadcasting (a radical suggestion even seventy years later), animal diseases and civil aviation, then those proposals should be submitted to the UK party leader for approval, the time being 'ripe for a declaration of Unionist policy for Scotland' (CPS 1946).

A 'special meeting' of the SUMC soon took place. Members included Lord Tweedsmuir, the late John Buchan's eldest son, and Sir Arthur Young, author of previous Unionist publications on Scottish affairs. The first full meeting of the SUMC sub-committee, meanwhile, ruled out a 'Stormont' solution given the slim chances of Scotland securing the 'favourable financial agreement' that existed in Northern Ireland. Rather it agreed to (a) extend use of the Scottish Grand Committee, (b) appoint a third under-secretary, (c) 'upgrade' civil servants in Scotland, (d) further utilise the Upper House in initiating 'Bills of particular Scottish interest', and (e) determine 'what further measures, if any, of devolution are desirable' from Whitehall to St Andrew's House in Edinburgh (SUMC 1946).

These modest proposals would set the frame – if not the precise detail – of the Unionist 'offer' until 1949, and in the meantime veteran nationalist unionists got to work in rhetorical terms. When Walter Elliot, who had lost his seat at the 1945 election, contested a Scottish Universities by-election in November 1946, he stressed that the legislative Union between Scotland and England 'was never meant to entail, and should not entail, a complete swamping of the economic identity of the Northern Kingdom such as is now being conducted in the name of nationalisation'. This transfer of Scottish industrial control to Westminster was not nationalisation, he added in a memorable phrase, but amounted to 'de-nationalisation' (Elliot 1946).

In March 1947, the SUMC submitted its proposals to Churchill, its chairman informing him of 'a considerable growth of Scottish Nationalist feeling', together with the 'persistent propagation of the idea that Scotland has not got adequate control over her own affairs'. The letter ended by expressing 'hope' that if the Shadow Cabinet concurred with the proposals then Churchill might 'make some reference to them' during his forthcoming speech at the SUA conference in Ayr on 16 May (SUMC 1947a).

This letter coincided with a gathering of the self-styled 'Scottish National Assembly' (SNA), a product of MacCormick's Scottish Covenant Association, in Glasgow. Interestingly, the role of Unionists in the SNA has generally been played down, Mitchell believing those involved to have been 'cynically using it' (Mitchell 1990: 27). But a *Scotsman* account of the meeting suggests a more sincere level of engagement. The Unionist MP for Perth, Colonel Gomme-Duncan, expressed his 'hearty belief that Scotland was having and had had, an exceedingly raw deal' and in future it 'should be recognised as a partner and not occupy the position of office boy'. The Earl of Selkirk, meanwhile, said the interests of the UK 'as a whole were by no means always identical with those of Scotland', and Lord Polwarth, the Unionist industrialist, supported the idea of a Royal Commission on Scottish affairs (*Scotsman*, 24 March 1947), something that would later form part of Unionist strategy.

Polwarth later wrote to Colonel Blair of the SUA praising a memorandum by the Unionist MP and lawyer J. L. Clyde on Scottish nationalism. Entitled 'The Importance of Scottish Nationalism', Clyde explored the 'prospect of alignment' between nationalism and Unionist Party policy. Channelling his 'legal nationalism', Clyde argued that Scots Law demonstrated that in certain areas of government 'independence' was both 'practicable and advantageous', going on to draw a distinction between the 'extreme view' of nationalism (full independence) and the 'moderate' stance (a devolved parliament within the Union). It was 'on the Executive side of government', however, where he believed an opportunity lay 'for the practical realisation of Scottish Nationalist aspirations' which, usefully, would not interfere with the sovereignty of Parliament.

As Clyde correctly observed, this represented 'no real departure' from the fundamental Unionist approach since between the wars, identifying 'increasing independence' for executive administration at St Andrew's House, Sir John Gilmour's creation of a 'Scottish Civil Service' (*sic*) and his elevation to Secretary of State rank as 'essential' reforms 'if Scotland was to be saved from being a mere province of England'. Thus 'socialist centralisation' could be halted by making 'every use we can of our peculiarly Scottish institutions' and preventing the 'dull pattern of the English system to be blindly applied for the sake of bureaucratic uniformity to the whole country'. Most striking was Clyde's conclusion, the original draft of which asserted that the Scottish Unionist Party had 'always agreed with the underlying objects of Scottish Nationalism'. This was then altered to state that Scottish Unionist policy was 'not inconsistent with the fundamental objects of Scottish Nationalism' (Clyde 1947).

This was typical Tory statecraft at work, an attempt to convince political nationalists that 'nationalist unionism' could address their grievances without the need for legislative autonomy. Clyde's memorandum was widely circulated and clearly influential in the elite debate that took place within Scottish Unionist circles (every Unionist MP received a copy), while it also achieved a wider audience when the sympathetic editor of the *Scotsman*, Murray Watson, decided to publish it in several parts during April 1947. Responding to these articles, the Duke of Montrose, the prominent Liberal nationalist, made the interesting observation that 'Tory opposition to devolution' since 1920 had been 'inherited from the rancour of the Irish episode' (*Scotsman*, 23 April 1947).

The Earl of Selkirk, however, wrote to Colonel Blair of his belief that the revival in Scottish nationalism went beyond mere 'sentiment',[1] and that he thought it 'a pity' to view the question 'too narrowly on the present structure of nationalised industries', believing that devolved control of those would 'require a Parliament in Scotland'. And although he was willing to 'accept' an executive solution as proposed by Clyde, it was 'no good talking about executive administration unless you have a high measure of financial discretion' (Selkirk 1947a), a point that anticipated early-twenty-first-century debates regarding 'fiscal responsibility' (Torrance 2012). Politically, therefore, Selkirk believed it of 'very great importance that it should be clear in Scotland that the Unionist Party is a distinct entity, however closely it may be associated with the Conservative Party in England' (Selkirk 1947a).

Colonel Blair concurred with the final point, pencilling 'Yes' next to Selkirk's plea for organisational independence and agreeing 'very strongly' that the SUA should 'retain its identity', distinct from the National Union of Conservative and Unionist Associations in England. 'As you know,' Blair added in reply, 'the Scottish Unionist Members of the House of Commons do preserve a very distinct entity, and their Committee, everyone must agree, has done great service to Scotland' (Blair 1947a). This exchange anticipated a row over party autonomy the following year (see below).

This organisational autonomy – a key feature of nationalist unionism since the 1910s – was further bolstered by the routine substitution of 'Unionist' for 'Conservative' in party literature emanating from London; the Eastern Divisional Council (EDC) even inserted pictures of SUA leaders to give one leaflet 'a distinctive Scottish character' (EDC 1948). The following year the EDC also suggested using 'distinctively Scottish' 'national symbols' on Unionist posters (EDC 1949). The official logo of the Scottish Young Unionists was changed to a large Scottish thistle.

Sir Arthur Young, meanwhile, suggested Churchill draw on the Clyde memorandum in his forthcoming conference speech, emphasising 'the desirability of further devolution in administration as distinct from a separation in legislation' (Young 1947). The SUMC proposals came before the Shadow Cabinet at two meetings in April and May 1947, with Scottish Unionist MPs in attendance. They expressed the view that it would 'both be in the interests of Scottish administration and to the political advantage of the Unionist Party if Scottish estimates [public spending] were considered in the Scottish Grand Committee'.

At the same time, there was a clear concern about creating a slippery slope, this 'initial concession' perhaps later compelling them to 'concede the principle of a Scottish Parliament' (Consultative Committee 1947). Indeed, the Anglo-Scottish Iain Macleod, a future Chancellor of the Exchequer then responsible for Scottish policy in the Conservative Research Department, believed that as legislative devolution was already Labour and Liberal policy, then it might be 'good tactics' for Unionists 'to concede a little of the ground' (Macleod 1947). 'As well as marking out a distinct position in relation to Labour,' concluded Hutchison, 'the Tories used this anti-Whitehall posture to counter the threat of Scottish nationalism and pull back Liberals into the fold' (Hutchison 2001: 78).

'Scotland and the Union'

Work was also under way to prepare and issue in pamphlet form a renewed statement of Unionist policy on Scotland. Blair's initial draft opened with a robust assertion of nationalist unionism, the claim that the Unionist Party was 'very much alive to the nationhood of Scotland', its 'character and environment, tradition and history, and the ties of blood relationship', all of which had produced a 'nationality' which found its expression in 'social customs and legal systems and in art, literature and music . . . its own national regiments with their own dress and customs'. All these things, it continued, 'in so far as they represent an unchanging national character, must and will remain separate, and will be upheld by the Unionist Party'.

Blair's draft went on to highlight the usual grievances regarding 'authorities in London which have little knowledge of Scottish conditions and Scottish interest'. Furthermore, Unionists were 'looking along the lines of independence for the Scottish Executive for improvement in the supervision of Scottish interests', clearly drawing on the Clyde memorandum in believing that the 'dull pattern of bureaucratic uniformity' should not be blindly 'applied [to] the whole country of Great Britain' (Blair 1947b).

The SUMC, however, did not consider Blair's draft 'to be suitable for general publication' (SUMC 1947b), while the Western Council Executive of the SUA feared its caveated rejection of a Stormont solution (on the basis that Scotland would not 'obtain the favourable financial arrangements secured by Northern Ireland') implied that a 'Parliament on the lines of the one in Ireland was practicable and desirable', so long as it was backed up with money from London (Blair 1947c). This might be called the Stormont Question – if devolution was good enough for Northern Ireland and posed no threat to the Union, then why not for Scotland?

Drafts of a separate pamphlet – 'SCOTLAND and THE UNION' – by the Tory propagandist Colm Brogan also caused problems. This was florid in tone, approvingly referencing Sir Walter Scott's sense of 'a very serious threat to the vigour of Scottish nationality long before it became plain to all'. Brogan also conceded that 'much in the negative criticism of Nationalists' was 'manifestly just', thus by opposing Labour's centralisation Scottish Unionists were 'working to preserve and restore the practical independence of Scotsmen in the conduct of their own affairs'.

'The Scottish Unionist Party has no fears for the survival of the Scottish nation', continued Brogan. 'A nation so ancient, vigorous and tenacious will not die.' Rather Unionists believed 'the independence of Scotsmen as responsible citizens' needed protection 'from the devitalising effect of Socialism', characteristic 'Scottish virtues' being blunted by the 'unScottish doctrine of egalitarianism' (a very different argument than that deployed by the SNP a few decades later). Thus, the party hoped to restore to the people of Scotland 'the truest form of independence', the right of free men to 'mind their own private business and to help themselves' (Brogan 1947).

On 29 October 1947, however, Sir George Clark-Hutchison wrote to all members of the SUMC asking them to destroy their copies of Brogan's pamphlet, it being 'most important' that they did 'not get into unauthorised hands'. Blair, meanwhile, was 'spitting blood', believing it would 'do more harm than good' were it to reach the public domain (Clark-Hutchison 1947). They were concerned that readers would derive neither a 'clear impression' of 'why a separate Scottish Parliament' was 'undesirable', nor what Unionists were advocating as an alternative. Blair highlighted several sentences which 'might legitimately cause the reader to ask the question: "Why then not have a separate Parliament in Scotland?"' In other words, it was too national-ist, merely denying 'disadvantages ascribed by the Nationalists to the Union without sufficiently pointing out the many advantages that have accrued to Scotland from the Union' (Blair 1947d).

Scottish Unionists, however, had simply been caught out by the logi-cal extension of their own argument: if administrative devolution were so desirable, then why not also the legislative variety? In promoting the former so zealously, they had unwittingly given credence to some of their opponents' points. Brogan's draft statement of Unionist policy had merely highlighted this logical inconsistency a little too clearly, thus it was killed off and an alternative document (by the more reliable Colonel Blair) com-missioned in its place.

A House of Lords debate on Scottish Affairs in November 1947 also highlighted internal tensions, particularly among Scotland's representative peers, always of a more nationalist inclination. The Earl of Airlie said the recent Edinburgh Festival had revealed 'a re-birth in Scotland', leading him to believe that 'some form of Dominion status' would in future be nec-essary. Lord Polwarth, meanwhile, warned that if the Labour government failed to establish a committee of inquiry into Scottish affairs then they did so 'at their own peril' (HL Deb 13 November 1947 Vol 152 cc647–93). The veteran Unionist MP Bob Boothby echoed Polwarth's point in his 1947 book *I Fight to Live*, saying the English 'had better take care' in its handling of Scottish sensitivities (Boothby 1947: 55) lest Scotland opt for more dras-tic action in response.

Conveniently, however, by early 1948 the focus was on the Labour gov-ernment's proposals for Scottish administration rather than Unionist pol-icy. Arthur Woodburn, Labour's Secretary of State for Scotland, published a White Paper which was met with general criticism, not only from Unionists but from Labour's own ranks. Among the former group, Clyde dismissed it as mere 'tinkering', while the Unionist MP Sir William Y. Darling quipped that 'after a great deal of labour the mountain has brought forth a mouse'. Scotland, he added, 'expected something with more substance' (*Scotsman*, 30 January 1948).

It made sense, of course, for the Unionists to exploit Labour's difficul-ties in this regard, for it bolstered their argument that they were the only true defenders of Scottish interests, a posture given even greater credibility by Labour's recent retreat from its historic support for Home Rule. Blair, meanwhile, had circulated his draft policy document on 10 January 1949, eventually published under the rather verbose title 'Scotland and the United Kingdom: The Unionist Party's Practical Policy for Scottish Administration of Scottish Affairs and Scotland's Part in Great Britain'.

It opened with the usual quotations from Messrs Rait and Horne before rehashing the 1945 policy statement in asserting that there was 'undoubtedly a Scottish nationhood to which the Unionist Party is very much alive'. If 'Scotland unmistakably desired' Home Rule, the pamphlet continued, then 'it could have it', while next came a commitment to an 'executive' response to Labour's nationalisation policy, something 'in the traditional sequence of Unionist policy'. 'In all nationalised industries Scottish independence for the Administrative Boards must be secured', it declared, while rehearsing by now familiar arguments about 'extended use' of the Scottish Grand Committee, the appointment of additional under-secretaries and more effective departmental liaison between Whitehall and St Andrew's House.

Lengthy sections also rebutted SNP arguments, warning that 'greater political nationalism' would 'inevitably bring more economic nationalism' with 'disastrous results'. And rather than a Scottish Parliament being dominated by 'alien' Irish and other foreign nationals, as Unionists had argued in the 1920s, now the argument became ideological, the fear being that 'Socialist' members of a Scottish Parliament would 'follow the lines of policy and directions issued from that London headquarters'.

'Above all', what was required was not a return to 'narrow tendencies of political self-sufficiency' but 'a revival of the old Scottish characteristics':

> Scotsmen used to be noted for their independence, their hard work, their thrift, their desire to lay by something of their own for their children, their belief in sound education, their regard for Scotland's traditions of loyalty and service. These are what the Unionist Party believes in fostering, not the pernicious fallacies of imported Socialism that are founded on envy and malice or at the best misguided sentimentalism.

Scotland, it concluded, 'must take her full share in the United Kingdom Parliament in building up a property-owning democracy at home and in maintaining in the British Empire its ideals of Liberty, Humanity and Justice' (Blair 1948a: 3–19).

This rallying cry revived the three main strands of 'nationalist unionism' first articulated the 1910s and 1920s, a fusion of Scottish, British and imperial identities, but *Scotland and the United Kingdom* also invited criticisms along the lines identified privately by Unionists during the preparation of Blair's tract. Many of these were made by the Unionist-turned-Covenanter James Porteous in a detailed rebuttal published soon after.

Sarcastically referring to administrative devolution as 'our old friend', Porteous argued that without legislative devolution it could 'only apply within a very limited sphere', while the existence of Stormont undermined hyperbolic Unionist opposition to a Scottish equivalent. He also mocked the obvious co-option of nationalist language such as 'proper independence for Scotland' ('a nice phrase!'), and concluded by arguing that a 'true conception of Unionism' had to consist of 'voluntary and willing unity of action for common purposes, not in the merging of the numerically less in the numerically greater'. The policy of the Scottish Convention, he added, was 'in the true tradition of Unionist principles' (Porteous 1948: 8, 9, 23).

Nevertheless, by this stage Unionists were playing 'the nationalist card to full effect' (Mitchell 1990: 27). As Bogdanor put it, Scottish nationalism was thus 'harnessed' by Unionists 'to the anti-socialist chariot' (Bogdanor 1980: 78).

The 'Paisley Declaration'

This strange association between nationalism and unionism was drawn into sharper focus when the death of former Conservative Prime Minister Stanley Baldwin elevated his son Oliver, a Labour MP, to the House of Lords, therefore initiating a by-election in the new Earl Baldwin's former constituency of Paisley in February 1948. A group of Paisley Unionists active in the Scottish Convention persuaded the SUA not to field an official candidate but instead support the Independent Nationalist John MacCormick in a straight fight against Labour's Douglas Johnston. The Scottish Liberals also supported MacCormick, and senior English (Peter Thorneycroft) and Scottish (Walter Elliot and Lady Grant) Conservatives even shared a platform with him during the campaign, leading the Labour Scottish Secretary Arthur Woodburn to believe that MacCormick's Scottish Convention was little more than a Tory plot (Keating and Bleiman 1979).

A joint Unionist–Liberal 'Paisley Declaration' issued during the by-election campaign dealt with Home Rule in clear nationalist-unionist terms:

We believe that the distinctive national traditions and characteristics of Scotland are of great value to the United Kingdom and to the world and that they constitute a priceless heritage of the Scottish people. If the process of centralising the economic control of Scotland in Whitehall is allowed to continue, that heritage will be lost and our national existence endangered. We therefore consider that a measure of devolution in the government of Scotland is a matter of urgency.

'So complete was Unionism's domination of the centre-right', judged Dyer, 'that its clients had come to include the most significant figure in the Scottish nationalist cause' (Dyer 2003: 300, 307). It was also a natural extension of the Unionist policy of 'containment', controlling Scottish nationalism by co-opting its language, ideas and even its leaders.

Johnston, however, emerged the winner, with 27,213 votes to Mac-Cormick's 20,668. At a meeting of the Scottish National Assembly the following month, Unionist MPs again took part. Niall Macpherson, the MP for Dumfries, felt able to support the main resolution, largely because it fell short of the Dominion status desired by SNP participants. 'What is it we are really after?' he asked rhetorically.

> Is it just to make certain that the Scottish ethos is maintained, that the Scottish character continues to remain such as it is, and that Scottish social progress continues along its own lines? We are members of a great Empire. It would be very strange, indeed, if we were to cut ourselves adrift at this particular moment. (*Glasgow Herald*, 22 March 1948)

According to the *Scotsman*'s account of the same gathering, Macpherson even supported working towards a 'common policy where there would be a Scottish Parliament providing for the social needs of the country, but not cut off from the United Kingdom as a whole' (*Scotsman*, 22 March 1948). For some Unionists, as Somerville put it, 'a devolved Britain was more palatable than a socialist Britain' (Somerville 2013: 36).

The SUA conference in Perth, meanwhile, unanimously urged the party leadership to give 'serious consideration' to 'a positive undertaking for a large measure of devolution for Scotland', although speakers emphasised that this did not mean 'a separate Parliament for Scotland'. The Earl of Mansfield revived the idea of a Royal Commission comprising 'eminent Scots men and women in all walks of life', while J. S. C. Reid, the MP for Glasgow Hillhead, said 'it was Unionist policy that, where there was a separate Scottish interest, feeling, or problem, there should be administration by Scotsmen in Scotland' (*Scotsman*, 29 May 1948).

Privately, however, there were dissenting voices. Viscount Elibank believed Colonel Blair's pamphlet emphasised the Union 'too much' and was not 'strong enough meat for the state of feeling in Scotland today', leading him to urge a 'more drastic policy' involving 'some sort of Scottish Assembly in Edinburgh' (Elibank 1948). Blair replied in emollient terms, though adding that it was 'important not to give way to sentimental or superficial clamour on the subject', being quite satisfied that 'anything in the nature of Home Rule for Scotland would be a complete and utter disaster for Scotland' (Blair 1948b).

Unfortunate in its timing, meanwhile, were press reports that a review of Conservative Party organisation by Sir David Maxwell-Fyfe intended to end what one newspaper called the Scottish Unionist Association's 'home rule' (*Daily Graphic*, 19 October 1948). Senior Unionists moved quickly to kill the story, a 'leading' figure telling the *Scotsman* that there was 'no likelihood of Scotland losing her own identity' (*Scotsman*, 19 October 1948). Indeed, the press coverage often conflated party and country, the *Daily Telegraph* talking of ending 'Scotland's Independence' (*Daily Telegraph*, 18 October 1948). This even prompted a rebuttal from UK party chairman Lord Woolton, who pointed out that Maxwell-Fyfe's committee had no jurisdiction over party organisation in Scotland:

> There has never been any suggestion of ending Scotland's political independence. Why shouldn't they be independent if they want to be? . . . I am anxious that both in England and Scotland it [the Tory organisation] should work more effectively, but I have no desire to impinge on the right of the Scottish Unionist Association to control their own affairs. (*Daily Telegraph*, 20 October 1948)

The 'Psychological Appeal of Scottish Nationalism'

What MacCormick called 'the national awakening in Scotland' (MacCormick 1955: 119), meanwhile, continued apace. Not only were meetings of the Scottish National Assembly receiving widespread and generally positive publicity, but surveys – as in 1945 – indicated broad-based support for further autonomy.

One survey conducted by Edinburgh University's psychology department found that more than 75 per cent believed Scots should run their own affairs, which suggested a large proportion of Unionists agreed. The Plebiscite Society in Kirriemuir, meanwhile, found 92.3 per cent support for a Scottish Parliament (23.3 per cent for independence) in a strongly Unionist part of Scotland in early 1949. Understandably emboldened, the SNA began to press Westminster for a national referendum on legislative devolution, an initiative supported by *The Economist*, *Scotsman* and the *Bulletin*, and which clearly concerned the SUA and SUMC. The senior Scottish Unionist James Stuart told MacCormick (on behalf of the SUMC) that if 'the people of Scotland were ultimately to decide in favour of a Scottish Parliament' then 'no one could gainsay them', although he advocated a parliamentary route rather than a plebiscite (MacCormick 1955: 139).

The Kirriemuir referendum also prompted the Earl of Airlie to tell a group of Dundee businessmen that he believed a Scottish Parliament 'would come one day', Scotland requiring 'the right to handle and give decisions on the domestic side of her business' (*Dundee Courier*, 3 February 1949), although the Unionist MP Sir Arthur Young cautioned against the party allowing itself to be 'stampeded' by the informal plebiscite. He clearly felt under pressure from members of the SUA policy committee, while at least one former Unionist candidate, now an 'ardent member' of the Scottish Convention, was also 'bombarding' Young with letters about a Scottish Parliament. All he would concede was that Unionists would not be in a 'strong position' at the next general election 'if it is purely upon the defensive' and looked as if it 'was not concerned about the good of Scotland' (Young 1949).

At a special meeting of the SUMC on 15 February 1949, panic in the Unionist ranks was clear, their restatement of party policy having apparently had little impact. Colonel Gomme-Duncan thought 'the need to answer the Nationalists' was 'urgent', while Sir William Y. Darling believed the 'Nationalist movement' to be 'great and growing' (Sir Thomas Moore, however, believed it 'came in waves' and would soon die down). When the chairman reminded the committee that it rejected legislative devolution, Darling broke ranks to say he would be prepared to 'go as far as' the Scottish Convention's proposals, while Colin Thornton-Kemsley suggested that 'a Scottish assembly, representative of local authorities, M.P.s, peers, the churches, nationalised industries, etc' with 'advisory functions' and sitting at Parliament House in Edinburgh 'would appeal to the imagination of Scotsmen'.

Blair, meanwhile, identified four 'very different sources' of support 'for greater power for Scotland':

> (i) the Scottish Nationalists; (ii) the unthinking who seized on the tie with England as the cause of all difficulties; (iii) the Liberals who were vote-catching, knowing they would never have to put their policy into practice; (iv) Unionists who were disturbed by increasing administrative dictatorship from London. (SUMC 1949a)

Once again it fell to Blair to put something on paper, although it was clear that he found himself at odds with several Unionist MPs. In a subsequent memorandum, he stressed that Unionist agents did not believe Home Rule to be a 'burning' issue (with the exception of the agent in Angus shortly after the Kirriemuir plebiscite); all he was prepared to add to his previous paper was a line concerning local government. Blair, however, conceded that presentation was key: 'The public are more likely to understand and be attracted by what they consider a positive policy than by a negative one' (Blair 1949).

A few days later Thornton-Kemsley fleshed out his own thinking in another paper proposing what he called a 'Council of the Realm'. This referred approvingly to a recent pamphlet by the SNP leader Douglas Young proposing a 'Scottish National Congress', something he believed demonstrated that even 'extreme' nationalists were 'coming round to a more sensible view of what is possible or desirable in the near future'. Thornton-Kemsley judged it a 'grave mistake to under-rate the psychological appeal of Scottish nationalism', adding that Unionist policy might 'be sound enough in theory' but would not 'cut much ice with the unattached voter who genuinely desires that Scotland should be given a greater share in working out her own destiny'. Style, in other words, was just as important as substance, if not more so.

He proposed, therefore, an indirectly elected 'Council of the Realm' with advisory functions, a halfway-house with which Scottish Conservatives were still toying twenty years later. And although he conceded this would satisfy neither 'confirmed Scottish Nationalists' nor 'extreme elements' in the Scottish Convention, taken in conjunction with the proposals set out in Scotland and the United Kingdom, they constituted 'a line of policy which Scottish Unionists and Liberal-Unionists could claim with confidence to be a practical and realistic approach to the problem of Scottish administration' (Thornton-Kemsley 1949).

At a further meeting of the SUMC on 29 March, Gomme-Duncan agreed that the 'psychological' aspect of any proposal would be 'of value as a counterweight to the suggestions of the Scottish Nationalists', but most Members present believed a Council of the Realm would 'be of an unwieldy size' and probably end up constituting the 'first step to a further demand for a Scottish Parliament' (SUMC 1949b), indicating continuing concern about slippery constitutional slopes.

At the SUA conference two months later, a resolution calling for a 'large measure' of devolution was once again passed without dissent, while Churchill's keynote speech evoked Baldwin in referring to the 'keen intellect of the Scottish race'. He described the 'whole process of nationalisation' as particularly 'detrimental and offensive to Scotland', affecting not only its 'prosperity' but the 'independence' it had 'exercised in so many fields'. 'No sharper challenge should be given to Scottish nationalist sentiment', added Churchill, 'than is now launched by the Socialism of Whitehall.' He therefore promised 'separate' Scottish boards for rail transport and electricity, as well as the prospect of additional under-secretaries to aid the Secretary of State for Scotland, a position he recognised as one 'of high honour in the Cabinet'. In short, a future Conservative government would take steps to 'see that Scotland is no longer treated as though she were some province or appendage of England' (Churchill 1949).

Another committee was subsequently instructed to draw up a more advanced set of policy proposals for presentation to a special conference later that year. In his private submission to that committee, Walter Elliot emphasised his long-held view that the Union of 1707 had represented a partnership of equals rather than 'a policy of amalgamation'. Furthermore, he supported a Church of Scotland proposal for an inquiry into the financial relationship between Scotland and England, as well as the idea of a Scottish Minister of State presiding over an annual meeting of Scottish councillors in order to 'cope with the undoubted feeling that no Scottish forum or meeting place exists for the general consideration of specifically Scottish problems' (Elliot 1949).

Indeed, the following month the broadly unionist Convention of Royal Burghs suggested creating a 'new central authority' comprising representatives from local and regional bodies as well as Scottish MPs in order to meet the desire for a Scottish forum identified by Elliot (*Scotsman*, 30 June 1949). But having engaged with another such body, the Scottish National Assembly, for the last couple of years, Unionists now cooled on what Tom Galbraith called 'Mr. MacCormick and his friends', Galbraith being 'genuinely concerned' at some of the Unionist-aligned names attending the SNA, lest it 'provide material for advertisement' among political opponents (Galbraith 1949).

A new edition of the Conservative Party's *Campaign Guide* published at around the same time quoted a speech in Dalkeith by Anthony Eden, a future party leader and Prime Minister, on the 'particular problems that Socialism brings to Scotland'. A political philosophy, he had argued, that denied 'individuality either in men or in nations' would 'not for long retain its hold on these islands' (CUCO 1949a: 67). Referring to this, the *Scotsman* had approved of Eden's acknowledgement that nationalisation 'inflicted a double penalty on Scotland', suffering from not only 'reduced efficiency' but the 'penalty of control from London, which offends her national feeling' (*Scotsman*, 20 June 1949).

Unionist-supporting newspapers such as the *Scotsman* were, as ever, important in communicating this nationalist unionism to a wider audience, while the major statement of post-war Conservative policy, *The Right Road for Britain* (1949), placed it in the context of broader Tory philosophy, that of creating a society 'decentralised, diversified, neighbourly, resourceful and resolute' (CUP 1949: 26), a recognition, in Quintin Hogg's phrase, of the cardinal Tory principle that 'if power is not to be abused it must be spread as widely as possible throughout the community' (Hogg 1948: 74).

'Scottish Control of Scottish Affairs'

Finally, in November 1949, the Scottish Unionist Association published its definitive statement of Unionist policy on Scotland, complete with the ostentatiously nationalist-unionist title 'Scottish Control of Scottish

Affairs'.[2] 'Union is strength', it declared confidently, but 'union' was 'not amalgamation'; rather Scotland was 'a nation', something 'recognised' by those who had forged the Union in 1707 by their careful safeguarding 'in symbol and in reality' of its 'national character and distinctive traditions'.

Only since 1945 had a socialist 'policy of amalgamation' superseded that 'balance between union and nationhood', a balance that militated against any proposal for 'the political separation of our two nations'. Furthermore, the Act of Union had 'never contemplated' such an 'unnatural state of affairs' in which management and control of state-owned industries were being transferred to Whitehall. It was therefore Unionist policy, 'while maintaining the Union of the two countries', to ensure that 'responsibility for managing Scottish Affairs in a manner best suited to the desires and the traditions of the people of Scotland' was retained, 'where it belongs, in the hands of Scotsmen' (SUA 1949: 2–10).

The language was markedly more confident – and indeed more 'quasi-nationalist' (Phillips 2008: 7) – than that which had characterised Unionist publications since the war. It then proceeded to set out detailed proposals, including a 'Deputy to the Secretary of State for Scotland' with Cabinet rank and usually based in Scotland, an additional under-secretary, a Royal Commission on Scottish Affairs, separate Scottish boards for nationalised industries, closer liaison between UK departments and the Scottish Office, more 'freedom' for local authorities and, when necessary, separate Scottish Bills in Parliament.

In conclusion, the 'essential preliminary' to 'securing recognition for Scotland and Scottish affairs' was the 'defeat of Socialism', after which a Unionist government would carry out 'administrative' rather than 'political' devolution, recognising Scotland 'not as a region but as a nation, in free but not subordinate partnership with England' (SUA 1949: 2–10).

Unionist policy would not deviate significantly from these aims and language for nearly twenty years. It was both a response to (political) nationalism and a (unionist) statement of it, conveniently framed by the Conservatives' broader ideological battle against socialism. Indeed, the *Manchester Guardian* was clear that the proposals were 'yet another tribute to the strength of the nationalist movement in Scotland' (*Manchester Guardian*, 29 November 1949).

But as Jackson observed, if the new statement of policy was intended as 'a means of dividing nationalists, then it also served to divide unionists' (Jackson 2012: 260), for the party was still not of one mind. Some Unionist MPs continued to look at the Northern Irish model, while John Cameron, the Dean of the Faculty of Advocates, said it seemed 'strange' for the party's proposed inquiry to have ruled out the 'logical and, indeed, democratic conclusion' (Mitchell 1990: 29), i.e. legislative as well as administrative devolution. The *Guardian* quoted one 'responsible Scottish Conservative' as grumbling that 'all this emotion' being generated in Scotland should 'properly be turned into the channel of getting rid of the Socialist Government' (*Manchester Guardian*, 1 February 1950).

It did not help that there was (perhaps deliberate) ambiguity regarding the remit of the Royal Commission. On this point there were mixed messages, Walter Elliot saying 'no door to further suggestion was shut', while J. H. F. McEwen claimed a Scottish Parliament was 'not within the purview of Unionist policy at the present time' (*Scotsman*, 29 November 1949). At a special conference in Glasgow on 6 December 1949, meanwhile, James Stuart spoke for most of those present in observing that there 'could be no finality about any proposals' (SUMC 1949a).

A *Scotsman* editorial praised the Unionist proposals as having the 'merit of being consistent' (*Scotsman*, 29 November 1949), while a *Times* leader column also alluded to the deep provenance of nationalist-unionist ideas. 'The spirit of Malachi Malagrowther is stirring again in Scotland', it declared, drawing a line between Sir Walter Scott's letters in defence of 'Scottish rights' and 'reports of speeches made in Scotland during the past few weeks', commending the Scottish Unionists for appealing to those who did not desire 'startling change' but rather 'clearer signs that Scottish affairs are considered and decided in Scotland by those who know the special conditions of the country' (*The Times*, 29 November 1949).

Whatever its inconsistencies, a 'distinctive Conservative position' had finally emerged of 'a de-centred but still united Britain' (Cragoe 2015), growing Scottish national sentiment having compelled Unionists – once again – to update their nationalist-unionist philosophy.

'Who Speaks for Scotland?'

By the end of the 1940s, the post-war government of Clement Attlee was not revered in the way it would be half a century later. Rationing and devaluation had taken their toll, and with an election due in 1950 it was by no means certain Labour would secure a second term. Indeed, over the next two years the Conservatives, still led by Churchill, would enjoy two electoral opportunities to challenge Labour and therefore deliver 'Scottish Control of Scottish Affairs'.

The party's 1950 manifesto, *This Is the Road*, acknowledged 'justifiable grievances' in Scotland (and Wales) against the 'immensely centralised control of their affairs from London', something that ignored its distinct 'national characteristics' (CUP 1950: 19–20). And speaking in Edinburgh on 14 February 1950, Churchill even argued that should England become 'an absolute Socialist state' then Scotland should never 'be forced into the serfdom of Socialism as a result of a vote in the House of Commons', for it would represent an 'alteration so fundamental' to the British 'way of life' that it would 'require a searching review' of the 'historical relations' between the two countries, an argument that anticipated the 'no-mandate' cry of anti-Tory nationalists in the 1980s.

Churchill's tone was respectful, speaking to Scottish Nationalists in words 'of great truth and respect', although he was also clear that 'Scotsmen would make a wrong decision if they tried to separate their fortunes from ours' at the very moment 'when by one broad heave of the British national shoulders the whole gimcrack structure of Socialist jargon and malice may be cast in splinters to the ground' (Churchill 1950: 7937–8). As Cragoe (2007) has shown, this rhetorical approach was mirrored to a lesser degree in Wales, where Churchill also evoked the principality's historical identity, thereby implicitly drawing both the Scots and the Welsh into the 'British nation's' opposition to socialism (see Chapter 9).

Scottish Unionists, meanwhile, wasted no opportunity in driving home the point that only they possessed 'a practical policy' enabling 'Scotland to regain her freedom and prosperity' and returning the Anglo-Scottish Union to a relationship 'based on equal partnership' (SUA 1950). During a set-piece debate between the Labour Scottish Secretary Arthur Woodburn and his de facto Unionist shadow Walter Elliot, this newly confident nationalist unionism received a full airing. Elliot chided Woodburn for abandoning a formal commitment to devolution, taunted him for having 'to ring up London to get permission to have another bar turned on in his office radiator', and even criticised the fact that three Labour candidates in Scotland had been born in England. 'Let free Scots enterprise', he declared, 'be developed in Scotland by Scotsmen.' The *Daily Record* publicised this exchange under the headline 'who speaks for Scotland?', leading Miller to conclude that this had become 'a significant secondary theme' of the election, 'controls' from London being attacked in both ideological and 'Scottish' terms (Miller 1981: 22–5).

On polling day this tactic of associating local 'nationalist' discontent with the broader campaign theme of combatting centralisation appeared to serve the Scottish Unionist Party (and its National Liberal or Liberal Unionist allies) well, with it gaining four seats across Scotland. Correctly anticipating another general election before too long, Unionists kept up the pressure in the months that followed, so much so that in May Cyril Osborne, the Conservative MP for Louth, complained that too much time was being taken up with Scottish questions (Osborne 1950).

Also exploiting the nationalist atmosphere was the Scottish National Assembly, 'commissioners' from which met a group of Unionist MPs and peers nominated by Churchill to discuss their proposals for a Scottish Parliament in May 1950, an indication of the party's ongoing willingness to engage with its more strongly nationalist critics. The commissioners happened to include two former Unionists, Andrew Dewar Gibb and James Porteous, who were keen to emphasise that their aims differed from those of the SNP. The Unionist delegation was conciliatory, believing there to be 'a field for wide discussion', while reiterating their opposition to a legislative assembly in Edinburgh (SUMC 1950a). Rhetoric aside, however, there remained a huge gulf between the two movements. In a private note, J. N. Browne wondered if the Convention might 'split the Labour vote' more than that of the Unionists, and if it would therefore suit them 'best to encourage, ignore, or attempt to suppress' its political activity (Browne 1950).

In July 1950, the SUMC met with members of the Northern Ireland Parliament as part of their ongoing inquiry into the Stormont model. The Ulster Unionist MP Sir Hugh O'Neill gave them an overview of the 'Ulster system', expressing doubts as to whether Scotland would enjoy similar advantages, although another Northern Irish MP, Sir Ronald Ross, believed it would actually 'be advantageous to Northern Ireland for Scotland to follow her example' (in setting up an autonomous parliament). Others believed the existence of a 'separate legislature' enabled the 'Ulster system' to make 'quick administrative decisions' (SUMC 1950b).

Later that year there were other nationalist straws in the wind. The lesser-known Scotstoun plebiscite on 25 October 1950, like that in Kirriemuir, demonstrated high levels of support for a Scottish Parliament, while 'King John' MacCormick defeated the Unionist Sir David Maxwell-Fyfe to become Lord Rector of Glasgow University, later using his installation address to articulate Unionist-like frustration at the actions of a centralising Labour government (Torrance 2011: 126–8). Perhaps in response, Unionists redoubled their campaigning efforts, commissioning a short film ('made in Scotland and by Scots') on Scottish affairs (SUMC 1950c), while in a major organisational reform Churchill replaced the old London-based 'Scottish Whip' with a new 'Chairman of the Unionist Party in Scotland'. This was to be James Stuart, previously UK chief whip and, in a doubtless conscious piece of historical symbolism, a descendant of Scotland's early Stuart monarchs.

The Scottish Unionist Party's growing confidence and autonomy was also reflected in its 1950 publication of the *East of Scotland Year Book* ('being a political reference annual for the year 1950'), the first of a series of almanacs issued by the Scottish Unionist Association over the next decade-and-a-half. That year's SUA conference, meanwhile, declared socialism to be 'completely contrary to the interests of the Scottish people' (WDC 1950), while the 1951 Conservative manifesto, *BRITAIN Strong and Free*, once again played the Scottish card, detailing 'measures designed to give Scotland greater control of Scottish affairs and to enable her to maintain and develop her own national way of life' (CUP 1951: 33). Opening the Exhibition of Industrial Power in Glasgow (part of that year's Festival of Britain), Princess Elizabeth echoed this 'official' nationalism in describing herself as 'a lover of Scotland' and referring to the exhibition as 'a well-deserved compliment to the land of so many famous engineers and inventors' (BBC, 28 May 1951).

The party, however, actually approached the 1951 campaign with an almost identical set of policies for Scotland. On a visit to Melrose in July that year, Anthony Eden declared that 'Scotland is no mere region, as some socialists seem to imagine. It is a nation, and a proud one and justly so' (*Scotsman*, 16 July 1951). But it was Churchill who again took the lead in merging all these policies within a grand narrative of Conservative decentralisation. 'All of our lives, whether Scottish, Welsh, or English, whether as nations or as individuals', he told an audience in Glasgow, 'are being hobbled by the interferences and restrictions of Socialism' (Cragoe 2007).

On polling day, not only were the Conservatives returned to office, but in Scotland the Unionists and their allies secured an additional three seats and almost 40 per cent of the popular vote which, given the new government's slim overall majority of seventeen, gave added weight and influence to the Scottish party. Victory also presented Unionists with a challenge: 'nationalist unionism' was all very well in opposition, but could it be implemented, and indeed sustained, now Labour had been vanquished?

Conclusion

To return to Smith's (1991) definition of nationalism as 'an ideological movement for attaining and maintaining the autonomy, unity and identity of a nation' (Smith 1991: 74), the period between the outbreak of the Second World War and the general election of 1951 found Scottish Unionists at first neglecting their 'nationalist-unionist' project, confident that the symbolic opening of St Andrew's House in 1939 had settled the constitutional debate for a generation, and subsequently rejuvenating it in response to the twin challenges of socialism and demands for legislative devolution.

But while the policy process that culminated in the publication of 'Scottish Control of Scottish Affairs' was more pungent in rhetorical terms, it was consistent with the nationalist unionism of the inter-war period, further extending 'administrative devolution' (although several Unionist MPs and peers privately favoured going much further). It was, therefore, predominantly civic in nature, markedly less ethnic and imperialist than it had been before the Second World War. And while Unionists still played on Scotland's 'myths, memories, symbols and values' (Smith 1986: 3–4), they placed greater emphasis on a decentralist agenda that conveniently dovetailed with similar proposals in England and Wales to resist centralised 'control' from London. As ever, the unionist 'centre' was content to let the Scottish 'periphery' take the lead, although in terms of policy-making it was a collaborative process.

This also allowed Unionists to pursue a rapprochement of sorts with those who supported legislative devolution, joining forces (most formally at the 1948 Paisley by-election) with the non-partisan Scottish Convention. In Bogdanor's words, Unionists could then 'respect the feelings which animated Scottish nationalism'. 'In Scotland', he added, 'it was the Tories who were the nationalists' (Bogdanor 1980: 76–7). And although, as we have seen, this was nothing new, the party shrewdly viewed Labour's centralisation agenda as an opportunity to 'politically solidify its Scottishness' (Ward 2005: 32). In other words, Unionists wished to protect Scotland's distinctive identity while Labour appeared intent on forcing it to capitulate to the dull hand of bureaucratic British uniformity. Scotland's distinctiveness was, therefore, constantly 'flagged', with Unionist leaders co-opting parts of the nationalist lexicon, weaponising words like 'control', 'independence', 'devolution' and even 'freedom' in day-to-day political discourse.

At the same time, by building upon the administrative devolution enhanced by Tom Johnston during the war, it also became clearer that Unionists were unintentionally fostering a greater sense of separate Scottish governance just short of legislative devolution, a 'discursive strategy', certainly, but one with unintended consequences (McAdam et al. 1996). As Miller argued, by the early 1950s this approach had been pushed 'almost to the limit' within the unitary British state, thus the Unionists' more strongly articulated guarantee of 'internal independence' for Scotland unwittingly contributed to 'an argument for Scots political control' of that increasingly devolved administration (Miller 1981: 23). Unionist officials privately acknowledged this 'slippery slope' analysis, while the next two decades would witness a long-running battle between Labour and the Unionists as to which could be the most Scottish, the most capable of 'standing up for Scotland' within the United Kingdom.

FIVE

Scottish (Conservative and) Unionist Party: Rise and Fall

If the period between 1912 and 1939 found 'nationalist unionism' in the ascendancy, and 1940–51 saw it evolve into the more robust 'Scottish Control of Scottish Affairs' agenda, then the final phase, between Churchill's 1951 general election victory and a belated shift in Conservative constitutional thinking in 1968, were two decades in which it rose – achieving a majority of seats and votes in 1955 – and fell, losing electoral ground to both Labour and the SNP, a decline which continued until 2014.

Even then, most of the standard tenets of nationalist unionism remained in place: promises of further administrative devolution, patriotic appeals and use of Scottish myths and symbols. But back in office, this no longer resonated as strongly as it had between the wars and in the context of the early 1950s, when popular support for some sort of legislative devolution had reached its height. If nationalism, to return to Smith's definition, required a 'political project', then it was during this period that it became subject to the law of diminishing returns.

There were also external pressures, a 'wind of change' abroad and halting attempts to find an alternative European role at home. Not only did these weaken the multi-layered Scottish/British/imperial Unionist identity, but what Bulpitt identified as the Union's 'territorial code' began to break down. The Scottish 'periphery' was increasingly viewed from the 'centre' as organisationally inept and an electoral headache, while other unionist parties, particularly Labour, became more confident in their own nationalist unionism.

'Ancient Traditions'

'Politicians concerned with Scotland are almost nationalistic when they are out of office', observed Paton, but 'when they form a government they become obstinately and even blindly unionist' (Paton 1968: 10). Although

. he overstated the point, a comparison of the period covered in the previous chapter and that surveyed in this illustrates that phenomenon, for although the measures set out in *Scottish Control of Scottish Affairs* and subsequent 1950 and 1951 Conservative Party manifestos were honoured to some degree, the approach of Churchill's first (and only) peacetime government was certainly less ostentatiously Scottish.

In 1951, James Stuart began a long tenure as Scotland's man in the Cabinet (or the Cabinet's man in Scotland), although perhaps more significant given his future career trajectory was the appointment of Lord Home as Minister of State at the Scottish Office, effectively Stuart's deputy. He was tasked with raising the political profile of the new government in Scotland and was therefore to spend most of his time in Edinburgh rather than London. Churchill, punning about 'your Home, sweet Home', joked that his real purpose was to 'quell those turbulent Scots' (Ramsden 1995: 245–6).

Walter Elliot, however, remained the rhetorical guardian of nationalist unionism at Westminster. In the Debate on the Address that followed the election, he channelled Sir Walter Scott in speaking of Scotland as a 'country with a great purpose, ancient traditions and full of power and force' which could 'yet make a great contribution' to solving 'modern problems'. 'Without her special gifts we should all be much the poorer', he told MPs. 'As Sir Walter Scott said: "Un-Scotch us, if you will; but if you do, you will make us damned mischievous Englishmen"' (HC Deb 8 November 1951 Vol 493 c45).

Elliot also shored up the Conservative government during controversy about the designation of the new monarch, which became something of a focal point for nationalism in the early 1950s. When John MacCormick (Rector of Glasgow University) contested the numerical accuracy of 'Elizabeth II', it fell to Lord Cooper, a former Scottish Unionist MP, to consider an appeal, Lord Guthrie having previously dismissed the case. As Jackson (2012) has observed, more attention has been paid to the judgment rather than the judge, but a glance at his CV reveals Lord Cooper to have been a 'legal nationalist' (see Chapter 3), a founder of Stair, the Scottish Legal History Society, and active within the Scottish Historical Society.

This surely influenced Cooper's opinion, thereafter much quoted by Scottish nationalists, that 'the principle of unlimited sovereignty of Parliament is a distinctively English principle' and had 'no counterpart in Scottish constitutional law'. He also articulated the classic Scottish Unionist view that Scotland and England had formed Great Britain in 1707 on equal terms, criticising those who acted 'as if all that happened in 1707 was that Scottish representatives were admitted to the Parliament of England. That is not what was done' (*MacCormick v. Lord Advocate* (1953) SC 396).[1] Scottish Unionist

MPs, meanwhile, lobbied for the 'II' to be omitted from pillar boxes, and Churchill acquiesced in changing the royal style in Scotland more generally to, simply, 'ER'.

In February 1952, the Cabinet had also considered the 'Stone of Scone', upon which Queen Elizabeth was to be crowned. It had been removed from Westminster Abbey more than a year earlier by four nationalist students, and Scottish Unionist MPs were acutely conscious that its recovery and future use would have to be handled with care. On 26 February 1952, for example, the Scottish Unionist Members Committee informed the media that while it believed the stone 'should be available for use at the Coronation Service . . . there was no unanimity as to where it should be kept at other times' (SUMC 1952). Scotland's 'representative' peers, always more nationalist than their elected colleagues, had expressed support for returning the stone to Edinburgh during a House of Lords debate on 9 May 1951. Lady Airlie even wanted to hold a separate Scottish coronation ceremony, but Churchill demurred, instructing the Cabinet to do 'nothing' until after King George VI's funeral and then 'without public fuss' (Churchill 1952).

The new monarch's 'State Visit' to Edinburgh in the June of that year was a masterclass in 'official nationalism'. In his foreword to the official souvenir programme (adorned with thistles, saltires, lions rampant and the Scottish coat of arms), James Stuart said the 'Honours of Scotland' to be carried before Her Majesty were 'symbolic but striking proofs' of the 'special place' Scotland held in relation to the Crown and Commonwealth. It was also repeatedly emphasised that the young queen was 'sensitive to the alert national consciousness of her Scottish subjects', having personally requested that the Honours 'be borne before her' (State Visit 1953: 11, 16).

As Jackson concluded, during this period there was 'much evidence, both private and published, to suggest a deep-seated concern for the sentiment, symbols, and culture of Scottishness' (Jackson 2012: 253). Indeed, MacCormick believed that as the influence of his Scottish Covenant movement declined, nationalist sentiment became more 'readily expressed' in 'symbols', noting in his memoir that saltires outnumbered every other flag during the 1953 coronation celebrations and at the Scottish Industries Exhibition the following year (MacCormick 1955: 198).

Implementing 'Scottish Control of Scottish Affairs'

The SNP's Robert McIntyre, meanwhile, spoke of 'consequences' flowing from the Unionists' failure to honour pre-election 'pledges' about easing 'remote control from London' (Somerville 2013: 59), and it did not take long for newspapers to take up this accusation of backsliding. In relation to transport, for example, the *Scotsman* noted that the 'change in party fortunes' had 'modified' the attitude of Scottish Unionist MPs, their 'zeal' for devolving control of 'nationalised concerns' having 'apparently weakened' (*Scotsman*, 12 December 1952).

Another *Scotsman* article in February 1953 criticised Scottish Unionist MPs for absenting themselves from a debate on their own proposals, noting the difficulty of reconciling that with the 'unequivocal undertaking' there would be 'separate executive authorities for the nationalised industries in Scotland'. 'No conceivable exercise of ingenuity', continued the article, 'appears to be capable of showing that the Minister of Transport has redeemed this pledge' (*Scotsman*, 17 February 1953).

The Scottish Covenant Association (SCA), with whom the Scottish Unionist Members' Committee maintained surprisingly diligent correspondence, also alluded to 'fraud and failure' when it came to Unionist election pledges, urging them to remember that it was 'a Scottish Party and that COUNTRY BEFORE PARTY is not just another shallow platitude' (SCA 1953). But if Scottish Unionists were guilty of 'fraud and failure', it appeared to have little impact, its sensitivity to Scottish national symbolism and the reversal of some Labour nationalisations apparently 'sufficient to meet Scottish aspirations at this time' (Miller 1981: 24).

Even MacCormick acknowledged that Churchill's government, 'although slowly and unwillingly', had begun to 'show signs of activity in Scotland in response to the pressure of [nationalist] propaganda', most significantly in delivering on its late-1940s promise to establish a Royal Commission on Scottish Affairs. With that, judged MacCormick in his memoir, 'the wind was taken out of our sails' (MacCormick 1955: 185–6), which, of course, had been its object.

The Royal Commission's remit, of course, was deliberately narrow, with nationalist unionism maintaining its legislative glass ceiling. Indeed, Scottish Unionist publications in 1953 and 1954 exuded confidence that the nationalist tide had receded, the 1952 Catto report (commissioned by the previous Labour government) having provided an evidential basis for Unionist claims that Scotland benefited financially from the Union.

One pamphlet quoted a speech from the senior Conservative Rab Butler, 'Scotland under the Unionist Government', on 19 February 1954. Reiterating the party's 'declared policy' to ensure Scotland's 'just rights and aspirations' were 'met and satisfied', Butler said his government had 'cut back those infringements on Scottish nationhood' that had been 'so marked and keenly felt':

We have fulfilled our pledge to strengthen and reorganise the Scottish Office. We have kept our promise to establish a Royal Commission to advise on administrative and other problems. We are providing in transport, in broadcasting and now in electricity, better Scottish control over public corporations north of the border. (SUA 1954: 1)

The Royal Commission reported in 1954. Mitchell saw Lord Balfour (whose father had mused on 'Nationality and Home Rule' three decades earlier) as having presided over 'an unexceptional enquiry with unexceptional conclusions' (Mitchell 2009: 26), but, significantly, he observed that 'in the absence of convincing evidence to the contrary the machinery of government should be designed to dispose of Scottish business in Scotland', also urging an 'essential principle' that Scotland's 'needs and points of view should be known and brought into account at all stages in the formulation and execution of policy'. Balfour also ruminated on the source of recent nationalist 'discontent', concluding that it had been 'aggravated by needless English thoughtlessness and undue Scottish susceptibilities'.

Even beyond that, argued Balfour, there existed 'more tangible causes', not least the significant expansion of the state since the beginning of the First World War. Whereas before the war the state's 'interference with the individual' had been 'insignificant' and therefore 'it mattered little to the Scotsman whether this came from Edinburgh or London', subsequent expansion had left him (or her) wondering 'why orders and instructions should come to him from London, to question whether Whitehall has taken sufficient account of local conditions and to criticise not government but what he regards, however erroneously, as English government' (Balfour 1954: 74).

Miller had a point in observing 'a sharp contrast between Balfour's diagnosis and its prescription' (Miller 1981: 23), but the Royal Commission and its underwhelming recommendations had, of course, been contrived to allow Scottish Unionists, as Somerville later put it, to 'take the moral high ground of claiming to listen and to act upon nationalist concerns by means of establishing a Royal Commission, but without the drawback of actual delivery' (Somerville 2013: 76).

Indeed, when the SUMC considered Balfour's report towards the end of 1954, it observed with satisfaction that its 'clear and objective picture' showed 'no cause for complaint on the relative position between Scotland and the rest of the United Kingdom'. Paradoxically, however, the SUMC also wondered if the Appellate Committee of the House of Lords might 'meet in Edinburgh to hear Scottish Appeals' and if the 'reconvening' of Tom Johnston's wartime 'Council of State' might be 'held in reserve as an emergency measure' (SUMC 1954), a subconscious acknowledgement that the Royal Commission might not have the desired impact.

Indeed, conscious there were no 'earth-shaking recommendations', James Stuart urged a speedy response in order to 'prevent a possible public campaign in which the Royal Commission's recommendations, as well as procrastination by the Government, would be called in question' (Stuart 1954). Writing in 1959, the nationalist-inclined journalist J. M. Reid was in two minds, acknowledging that the gradual extension of administrative devolution had recreated 'the framework of a state' but that Scottish Office ministers remained, in essence,

> managers of a country with an obstinately individual life of its own which is apt to fret against the increasingly rigid framework of modern government from a distance . . . Devolution which is merely administrative begins to look more and more anomalous as the years go by. (Reid 1959: 147, 174)

The 1955 General Election

Publication of Lord Balfour's report in 1954, however, allowed Unionists to fight the forthcoming general election on the basis of having met its earlier manifesto pledges. As Somerville observed, the Scottish Unionist Party 'wore tartan on its sleeve by flying the Saltire at election contests and its Scottish conferences and by using Scottish symbolism generally to promote the party's appeal to Scottish sentimentality and its desire to safeguard Scottish interests and traditions' (Somerville 2013: 82).

A by-election in Edinburgh North in January 1955 set the tone for the general election that followed. Sparked by the appointment of James Clyde (a key figure in developing the 'Scottish Control of Scottish Affairs' agenda) as Lord President, it found (what remained of) the Scottish Covenant Association hassling the Unionist candidate, W. R. Milligan, as to his stance on devolution. He was opposed to a Scottish Parliament but said that as 'statesmen and politicians the Scots are perfectly capable of controlling their own affairs' (*Scotsman*, 21 January 1955).

One of his election meetings was disrupted by a young man wearing a kilt, who 'waved the Lion Rampant and St Andrew's Cross'. Milligan was indignant: 'Do you dare say I am not pure Scots? These are my flags, as yours.' This remark was 'warmly applauded' (*Scotsman*, 26 January 1955), while the press had great fun with the fact that the meeting was chaired by Sir William Wallace who, according to one headline, had quelled 'a Nationalist at election uproar' (*Evening Dispatch*, 26 January 1955). Milligan won the by-election.

As in 1950 and 1951, the 1955 Conservative general election manifesto, *United for Peace and Progress*, devoted a substantial section to 'Scottish Affairs' (three times as long as that in 1950), highlighting a 'general theme' that within the Union 'responsibility for managing Scottish affairs' would 'be in the hands of Scotsmen'. In accordance with the recent Royal Commission, it continued, the Secretary of State was to assume 'care of Scottish roads and bridges', and where 'further measures of this kind' were shown to be 'in the best interests of Scotland', then Conservatives would 'not hesitate to adopt them' (CUCO 1955a: 28–9).

Pagination proved important, the *Glasgow Herald* comparing the Conservative manifesto's 'one and a half pages' on Scottish Affairs with a 'meagre reference' in Labour's (*Glasgow Herald*, 30 April 1955). The *Scotsman* also judged that in terms of 'administrative devolution the Unionists have indisputably gone farther than their predecessors', and while it 'may not have been wholly fulfilled', they had 'applied the principle, whereas the Socialists cannot get away from centralised control' (*Scotsman*, 30 April 1955). In competition with Labour, the Liberals and the then tiny SNP, Unionists appeared the most effective defenders of Scottish distinctiveness – the most nationalist of the three major parties.

That year Scotland also got its own dedicated chapter in the Conservative Party's *Campaign Guide*. This quoted from a 1952 speech by Anthony Eden, who in 1955 had succeeded Churchill as UK Conservative leader and Prime Minister, and another from the Anglo-Scots Harold Macmillan articulating a specifically Tory view of the multi-national UK. He argued that the Union of 'our two great Kingdoms and the Principality of Wales' must be that 'of the wedding ring not of the handcuff'. Unionists, added Macmillan, did not believe the 'Scottish partner' had been 'well treated' by the previous Labour government; the 'balance' had not been 'evenly held', offending Scotland's 'nationhood' and touching 'her pride'.

The *Campaign Guide* went on to compare the Conservative record with that of Labour, castigating the opposition's 'uninspiring statement on Scotland' in its manifesto and thus its 'scant attention' to Scottish problems (CUCO 1955b: 308 and 319). The 1955 *East of Scotland Yearbook* also drove home the message that Unionists, rather than Labour MPs, were the guardian of Scottish interests within the Union, so much so that 'allegations of neglect by the Government of Scottish affairs are clearly unfounded and misleading' (SUA 1955: 17).

The general election campaign caught the Scottish Unionist Party at its height, doubtless aided by the novelty of a new Prime Minister (Eden) and rising living standards. Unionists secured a majority of both seats (36) and the popular vote (50.1 per cent), marginally ahead of the Labour Party on both counts. Although Mitchell (2014) was correct in observing that that majority relied upon a Unionist alliance with other parties such as National Liberals and Liberal Unionists, only sixty years later would another party come close to winning a majority of the popular vote. Scottish Unionism, and its nationalist-unionist ideology, had peaked.

'An Important Matter of Principle'

Writing in 1954, Pryde acknowledged the difficulty in assessing the true strength of nationalism in mid-twentieth-century Scotland, for although supporters of 'self-government' were 'enthusiastic and single-minded' and 'perhaps a majority' of Scots were willing to 'acquiesce' in 'a separate parliament as the symbol of nationhood', this sentiment existed to such 'a mild degree, with such lack of fervency, as not to shake their political habits or their adherence to the two major parties, neither of which subscribes to legislative devolution' (Pryde and Rait 1954: 151).

In the months that followed the 1955 election, Unionists continued to co-opt and therefore 'contain' this sentiment. Lord Home spoke 'of Scotland as a country' joined now for 250 years 'in friendly union with a great and powerful neighbour', while also invoking Sir William Wallace, 'who in the 13th century, first rallied his countrymen to resist a forceful union with England' (SUMC 1955). In 1953, a cross-party group of Scots, including several Unionists, had proposed a London memorial (at the location of his execution) for Sir William. Walter Elliot's papers reveal concerns of 'too strong a Scottish Nationalist element' creeping into the project, thus Elliot was drafted in to give reassurance that it was backed 'by people whose patriotism has sanity as well as sincerity', a standard expression of the distinction between 'good' and 'bad' Scottish nationalism.

At the memorial's unveiling on 8 April 1956, Elliot gave a stirring address which drew upon some familiar themes:

> Sir William Wallace was our countryman. It was for the freedom of our land that he took up arms. It was our countrymen who answered his call to battle. Within four months of his execution at this spot, a successor arose – Robert the Bruce; whom again our country supported; till the object of both was won.

The proceedings, however, were marred by a protest, the chairman of the London branch of the SNP calling those present 'traitors to Scotland' for daring to sing the (UK) national anthem. He proceeded to jump onto the platform, but the elderly Elliot sent 'him flying to the back of the platform with a tackle worthy of a Border Rugby forward'. Two sorts of nationalism had literally collided in the imperial capital (Elliot 1956).

In March 1957, the Scottish Unionist Members' Committee considered a letter from a 'rabid nationalist' whom it nevertheless concluded had 'a pretty strong case' in arguing that the Church of Scotland ought to have a representative – like the Anglican Church – in the House of Lords. Lord Balfour had commended the claim of Scotland's 'national' church to 'an appropriate share in representation' in the Upper House (Balfour 1954: 38), and the Conservative Research Department could see 'no reason why this claim should not be granted'. 'If we could do something about this matter it would greatly please the Church of Scotland,' it added, 'which carries throughout Scotland a good deal more influence and prestige than does the Church of England throughout England' (SUMC 1957). Nothing, however, came of this proposed sop to Scottish sensibilities. But then as Cameron observed, the 'almost institutional connection between the Kirk and the Unionists' in the 1920s had 'melted away' by the post-war era (Cameron 2010: 265–6).

The Conservative Research Department, at that time a relatively new yet increasingly influential organ of the UK party, also made a point of arguing that Scotland was entitled to preferential treatment over Wales. Not only was Scotland 'a more populous and more wealthy country than Wales', but it possessed 'her' own legal system and 'Parliamentary legislative procedure', as well as a system of local government which followed 'a different pattern' from that in England and Wales (SUMC 1956a). There was a clear hierarchy within the 'territorial code' of unionism.

By the mid-1950s, however, some Unionists began to feel the maintenance of a distinct party identity north of the border was not necessarily to its advantage. At the 1956 SUA conference, the East Renfrewshire Unionist Association submitted a resolution seeking to change the name of the party in Scotland to 'Conservative'. Others, however, believed this 'would not be advisable' as the word 'Unionist' involved 'an important matter of principle' (SUMC 1956b), sparking an internal debate that would only be resolved nearly a decade later. For example, the Unionist MP for Stirling and Falkirk, J. S. C. Reid, believed that not only should Unionists ostentatiously 'appeal to the sentiment of the Scottish nation' but also 'stress our individuality as a Unionist party in Scotland apart from the Conservative party' (Jackson 2012: 253–4).

In response to those who believed the word 'Unionist' to be 'out of date', the 1957 *East of Scotland Yearbook* argued that it now possessed a 'new connotation' unconnected with Home Rule for Ireland, saying that it 'may be taken to mean the unity of all classes in a property-owning democracy and the unity of the Commonwealth'. To many, it added, Unionist was preferable to 'Conservative' in that it more fully captured 'Unionist philosophy' as epitomised by Edmund Burke, chiefly the 'disposition to preserve with the ability to improve' (SUA 1957: 25).

Increasingly, however, many doubted the Scottish Unionist Party's 'ability to improve' following its 1955 triumph. During 1957, the 250th anniversary of the Anglo-Scottish Union, a sense of frustration permeated some Unionist statements. Writing in the *Spectator*, Sir Robert Boothby argued that in Scotland a 'political revival' was 'urgently required', not least in symbolic terms:

> If I had ever been offered the Scottish Office – and at one moment, long ago, it was conceivable – I should have asked for an official residence in Edinburgh; and, with the assistance of my old friend Sir Compton Mackenzie, striven to revive the pristine glories of a society which once dominated Europe. I should have driven round Scotland in an enormous black car, with the rampant lion flying proudly in the wind, and – if possible – outriders on motor-cycles. I should have cruised off the West Coast every year in the Minna, rechristened a yacht for the purpose, with more flags.

'Without Scotland the English would be sunk', added Sir Robert. 'They should be made to realise it' (*Spectator*, 30 May 1957).

In his foreword to the 1958 *East of Scotland Yearbook*, the SUA president Philip Christison warned that 'Unionists, Conservatives, and National Liberals, must stand united to prevent our country falling once more into Socialist hands with all that entails' (SUA 1958: 7), quite a statement only a few years after that coalition secured more than 50 per cent of the Scottish vote. Some MPs, inevitably, blamed the media, the SUA chairman expressing concern that letters to the *Scotsman* 'seem to indicate among some people a misapprehension' that 'Scotland is being unfairly treated and is being mulcted of money for the benefit of England' (SUMC 1959).

There was also a hint of desperation in party literature. In the Argyll by-election of 1958, Michael Noble's election address pictured him in a kilt petting a Highland cow in front of rolling glens. 'I believe in Scotland', he declared. 'There is greater prosperity and hope for the future to-day in the Highlands than at any time in the last century' (Noble 1958).

'A Scottish Economy'

Another Scottish Unionist Association publication quoted Harold Macmillan, Prime Minister since Eden's resignation over Suez, saying that the 'greatest improvement' in UK employment figures had taken place in Scotland.

Never, he added, had 'so effective an effort been made by any Government to help the development of the economic and industrial life in Scotland' (OCUPS 1959: 21–4), pointing to the recent decision to locate the Ravenscraig steel strip mill in Lanarkshire.

The chairman of the SUMC had written to Macmillan in November 1958 'earnestly' hoping any decision would 'be favourable to Scotland'. In response, the Prime Minister played up his Highland provenance. 'Of course, with so many Scots in the Cabinet it would be surprising if Scotland did not get her full share!' he quipped. 'Even when we emigrate, we do not forget the land of our Birth' (SUMC 1958).

As Ramsden (1995) observed, in Scotland the need for economic modernisation took on a clear political dimension. As Cairncross had emphasised in 1954, although the 'Scottish economy' was an 'integral' part of the UK economy, one 'segment' of a common market with the same currency and identical rates of tax, it also constituted 'a distinct society . . . in which the fire of nationalism still burns . . . differing from England and Wales in memories and aspirations, temperament and tastes, institutions and culture', nothing less than 'a Scottish economy' functioning 'as a unit and with an independent momentum' (Cairncross 1954: 1).

Although in the 1950s pragmatic Scottish Unionism had 'effectively adapted some of Labour's statist policies for its own ends', particularly when it came to public housing and support for New Towns (Jackson 2012: 261), during the 1955–9 Parliament the economic boom that manifested itself in other parts of the UK was not as pronounced in Scotland. And given that Unionists had spoken the language of 'Scottish solutions' to Scottish problems, inevitably they ended up being held responsible.

SUMC notes and briefings concentrated on rebutting SNP claims to a greater extent than ever before, emphasising that Scotland was 'not so wealthy a country as England' and therefore received 'financial help' that 'would no longer be available' if it pursued independence. They also revived an old divide-and-conquer argument from before the war: the notion that the Highlands would be marginalised in any Scottish Parliament and receive less financial 'aid'. Paradoxically, Liberal proposals for a devolved Scottish Parliament were attacked on the basis that 'without the power of the purse a Parliament becomes a mere "talking shop"' (SUMC 1959b), which rather suggested Unionists might support legislative devolution so long as it included fiscal powers.

At the general election in October 1959, Scottish Unionists lost five seats and around 14,000 votes (although it retained a lead over Labour in terms of the popular vote), which in the context of steady advances since the 1920s most likely reflected negative economic developments which had not been present four years earlier. Nationally, by contrast, the Conservatives had increased their majority over Labour to 100 seats. 'The Conservatives all but forgot Scotland in the 1959 election', was Miller's diagnosis (Miller 1981: 29), while after the election Ramsden saw as a display of 'indifference' Macmillan's promotion of one defeated Scottish MP to the Lords and allowing 'him to take the name of the constituency that had just refused to elect him' (Ramsden 1996: 232). From 1945 until 1959, election results had generally followed UK trends, but now there was a clear divergence between Conservative fortunes north and south of the border.

Electoral Divergence

In its annual report for 1959, the Western Divisional Council reckoned the 'prosperity theme, so effective in England, was not quite in tune with conditions in West Scotland and other areas similarly affected by unemployment and under-employment'. It also felt the 'Scottish vote' reflected 'the anxiety felt in some areas about the employment situation', which meant pressure on the government to 'redouble' its 'efforts to close the gap between the workless figures in England and Scotland' (WDC 1959).

The Scottish economy would be one of the dominating themes of the next six years, along with ongoing discussions about party organisation, the (relative) rise of the SNP and the decline of empire. In 1960, Harold Macmillan spoke of a 'wind of change' blowing across Africa, an allusion to the emergence of several newly independent states. This, as McLean and McMillan concluded, 'threatened Unionism . . . the end of empire imperiled the ideology and weakened the glue of barely articulated popular Unionism' (McLean and McMillan 2005: 10).

Of more pressing concern for Scottish Unionists was the domestic revival of interest in Home Rule, dormant since the early 1950s (Miller 1981: 24). Speaking notes prepared for the Glasgow MP Tom Galbraith struck a pragmatic tone, conceding that greater 'separation' had 'its attractions' as 'a nice, easy solution', and that 'of course' it would 'be possible to work out something on these lines for Scotland' (i.e. a Stormont-like devolved Parliament). Even 'Dominion status' was 'an attractive proposal', although the fact remained that 'at present we in Scotland get more out of the United Kingdom Exchequer than we put into it', something that was 'only fair since our needs are greater' (SUMC 1960).

As Phillips (2008) has demonstrated, by this point the Unionist-dominated Scottish Council (of) Development and Industry (SCDI) began moving in an overtly devolutionist direction out of frustration at the London-centric nature of economic decision making; prominent figures included the Lords Polwarth and Clydesmuir. By way of a response, the UK government's Toothill Report (1962) constituted the last gasp of administrative devolution, rejecting economic powers for the Scottish Office but recommending a new 'department' to co-ordinate regional development measures. 'There was nothing nationalist about the Report,' judged Kellas of Toothill, 'in fact it was less romantic than the Balfour Commission' (Kellas 1980: 77).

Drucker and Brown were clear that Nationalist parties (in Wales and Scotland) made 'headway by pointing out how ineffectively the British state was serving the needs of the Scottish and Welsh economies' (Drucker and Brown 1980: 30). Not only did this damage Scottish Unionists in electoral terms, but party organisation suffered from the withdrawal of business support. Long-standing party staff retired amidst personality-based infighting, while the practice followed since 1951, by which the Scottish party chairman was also Secretary of State for Scotland, 'did not allow a separate identity to be claimed for the Scottish Party at times when the Government was unpopular' (Ramsden 1996: 135).

Some Unionists tried to compensate with symbolism. In the early 1960s Lord Clyde, a former Unionist MP and Lord President of the Court of Session, launched a worldwide appeal for funds to erect an equestrian statue of Robert the Bruce to commemorate his 1314 victory over Edward II at Bannockburn. Installed near Stirling in 1964, it continued a tradition of 'unionist nationalism' dating back to the mid nineteenth century but, ironically, later became a rallying point for supporters of independence.

'A Scot from the Borders'

At the 1963 Dumfriesshire by-election, Unionist David Anderson (recently appointed Solicitor-General for Scotland) tried to fend off his SNP and Labour opponents by warning that it was 'no time for "protest" voting', citing the new Prime Minister (Sir Alec Douglas-Home), 'a Scot from the Borders', as someone ('a Scottish M.P. for 15 years in Lanark and our Scottish Minister of State for 4 years') who 'knows our problems here' (Anderson 1963).

Ramsden believed Sir Alec's presence demonstrated that Scotland remained 'at the heart of Tory politics' (Ramsden 1996: 251), but while Home's Scottish credentials were clear, they did little to halt Unionist decline. At the 1964 Rutherglen by-election, the Unionist candidate Iain Sproat even implied that 'British influence' was 'personified' by two Scotsmen, Harold Macmillan and Sir Alec Douglas-Home, who had 'brought about the signing of the famous Moscow Test-Ban Treaty just under a year ago' (Sproat 1964). But this seemed an inadequate substitute for the once-strong imperial strand of nationalist unionism.

In the run-up to the 1964 general election, meanwhile, there was a sense that the Unionists, their name, representatives and reputation had come to be regarded as something of a joke. Labour MPs sneered about the 'merits or demerits of Scottish Unionist Members, as they like to call themselves' (HC Deb Vol 694 c1551 and v697 c549), while the *Daily Record*, which had switched to supporting Labour in the early 1960s, took to caricaturing its new opponents, something Seawright reckoned might have given 'public portrayal to the negative image of the Tory Party in Scotland as the "Hooray Henrys" of the grouse moor', instead equating 'Scottishness' with Labour (Seawright 1996).

'In Britain, 1964, while Sir Alecs enjoy a day's shootin' on the empty moors,' observed one article on the eve of the election, 'old folks go hungry and young folk seek vainly for a job' (*Daily Record*, 14 October 1964). This added a clear class dimension to the guardianship of Scottish national identity, which would become more pronounced in the following decades. In their 1966 'Craigton Survey', for example, Budge and Urwin discovered 'elements of a class comparison', with voter perceptions characterised as a 'struggle between underprivileged Scots and wealthy Southerners' (Budge and Urwin 1966: 124, 131).

The 1964 Conservative Party *Campaign Guide* made strenuous efforts to combat this image, highlighting economic advances since the last election ('Scotland's economy is at present undergoing a transformation'), reviving the 'Scottish Control of Home Affairs' slogan, rebutting (at length) 'Scottish Nationalist Claims' and ironically, given its own tactics since the Second World War, accusing the Liberals of attempting to 'gain popularity by playing up to Scottish nationalism' (CUP 1964: 362, 383–4). At the 1964 election, Scottish Unionists (although many now called themselves Conservatives) lost another six seats, meaning the party had shed a fifth of its vote and a dozen MPs since its electoral triumph in 1955.

Senior Unionists blamed 'organizational weakness' (Fry 1991: 225), and it was on that the party fixated as it sought a recovery. Although the Western Divisional Council believed 'it was beneficial in Scotland not only to boast of an organisation independent of London but to boast of an organisation independent of other areas in Scotland' (Seawright 1998: 34), in April 1965 the Eastern and Western Divisional Councils were scrapped and the Scottish Unionist Party, in existence since 1912, was reborn as the 'Scottish Conservative and Unionist Party' (Torrance 2012).

Seawright concluded that the party had 'exchanged a form of discourse that tapped a rich vein of Scottish culture for one that ran the danger of sounding dangerously English' (Seawright 1996: 33). Urwin's view was more nuanced, observing that while much Scottish Unionist 'energy' had in the past been 'devoted' to the defence of their 'independence', it had been 'essentially an unreal struggle', their 'attitudes' and organisation not 'commensurate with the responsibilities which "independence" implies' (Urwin 1966: 146). Over time, however, the change in nomenclature took on a heightened significance, a convenient scapegoat for subsequent electoral decline. The official Tory historian Lord Lexden, for example, believed Edward Heath's 'arrogantly imposed' change had 'demoted Scottish national pride' (*Daily Telegraph*, 13 February 2014).

The 'Declaration of Perth'

So just as a more overt nationalist dynamic began to manifest itself, the newly renamed Scottish Conservative and Unionist Party appeared to have downgraded its own Scottishness. After the 1966 election, at which Labour increased its majority, the UK party's Opinion Research Centre (ORC) found that voters in Scotland and Wales perceived the Conservatives as 'a uniquely English party of the Squirearchy, the Establishment, the Church of England and Westminster'. Not only that, but Conservative voters in Scotland might be persuaded to vote SNP, while a majority of Scottish voters in general said they would support Home Rule even if it made them worse off. In other words, the SNP, which had won just 5 per cent of the vote at the recent election (twice its share in 1964), posed a direct challenge to the predominant party of the Union (Cragoe 2015).

A separate report for the Conservative Research Department in July 1966 had even wondered, apparently unaware of developments since the 1920s, whether it was a 'weakness' that the party in Scotland and Wales did 'not make a specifically nationalist appeal'. Could it be dealt with by changes to local government, it wondered, or was something more targeted, 'an opium for disenchanted Celts', required (CPA 1966)? Although Edward Heath, UK Conservative leader since 1965, privately acknowledged nationalism as the 'biggest single factor in our politics today', he fluctuated between dismissing the SNP as 'flower people, with flower power' (MacDiarmid 1968: 354) and legitimising aspects of their demands following Winnie Ewing's success at the 1967 Hamilton by-election.

And while Heath's commitment – the 'Declaration of Perth' – to a directly elected Scottish Assembly at his Scottish party's conference in Perth in 1968 was 'at root, a calculation made with an eye to electoral success', it also possessed a deeper provenance. As Cragoe observed, Conservatives had always had 'much greater natural sympathy with the claims of Scottish nationhood' than in Wales or Ireland and 'consequently recognised the potential strength of nationalism's appeal for those who might otherwise consider themselves "natural" Tory voters' (Cragoe 2015: 30).

There was, in other words, a degree of intellectual consistency in this belated commitment to legislative devolution, hitherto presented by Conservatives as the unacceptable face of nationalism, for it could be viewed as the logical conclusion – or what Pentland called a 'matured endpoint' (Pentland 2015: 271) – to a long-standing Unionist commitment to administrative devolution; Arnott and Macdonald viewed it as 'less of an aberration' and more of a 'missed opportunity to take a long-held commitment to administrative devolution all the way to a legislative end' (Arnott and Macdonald 2012: 45). The historian Lord Blake, for example, referenced Lord Carnarvon's support for Home Rule in the 1880s in order to depict Heath's proposals as 'quite consistent with the Conservative tradition' and in no way detrimental to 'the principle of the Union' (Blake 1968).

Indeed, further research commissioned by the party before Heath's declaration found that 'the desire for a greater say by Scotland in her own affairs, greater autonomy of some sort, runs right through the nation'. Even 'anti-nationalists' who remained 'loyal' to the Conservative Party shared 'this feeling in a subdued form' (CPA 1968: 32). The MP Jock Bruce-Gardyne acknowledged this in an article for the *Spectator*, 'We're all nationalists now', he declared, writing that the 'real secret' of the SNP's success was that Scots were 'nationalist', albeit 'not in the SNP sense': 'We are turning to the SNP because the United Kingdom has ceased to satisfy us as a focus of national pride, and we demand more of our politicians than the satisfaction of our material expectations' (*Spectator*, 16 May 1968).

This was insightful. That year the Scottish Tory MP (and future Scottish Secretary) George Younger had also led a nationalist-unionist campaign to 'Save the Argylls', one of Scotland's oldest regiments (Torrance 2008), writing in the *Scotsman* that

> Most of us . . . have a strong desire to see many more decisions on Scottish matters made by Scotsmen in Scotland . . . I believe we should turn our energies to bringing government at all levels nearer the people . . . We should have televising of Scottish business at Westminster . . . Scottish Conservatives have never regarded the process of devolution as complete . . . The sole criterion must be the good of Scotland, and we are patriots no less than anyone else in Scottish politics. (*Scotsman*, 15 December 1967)

A group of younger Scottish Conservatives responded to this mood by forming the nationalist-unionist 'Thistle Group', which was 'determined to give the Scottish Conservatives a more distinctly Scottish flavour' (Hanham

1969: 195). 'In the eyes of any Scotsman, Scotland is The Priority', declared the ginger group's first pamphlet, 'and it is only by concentrating on priorities that any political party can hope to gain the confidence of the electorate. This the Scottish Tory Party has failed to do' (Marr 1995: 124).

But as Pentland observed, 'an historic Unionism, with its strong appeal to Scottish nationality', had already 'lost out' to the endorsement of a 'narrower unitary British patriotism, which held little attraction for many Scots' (Pentland 2015: 273). With most of the empire disbanded, Scottish Unionists had ended up emphasising the British strand of its nationalist unionism at the expense of the Scottish dimension, and even then not very effectively. According to the nationalist journalist J. M. Reid, a 'share' in the old British Empire had been the 'chief reward' offered to Scots by the 1707 Union, but now that it had 'vanished', national 'independence' had 'become the basis of the Commonwealth which has replaced it' (Reid 1971: 184).

Indeed, some Conservatives attempted to substitute the British Empire with another supra-national union, the European Common Market. Most striking in this respect was Lady Tweedsmuir, daughter-in-law of the late John Buchan (Ward 2005), while the Earl of Dalkeith, the first disabled Member of Parliament following a riding accident, declared that Scotland and the UK 'must join Europe . . . to become "great" again' (*Edinburgh Evening News*, 29 June 1971). But although the 'end of Empire' thesis in relation to the decline of the Scottish Conservative Party has been overstated (Pittock 2001), Europe did not pull at Scottish heartstrings in the same way as Malawi, Malaysia or India.

A Scottish party commission chaired by Lord Home had, meanwhile, fleshed out Heath's proposals and left the Conservatives – who returned to government in 1970 – with a commitment to devolution. In office (much like Liberal and Labour governments in the early twentieth century), however, this pledge was not considered a priority, even once the Royal Commission on the Constitution concurred towards the end of 1973. Heath's government was so consumed with the 'high politics' of economic turbulence and industrial unrest that 'low politics' fell off the agenda, with the peripheral Scottish Conservative Party struggling to compete with Labour and a resurgent SNP.

Writing in 1975, the MP and Thistle Group veteran Malcolm Rifkind urged his party to 'develop a new Scottish Unionism relevant to the needs and aspirations of modern Scotland'. It must, he added,

> also become the champions of devolution, an objective quite consistent with the Union. One of the curses of the devolution debate is that it has been argued to too great an extent in terms of nationalism, the S.N.P. and political tactics. Devolution, however, is in sympathy with basic Conservative philosophy. (*Question*, November 1975)

Scottish Conservatives, however, were split, with the unionist wing – which viewed devolution, like Labour unionists, as a 'slippery slope' – winning an internal battle in late 1976, when Mrs Thatcher ordered her MPs to vote against the second reading of the Scotland and Wales Bill (which implemented Labour's proposals for a Scottish Assembly). Thereafter, the party's nationalist-unionist tradition went into marked decline; the Overton window had shifted, meaning that legislative devolution was now well within the acceptable parameters of political discourse.

Party literature illustrated this shift. 'Did you know', asked a Scottish Conservative flyer produced in the mid-1970s, that 'since 1938 Scotland has had Devolution?' 'From St. Andrews House in Edinburgh we control most of what goes on in Scotland', including 'devolved' policy areas such as health and education. 'On top of all that Scotland has its own Legal System', it continued. 'ALL THIS and more is already run by Scots for Scots in Scotland – with one great advantage. We can plug into the larger U.K. resources as and when we need.' Join the Scottish Conservatives, it implored in capital letters, 'and back the United Kingdom' (Scottish Conservative Party 1970s).

As in the 1930s, however, the party continued to affect an open mind when it came to legislative devolution, with Lord Home (in)famously promising that the 1979 referendum would not be 'Scotland's last chance' for a Scottish Assembly (*Scotland*, 5 January 1979).[2] Certain Scottish Conservatives, such as the Edinburgh councillor Brian Meek, involved themselves in the 'Yes for Scotland' campaign, but more aligned with 'Scotland is British'. The referendum was won, but also lost, failing to satisfy the required 40 per cent threshold (of the total Scottish electorate) for the Scotland Act 1978 to take effect.

As Secretary of State for Scotland after 1979, George Younger presented himself as mitigating Thatcherism's harsher edges (as did Peter Walker in Wales). In 1981, he and others fought a nationalist-unionist battle to prevent the HSBC from taking over the Royal Bank of Scotland, while Younger's successor, the previously pro-devolution Malcolm Rifkind, promoted Gaelic education and broadcasting. Although she acquiesced at the time, Mrs Thatcher later wrote in her memoirs that Rifkind *et al.* 'regularly portrayed themselves as standing up for Scotland against me and the parsimony of Whitehall', although 'in adopting this tactic' she – not unreasonably – believed they had 'increased the underlying Scottish antipathy to the Conservative Party and indeed the Union'. Of the Scottish Office, she complained that it 'added a layer of bureaucracy, standing in the way of reforms which were paying such dividends in England' (Thatcher 1993: 620).

Nevertheless, emphasis on Thatcher's 'assimilationist' proclivities (Mitchell 1998) has been overdone; whatever her private views, as Prime Minister she did not seriously erode the department's autonomy or spending power, even creating new Scotland-only agencies (for example, Scottish Enterprise) and acknowledging the 'Scottish dimension' of industries such as steel-making (Torrance 2009). Still, in 1988 the centrist Tory Reform Group, conscious that opponents equated the Scottish Conservative Party with 'all that the Scots dislike most about "Englishness"', recommended attempting to 'equate Scottish Toryism with Scottish culture and consciousness' (MacKenzie 1988: 5).

Mrs Thatcher had tried. In a 1982 speech she spoke of 'traditional Scottish values of thrift and application, of fair-dealing and self-advancement' (26 November 1982), although a year later she added that these 'values' could equally be English as they were 'not tied to any particular place or century' (she had, however, called them 'Victorian values') (28 January 1983). Most boldly, at the 1988 Scottish Conservative conference the Prime Minister declared:

> Tory values are in tune with everything that is finest in the Scottish character and with the proudest moments in Scottish history. Scottish values are Tory values – and vice versa. The values of hard work, self-reliance, thrift, enterprise – the relishing of challenges, the seizing of opportunities. That's what the Tory Party stands for – that's what Scotland stands for. (13 May 1988)[3]

Crucially, however, this did not appear to many voters as credible, the Conservatives remaining 'a strongly British nationalist party' but having 'lost the classic unionist nuances' (Keating 2009: 65). Opposition to Thatcher also assumed a nationalist form: under her watch the 'holy trinity' of Scottish national identity was perceived to be under assault – Scottish education was being 'Anglicized', Presbyterian values insulted by the Prime Minister's 'Sermon on the Mound' and Scots Law deregulated (Torrance 2009).

Nationalist Unionism Redux

As Prime Minister after 1990, John Major attempted to reset the Anglo-Scottish relationship to an earlier, more territorially sensitive dynamic, referring to Scots during the 1992 general election campaign as 'an intensely proud, patriotic race' (*The Times*, 28 March 1992). He and Scottish Secretary Ian Lang's subsequent publication, *Scotland in the Union: A Partnership for Good*, echoed earlier Scottish Unionist publications. Major's introduction declared that 'no nation could be held irrevocably in a Union against its will',[4] while promising the creation, 'when appropriate', of 'new bodies to take account of the distinctive Scottish identity'. The Union, it added, far from diminishing Scotland had

> in fact allowed the development of a stronger Scottish identity shaped, as it is, by Scotland's place in the United Kingdom and in the wider world. That such a development has taken place since 1707 is a tribute to the nature of the Union and the way in which it avoids imposing uniformity throughout these islands. But the strength of Scottish identity poses a challenge to government; to respect and cherish the differences between each of the constituent parts of the United Kingdom. Fundamental to that is a need to recognise the individual needs of each and to respond sensitively to them. (Scottish Office 1993: 6, 38–9)

This was an attempt to update Thatcher's 'composite' territorial code, though it brought to mind the 1954 Balfour Commission with relatively weak policy proposals: the 'devolution' of responsibility for the Scottish Arts Council, as well as some 'control' of training, industrial support and airports in the Highlands and Islands. Full legislative devolution, however, remained beyond the pale, although Major was simultaneously committed to restoring 'consociational' devolution in Northern Ireland as part of the ongoing peace process. The Prime Minister tried to square this circle by arguing that Northern Ireland was exceptional, which was both true and not an altogether adequate response to the long-standing Stormont Question.

Melding, however, located Major between Heath and Thatcher in terms of approach, likening his governments to those of Salisbury and Balfour in attempting to 'kill off' Home Rule 'with kindness' (Melding 2009: 123). In 1993, the UK government made great play of the European Summit taking place in Edinburgh, the intention being to stress the Scottish capital's status within both the British and European Unions, much as the Empire Exhibition of 1938 had emphasised Glasgow's import to the British and imperial families of nations.

Meanwhile the Thatcherite Michael Forsyth, Secretary of State after 1995, reinvented himself as 'a benign manager *cum* cultural nationalist', adopting a lion rampant party logo, courting the pro-devolution Campbell Christie (of the STUC), appointing the former SNP MPs Jim Sillars and Dick Douglas to Scottish quangos, proposing a Scottish History Higher qualification and attempting to capitalise – less successfully than the SNP – on Mel Gibson's *Braveheart*, recruiting the Australian actor to advise on film policy (Harvie 2004: 231). The apex of this nationalist-unionism redux came on St Andrew's Day 1996, when a bekilted Forsyth 'returned' the Stone of Destiny to Edinburgh Castle, having been convinced by his daughter that the argument for doing so was unanswerable (Torrance 2006). 'My mother was a Tory but she was also a nationalist', he later recalled. 'And I can remember my mother used to tell me about the Stone of Destiny when I was a child, and tell me it should be in Scotland' (*The Times*, 15 November 2016). Forsyth's most radical proposal, that votes on legislation in the Scottish Grand Committee should be considered binding, did not win Cabinet agreement (Torrance 2009).

Writing in 1995, Nairn viewed Scottish politics as an 'orthographic battle' between 'the upper and the lower cases':

> Almost everyone is some sort of nationalist . . . In retreat, the Conservatives have discovered that true Unionism awarded Scotland just as much nationalism as was good for it, via Scots Law, institutional autonomy and new devices like the National Health Trusts. Many of their speeches these days are devoted to extolling the modest merits of enough-as-is-good-for-you national self-reliance. One might almost think that the aim of Union and Empire had all along been to foster this better class of Scottish and Welsh nationalism.

Nairn then touched upon the inherent tension in such an approach:

> Some in their audience are of course bound to think, if it has been so marvellous then might not more be better still? Ah, it would bring disaster! is the official reply – the agonising abyss of separatism etc. But just why would healthy self-management lapse so swiftly into chaos? (*London Review of Books*, 24 August 1995)

'The Wrong Side of History'

The events of 1997 are well known: the complete wipeout of Conservative MPs in Scotland had been long predicted but finally came to pass. In the devolution referendum that followed, the party ignored calls to do a volte-face and instead maintained its anti-devolution stance under the banner 'Think Twice'. Although turnout was surprisingly low (60 per cent) and a quarter of those voting rejected legislative devolution, it represented a humiliation for a party which, just four decades earlier, had commanded Scotland's political mainstream.

Even once the Scottish Parliament was established in 1999, seventeen newly elected Conservative MSPs often appeared grudging participants. Senior party figures periodically floated the idea of restoring the party's pre-1965 autonomy or supporting 'fiscal autonomy', but Scottish Conservatives made little progress over the next eight years. Following the election of a minority SNP Scottish Government in May 2007, the party attempted to 'detoxify' by co-operating with both the SNP at Holyrood and the other unionist parties – Labour and the Liberal Democrats – in formulating a scheme for greater devolution via the cross-party Calman Commission.

During a December 2007 debate on the establishment of the latter, David McLetchie, Scottish Conservative leader between 1999 and 2005, attempted to redraw the party's constitutional 'line'. In a list of the Union's 'fundamental characteristics', he included 'common taxes' and social security and welfare programmes 'that promote cohesion and unity and ensure equitable treatment across the nation as a whole'. If those were maintained, he argued, then unionists would 'achieve two highly desirable objectives': 'First, we define the essential difference between unionism and nationalism, and what that means in modern Scotland. Secondly, we are able to have a sensible debate about the distribution of competencies and responsibilities up to that line' (Scottish Parliament Official Report, 7 December 2007). That 'sensible debate', however, was soon overtaken by events, chiefly the SNP's victory at the 2011 Holyrood election and ensuing independence referendum. In 2010 the new Anglo-Scottish Prime Minister and UK Conservative leader ('I'm a Cameron', David told the BBC in 2006, 'there is quite a lot of Scottish blood flowing through these veins') had attempted, Balfour-like, to kill Home Rule with kindness, travelling north to meet Alex Salmond (First Minister since 2007) and promising a 'respect agenda'.

Further losses in 2011 necessitated another party commission – grandee Lord Sanderson concluded that the party was still considered 'anti-Scottish' (Sanderson 2010) – and a new Scottish leader. Murdo Fraser harked back to 1965 with his proposal to secede from the UK party ('We were not the Conservative Party then. We were a party which had a distinct Scottish identity'), while offering a mea culpa for previous thinking on constitutional change ('The idea that devolution is inevitably a slippery slope to separation and that any power devolved is a step closer to independence . . . was too simplistic). A 'New Unionism', he suggested, would 'be enthusiastic about the evolution of devolution' (Fraser 2011).

Fraser's rival, Ruth Davidson, spoke of a 'line in the sand', by which she meant the partial fiscal and welfare powers enshrined in the Scotland Bill then making its way through Westminster. 'When the [independence] referendum is done', she added, 'and Scotland in the Union has won the day, let that be an end to it' (Davidson 2011). Davidson's line, however, was quickly washed away. In January 2012, Cameron offered to facilitate the independence referendum while further extending devolution if a majority of Scots voted No. 'The shadow of Sir Alec Douglas-Home . . . is cast very large over this', was

Alex Salmond's historically minded but sceptical response. 'Scotland, I don't believe, will be fooled twice' (*The Times*, 17 February 2012).

The Conservative-led Coalition, however, made a point of appearing 'reasonable', diligently avoiding any activity that could be depicted as 'anti-Scottish' by the SNP (Torrance 2013). Ruth Davidson campaigned for the Union under the 'Better Together' banner and offered further repudiations of the Scottish Conservative record. In one speech she spoke of finding themselves 'on the wrong side of history in 1997', resisting devolution long after it had become 'the settled will' of the Scottish people: 'It made us look as if we lacked ambition for Scotland' (Davidson 2013a).

This signalled a shift in Scottish Conservative discourse, which rediscovered something of its earlier feel for the nuances of Scottish nationalism. 'I am a Scot, and I am proud of my country', declared Davidson in another significant speech.

> I understand what drives those who say they want independence for Scotland ... Love of country ... Patriotism ... The hope and belief in a better future for all our people. I don't believe there is a single person in Scotland who does not understand those feelings; who does not share in that hope, belief and ambition for a better tomorrow. I know I do, and I know you do too. But no political party – and no side in the constitutional debate – has a monopoly on patriotism.

She went on to reject 'the notion we are somehow incapable of governing ourselves', but 'just because we could stand alone in the world, is not a reason for doing so' (Davidson 2013a). Conservatives shared 'the nationalists' faith in Scotland's future', Davidson said elsewhere, although their 'faith' was 'not blind to the facts' (Davidson 2013b). Similarly, David Cameron argued that not

> only can you love Scotland and love the United Kingdom, not only can you drape yourself in the Saltire and the Union Jack, but you can be even prouder of your Scottish heritage than your British heritage – as many in Scotland are – and still believe that Scotland is better off in Britain (Cameron 2012).

All these were examples of nationalist unionism having been 'revived and entrenched' in Scottish political discourse, the Scottish Parliament having provided it with 'a concrete, institutional means of expression' and Scottish Conservative deliberations on national identity once again resting on 'concentric circles of identities, with British identity wrapping the Scottish one and the British state supporting both' (Ichijo 2012: 33, 35).

The referendum, however, also brought challenges, requiring Scottish Conservatives not only to flaunt their Scottishness but also to make arguments *for* the Union, overcoming decades of 'banal' or 'unthinking' unionism.[5] Nevertheless, for the first time since 1968 the party presented itself to the Scottish electorate as enthusiastic devolutionists. One journalist wrote that the 'buzz-phrase' in the Davidson 'camp' ahead of local government and general elections in 2017 was behaving like 'nationalist-unionists'. 'As paradoxical as this may sound', wrote Chris Deerin, 'it is quite a simple thing: to be seen to stand up for Scotland without wanting to rip it out of the UK' (*The Times*, 27 April 2017).

Conclusion

Since the 1920s, nationalist unionism had thrived, in the words of Jackson, 'by cultivating Scottish institutions, administrative devolution, and making patriotic appeals within the wider framework of union' (Jackson 2012: 279), but between 1951, when the Conservatives returned to office, and 1964, when it again entered opposition, there occurred a gradual weakening of the basis for the Scottish Unionist Party's inter-war and post-war success. By 1997 the Scottish Conservative and Unionist Party (as it became in 1965) had no MPs in Scotland, with only a modest recovery (aided by proportional representation) in the Scottish Parliament between 1999 and 2014.

Part of the decline was down to a deterioration in what Bulpitt called the Conservative Party's 'territorial code', the 'Dual Polity' having been weakened by economic decline in Scotland and Wales and increasing nationalist discontent – of different forms – there and in Northern Ireland. Edward Heath attempted to rejuvenate the code in the late 1960s with a commitment to a Scottish Assembly, while Margaret Thatcher adopted a 'composite' code which maintained elements of the old (administrative devolution) while reasserting 'centre' autonomy and influence (economic reform, international prestige). Back in power after 2010, and with the previous glass ceiling of legislative devolution shattered, David Cameron attempted to formulate a new form of territorial management that could cope with a resurgent SNP and associated demands for independence.

During this period (1951–2014), the Conservative Party's nationalist unionism was both civic and cultural in basis but also increasingly ineffective. Scottishness, concluded Cameron, 'may have assisted the Unionists in the 1950s when Labour was highly centralist and the SNP marginal, but the picture changed in the 1960s, even more in the 1970s' (Cameron 2010: 266). By helping promote a nationalist frame within an increasingly distinct Scottish political system, Unionists fell victim to their own rhetoric: by the late 1950s, Scotland did not appear to have 'control' of its own affairs, especially economic, while Labour accused it of anti-Scottish 'neglect', just as Conservatives had Attlee's government in the late 1940s. Heath, Thatcher and Major all attempted to 'play the Scottish card', but the party came to be perceived (like that in Wales) as essentially English and therefore not a credible 'guardian' of Scottish national aspirations.

Nevertheless, at no point did the party deny the reality of Scottish nationhood, predicating most of its rhetoric, administrative devolution and symbolic concessions on that essentially nationalist basis. In another era, Michael Forsyth's revived nationalist unionism of the mid-1990s might have been more effective, but by then the Overton window had shifted; legislative devolution had become the 'settled will' of the Scottish mainstream and, therefore, could no longer be pushed to the periphery of acceptable discourse.

Only after 2011, with the SNP in devolved power and an independence referendum imminent, did the party reconcile itself to the new constitutional order and seek a role as Scotland's main 'unionist' party, one led by an ostentatiously Scottish leader, Ruth Davidson. Ironically, not only did the 2014 independence referendum boost the fortunes of the losing side, but it also instigated a long-awaited revival in Scottish Conservative fortunes, allowing the party to once again claim to 'stand up for Scotland' from within the United Kingdom.

SIX

The Liberals and 'Scottish Self-Government'

Perhaps the original exponents of 'nationalist unionism' were the Scottish Liberals. Scotland's dominant party for around half-a-century following franchise reform in 1868, it – alongside the Scottish Conservatives – campaigned via the Convention of Royal Burghs for a Scottish Secretary in 1884. And after the Liberal split over Irish Home Rule in 1886, the party grappled with pressure to follow its own logic and establish a devolved Parliament in Scotland as well as Ireland.

For much of their electoral ascendancy, the Scottish Liberals presented themselves as the natural party of Scotland, defender of its distinctive position within the Union and more intuitively 'Scottish' than the Conservative and, later, Labour parties. Its nationalism, meanwhile, evolved, from support for administrative devolution that it shared with the Scottish Conservatives in the 1880s, to a sudden conversion to legislative devolution in 1886, something it (and its various permutations) continued to champion – to varying degrees – until into the early twenty-first century.

Although Liberal nationalism went beyond that of the Conservatives, it still counted as 'nationalist unionism' in that it did not countenance an end to the Anglo-Scottish Union, with even legislative devolution posited as a means of strengthening the UK and its empire, chiefly by keeping Ireland as part of the colonial metropole. In keeping with this book's broader thesis, it will also argue that the Scottish Liberals were the main 'carrier' of this nationalism in the late nineteenth and early twentieth centuries, before the mantle was taken up by Scottish Labour and the Scottish Unionists.

Combining the historical and theoretical approach of the previous chapters on the Scottish Unionist Party, this chapter will highlight the Liberal claim to 'stand up for Scotland', examine how the Scottish and UK Liberal parties interacted over Home Rule and examine whether the nationalism in question was civic or ethnic in nature. In doing so, it will firmly refute the notion (see Nairn 1981) that nationalism was somehow 'absent' from late-nineteenth-century Scotland.

The Scottish Liberal Ascendancy

From 1881, the Liberal Party in Scotland was organised on a 'national' basis, following the merger of the Liberal Associations in the 'East and North' and 'West and South' of Scotland. This produced the 'Scottish Liberal Association' (SLA), which, unlike the Welsh Liberal Federations, were not linked to the (English) National Liberal Federation. This organisational 'independence' would often be referenced by Liberals in the context of debates concerning Scottish autonomy, much as Scottish Unionists would theirs after their 'fusion' with the Liberal Unionists in 1912.

Scottish Liberals were also strong in electoral terms, winning a majority of seats in Scotland at every general election between 1832 and 1895 and, on all but one occasion, a greater share of the vote than that polled in England. The party's nationalism, however, only appears to have manifested itself towards the end of that century, the National Association for the Vindication of Scottish Rights of the 1850s having been a predominantly Tory affair. Keating and Bleiman believed this 'link' of 'Scottish nationalism and radicalism' to have been established between the franchise reforms of 1867 and 1884 (Keating and Bleiman 1979: 27).

During this period, key tenets of Scottish nationalism took root in Liberal discourse and ideology: the belief that Scotland was a naturally radical country which, if it had a parliament of its own, would adopt progressive policies, a reflection, among other things, of an accompanying belief in egalitarian Scottish democracy, derived from the Highland clan system, the General Assembly of the Church of Scotland and the distinct Scottish education system. This radicalism was believed to be stifled by Westminster, particularly the House of Lords' inbuilt Conservative majority.

A key figure in all of this (though not opposition to the Upper House) was the fifth Earl of Rosebery, who first came to national attention in 1879 through his supporting role in William Ewart Gladstone's first Midlothian campaign.[1] Like later Scottish Unionists, Rosebery's political identity comprised Scotland, Britain and its empire, of which he was an enthusiastic champion. Rosebery could be seen as the Scottish equivalent of Thomas Edward Ellis in the Welsh Liberal Party (see Chapter 9) – both were the informal leaders of their respective parties' 'nationalist' wings.

Rosebery's nationalism was never properly defined, although its general character was clear from orations such as an 1882 Rectorial address on 'The

Patriotism of a Scot'. He was also instrumental in adding a dedicated university chair in Scottish history to the roll call of Scottish nationalist demands. In his 1880 Rectorial address at Aberdeen University, Rosebery said he regarded it as a 'stain' on Scottish universities that there was no provision for the teaching of Scottish history. 'The history of Scotland is not a cold register of dates and treaties,' he declared, 'it stirs the blood like a trumpet; no stranger can read it without emotion' (Anderson 1902: 231). And like 'all previous nationalists, like Scott or Burns, like Chalmers or Aytoun', observed Coupland, Rosebery 'stood staunchly by the Union' (Coupland 1954: 294).

Aware of his appeal in Scotland, Gladstone put Rosebery in charge of Scottish Affairs at the Home Office, a position he used to badger the Grand Old Man into action. On 18 May 1882 he wrote to remind him that Scotland was 'the backbone of the Liberal party', and that there was 'some discontent as to her treatment'. He charged the government with 'neglect', complaining that 'not one minute of Government time has been allotted to Scotland or Scottish affairs'. Furthermore, Rosebery had understood his appointment as an under-secretary to be a temporary measure, 'intended to mark a new departure, to be a step in the right direction, and to contain the germ of a new office which would satisfy the country'; instead, Gladstone seemed intent upon heading into the next session of parliament with no changes (Crewe 1931: 153–8).

The 'new office' to which Rosebery referred was the idea of a specifically Scottish department and minister, similar to those already in existence for Ireland. This reflected a 'civic' aspect of nascent Scottish nationalism, an emphasis on distinct institutions.[2] Writing in 1883 on Scotland's 'version' of Home Rule, Scott Dalgleish said distinct Scottish institutions were 'the mainstays of the national sentiment'. 'The institutions of a country are like the features in the human face,' he added, 'they are at once an expression of character and the marks by which individuality is recognised' (Dalgleish 1883: 20). This contrasted with the view of Conservatives like Lord Salisbury, who believed Scotland to be 'an example of the contentment with which a nation, as high-spirited as Ireland, has accepted the extinction of its nationality'. For half-a-century Scotland had fought against Union, he argued, yet now the 'Union is Scotland's proudest boast!' (*Scottish Review*, March 1888).

Yet other Scottish Conservatives desired reform and joined forces with Scottish Liberals in January 1884 at the meeting convened under the auspices of the Convention of Royal Burghs (see Prelude). Separate management of Scottish affairs at Westminster was not new. For decades the Lord Advocate had 'managed' these on behalf of the Prime Minister, while a Liberal commentator later observed that an old 'Tea Room' compact already meant English MPs had 'practically left Scottish members to manage their own affairs, and thus virtually, though not formally, conceded a limited Home Rule to Scotland' (Kinnaird Rose 1895: 513, 533). What Bulpitt later called the Conservatives' 'territorial code' had its nineteenth-century, and Liberal, antecedents.

The original Liberal-introduced Bill to establish a 'Secretary for Scotland' fell, but it was taken up by the Conservatives during the 1885 general election,[3] although the Liberals were soon back in government. But rather than fill the new office himself, Rosebery joined Gladstone's administration as Foreign Secretary. Coupland compared his 'position as a Scottish nationalist' with that of Lloyd George in Wales: 'He could and did support the cause on occasion, but he could no longer be its leader' (Coupland 1954: 296). Soon there was another election, in which the Liberals lost office for the second time in as many years,[4] leading some Scottish Liberals to conclude that Home Rule for Scotland had become a priority.

Many of the arguments put forward in 1886 by the National Liberal Federation of Scotland (founded by Joseph Chamberlain as a rival to the mainstream Scottish Liberal Association) were to become mainstays of Scottish nationalist discourse:

> Scotch business gets scant justice at Westminster; Scotch private Bills put large fees in the pockets of English lawyers; and social reforms, demanded for more than a generation, now ripe for legislation, cannot be approached so long as the mind and purpose of the Nation are smothered by the overpowering Conservatism of England. The leading Metropolitan Press does not scruple to exult over this fact; but Scotland cannot quietly submit to be so treated. The true remedy lies in Home Rule – allowing the Scottish people to manage their own affairs (NLFS 1886).

Hutchison highlighted the 'inherent contradiction' in such complaints, on the one hand claiming that Westminster 'passed laws which aimed to Anglicise Scottish institutions' while simultaneously being 'charged with neglected Scottish legislation' (Hutchison 2005: 252). Nevertheless, it was striking how quickly even the Scottish Liberal Association shifted from what Armstrong called 'conservative' to 'liberal unionism'. Some argued that Scots should naturally rally behind their Irish 'brethren'. Robert Wallace, Liberal candidate in Edinburgh East at the 1886 election, said he should think it

> surprisingly strange if the Scotch people refuse to recognise in another people the right to govern themselves. For what did our ancestors lay down their lives

> on the bloody fields of Falkirk and Bannockburn . . . if it were not to affirm
> the principle that a people, if they will it, have the right to be emancipated
> from an alien or unjust authority? (Lloyd-Jones 2014)

Gladstone's rhetoric did not necessarily lower expectations in this regard,
many Liberals as well as the Scottish Home Rule Association (SHRA, which
had been formed in 1886) believing him to have stated 'that Scotland can
have Home Rule if she desires it'. Anti-Home Rulers – the 'Liberal Unionists' – believed, on the other hand, that their erstwhile leader had helped
generate dangerous nationalist rhetoric. Arthur Elliot, the Liberal Unionist
MP for Roxburghshire, saw the SHRA's emergence as a consequence of Liberal losses, which had 'forced' Gladstone to 'flatter on every occasion anti-
English prejudices' (Lloyd-Jones 2014). A. V. Dicey, meanwhile, warned
against 'unilateral devolution' in *England's Case Against Home Rule* (1886), a
text which was to shape unionist thinking for many decades to come.

Not all Scottish Liberals supported Gladstone's new-found zeal for
Home Rule; indeed opponents came from surprising quarters of the party.
Duncan McLaren, a nationalistic Edinburgh MP and veteran of both the
National Association for the Vindication of Scottish Rights in the 1850s and
the 'national meeting' in 1884, accepted the validity of Irish grievances but
believed the 'three kingdoms' – Scotland, England and Ireland – should be
treated equally, and in administrative terms rather than legislative. When
the Edinburgh South Liberal Association, of which he was honorary president, declared for Home Rule, McLaren resigned, even pledging to vote
locally for whomever (and of whichever party) pledged their opposition
to an Irish parliament (Pickard 2011: 264–5). Nationalist unionists often
reached surprising conclusions.

Commenting on the 'immediate upsurge' in 'nationalist sentiment'
among Scottish Liberals after the 1886 Liberal Party split, Hanham also
noted the tensions between the party and the SHRA:

> The leaders of the Scottish Home Rule Association soon recognized that they
> were stronger nationalists than they were Liberals and resented the fact that
> the Scottish Liberal Association was determined to keep the leadership of the
> Home Rule movement in its own hands. (Hanham 1969: 119)

In the autumn of 1887, the Scottish Liberal Association executive dispatched
a delegation of Scottish Liberal 'Deputies' to Ireland, where they were 'met
at the chief [railway] stations by eager crowds of people . . . thanking them
for the sympathy of Scotland, and for the practical interest taken by her
in their struggle for constitutional rights'. In Dublin they met Nationalist

leaders and spoke to thousands from the window of the Imperial Hotel. The deputies also experienced 'manifest hostility' from Dublin Castle (the seat of British rule), 'whose spies and detectives were in constant attendance upon them'. Returning to Scotland, the deputies had no doubt Ireland could govern itself while the Union and empire would 'rest on the sure basis of mutual interest and goodwill, and would be clung to by the Irish people as an element vital to their prosperity and to their very existence as a nation' (SLA 1887: 1–3). A copy of their report was sent to Gladstone, who naturally approved.

Sympathy with Irish Home Rule did not, of course, mean the Scottish Liberals were formally committed to legislative devolution for Scotland, whatever the views of certain MPs and activists. There is a sense the party approached this question with caution, generating apparently positive mood music in an effort to make Irish Home Rule more palatable in Scotland, where the Liberal Unionists had quickly established themselves as a major force. As Bulpitt observed, this ambiguity formed part of the Liberals' 'territorial code', allowing the party 'to assume the leadership of Scottish and Welsh nationalism for over thirty years without committing itself irrevocably to that cause in either section' (Bulpitt 1983: 126).

While a resolution in favour of 'the application of the principle of Home Rule to Scotland' was adopted at the SLA's annual General Council meeting in February 1888, Lord Elgin made clear the party executive's reluctance to commit themselves to any 'specific form' of Home Rule (Lloyd-Jones 2014). Yet the same Elgin also wrote to Charles Stewart Parnell on behalf of the SLA executive in 1889, hoping the 'day of triumph' was at hand, when the 'people of Ireland – emancipated, self-governing, and loyal – will enjoy, without let or hindrance, the sense and pride of nationality which the people of Scotland have never lost' (Elgin 1889).[5]

Even Rosebery equivocated, telling the Glasgow University Liberal Club that he supported a 'local-national' body of 144 members with certain powers delegated from the Imperial Parliament to Edinburgh (*Scottish Review*, April 1890), although he cautioned that Ireland had to take priority. One commentator observed that any arguments for Home Rule which did exist had 'given but scant consideration to the sentimental or national aspect of the agitation in which they are engaged' (*Scottish Review*, July 1888). The appeals were largely practical, often eschewing sentiment.

Yet by the time the SLA gathered for its 'national' conference in 1889, there were no fewer than seven Home Rule resolutions. And when Gladstone toured his Midlothian constituency in 1890, 27 of the 185 addresses he received included references to the same aspiration. As Lloyd-Jones points out, judging from his diaries, it is clear that Gladstone kept abreast of the Home Rule debate through articles in the *Scottish Review* (cited in this chapter), as well as pamphlets produced by the SHRA.

The Grand Old Man had recently acknowledged that were 'Scotland unanimously, or by a clear preponderating voice . . . to make a demand on the United Parliament to be treated not only on the same principle but in the same manner as Ireland', he could not 'deny the title of Scotland to make such a claim'. This was hardly unequivocal or enthusiastic, and on 21 October 1890 the executive of the SLA told Gladstone that it anxiously awaited 'the moment when our leader shall give us the word that shall rally us in the fight', the goal of self-government having 'long been dear to the Scottish people' (SLA 1890).[6] There was obvious tension between the Liberal centre and its periphery where, as in Wales, it derived much electoral support.

The Scottish Home Rule Association, which had initially hoped to achieve its aims via the Liberal Party, withdrew its support ahead of the 1892 general election out of frustration, thereby prioritising its nationalism over its liberalism. Even when the Liberals secured fifty out of seventy Scottish constituencies, there was little movement from the new government (which Rosebery joined, again as Foreign Secretary). Another influential figure was the Liberal scholar John Stuart Blackie, who made a point of sending Gladstone his pamphlet on *The Union of 1707 and Its Results: A Plea for Scottish Home Rule*, 'which presented the unionist-nationalist case in homely terms' (Wallace 2006: 259), after that election.

Blackie's nationalism went beyond that of Rosebery in advocating legislative as well as administrative devolution (he was also known to make anti-English remarks at public meetings). Like Rosebery, however, Blackie was a strong imperialist, enrolling Wallace and Bruce into 'the story of Britain and its empire', and presenting them as 'champions of "British" freedom' (Wallace 2006: 252). He also helped raise money for the Wallace monument in Stirling, anticipating the cultural nationalism of later Scottish Unionists. Gladstone was unmoved, privately assuring Queen Victoria that the cause of Scottish Home Rule had 'in no way been promoted by the leaders of the Liberal Party', and that he personally had 'used every effort in his power to temper, qualify and restrain' it (Lloyd-Jones 2014). This was, as the quotations above demonstrate, highly disingenuous.

A second Irish Home Rule Bill failed the following year, and in 1894 Rosebery succeeded Gladstone as Prime Minister, though (as would later prove the case with Ramsay MacDonald and David Lloyd George) his earlier support for a degree of Home Rule was trumped by more pressing considerations. His Scottish Secretary, Sir George Otto Trevelyan, established a Scottish Grand Committee, and while this had Conservative support, it hardly satisfied Scottish Liberal demands. In opposition after 1895, the Scottish Liberal Association continued to quote Gladstone's 1889 statement on not denying Scotland's 'claim' to Home Rule, but it was subject to the law of diminishing returns.

In 1900, however, party policy remained that freeing up Parliament (via Home Rule) to concentrate on matters of imperial concern would 'alone justify a scheme of devolution', while also combatting the 'great bogey' raised by Conservatives of 'Separation' (SLA 1900: 121–3). Liberals had long been irritated at being branded 'separatists' by both Liberal Unionists and newspapers like the *Scotsman*.[7] As a Liberal commentator had observed at the height of the Home Rule crisis, those who advocated 'Home Rule all round' were the true 'Unionists', and those who opposed it were really 'Separatists', in that failure to concede the measure (in Ireland at least) would likely lead to a more radical outcome (*Scottish Review*, March 1888).[8]

The Young Scots Society

The 1900 general election proved disastrous for the Liberal Party, even in Scotland, where it was deprived of a majority for the first time since 1832. That same year saw the formation of the Young Scots Society (YSS) by a group of Liberal activists determined to help the party recover, in part by infusing it with a stronger sense of Scottishness. An early YSS motto was 'For Gladstone and Scotland', which, as James Kennedy observed in his seminal study of the group, 'encapsulated the Society's dual aim: to promote both liberalism through support for radical reform and nationalism through support for Scottish Home Rule' (Kennedy 2015: 10).

Despite its close connection with the Scottish Liberal Association, however, the YSS was constituted as an autonomous organisation. J. W. Gulland, Edinburgh's YSS president from 1903 to 1905, rejected establishing a new Scottish national party as 'unnecessary' and 'unwise'. 'Let us rather make the Scottish Liberal members our Scottish party,' he urged, 'impregnate them with Scottish ideas, make them fight at Westminster for Scotland as the Irish members do for Ireland and the Welsh members for Wales.' The Parliamentary Parties of Ireland and Wales, sub-national lobby groups at Westminster, were clear models for this strategy, as was the Young Wales Society (Cymru Fydd). Another YSS supporter wanted the society imbued with 'Scottish ideals – of the country which produced a Wallace and Bruce, a Carlyle and Burns' (Kennedy 2015: 86). Young Scots frequently quoted the Italian liberal nationalist Giuseppe Mazzini (also an inspiration for Welsh Liberal nationalists), but did not question the unionist status quo. Instead it sought reform, a federal rather incorporating reworking of the 1707 Anglo-Scottish settlement.

Given its pursuit of legislative devolution, the society was critical of the 'administrative' status quo. One Young Scot deemed the Scottish Office 'too much of an alien organization', while the 'bureaucratic boards' in Edinburgh were 'at variance with democratic ideas and sentiment'. Another standard complaint was familiar from the late nineteenth century – a lack of parliamentary time to discuss Scottish matters. Legislation was, therefore, 'imposed on [Scotland] against her wishes and desires . . . Scotland comes as an afterthought. The proposed legislation is framed by an English minister with the assistance of English lawyers, and it is based on English experience, custom, and law' (Kennedy 2015: 124).

Liberals in Scotland recovered at the 1906 election, winning fifty-eight out of seventy-two seats, its largest victory since 1885. The YSS's contribution to this result was widely acknowledged, as it was again at the two elections of 1910 in which the party maintained its dominance in Scotland, but not in England, where it lost more than 100 seats. This meant the parliamentary Liberal Party was now overly dependent upon Scottish votes in the House of Commons. Sensing an opportunity, the society stepped up its efforts, this time more unequivocally in favour of legislative devolution which, according to Coupland, had been 'nailed' to the Scottish Liberal 'platform' in 1908 (Coupland 1954: 304).

James Myles Hogge, who contested the Camlachie Division of Glasgow at the December election, had declared himself a Scottish Home Ruler and, if elected to Parliament, intended to do all in his 'power to secure a scheme of devolution which would give to Scotland control of her own affairs' (Hogge 1910). And in the absence of that scheme, the YSS also became increasingly critical of the Liberal Party, just as the Scottish Home Rule Association had twenty years before, both groups deeming the party to be insufficiently nationalist.

In July 1911, the society published its *Manifesto and Appeal to the Scottish People on Scottish Home Rule*. The following year it produced a booklet, *Sixty Points for Scots Home Rule*, which became an important part of the YSS's propaganda work. There was also a lively internal debate as to how much emphasis should be placed on Home Rule, which Kennedy believed underscored 'a key dilemma for Young Scots: a belief that liberalism should not be subordinate to nationalism; rather, that nationalism should be subsumed within liberalism' (Kennedy 2015: 129).

A related concern among Young Scots was that the presence of so many Scottish Liberal MPs in the UK government represented an impediment to achieving Home Rule (though some had established a 'Scottish Nationalist' group in Parliament in 1910). Yet opening the Young Scots Club on Edinburgh's West Richmond Street, David Lloyd George – an important figure in the creation of 'welfare unionism' as well as Welsh nationalist unionism – smothered the society with praise:

> When the whole Scottish Liberal representation is inspired by the Young Scots national ideals, the day of Scotland's political salvation will not be far off. The whole tone of Scottish Liberalism has changed enormously for the better since the Society was founded in 1900, and with the change of tone Liberalism has greatly strengthened its hold on the country. Scottish Liberalism must be Radical and National. (Lloyd George 1911)

It demonstrated that the UK Liberal Party still saw the need to harness Scottish nationalism in order to maintain its electoral position, in Scotland (and Wales) if not south of the border. This nationalism, like its later Scottish Unionist manifestation, had an ethnic dimension. Some Young Scots objected to the imposition of English candidates in Scottish constituencies, a view endorsed by Harry Watt, the MP for Glasgow College since 1906. His concern was that 'alien' candidates would lack 'local patriotism' and know nothing of Scotland's 'institutions . . . customs and law and methods':

> Scotland can derive not the smallest gain or benefit from representation from Englishmen . . . No sooner do these men get back to London elected than they forget that they are Scottish members . . . they never think how this legislation will suit the Scottish people who have sent them there. These men of course only make the necessity for Home Rule for Scotland all the more marked. But how is that goal ever to be reached if we continue to import freely from all sorts and sizes of Englishmen?

Watt added that he would even support a Scottish Labour or Tory candidate 'in preference to one of these free imports' (Kennedy 2015: 133). Similarly, the society's *Manifesto and Appeal to the Scottish People on Scottish Home Rule* made repeated references to the 'Scottish race', which differed 'in character, custom, and law from the other peoples that make up the United Kingdom', and must therefore 'know their own requirements best'. Other arguments were more 'civic' in nature:

> For years and years Scotland has been clamouring for legislation on Land, Temperance, House-letting, Education, and Poor Law Reform, but to all these demands the Imperial Parliament turns a deaf ear – it has no time for Scottish affairs . . . Scotland's story since the Union is a story of legislative starvation . . . [it has] to submit to laws being imposed upon her in defiance of her wishes and desires. (YSS 1911: 2–3)

Home Rule, concluded the YSS, was an 'Imperial necessity', which spoke to its colonial unionism, a legacy of Rosebery *et al.* Contesting the Edinburgh East by-election in 1912, this time successfully, J. M. Hogge hailed the recent National Insurance Act as embryonic Home Rule:

> Scotland has her separate commissioners to adapt it to her national needs. To Scotsmen, reared by the hard discipline of economic conditions in habits of thrift, this Act comes as a great instrument of security against the accidents of life, and personally I am confident that Scotsmen can so use it as to achieve still further and useful extensions of its beneficence. (Hogge 1912)

At the same time, the newly created Scottish Insurance Commission and other 'Scottish' boards and offices acted to undermine the demand for Home Rule by demonstrating that the UK was capable of reform along 'national lines'. As Kennedy put it, 'the very success of administrative devolution effectively undermined the campaign for Scottish Home Rule by removing a central motive' (Kennedy 2015: 147).

The Liberal nationalist high watermark arguably occurred in November 1913, during a speech by Scottish Secretary Thomas McKinnon Wood at Edinburgh's King's Theatre. Billed as a 'National Conference and Demonstration', the morning consisted of a meeting of 500 representatives from what would later be called 'civic' Scotland, town and parish councils, school boards and trades councils, as well as the YSS and men's and women's Liberal Associations.

The afternoon 'demonstration', meanwhile, attracted around 3,000 people and 23 Scottish Liberal MPs, who listened as McKinnon Wood said 'he had the authority of the Prime Minister for stating that the Government accepted Scottish Home Rule in principle and that a measure would be prepared to carry it into effect' (SLP 1949a).[9] A correspondent writing in the *Scottish Nation*, one of a plethora of journals sympathetic to the YSS, rightly judged the statement to be for 'home consumption', the truth being that Home Rule was 'in the Government refrigerator at Westminster, and nothing will thaw it but public pressure from without' (Kennedy 2015: 146).

The Government of Scotland Bill was, however, introduced, and even passed its second reading in the House of Commons. Moving it, the Scottish Liberal MP Sir Henry Cowan conflated party and nation, arguing that the Scottish Liberal Association was

> so predominantly Liberal that, in the absence of a Scottish Parliament, that body can claim to be the most representative institution in the country [and] advocates without reserve Scottish Home Rule. At its annual meeting year after year it debates the question, and it passes resolutions, which become

only more urgent as time goes by, calling upon the Government to introduce a measure giving self-government to Scotland. At Aberdeen last November this great body declared in its resolution the urgent need for a federal system of Home Rule and demanded that a measure granting Home Rule to Scotland should be introduced and passed through all its stages without delay. The Scottish Liberal Members to a man are declared and convinced Home Rulers.

Cowan's wider point was aimed at those (mainly Conservatives) who doubted public support for legislative devolution. Scottish Liberal strength and unanimity, he concluded, seemed 'rather curious if there is no demand for Home Rule in Scotland'. Cowan also drew upon pre-Union history, boasting that the Bill would revive 'three ancient institutions – the Scottish Parliament, the Scottish Privy Council, and the Lord High Commissioner in his political capacity' (HC Deb 30 May 1913 Vol 53 cc474–5, 480).

The Bill, like its Irish equivalent, fell victim to wartime priorities, and as storm clouds gathered in Europe, the Young Scots marked the 'sexcentenary' of Bannockburn, a commemoration later taken up on an annual basis by more overtly nationalist parties. It was remembered not as a military anniversary but a 'symbol of Scottish nationality', Bannockburn having 'vindicated the nationhood of Scotland against the all but successful attempt of England to crush it'. Nevertheless,

Scottish nationality is persistent and unquenchable. To-day it is expressed in a hundred ways: in a separate body of laws, a separate national administration, a distinctive national temperament and political outlook, a separate national literature, a separate ecclesiastical organization, a separate educational system, &c.; but it is seriously impaired by the lack of a National Parliament to shape and direct the national life and ensure the steady progress of the country. Scotland has all the appanage of a kingdom except a legislature. (YSS 1914: 2)

Standing for re-election in Edinburgh East four years later, J. M. Hogge said Scotland had 'given lavishly of its young life in this Empire War' and therefore their name could 'best live for evermore in a new national life' (Hogge 1918). Yet the YSS struggled to adapt to the post-war political terrain, not least the growing popularity of the Labour Party and consequent decline of the once-mighty Liberals.

Instead, Young Scots found other outlets for their nationalism, either the revived Scottish Home Rule Association or the Scottish Labour movement, then at the height of its 'first' nationalist-unionist phase (see Chapter 7). Only J. M. Hogge, unable to reconcile himself with socialism, continued to press for Home Rule via the Scottish Liberals. Perhaps the most successful of the ex-Liberals was the Rev. James Barr, who joined the Independent Labour Party in 1920 and was elected the MP for Motherwell four years later, after which he unsuccessfully steered another Home Rule Bill through the House of Commons. As Prudhomme observed, the Young Scots Society had provided 'a breeding ground for nationalists or future Labour members' (quoted in Kennedy 2015: 242).

The Strange Death of Liberal Scotland

For the next few decades, the once-dominant Scottish Liberals experienced a long decline which mirrored the 'strange death' of the party in England. While the Scottish organisation was often more preoccupied with survival rather than constitutional matters, support for Home Rule remained, at least on paper. At its annual gathering in 1924, the Scottish Liberal Federation reaffirmed support for Scottish devolution within a federal framework, while the following year Scottish Liberal conventions in Edinburgh and Inverness declared that the 'case for Scottish Home Rule is overwhelming, both on Imperial and National grounds' (SLF 1925: 13). The decline of the Young Scots had been preceded by the formation of a 'Scottish National Committee' to press for Home Rule, chaired by R. C. Munro Ferguson, a keen supporter of imperial federation and a former Scottish Secretary (Hanham 1969).

One of the party's most articulate Home Rulers was Alexander MacEwen, who was between 1925 and 1931 the Liberal Provost of Inverness. His book, *The Thistle and the Rose: Scotland's Problem To-day*, appeared as MacEwen was abandoning the Scottish Liberals in favour of the Scottish (Self-Government) Party, which later merged with the National Party of Scotland to form the Scottish National Party, of which he became the first leader. Conceived 'in no spirit of narrow nationalism', he argued that correctly guided, the 'Scottish National Movement' should have for its aim 'something more than self-government for Scotland. It should aim at incorporating Scotland, England, and the Dominions in a great Federation of free peoples', the first stage of which would be a British Federal Parliament. One of MacEwen's election leaflets underscored the point, pledging no 'separation from England and the Dominions, except legislative and financial separation' (MacEwen 1932: 129). And his argument was not purely technocratic:

> Even before the present economic crisis became acute, there were evidences of a revival of the national consciousness – a desire that Scotland should have her own literature, her own music, drama and art, and that spiritually, politically, and economically she should vindicate her historic right to be a nation. (MacEwen 1932: 1)

By the late 1930s, the Scottish Liberals were basically on the same page. An interim report from its Industrial Policy Committee noted that while Liberals had advocated 'self-government' in the nineteenth century 'principally on the grounds that it would make for greater administrative efficiency and would relieve the congestion at Westminster', a Scottish Parliament was 'nowadays advocated, not merely as an administrative convenience, nor even as a concession to nationalist theory, but rather as an instrument which will enable Scotland to save herself by her exertions' (SLF 1937: 32). As Hutchison put it:

> The older nationalistic right to self-determination was now almost subsumed by the argument that urgent and radical action was needed if the social ills afflicting Scotland – notably rural decline and urban squalor – were to be redressed. A Westminster parliament was too clogged up with imperial business to handle competently Scotland's peculiar problems. National regeneration, a key social radical concept, was thus explicitly conjoined with Home Rule in the propaganda material produced by left Liberals in the last few years of peace. (Hutchison 2001: 7)

But the party was not as unanimous on this issue as it had once been. At the 1941 Scottish Liberal conference, Lady Glen-Coats' resolution calling for a parliament and plebiscite was opposed by the Aberdeen Liberal Association, which believed Scotland was 'not geographically suited for a Legislature of its own', fearing it would increase bureaucracy and 'sectional interests'. Devolution, it added, could be 'attained by Parliament through other effective means' (SLF 1941). A Scottish Parliament, however, remained official policy, while the party claimed its constitutional goals were reflected in its organisational status. 'It is as a Scottish Party, free from any external control, that it appeals to the people of Scotland', stated the 1950 manifesto. 'It believes that Liberalism is the natural political expression of the Scottish genius' (SLP 1950).

Scottish Liberals had been fully involved in the Scottish National Assembly convened by the Scottish Convention movement in 1947, even adopting the assembly's statement of policy as its own, chiefly that it had 'no desire to impair the essential unity of the United Kingdom', although without 'self-government a nation can have no adequate focus for the expression of its spiritual, cultural and economic life' (SLP 1949c: 1). It helped that John MacCormick, leader of the Convention, was an active Liberal having broken with the SNP in 1942.[10] 'We as Liberals can support these proposals not merely because we are Scots,' he told the Scottish Liberal executive in October 1947, 'but because we are Liberals and because they express the fundamental principles of Liberal policy' (SLP 1947). The following year MacCormick was chosen to fight, with tacit Unionist support, the Paisley by-election, with one Scottish Liberal viewing it as 'a rather unique opportunity of seeing a Scottish Liberal spokesman returned to Westminster, someone who could stand up for Scottish Liberalism and who could stand up for Scottish interests' (SLP 1948).[11]

The title of a pamphlet setting out Scottish Liberal policy, however, revealed tensions within the party. In keeping with long-standing nomenclature, it was to be called 'Home Rule for Scotland', although a Mr Meikle objected on the basis that it might be seen as 'breaking away from England'. He suggested 'Scottish Devolution', but after some discussion it was agreed the title be changed to 'Scottish Self-Government', which remained in use by the party until the 1980s. The party also rejected a request from the SNP to state that it would give 'priority to self-government' on taking office. They were 'asking the impossible', replied Andrew McFadyean. 'If ... a Liberal Government attained power at a moment of grave international tension, or even of threatened war, it is equally plain that Scotland would have to wait' (SLP 1949b).

Judging from other Scottish Liberal papers, however, the term 'Home Rule' remained in use for several years after that 1949 meeting. John Bannerman,[12] another strong Home Ruler within the party and its chairman after 1954, was also uncomfortable at the Convention having 'usurped' its political status. 'It was up to them as the Liberal Party in Scotland', he told the executive on 8 December 1951, 'to put it before the public that they – not [the] Convention – were the constitutional Party for Home Rule for Scotland' (SLP 1951).

By the following year, the Scottish Liberals appeared to be rediscovering something of their previous nationalism. At an executive meeting on 1 March 1952, the chairman referred to the 'fettered' (and recently stolen) Stone of Destiny as being 'symptomatic of the Scottish people who were struggling in chains in this so-called Elizabethan age of freedom and liberty to gain even the bare bones of their freedom'.[13] He called for a government commission, 'so long promised, to investigate the factors attendant on the Scottish demand for Home Rule' (SLP 1952). Yet when the Royal Commission on Scottish Affairs reported in 1954, the Scottish Liberal executive felt this product of Scottish Unionist nationalism to be of little value because its remit had not included devolution.

Throughout the 1950s, the Scottish Liberals had just one MP, Jo Grimond in Orkney and Shetland (later UK party leader between 1956 and 1967), so any press notices sent out by party HQ carried little weight, in the Scottish media and certainly among voters. And like all small parties, there were frequent internal disputes. In May 1953, Lady Glen-Coats, who had almost single-handedly sustained the party during its lean years, even resigned her membership because she felt the party 'was wavering in its adherence to Home Rule for Scotland' (SLP 1953). Support for a Scottish Parliament was later reaffirmed (and Glen-Coats readmitted) – and again at the party's 1957 Arbroath conference – yet the party gave the appearance of protesting too much, reflecting a long-standing ambiguity surrounding its constitutional stance. No more were party and nation at one, despite the lion rampant in its logo.

Recovery

Only in the 1960s did the Scottish Liberal Party become a more credible vehicle for nationalist unionism.[14] At the 1964 general election it won four MPs, which became five at another election two years later, several of whom were committed Home Rulers. This modest recovery also coincided with a periodic rise in Scottish nationalist sentiment like that in the early 1930s and late 1940s, only this time Liberals were more determined – and in a better position – to harness it.

Indeed, the tone of its 1967 statement of policy, *The Liberal Crusade: People Count – The Liberal Plan for Power*, was much more confident than in the past:

> A Scottish Parliament for Scottish Affairs within the framework of Britain is the first priority of our Scottish policy and we pride ourselves that the hard work and practical common sense of our Scottish MPs have brought its establishment much nearer. But the foundation and basis of all we do is the achievement of greater freedom and opportunity for the individual. (SLP 1967a: 32)

The previous year, two Scottish Liberal associations had urged the party 'to intensify its campaign for a Scottish Parliament for Scottish affairs and to strive for the day when 36 M.P.'s who support this policy, having been elected in Scottish seats, the Party can justifiably demand the immediate establishment of a Scottish Parliament', a motion which passed unanimously (SLP 1966). (Interestingly, this later formed the pre-2000 basis for what the SNP considered a 'mandate' for beginning independence negotiations rather than devolution.)

One of the party's existing MPs, Russell Johnston, introduced a Private Member's Bill to establish a Scottish Parliament the same year, reviving a Scottish Liberal tradition begun in the late nineteenth century. Importantly, this move pre-dated the SNP's surprisingly good performance at the Pollok by-election of March 1967, although it fell to Johnston to try to reach some sort of electoral 'pact' with the Scottish Liberals' emerging electoral rival.

This was discussed at length during the Scottish Liberal Assembly in Perth a couple of months later. The broadcaster Ludovic Kennedy and activist David Starforth (who had been behind the 1966 'intensify' motion) proposed 'official' talks with the SNP to avoid 'splitting' the 'Scottish Self-Government' vote in future by-elections. This was rejected, although an amendment passed in the name of James Davidson and David Steel – the latter having emerged as a strong advocate of devolution following his by-election win in 1965 – said the conference

> would welcome any indication from the leaders of the Scottish National Party that they are willing, in recognition of the need for both Parties to place the national interests of Scotland, before short term Party interests, to co-operate with the Scottish Liberal Party to achieve a Scottish Parliament. (SLP 1967b)

As in 1951, the Scottish Liberals were determined not to cede any ground to rival nationalists. The SNP demanded the Liberals prioritise self-government, while the Liberals insisted the SNP abandon independence and support federalism as a condition for any pact.

The Liberal–SNP talks also foundered on the basis that John Bannerman, while 'never anti-Scottish Nationalism' was 'highly suspicious' of some in the SNP. To Hanham, Bannerman 'looked at times to be a Home Ruler who happened to be a Liberal rather than vice versa' (Hanham 1969: 119), but this did not make him sympathetic to a party advocating independence. According to George Mackie, Ludovic Kennedy caused 'great harm' to the Scottish Liberals by quitting the party (over its unwillingness to prioritise self-government) without actually defecting to the SNP.[15] 'I suppose we should have been able to harness the surge of Scottish feeling instead of the Nats', reflected Mackie in his memoirs.

> But the Nationalists did it really by appealing not to a desire for a centre of power and excellence to promote Scotland, but to the anti-English chip on the shoulder which I am afraid many Scots have. I do not regard this sort of campaign as suitable for any Party with the name of Liberal attached to it. (Mackie 2004: 164–5)

In other words, their respective nationalisms were incompatible.[16] Besides, the SNP's breakthrough in the November 1967 Hamilton by-election most likely convinced it that a pact with the Liberals was not, after all, necessary.

Instead, Jeremy Thorpe, Grimond's successor as UK Liberal leader, revamped the party's constitutional agenda, which moved more unequivocally towards federalism. Thorpe personally introduced a Federal Government Bill on 21 February 1968, while the West Aberdeenshire MP James Davidson introduced another Private Member's Bill, the Scotland and Wales (Referenda) Bill, which offered the people of Scotland and Wales four 'clear' choices: maintaining the status quo; devolving additional powers to the Secretaries of State for Scotland and Wales and Scottish and Welsh Grand Committees; establishing devolved parliaments within a federal UK; and, finally, 'complete independence within the British Commonwealth'. If a majority backed the fourth option, declared Davidson, 'then that is surely the will of the people' (HC Debs 14 Feb 1969 Vol 777 c1735).

It was a clever attempt to neutralise the SNP while maintaining the Scottish Liberals as the principal 'carrier' of nationalist unionism, although in 1968 Edward Heath had also entered the field with his Declaration of Perth (Labour, meanwhile, had kicked the issue into the long grass via a Royal Commission). Although the Bill failed on its second reading, it enjoyed strong support from the *Scotsman* newspaper, which published a series of articles on devolution in pamphlet form, *How Scotland Should Be Governed*.

A 1968 leaflet entitled 'Self Government', meanwhile, set out to distinguish the party from the Conservatives, Labour and the SNP. Scotland, it claimed, was neglected, because 'London doesn't care and isn't interested in Scotland'. Heath's Scottish Assembly would 'just tinker with the problem and still wouldn't bring decision to Scotland', while the SNP wanted 'complete separation' and were 'prepared to see customs posts on the Cheviots' (Hanham 1969: 190). The UK and Scottish Liberal parties also held a joint 'Assembly' in Edinburgh during September 1968, again with much talk of devolution, while in 1970 the Scottish party republished its 1949 (already updated in 1962) pamphlet, *Scottish Self-Government*.

The 1970 general election, however, saw the Scottish Liberals lose two of its five MPs, while the SNP increased its share of the vote and gained its first MP at a UK election. Thereafter the devolution issue stagnated for several years. Liberal conference resolutions illustrated the party's efforts not to lose residual nationalist votes, calling for 'special arrangements' to 'safeguard Scottish interests' during the UK's negotiations to join the European Economic Community (1971), as well as 'direct [Scottish] representation at all levels in the Community' (1972). The latter gathering called on all Scots 'to rally to the cause of the Scottish Liberal Party as the only feasible means of achieving self-government', while condemning 'the betrayal of promises and the gestures on self-government made by the Labour and Conservative Parties'. The party also demanded a Scottish Oil Development Corporation and supported the

Kilbrandon Commission's proposals for a Scottish Assembly as 'a first step towards a full democratic European Federation in which Scotland would be a unit' (SLP 1971-4).

Scottish party leader Russell Johnston's Assembly speeches during the 1970s also represented a sustained intellectual attempt to differentiate his and his party's 'good' nationalism from the SNP's 'bad' variety. In one peroration, Johnston said he understood the SNP's motivation in his 'gut', but his 'reason' rejected their proposed solution (i.e. independence) (Johnston 1979: 15), while in 1974 he said of the SNP:

> Here one finds, in the main, not Liberals, but frustrated Tories and Social-ists – and the areas of their electoral success demonstrate this – who give priority to the need for a national identity over the long established cen-trist view of the Parties with which they have been traditionally linked. For us this has never been an issue because we have always been a Home Rule Party. The recognition of national identity is a basic part of the whole Liberal ethos as spelt out by Gladstone and Asquith and Sinclair and MacCormick and Bannerman . . . I see the SNP as a pressure group – a pressure group which is doing a good job, but a one-ticket movement not-withstanding. (Johnston 1979: 39)

This cast Gladstone *et al.* as more enthusiastic devolutionists than had been the case, while in another speech, Johnston said the fact that the SNP might 'temporarily outstrip' the Scottish Liberals did not 'worry' him because

> while their leadership has a commitment to total independence, I believe that given a Parliament controlling our own affairs, we would shed outright nationalism and turn back to the political options, right, left and centre, which the Nationalists now contain temporarily in their ranks . . . Because Liberalism is bigger than Nationalism. It is a world philosophy. (Johnston 1979: 40)

It was an obvious attempt to contrast the moderate, achievable aims of the Scottish Liberals (a devolved Scottish Parliament with representation in Europe) with the SNP's anti-EEC independence:

> Those who see the SNP as a vehicle for genuine change in our society should think very hard about this. Firstly, real, lasting change does not happen quickly. It is a foolish self delusion to believe it: it is a cruel deception to seek support by suggesting it. Secondly, a change which simply replaces one power grouping by another is no change at all. It is simply history repeating itself. (Johnston 1979: 57)

Although the Scotland Act 1978, which Scottish Liberals supported as the first step towards a federal UK, proved another false dawn, the debates of the 1970s helped keep the party in the constitutional bidding game, even though Scottish Liberal voters had moved 'strongly to the status quo' by the 1979 referendum, suggesting the leadership was out of touch with its base (Kellas 1989: 150).

After 1979, when devolution once again went on to the backburner, Liberal support did not require restating as it had a few decades before, although Ray Michie (daughter of John Bannerman and a future MP) made the surprising observation that 'self-government was nothing to do with nationalism or patriotism' (Ascherson 1980: 6). It helped the party that so many of its elected representatives were prominent at a UK level, not least David Steel, 'federal' leader since 1976. At the party's 1982 UK Assembly, Russell Johnston even suggested that devolution for Scotland ought to be prioritised above Wales or the regions of England.

By 1982, the Liberals also had competition in the form of the Social Democratic Party (SDP), whose first 'consultative assembly' in Scotland embraced 'Home Rule all round', a goal recognisably Liberal in that it combined 'the case for decentralization' as well as 'a keen sense of national identity':

> The SDP sees Home Rule neither as a halfway-house to separation, (as does the SNP), nor as an expedient adopted only to preserve electoral support, (as does the Labour Party), but as the logical fulfilment of deeply held political principles. (SDP 1983)

At the 1987 Scottish Liberal Assembly, meanwhile, soon-to-be MP Menzies Campbell proposed a 'Scottish Home Rule Declaration', believing that the case for a devolved Scottish Parliament had 'never been stronger' (SLP 1987).

Only after the 1987 general election, in which a Conservative government was once again returned with a minority of Scottish seats (the Liberal–SDP 'Alliance' won nine, the SNP three), did devolution assume a sustained high profile. Russell Johnston warned that Scottish resentment could even 'boil over into [a] form of violence' if the UK government continued to ignore demands for a Scottish Assembly, with 'hotheads at the extremes of politics' pursuing civil disobedience (*Financial Times*, 16 June 1987). Scottish Labour, at this time the main carrier of the nationalist vote (see Chapter 7), deployed less controversial language but spoke in similarly emotive terms.

The Alliance called for cross-party devolution legislation given that the overwhelming majority of Scottish MPs supported what was now routinely called a Scottish Parliament rather than 'Assembly', but Scottish Labour was not keen, leading Ronald Waddell, organising secretary of the Scottish Liberal Party, to call on Labour to 'stop acting as though it was the only party to represent Scotland' (*Guardian*, 16 June 1987), a little hypocritical given past Liberal form and rhetoric. By this stage the SDP posed minimal threat, the Scottish party warning HQ in London that once 'the party is labelled as English it will never be able to re-establish itself North of the Border' (SDP 1988).[17]

As the 1980s drew to a close, however, Labour and the Liberals reached an accommodation that culminated in the 1989 'Claim of Right' and Scottish Constitutional Convention (SCC), both of which were overtly nationalist-unionist in tenor. The former, signed by most Labour and Liberal (or 'Democrat') MPs, acknowledged 'the sovereign right of the Scottish people to determine the form of Government best suited to their needs', thereby popularising a key nationalist rallying cry later taken up by the SNP. The SCC drew a clear line with two earlier Claims of Right, while Canon Kenyon Wright said he felt the 'guardian presence' of the signatories of the Declaration of Arbroath (Kearton 2012: 37). The SNP, meanwhile, by 'standing outside' the SCC, 'refused to give up its claims to be the monopoly voice of the national movement' and thus relinquished that territory to Labour and the Liberal Democrats (McCrone 1992: 214).

The SCC completed its work before the 1992 general election, in advance of which two members of what was now the Scottish Liberal Democrat executive declared their support for independence rather than federalism. One of them, Bob McCreadie (a party vice-chairman), cited a 'growing convergence' between self-determination and the SCC, while the other, Denis Robertson Sullivan, agreed that independence should become the party's long-term objective. 'There has always been a strong thread of independence running through the party', explained Sullivan, although neither he nor McReadie intended to join the SNP. Malcolm Bruce, the Scottish Liberal Democrat leader, attempted to square the circle by arguing that the party had always maintained the right to self-determination, including independence if the people of Scotland so desired (*Guardian*, 7 February 1992).

Perhaps in response, the former UK Liberal leader David Steel attacked nationalism during the 1992 election campaign as 'an aggressively destructive force', basing his argument on an age-old nationalist-unionist distinction between 'negative nationalism' and 'positive patriotism' (*Herald*, 26 March 1992). When another Conservative government opposed to devolution was elected the following month, the Scottish Liberals, Labour and the SNP were compelled to spend another five years vying for nationalist supremacy.

In January 1995, Menzies Campbell introduced another devolution Bill and was at once assailed by SNP leader Alex Salmond, who said the Liberals had achieved 'precisely nothing' in spite of a century-old commitment to

'Home Rule'. Campbell retorted that the SNP clearly regarded themselves as the 'exclusive brethren' of Scottish politics (*Herald*, 18 January 1995). Thereafter the Scottish Liberal Democrats presented themselves as the 'guarantors of home rule' in response to an apparent cooling in Labour's devolution position. New leader Jim Wallace said:

> No-one looking at Scottish political history can be in any doubt about the commitment of the [Scottish Liberal Democrats] to the Scottish Parliament, to home rule, and if there is any question or uncertainty about whether the Labour Party under Tony Blair will deliver, then what better guarantee than to ensure that there are a good number of Scottish Liberal Democrat MPs backed up by a solid number of SLD votes in the next UK Parliament?

Interestingly, Wallace acknowledged that a number of his party's supporters felt that when it came to devolution, there had been an element of 'me too-ism' between them and the Labour Party (*Herald*, 21 August 1995). And when, that same year, the Conservatives belatedly tried to get in on the act by returning the Stone of Destiny to Scotland (Shadow Scottish Secretary George Robertson said Scots would not 'be bought off by symbols of ancient power'), Wallace accused Prime Minister John Major of hypocrisy, supporting devolution for Northern Ireland but not Scotland, and preaching 'subsidiarity' in Europe but not in the United Kingdom (*Herald*, 6 July 1996).

Guarantors of Change?

After the first Scottish Parliament elections in 1999, the Scottish Liberal Democrats forged an electoral pact with Scottish Labour rather than the SNP, as had been envisaged thirty years earlier, two nationalist-unionist parties making common cause now that devolution had been delivered. Rather than being punished, as later orthodoxy dictated for smaller parties in coalitions, the Liberal Democrats performed well at the next elections in 2003, both in terms of personnel but also in being seen to have won concessions from Labour – on tuition fees, PR for local government and a Borders railway. At the 2005 Westminster elections, the Liberal Democrats became Scotland's second party with 22.6 per cent of the vote.

In 2006, Lord (David) Steel, a former UK party leader and the Scottish Parliament's first Presiding Officer, published *Moving to Federalism: A New Settlement for Scotland*, which advocated greater fiscal autonomy for the Scottish Parliament, an indication the party was thinking ahead to the next Holyrood election, when it anticipated the need to provide a constitutional 'offer' for voters, perhaps also conscious that the SNP – led once again by

Alex Salmond – might outbid the coalition parties when it came to the Scottish Question. But instead of coalescing with Salmond's party following the 2007 election, the Liberal Democrats entered opposition on the basis that it could not countenance an independence referendum. One of its MSPs, Jamie Stone, had also created bad feeling by attacking the SNP as 'xenophobic' before polling day.

Between 2007 and 2014, the Liberal Democrats tried to keep themselves in the game by co-operating with Labour and the Conservatives in the cross-party Calman Commission and, later, Better Together, but this served to cast them as one of three 'unionist' parties rather than 'guarantors' of devolution. Another coalition, this time at Westminster with the Conservatives, in 2010 did not help the party's fortunes, generally or in Scotland (although it did mean the position of Scottish Secretary went to a Liberal for the first time since 1945). Contesting the Scottish party leadership in 2008, Scottish Liberal veteran Ross Finnie had complained that he and his colleagues had been left responding to a debate, 'the terms of which have been set by another party' (BBC News online, 25 July 2008). In a radio interview Tavish Scott, the winning candidate, suggested that politicians and the media were 'too obsessed by endless talk about referendums and the constitution'.

Alex Salmond's prediction that the coalition would spell disaster for the Liberal Democrats at the next Scottish Parliament election proved brutally accurate: the party lost all its mainland constituencies amid an SNP tsunami, retaining only Orkney, Shetland and three list MSPs. In the long build-up to the independence referendum, Willie Rennie, the party's new leader, did his best to push the idea of a 'strong Scotland' within a 'federal UK' (*Telegraph*, 4 March 2012), while asking former UK leader Sir Menzies Campbell to lead yet another commission. 'A rejection of independence', argued Sir Menzies, 'will enable Scotland to continue down the track towards a modern, pluralist and federal relationship with the other parts of the United Kingdom' (Campbell 2012: 19). Rennie said the party would act as 'the guarantors of change', reviving a pre-1997 Scottish Liberal Democrat argument.

'Liberal Democrats have wanted home rule for a hundred years', declared Rennie at the party's 2012 Scottish conference. 'A Scotland with the powers to run our home affairs but proud to share the wins and share the risks with the United Kingdom family of nations' (*Telegraph*, 4 March 2012). But like Scottish Labour, the Scottish Liberal Democrats had a nationalist (or 'Home Rule') wing – most prominently Judy Steel – and watched as many of their once-loyal voters were wooed by Alex Salmond, who in one referendum speech made a direct pitch to Liberal Home Rulers.

The old Liberal refrain of 'federalism' had a certain profile during the campaign, but it was ill-defined and unlikely to be delivered; 'independence' was, for many, a more beguiling tune. Although the No vote in 2014 was swiftly followed by the cross-party Smith Commission and further devolution (along Liberal Democrat lines), which took legislative form as the Scotland Act 2016, the party got little credit. At the 2015 general election it, like Labour and the Conservatives, emerged with just a single MP. Only one party was now seen to 'stand up for Scotland', and that was the SNP.

Conclusion

As Biagini observed, under leaders from Gladstone to Asquith, the Liberal Party had proved itself 'good at managing and absorbing Celtic separatism, turning a potentially destructive force into an important asset for both the stability of the United Kingdom and the electoral success of their own party' (Biagini 1996: 14). In the late nineteenth century, therefore, Liberals often functioned 'as the party of Scottish aspirations', the main 'carrier' of nationalist unionism and its commitment to legislative devolution, although this was not as unequivocal as later Liberals liked to claim.

By the 1920s, this 'aspiration' had largely passed to the emerging Scottish Labour movement, while the Scottish Unionist Party also appropriated aspects via its Liberal Unionist contingent. Although the Scottish Liberals retained a commitment to 'Home Rule' throughout the mid twentieth century, it had little support. As Ward concluded, 'Scottish nationalism alone was not enough to secure Scottish votes' (Ward 2005: 13). It was, in other words, a necessary but not sufficient aspect of electorally successful nationalist unionism.

Only in the late 1960s, when Scottish party politics became more competitive on the basis of the constitutional question, did the Scottish Liberal Party re-emerge as a nationalist-unionist player. Its goal had evolved from 'Home Rule all round' to 'federalism', and it worked hard in the 1970s and 1980s to regain its historic position as Scotland's main 'carrier' of the 'Home Rule' vote, especially against competition from the SNP. In doing so, it contrasted its moderate desire for devolution with the SNP's extreme and, it was often implied, anti-English motivation of full independence. Its nationalism, however, was never really banal, existing more in the Scottish Liberal mainstream than that of Labour and the Conservatives.

Between 1989, when the Scottish Constitutional Convention met for the first time, and the 2007 Scottish Parliament election, the Scottish Liberal Democrats and Scottish Labour Party formed a successful nationalist-unionist alliance, not only implementing the long-standing goal of a Scottish

Parliament but governing together for eight years. Thereafter, however, nationalist unionism found it difficult to adapt to the 'new politics'. The Liberal Democrats were keener on extending the settlement than Labour, but both suffered in the face of a challenge from another party which claimed to 'stand up for Scotland', both as the new 'defenders' of the devolution settlement and in arguing that Scotland's 'Home Rule' journey had to be 'completed' with independence.

SEVEN

The Scottish Labour Party and 'Crypto-Nationalism'

Whatever the efforts of the Scottish Liberal Democrats to harness Scottish nationalism in the 1980s and early 1990s, the Scottish Labour Party remained its primary 'carrier'. One need look no further than Donald Dewar's memorable speech at the opening of the Scottish Parliament on 1 July 1999:

> This is a moment anchored in our history.
>
> Today, we reach back through the long haul to win this Parliament, through the struggles of those who brought democracy to Scotland, to that other Parliament dissolved in controversy nearly three centuries ago . . .
>
> This is about more than our politics and our laws. This is about who we are, how we carry ourselves. In the quiet moments today, we might hear some echoes from the past: The shout of the welder in the din of the great Clyde shipyards; The speak of the Mearns, with its soul in the land; The discourse of the enlightenment, when Edinburgh and Glasgow were a light held to the intellectual life of Europe; The wild cry of the Great Pipes; And back to the distant cries of the battles of Bruce and Wallace. The past is part of us.

And so it continued, invoking Walter Scott ('only a man with soul so dead could have no sense, no feel of his native land'), Robert Burns (who 'believed that sense and worth ultimately prevail') and the 'symbolic thistles' on the new Parliament's mace together with the words: 'Wisdom. Justice. Compassion. Integrity' (Dewar 1999). Many of these names, symbols, themes and arguments would have been familiar to any nationalist unionist of the previous century.

But Dewar's speech – rich in ethno-symbolism – also appealed to supporters of independence – it would be referenced over the next two decades by Alex Salmond and Nicola Sturgeon – while Robert McLean (a leading light on Scottish Labour's nationalist wing) noted the 'difference in tone from that struck by the cautious reformer of the late 1960s', something he suggested reflected 'the changes in Scottish society, and Donald Dewar's perspective, over the past thirty years' (McLean 2001: 10).

This chapter examines three distinct phases of Labour's 'nationalist unionism': (1) its strong support for Scottish Home Rule in the early twentieth century; (2) the devolution debate of the 1960s and 1970s; and (3) that which re-emerged in response to the twin challenges of the SNP and Thatcherism in the 1980s. Unlike the Scottish Unionists and Liberals, Labour's claim to 'stand up for Scotland' has been the subject of extensive academic attention.

Keating and Bleiman dealt comprehensively with the first and second phases, as did McLean (1991), who extended his narrative ('a positive assertion of Labour's nationalist traditions') to include the third, also covered by Geekie and Levy (1989). Bulpitt's 'territorial code' can be applied here, as can Smith's 'ethno-symbolism' and Billig's 'banal nationalism', particularly Labour's tendency to push the nationalism of its opponents (i.e. the SNP) to the periphery. And like the Scottish Unionists, Labour made a distinction – often muddled – between 'good' and 'bad' nationalism.

Labour's First Home Rule Phase

'From its emergence as an independent political force in the 1880s,' wrote McLean in his two-volume survey of 'Labour and Scottish Home Rule', 'Labour was the natural standard bearer of Scottish national sentiment' (McLean 1991a: 3). Indeed, the concurrent emergence of the Scottish Home Rule Association (SHRA) and independent Labour representation in the 1880s meant Labour in Scotland promoted legislative devolution as part of its platform. Members of the SHRA also included prominent figures on the left, including G. B. Clark (of the Crofters Party), R. B. Cunninghame Grahame (later the SNP's first president) and Ramsay MacDonald (later the UK's first Labour Prime Minister).

Others emerged from the Scottish Liberal movement, such as Keir Hardie, who stood as the independent Labour candidate in the Mid-Lanark by-election of 1888 (though he still intended to support Gladstone if elected). MacDonald wrote to say that if Hardie was unsuccessful, then the 'cause of Labour in Scotland and of Scottish Nationality will suffer much thereby. Your defeat will awaken Scotland and your victory will re-construct Scottish Liberalism' (Stewart 1925: 42). As McLean and McMillan pointed out, MacDonald's letter mentioned Liberalism, Labour and Scottish nationality 'as if they were the same, or at least overlapping'

(McLean and McMillan 2005: 120). The *Scotsman*, meanwhile, attacked Hardie as a representative of the 'social divisions and Scottish separatism inherent in the Gladstonian ranks in Scotland'.

Hardie lost the election and instead formed the first Scottish Labour Party (SLP), one aim of which was Home Rule for 'each separate nationality or country in the British Empire, with an Imperial Parliament for Imperial affairs', demonstrating that Labour's early nationalist unionism, like its Scottish Unionist corollary, included an imperial dimension. McLean viewed the SLP, which merged with the Independent Labour Party (ILP) in 1894, as 'a key intermediary in passing the mantle of Scottish Home Rule from the Liberal Party to an infant labour movement' (McLean 1991a: 12–13).

As with Scottish Liberalism, Home Rule lost its salience within the Labour movement towards the end of the nineteenth century, only returning after 1914. In 1915 the Labour Party formed a Scottish Advisory Council (generally known as the 'Scottish Council'), MacDonald believing the movement had not 'been Scotch enough'. As Home Rule sentiment increased during the First World War, however, he was confident there now existed 'an organisation ready to direct it'. By 1918, 'a distinctively nationalist tone' had crept into Scottish Council debates (Keating and Bleiman 1979: 56, 60). The Labour Party's 'Scottish Programme' at the 1918 general election promoted 'the self-determination of the Scottish people' (McLean 1991a: 15). That same year, Roland Muirhead of the ILP formed a new Scottish Home Rule Association, this time with more of a Labour (rather than Liberal) bent. Until 1923 the Scottish Council of the Labour Party regularly passed motions in favour of Home Rule, while legislation was drafted and promoted in Parliament, just as it had once been by Liberals. This culminated in George Buchanan's 1924 Government of Scotland Bill, although by then the recent formation of the Irish Free State had largely laid to rest Liberal (and Labour) talk of 'Home Rule all round'.

John Maclean, meanwhile, was a nationalist for reasons both tactical (he believed a devolved Scotland would more quickly attain socialism) and sentimental (a belief in Celtic 'clan' communism). That tactical rationale resonated in the Labour movement, just as it had among Liberals in opposition. If Scotland had possessed Home Rule in the 1920s, the argument ran, then it would have had a socialist government. Instead, Scottish radicalism was being held back by Tory England, a counterfactual asserted in a variety of ways (and by a variety of parties) over the next century. As the fraternal delegate from Labour's National Executive Committee remarked to the Scottish Council in 1923, 'the Celtic fringe' could save 'Saxon England from the folly of its own Conservatism' (Keating and Bleiman 1979: 81).

According to Keating and Bleiman, Labour's nationalism peaked in 1922 along with the Scottish economy, with both slumping thereafter, although the Red Clydesiders – and associated mythology – kept the issue on the agenda. Arriving in London to take up his seat after the 1922 general election (at which Labour became Scotland's largest party for the first time), John Wheatley told reporters that no subject aroused 'such enthusiasm' as 'the subject of Scottish Home Rule'. Speaking at an SHRA rally in support of the Buchanan's Bill in Glasgow during 1924, James Maxton said he would 'ask for no greater job in life (than to make) the English-ridden, capitalist-ridden, landlord-ridden Scotland into a Scottish socialist Commonwealth' (Keating and Bleiman 1979: 81).[1]

Finlay reckoned one of the main reasons self-government was popular within the Scottish Labour Party was that

> it appealed to popular nationalist sentiment and, in the absence of properly defined policies, could be used as a panacea for a whole range of social, political and economic problems. Also, it acted as a unifying force, bringing together disparate elements, such as the Rev. James Barr and James Maxton, together in common cause. The use of nationalist rhetoric was a speciality with Labour politicians when addressing large audiences who, probably because of the simplicity of the Home Rule idea, responded enthusiastically to the demands for a redress of Scottish grievances. (Finlay 1994: 9)

Bulpitt drew a line between Labour's approach and that of the Liberals after 1886, both posing 'as a party of peripheral defence whilst at the same time pursuing a fundamentally centrist strategy' (Bulpitt 1983: 130). Like earlier Radicals, Labour politicians also appropriated standard nationalist-unionist 'heroes'. In June 1923, the ILP organised a Bannockburn Rally with David Kirkwood as the main speaker, while in Ederslie a few months later, Tom Johnston and James Maxton addressed a Wallace rally (McLean 1991a: 18).

The Buchanan's Bill was talked out by Conservatives during the first (minority) Labour government in 1924. In response, the SHRA summoned a 'National Convention' and appointed a committee to draft another Home Rule Bill, which was introduced by the Rev. James Barr (previously a member of the Liberal-aligned Young Scots Society) in 1927. This reflected both its sponsor's political priorities ('matters of temperance, matters of religious equality and the great principles of moral and social advance') and a hardening of nationalist demands, advocating Dominion status for Scotland and the withdrawal of its MPs from Westminster.

As Keating and Bleiman put it, the SHRA was

an alliance of two very different kinds of Home Ruler: on the one hand, Labour men, trade unionists and Co-operators, for whom Home Rule was part and parcel of Labour's advance; on the other, committed nationalists, for whom the alliance with the Labour movement was useful only to the extent that it served the national cause. (Keating and Bleiman 1979: 102–3)

For a while this balancing act worked well enough, but the division became more obvious as Labour's national priorities changed, particularly now it was out of government. Disillusioned at Ramsay MacDonald's failure to deliver in government, the 'committed nationalists' in the SHRA quit Labour and formed the National Party of Scotland (NPS) in 1927, believing a dedicated nationalist party to be the more realistic means by which to achieve its constitutional ambitions. The SHRA was formally dissolved in 1929.

At its 1928 UK conference, Labour endorsed *Labour and the Nation*, which called for 'the creation of separate legislative assemblies in Scotland, Wales and England with autonomous powers in matters of local concern', but this was little more than a formal reaffirmation of its 1918 commitment. In office again the following year, 'the fading light of Ramsay MacDonald's nationalism flickered up for a moment and went out' (Coupland 1954: 400). He had promised an inquiry into Scottish governance during a speech in Glasgow, something he reiterated in the Commons:

That inquiry will be ... primarily into local administration, but I should be very sorry indeed if from the view of that committee the larger question of Scottish self-government were to be excluded. If the House will agree to my suggestion and we set up such a committee, it will not be my fault if the terms of reference are so narrow that the larger question of Scottish self-respect and the recognition of Scottish historical authority are excluded from the view of the Committee. (HC Debs 10 Jul 1929 Vol 229 cc933–4)

No inquiry took place. As Keating and Bleiman observed, 'nationalism might be an appropriate ideology for a movement of the periphery, but, as soon as that movement became serious about capturing power at the centre, its nationalist credentials became suspect' (Keating and Bleiman 1979: 84). The same had been true of the Liberals, with Lloyd George having 'shown himself no more ready than Ramsay MacDonald to devolve power' while in office. Although prepared to accommodate aspects of Scottish nationalism, in the absence of a significant electoral threat from the new NPS, Labour could also 'suppress the nationalist dimension in Scottish politics while claiming itself to represent Scotland's best interests' (Keating and Bleiman 1979: 107–8).

By 1932, even James Maxton believed the struggle 'for mere political liberty' to be 'out of date', be it in Ireland, India or Scotland, while the 1931 Statute of Westminster removed the idea of Dominion status for Scotland as a credible defence against charges of 'separatism' from Labour's unionist opponents. As the 1930s progressed, meanwhile, nationalism became tainted through developments on the Continent, so as Labour retreated from its first nationalist phase, it dovetailed with the Conservative 'territorial code' and its commitment to 'administrative devolution', for it 'expressed a continuing concern with the promotion of Scottish goals and benefits while avoiding the dangers of constitutional change' (Keating and Bleiman 1979: 114).

Those goals included aspects of contemporary socialism, i.e. centralised economic planning and protectionism. Tomlinson and Gibbs identified an 'economic unionist-nationalism' as the predominant ideology of industrialists in the Scottish National Development Council (created in 1931). This envisaged the 'rationalisation and diversification' of Scottish industry, an objective to be achieved within the framework of the British state, in particular an enlarged and empowered Scottish Office (Tomlinson and Gibbs 2016), which in due course 'led the way in promoting this notion of a Scottish national economic interest' (Paterson 1994: 118).

Thus the myriad of nationalist parties formed between 1928 and 1934 represented not the advance of political nationalism but rather its retreat from sections of the Labour and Liberal movements in Scotland. Some maintained their nationalism in largely rhetorical form. David Kirkwood, for example, spent the 1930s urging successive Scottish Secretaries to 'stand up for Scotland' within the British Cabinet, while Tom Johnston (involved, like the Unionist Walter Elliot, in the Saltire Society) kept up pressure via a London Scots Self-Government Committee, which complained that Scotland was 'neglected' by Westminster and held back by Tory England.

Thomas Burns' federalist 1938 *Plan for Scotland* noted that 'Scotland has . . . been ruthlessly exploited and bled white, not by England, but by her own industrialists'. Interestingly, a preface by UK Labour leader Clement Attlee recognised that 'nationalism has an immense attractive force for good or evil':

> Suppressed, it may poison the political life of a nation. Given its proper place it can enrich it . . . Nothing is easier than to make windy speeches on the right of Self-Government, in which little attention is given to construction, but much to the fomenting of ill between nations . . . plenty of spadework to be done in working out the best means of effecting the most fruitful co-operation between the three nations inhabiting Britain. (Burns 1938)

This was not so different from standard unionist distinctions between 'good' and 'bad' nationalism, though naturally Attlee's conception of the former was more concerned with economics and welfare than the Conservatives' patriotic imperialism.

Economic considerations also weighed heavily on Tom Johnston, one of Labour's most prominent pre-war nationalist-unionists, although imperialism was not completely absent. As Johnston told the Commons in 1922:

> ordinary business and public-spirited men in Scotland desire that they should be associated more closely with the administration of Scottish affairs, that Scottish business should be done in Scottish ways, and that the Scottish people should have more control than they have at the present time . . . We do not want to break away from the Union. We are . . . proud of the Union and the Empire . . . Scottish people have been among the pioneers in building up the Empire and have been proud to be associated with England in building the Empire. (HC Debs 26 May 1922 Vol 154 c1645)

Long a supporter of Home Rule (in 1923 he had extracted an apology from premier Andrew Bonar Law for referring to 'England' rather than 'Britain' in diplomatic correspondence), by the late 1920s he had come to the conclusion that a Scottish Parliament could only succeed on the basis of a strong economy. As he memorably put it in his memoirs, what 'purport would there be in getting a Scots Parliament in Edinburgh if it has to administer an emigration system, a glorified Poor Law and a graveyard?' (Johnston 1952: 66).

So as Scottish Secretary between 1941 and 1945, Johnston pursued a consensual approach to preparing Scotland's economy for the post-war era, containing nationalism through a 'patriotic style of politics which still avoided legislative devolution'. His press office 'cultivated journalists who had always shown nationalist sympathies', including G. M. Thomson and J. M. Reid, while Johnston's rhetorical 'declarations of nationalism', according to Harvie, were 'the most explicit ever to have come from a Secretary of State' (Harvie 1981: 15). Johnston's success not only represented 'a great vindication' (Keating and Bleiman 1979: 129) of administrative devolution, but even satisfied some in the SNP (Finlay 1994).

In Cabinet, Johnston was also adept at wielding the threat posed by 'extreme' nationalism in order to promote the nationalist-unionist variety. 'He would impress on [a Cabinet] committee that there was a strong, nationalistic movement in Scotland', recalled Herbert Morrison, 'and it would be a potential danger if it grew through lack of attention to Scottish interests' (Galbraith 2018: 270). Johnston's concern was not necessarily misplaced, for the SNP (though hardly extreme) polled well in a series of wartime by-elections. In 1943, Lord Reith recorded a meeting with the Secretary of State in his diary:

> He thinks there is a great danger of Scottish Nationalism coming up, and a sort of Sinn Féin movement as he called it. The Lord Justice Clerk (Lord Cooper) had said in a letter that if he left off being a judge and went back to politics, he would be a nationalist. (Reith 1975: 300–1)[2]

Thus Johnston gave competing nationalist initiatives short shrift. When John MacCormick, who in 1941 was yet to break with the SNP, sought a meeting with Arthur Greenwood, the minister responsible for post-war reconstruction, to work 'out a plan for self-government in Scotland immediately after the war', Johnston replied that Scottish interests were being adequately safeguarded by him as Secretary of State (Galbraith 2018: xx). Indeed, the relative autonomy granted to Johnston by Churchill – he agreed to facilitate anything agreed by Johnston's cross-party 'Council of State' – meant the Conservative/Labour 'territorial code' functioned even in the challenging circumstances of wartime. 'We were now no longer representatives of an old nation in decay,' Johnston reflected in his memoirs, 'but of a young virile people lit up with the assurance that whatever men do in unison they can do' (Johnston 1952: 99).

Out of office in 1945, Johnston's support for Home Rule reasserted itself, even to the degree that Alastair Dunnett, a future editor of the *Scotsman* and his press officer during the war, claimed to have heard, in a film on post-war Scotland,[3] 'Tom Johnston declaring his belief that Scotland's future rested upon her obtaining full independence'. This was perhaps a hopeful misinterpretation of an emotive statement of support for devolution, but Dunnett concluded that he 'had always known that [Johnston] was a nationalist in the real sense' (Galbraith 2018: 316).[4]

'Unionist Interregnum'

Home Rule was not mentioned in Labour's manifesto for the 1945 general election, although speakers' notes issued by the Scottish Council included it, a compromise recommended by Harold Laski (McLean 1991a: 24). Twenty-three of the party's thirty-seven Scottish MPs had included Home Rule in their election addresses, which Bob McLean took as proof that Labour's 'nationalist tradition' remained intact but, just as in 1924, this cooled on entering government, even more so given the size of Attlee's majority. Thus Labour entered what McLean called a 'unionist interregnum', from which it 'only slowly and reluctantly' emerged in the late 1960s (McLean 1991b: 3).

As Labour turned away from nationalism, it also refashioned unionism in its own image. As Moran has observed, a 'new sense of civic identity' emerged after the Second World War, one based upon 'the notion of universalism – a new way of thinking of ourselves as British, involving common social entitlements and common social obligations' (Moran 2017: 23–4). This identity was anti-imperialist and not terribly interested in accommodating Scottish nationalism, and thus posed a challenge to two key elements of pre-war Scottish Unionist identity.

At the same time, the 'greatest emblem' of this new 'welfare unionism' (McLean and McMillan 2005), the National Health Service, was separately administered (and legislated for) in Scotland, in part a recognition of Tom Johnston's wartime reforms which had created a nascent universal health service in the west of Scotland. Crucially, the Conservatives came to embrace much of this 'reimagined state', its four distinctive elements being 'social citizenship, metropolitan dominance, world state destiny and a Unionist settlement' (Moran 2017: 29). But as Moran also observed, all four elements would eventually 'decay', with consequences for inter-party nationalist-unionist competition.

The reduced salience of the Scottish dimension was reflected in Attlee's choice of Scottish Secretaries, the first two of which – Joseph Westwood and Arthur Woodburn – were hardly figures of standing and energy in the mould of Tom Johnston. It fell to Woodburn to grapple with the rise of the pro-devolution 'Scottish Convention', which became the main repository of non-party political nationalism in the late 1940s and early 1950s.

At the close of Labour's Scottish conference on 26 October 1947, Woodburn warned that Scotland 'must be careful not to follow some of the Pied Pipers of Nationalism over the brink that leads to disaster' (*Scotsman*, 27 October 1947). Later, in an illuminating Cabinet paper dated 6 December 1947, he observed that as a result of the Convention's activities, all political parties in Scotland, 'including the Labour Party, are taking part in an agitation for a greater measure of Scottish control over Scottish affairs'. This agitation, he added, did 'not follow party lines'. Woodburn then categorised different groups of support, by 'far the largest' being

> one which has strong emotional feeling behind it in Scotland, asks that Parliament should give more time to Scottish affairs and that, within the British constitution and the unity of the two countries, the Scots themselves should have further opportunities of administering in Scotland the business of Government and of the socialised industries and other Government-appointed organisations.

Woodburn believed this sentiment had 'for long been latent', although the 'exploitation of Scottish sentiment about the organisation of socialised industries on a Great Britain basis' by the Unionists had 'been largely responsible for bringing matters to a head'. He added that the

> danger of this widespread feeling in Scotland is that it is hidden to some extent by the fact that elections are fought between the main parties. But it betrays itself in the general uneasiness that Scotland is held to be of no account by British Governments. There is, therefore, a kind of smouldering pile that might suddenly break through the party loyalties and become a formidable national movement. (Woodburn 1947)

This was prescient stuff, although Woodburn's proposed remedy – a reorganisation of Scottish business at Westminster, a Scottish Production Council and an inquiry into Scottish governance – met with opposition from Herbert Morrison, who believed such an approach (especially an inquiry) might 'set afoot an agitation for concessions on a lavish scale which you will not be able to control' (Levitt 1992: 113). The Scottish Secretary compromised, retaining parliamentary reforms (a beefed-up Scottish Grand Committee) and what was now called a Scottish Economic Conference, but no formal inquiry. He then set to work on a much-anticipated white paper.

'We want to be ourselves, and will be ourselves', Woodburn told reporters in early December 1947. 'We have our own culture, education and laws, and our own contribution to make . . . The problem to be solved was how to remain ourselves and also part of a corporate community' (Scotsman, 1 December 1947). His solution was published on 29 January 1948 (the day on which the Indian nationalist Ghandi was assassinated, a symbolic link made by some newspapers), but the reaction was swift and critical, from the press, the Convention, Liberals and even Labour colleagues; only Scottish Unionists appeared supportive, as they were yet to come up with proposals of their own (see Chapter 4), although the Unionist MP for Ayr, Sir Thomas Moore, condemned it as a 'nonsensical . . . sop to Scottish Nationalists' (Scotsman, 29 April 1948).

The reconstituted Scottish Grand Committee met and the Economic Conference was convened, and just as it seemed the moment had passed (as it often had in the past), the Convention movement resurfaced in 1949 as the Scottish Covenant Association, its petition in support of legislative devolution attracting thousands of signatures. Woodburn came under further pressure to concede a government inquiry, although this was firmly rejected by Labour's Scottish Council during its annual conference.

Already convinced the Convention was a Tory front given John MacCormick's Unionist-backed Liberal candidacy in the 1948 Paisley by-election (see Chapter 4), Woodburn then blundered by depicting MacCormick as a nationalist extremist ('on three occasions he mentioned the word "bomb"') during an adjournment debate on Scottish devolution (HC Deb 16 Nov 1949 Vol 469 c2097). The media added mockery to their long-standing criticism of Woodburn, from which he never really recovered. Meanwhile, Unionists had unveiled their own proposals, out-bidding Labour with a new Minister of State and a Royal Commission on Scottish Affairs.

So in the midst of its unionist interregnum, Labour proved unable to harness Scottish nationalism in a way it had managed just twenty-five years earlier. Hector McNeil, appointed Woodburn's successor in February 1950, did not fundamentally disagree with his predecessor's analysis of the situation, but he realised the need for a different tone. 'There always will be a concern and a zeal among Scots people to protect these Scottish characteristics', he told the Commons in his first outing as Secretary of State. 'There has been a gradual transfer [of autonomy], and it is unlikely that that transfer will be stopped at any one stage' (HC Deb 10 Mar 1950 Vol 472 c635).

By May 1950, the Scottish Covenant claimed more than a million signatures, but still the Prime Minister refused to legitimise what Labour regarded as 'bad' nationalism by meeting a delegation led by MacCormick. Instead McNeil did so, flattering them with sympathetic words but no real intention of acceding to their demands, although he made one concession: a fact-finding inquiry into financial relations between Scotland and England. The Catto Report (published in 1952, by which point Labour and therefore McNeil were out of office) estimated that while Scotland received 12 per cent of government expenditure it contributed 10. McNeil also published a handbook on Scottish administration, intended to demonstrate just how much 'Home Rule' Scotland already enjoyed.

Thereafter, the Covenant movement fizzled out, and Labour's unionist interregnum hardened. In the STUC's evidence to the Royal Commission on Scottish Affairs (which Scottish Labour had belatedly supported on the eve of the 1951 general election), it urged administrative rather than legislative devolution, a stance reiterated in 1954 and again in 1955. And with the publication of *Let Scotland Prosper*, its first separately published policy statement on Scotland, the Scottish Council of the Labour Party turned decisively against Home Rule. In 1958, it was formally removed from the party's platform; UK party leader Hugh Gaitskell explained that what Scotland needed was a Labour government rather than legislative devolution.

Labour's Second Home Rule Phase

Labour's second Home Rule phase, therefore, initially took on a different form, playing the 'Scottish card' almost as vigorously as Scottish Unionists had in the late 1940s and early 1950s, but shorn of Labour's historical commitment to a Scottish Parliament. This second phase was also animated by a deep, increasingly tribal hatred of what it regarded as the 'bad' or 'extreme' nationalism represented by the Covenant movement and the Scottish National Party, the attacks of the former on Labour having 'left a bitter aftertaste' (Keating and Bleiman 1979: 150).

Channelling that anti-nationalist tribalism was the Labour MP Willie Ross, who combined strident attacks on the SNP with accusations of Tory neglect and breaches of faith on Scottish autonomy, cleverly turning the tables on Unionists who had levelled the same charge against Labour during its 'Scottish Control of Scottish Affairs' phase. To this Ross added his own cultural nationalism, not unlike that of his later successor as Scottish Secretary Donald Dewar, infused with Presbyterianism and articulated with lashings of Burns and a skilful appropriation of Ayrshire dialect in his parliamentary performances. In 1962, Gaitskell made Ross Shadow Secretary of State for Scotland in place of the less aggressive Tom Fraser.

Having successfully depicted the Scottish Unionists as the wrong 'sort' of Scots (i.e. tweedy and out of touch), by the time Labour returned to government under Harold Wilson in 1964, few would have disputed its claim to 'stand up for Scotland'. The collapse of the Covenant movement by the end of the 1950s also meant Scottish nationalism lacked an alternative outlet, which allowed Labour to 'command the centre of the Scottish political stage as never before and to turn the Scottish question to its own advantage' (Keating and Bleiman 1979: 149).

Labour's 1962 statement of policy, *Signposts for Scotland* (there were also 'signposts' for Wales and the 'New Ulster'), was full of rhetoric about the Conservatives having 'failed' Scotland, which could only be saved by a Labour government. 'Scotland has its own rich national culture', it added. 'Wise planning throughout Britain will seek to preserve this.' Labour's national plan (UK and Scottish), meanwhile, was to 'involve further measures of devolution in Scotland and a major increase in the powers and scope of the Scottish Office':

> Scotland will stand to gain more from this fairer sharing of both benefits and burdens just because of our present relatively greater needs. This is the answer to those who claim that Scotland should cut herself off from the rest of Britain and make herself economically and politically independent. Such a separation would give Scotland the worst of both worlds. (Labour Party 1962: 3, 12, 22–3)

The 1966 general election represented 'peak' Scottish Labour, with the party securing almost 50 per cent of the vote and forty-six out of seventy-one seats. As Scottish Secretary since 1964, Ross was of the view that he, like Tom Johnston, would be so effective in exploiting administrative devolution as to make the legislative variety unnecessary. And, like Churchill with Johnston, Wilson was content (*pace* Bulpitt) to let Ross do his own thing as long as it delivered electoral dividends.

What provided the impetus for the more recognisable aspect of Labour's second 'Home Rule' phase was the electoral rise of the Scottish National Party in the late 1960s, the 'smouldering pile' Arthur Woodburn had anticipated might break through in his 1947 Cabinet memorandum. The first indication came at the Pollok by-election of March 1967, at which a significant SNP showing split the anti-Tory vote and gave the rebranded Scottish Conservative and Unionist Party some welcome good news in the guise of historian Esmond Wright. Next were municipal elections and then, the biggest shock, the Hamilton by-election that November.

Initially the Labour response was attack. Ross stepped up his anti-SNP vitriol and resisted any concessions beyond a Scottish Affairs select committee (formed in 1968 with Donald Dewar as a member). Cabinet colleague Richard Crossman touched upon the paradox in his colleague's stance: 'Willie Ross and his friends accuse the Scottish Nationalists of separatism but what Willie himself actually likes is to keep Scottish business absolutely privy from English business' (Crossman 1977: 48).

As McLean and McMillan observed, Labour divided between 'hedgers and ditchers'. Wilson and Crossman led the hedgers, who believed that 'making some gestures to devolution would head off the Scottish Nationalist threat', while the ditchers, led by Ross, 'believed that any concession to the SNP was dangerous. For them, devolution was a dangerous precedent, a slippery slope, the start of the breakup of Britain' (McLean and McMillan 2005: 161).

A Royal Commission on the Constitution was, however, appointed in 1969, taking (illuminating) minutes and, if not wasting years, then effectively kicking the devolution issue into the long grass. The Scottish Council of the Labour Party's oral evidence restated the unionist case, warning that any form of 'assembly with substantial legislative devolution' would constitute a 'slippery slope towards total separation, or at least a form of separation which would set up divisions within the United Kingdom' (SCLP 1971). It even stated that a Conservative government would, in its view, be preferable to devolution.

After 1970, it appeared the SNP had peaked, and Ross reverted to pre-1964 form in presenting himself and Labour as defenders of Scottish interests against the ill-fated Conservative government of Edward Heath. Even after the Royal Commission recommended a Scottish Assembly and the SNP seized another Labour heartland in Govan towards the end of 1973, Ross held firm. The line only softened through fear of further losses to the SNP between February and October 1974.[5] As Hutchison noted, some Labour thinkers had also started to push for devolution 'as desirable in its own right, irrespective of party tactics'. John P. Mackintosh's *The Devolution of Power* (1968) had been influential, and by early 1970s his ideas had been taken up by young Scottish Labour modernisers such as Jim Sillars, Harry Ewing and Gordon Brown (Hutchison 2001: 129), some of whom added a cultural-nationalist dimension. And as the SNP electoral challenge manifested itself, Mackintosh's followers pushed this agenda even more firmly.[6]

The events at Dalintober Street in the summer of 1974 have been comprehensively charted elsewhere but, interestingly, Scottish Labour dug into its Home Rule-supporting past in order to legitimise its U-turn, just as Heath had done with his Declaration of Perth, presenting it as the natural culmination of several decades of nationalist unionism. 'Their old method of handling the Scottish question was failing,' judged Keating and Bleiman, 'they had conceded the devolutionists' case by their own advocacy of administrative devolution and had positively revelled in the argument that Scottish problems, being distinct, merited special treatment' (Keating and Bleiman 1979: 173). Barbara Castle recorded Ross saying in Cabinet in July 1974 that 'we ought not to have gone so far . . . but having started the whole [Kilbrandon] enquiry, we had aroused expectations we could not resist' (Castle 1980: 153).

Though reluctant to change course, Ross possessed sharp political antennae and realised something had to give. Alex Neil, later an SNP member of the Scottish Parliament but in the 1970s a member of Labour's National Executive Committee, recalled waking a dozing Willie Ross at Keir Hardie House (Labour's Scottish HQ), prompting him to declare: 'The way to deal with the SNP is to be more nationalist than the nationalists!' (interview with Alex Neil, 25 May 2016).[7] As John Pollok later reflected, Ross was 'almost the archetypal Scot' and would have been seen 'outside of Scotland as one of the strongest nationalists there has ever been' (Pollok 1997).

That said, the party's sudden conversion to legislative devolution remained generally free of overtly nationalist rhetoric. A 1975 white paper was dry and technocratic, Labour having ignored Nairn's call to build up their own 'socialist nationalism' in order to compete with the SNP's (Nairn 1981). John P. Mackintosh, meanwhile, calmly articulated the old nationalist-unionist argument about nationalist forces being channelled in either a 'destructive' or 'positive' direction. Nationalism, he had told the Commons towards the end of 1969, 'is not altogether bad':

My constituency contains the site of the last battlefield on which the Scots defeated the English, at Preston-pans, and I have a certain mild form of national pride of my own. But this does not mean that I dislike other tribes, such as the Welsh, that I have any hostile feelings towards foreigners or that I lack pride in being British. It does not mean that I am not eager to join the European Economic Community or that I am not enthusiastic for the development of the United Nations. (HC Deb 28 Oct 1969 Vol 790 c12)

Europe had replaced the British Empire as the third, supranational strand of Mackintosh's 'dual' Scottish and British identity.

During the 1970s, however, what Keating and Bleiman called a 'neo-nationalist' element in the party began to emerge, comprising long-standing Labour Home Rulers such as David Lambie (who likely believed in full independence) and a group led by Jim Sillars, who had 'been moving in an increasingly nationalist direction' since his South Ayrshire by-election victory in 1970 (Keating and Bleiman 1979: 178). In June 1973, Sillars told Tony Benn he had become a 'convinced Scottish nationalist', and four months later that he would 'become a Scottish nationalist member' if the UK stayed in Europe. Sure enough, he finally broke with Labour following the 1975 referendum (Benn 1989: 46, 73).

Sillars was fascinating in that just a few years previously he had co-authored a pamphlet with Alex Eadie entitled, somewhat hyperbolically, *Don't Butcher Scotland's Future*. This rejected the 'separatist case' (which by implication included legislative devolution), but not because 'it is emotional': 'Pride in things Scottish, and a deep desire to see our nation prosperous, happy, and buoyant, are emotions to be encouraged as they have a creative value of their own.' Rather the rejection was utilitarian, the authors advocating a Scottish Affairs committee, a two-tier system of local government (both of which transpired) and a Scottish Ombudsman committed to 'righting grievances at all levels of government both national, regional and local' (Sillars and Eadie 1968). Eight years later and Sillars had split from Labour, establishing a 'Scottish Labour Party' (a nod to Keir Hardie's pro-Home Rule 1888 forerunner) committed to the very outcome – legislative devolution – he had previously argued would 'butcher' Scotland's future. It was, admitted Sillars, the 'political death or glory option' (*Scotsman*, 10 December 1975).

Others rejected the Sillars approach while believing Ross was making a strategic mistake. Speaking at a crucial Scottish Executive meeting on 17 August 1974, Brian Wilson 'thought the party should square up to the challenge of the SNP and not run away, instead of sheltering under the umbrella of a Scottish Assembly'. He thought, added Tam Dalyell in his diarised account, that 'it would lead to the destruction of the Labour Movement' (Dalyell 2016: 48). Dalyell, like Wilson an opponent of Labour's renewed compromise with nationalism, helped form the 'Scotland Is British' group in the summer of 1976 and later published a polemic entitled *Devolution: The End of Britain?* A more sincere advocate of devolution than Ross *et al.* was Mick McGahey, who in 1978 told his mineworkers union: 'We must never allow the Nationalists to appear to be the banner of the Scottish nation. That honour truly belongs to the Labour and trade union movement' (Gibbs forthcoming).

Again, the moment passed. The decline of the SNP during 1978 was as sudden as its rise four years earlier. Labour interpreted this as a vindication of its devolution conversion, but in truth enthusiasm for constitutional change had cooled. But by this point the government, now led by James Callaghan, was committed to a Scottish Assembly it did not really want, following a post-legislative referendum which had been foisted upon them by rebellious Labour backbenchers. Nevertheless, the Scottish Labour official Helen Liddell declared in January 1978 that the party 'must get the credit for delivering devolution', and that any involvement with 'separatists' would hand a propaganda victory to the No campaign (Bochel *et al.* 1981: 17).

Interviewed by Robin Day in February 1979, the new Prime Minister believed that the fifth of Scots who supported independence would 'begin to dwindle' once the assembly was up and running. He also claimed that without the Royal Commission and other steps taken by Labour, 'then perhaps the feeling of frustration in Scotland might have made for a bigger division between Scotland and the rest of the United Kingdom' (*Panorama*, February 1979). In a pre-referendum broadcast, meanwhile, Callaghan said there was 'room for much diversity' within British sovereignty, and that a 'yes' vote would constitute 'the first and most essential step to putting an end to a controversy that has distracted politics in Scotland intermittently for a century' (Marr 2016).[8]

Labour's Third Home Rule Phase

Following the referendum in March 1979 and the fall of Callaghan's government,[9] there was no unionist interregnum or disavowal of policy as in the 1950s, but neither did Labour's devolution policy enjoy the high profile of the previous five years. After the 1979 general election, however, the Labour Party gradually moved towards a much clearer commitment to a Scottish Assembly (and later Parliament), this time with the sort of arguments and rhetoric which had accompanied its support for Home Rule in the 1920s. This was nationalist unionism redux, markedly less unionist in tone and a clear attempt to acquire some of the SNP's 'natural' support by appearing a 'credible' vehicle for self-government (Kellas 1989: 139).

The party programme of 1982 accepted 'the decision of the people of Scotland who opted for an assembly' in 1979 and reaffirmed its commitment to devolution. In February 1983, an NEC statement committed the next Labour government to the creation of a directly elected assembly with revenue-raising and industrial powers. This commitment then appeared in Labour's 'suicide note' 1983 manifesto. A former Scottish Labour Cabinet minister told the *Scotsman* that although the party would likely 'return even more MPs from Scotland', it would be out of office 'down here' (Westminster) for another decade. 'We will have to play the nationalist card in Scotland', he added. 'We will have to go for an Assembly with substantial economic power short of independence, but not much short' (*Scotsman*, 28 July 1982).

Shortly before the 1983 election, the left-wing Scottish Labour MP George Galloway also urged his party and the STUC (whose official Bill Speirs was a high-profile devolutionist) to organise 'a representative Scottish convention which would debate and agree the tactical and strategic paths the campaign for devolution should take' (*Glasgow Herald*, 1 June 1983). Meanwhile Ernie Ross, the left-wing Labour MP for Dundee West, was confident Labour could embrace, lead and shape the 'Scottish dimension' while differentiating itself from the SNP:

> The Scottish nationalism of the Labour movement has recognised the differences in social class in the community, unlike the right-wing leadership of the SNP who tend to ignore this aspect. Part of the traditional message of the Scottish labour movement has always stipulated the need and the demand for Scottish self-government to attack social inequality in Scotland – together with the view that socialism would win the argument in Scotland before it did in England. (Ross 1983: 191)

Interviewed at around the same time, John Smith cautioned that a devolution argument which 'expresses itself in such a way that it appears like disguised nationalism' was 'not likely to succeed at Westminster' (*Radical Scotland*, February–March 1983). Interviewed by Nairn and the journalist Neal Ascherson in 1981, he denied ever having 'been a nationalist' but added that as a 'Scotch lawyer' he had become 'indignant at the dismissive English view of our system', thus moving towards devolution on a 'heavily pragmatic basis'. He also professed pride in 'Scottish institutions generally' and 'the Scottish style of life', wanting his children to have their 'cultural roots' and education in Scotland, although he did not believe 'considerations of this kind' were, 'in themselves, arguments for an independent, sovereign Scottish state' (*Bulletin of Scottish Politics*, Spring 1981).

There also existed the sort of tension between the party's Scottishness and Britishness which had led to inaction on devolution in the 1920s. Gordon Brown summarised it thus:

> the real problem for Scottish Labour was that it wanted to be Scottish and British at the same time. No theorist attempted in sufficient depth to reconcile the conflicting aspirations for home rule and a British socialist advance. In particular, no one was able to show how capturing power in Britain – and legislating for minimum levels of welfare, for example, could be combined with a policy of devolution for Scotland. (Brown 1982: 527)

Labour was trying not to consider this as it foregrounded its Scottishness. Central to its developing approach was the idea of the 'Scottish mandate', and the related belief that sovereignty rested with the 'people of Scotland' rather than the UK Parliament at Westminster. This view was not new, having first arisen under the Heath government (which enjoyed the support of only twenty-three Scottish MPs) and later being taken up by the left-wing "79 Group' within the SNP.

Arguably, however, it was Scottish Labour politicians who first popularised the notion that as Mrs Thatcher's governments only had (as between 1970 and 1974) a minority of Scottish MPs, then they had 'no mandate' to govern Scotland, a legitimacy which instead rested with Scottish Labour. This was reductive, for not only were the Scottish Unionists (and allies) the only party to have achieved more than 50 per cent of the popular vote in Scotland, but Labour's Scottish majorities owed more to the vagaries of a first-past-the-post electoral system than vote share. Furthermore, it therefore followed that Labour had lacked a 'mandate' to govern England on three occasions since 1964, a point often made by Mrs Thatcher.

Leading proponents of this analysis included John Maxton (a nephew of James), John Home-Robertson, Dennis Canavan, David Marshall and George Foulkes,[10] although even the more cautious Donald Dewar claimed that a Scottish Assembly would have protected the Scottish people 'from much damaging legislation which does not reflect Scottish priorities' (*Glasgow Herald*, 1 March 1985). The journalist James Naughtie called Canavan *et al.* 'wild boys in Parliament' and described how their 'anger' led them 'dangerously close' to a position the Scottish Labour leadership believed would hand the SNP an opportunity. 'When a Scottish mandate was accepted, where was the case against separation?' asked Naughtie rhetorically. The Scottish Labour group of MPs refused to formally endorse 'no mandate', although the 'wild boys' continued to make the argument regardless (Naughtie 1989: 162).

Talk of 'no mandate' also represented an updating of the previously Liberal (and early Labour) argument that Scotland was a naturally more 'progressive' or 'socialist' nation which was being held back or, worse, over-ruled, by Conservative England. As the Labour MP Norman Hogg put it in 1987, his party defended traditions with 'roots deep in Scottish history', reflecting 'the deeply held Scottish conviction that the sick, the poor and the disabled are our collective responsibility' (*Glasgow Herald*, 2 November 1987).

Thus Labour's third Home Rule phase emerged in opposition to Thatcherism and the SNP, resuscitating some old battle cries (for example, neglect), borrowing others from its nationalist opponents and creating new ones, a 'social nationalism' which presented devolution as the means to a socially just end (Scothorne et al., 2016). This approach became particularly salient following the 1987 general election, when the Conservative Party lost all but ten of its Scottish MPs and slumped to around a quarter of the Scottish vote. Labour, on the other hand, secured fifty MPs, quickly dubbed the 'feeble fifty' by the SNP's Alex Salmond, who had resolved in the late 1970s to rob Scottish Labour of its claim to 'stand up for Scotland'.

Salmond, who took Banff and Buchan from a Conservative at that election, later recalled going to the House of Commons' TV room in order to watch England playing in the European Championships:

> Just about every Scottish Labour MP [was] there raucously cheering on the other team against England, [something] they'd [have] in common with many Scots. I remember thinking to myself, here we are, the unionist manifestation of Scotland – unionist to their fingertips – and every one of them getting their sporting thrills by vicariously hoping that somebody else would beat England. (Salmond 2018)

Days after the 1987 election, the 'feeble fifty' met in Glasgow in an attempt to rebut the SNP's charge of powerlessness. Not only did they plan a devolution Bill (à la the 1920s) but Donald Dewar, the Shadow Scottish Secretary, said he would demand the government establish an assembly, scrap the Poll Tax and suspend privatisation. If he did not obtain a 'satisfactory response' to these quixotic demands, then Labour would 'initiate a programme of action aimed at making the Government come to terms with their impossible position in Scotland' (*Financial Times*, 16 June 1987). At another gathering two months later, George Galloway declared that 'as a nation, Scotland is entitled to as much self-determination as it wants', while Bill Speirs of the STUC spoke of 'a struggle for national liberation' (*Scotsman*, 31 August 1987).

To a degree, Labour had boxed themselves in with their 'devolutionary nationalism' and talk of a 'doomsday scenario' in which the Conservatives would continue to govern Scotland without any MPs (which had not, after all, come to pass). Now the Conservatives had been re-elected for the second time, Labour MPs had to match the expectations of radical action they had themselves created. As the once-unionist *Glasgow Herald* put it, Labour now found itself 'in a sense the custodian of the devolution consensus and will be expected to advance the cause' (*Glasgow Herald*, 13 June 1987).

Inevitably, Dewar's Scotland Bill failed while, as Geekie and Levy pointed out, Labour's co-option of nationalist arguments did not stop with the 'Scottish mandate', there being a 'range of ideological preconceptions, policies and strategies which Labour has inherited from the SNP and earlier nationalist Home Rule movements'. Jack McConnell, a district councillor in Stirling, argued that Labour could show voters that 'the control over their own lives, which Scots have been deprived of for almost three centuries, can be re-established' (*Radical Scotland*, February/March 1987). Dennis Canavan argued elsewhere that the people of Scotland had not given their 'democratic consent' to the Act of Union.[11]

As Brian Wilson later reflected, the Thatcher years 'made it hopeless to argue against devolution within the Labour Party' (interview with Brian Wilson, 2 May 2016). In August 1987, Robin Cook, once an opponent of devolution but now a front-bench spokesman, urged his colleagues to set up an alternative forum to Westminster 'somewhere in Scotland, and invite the MPs of other parties to join us there and vote on the Scottish issues' (*Glasgow Herald*, 31 August 1987).[12] This built upon George Galloway's idea of a Scottish 'convention', the sort of cross-party vehicle Labour had opposed forty years earlier.

On the fringe of the 1988 Scottish Council conference, a number of younger party activists (including McConnell) established a group called 'Scottish Labour Action' (SLA) to exert devolutionary pressure – in the manner of the Young Scots Society – on Labour. They argued that the Scottish people were sovereign and that Labour had to work with other parties to prepare for Home Rule. Shortly after the SLA was formed, Murray Elder informed Charles Clarke (who worked in UK Labour leader Neil Kinnock's office) that it had been clear 'for some time that there is an increasing Nationalist tendency amongst the activist membership in Scotland' (Elder 1988a). In a similar missive to Larry Whitty, the SLA were framed as

a quasi-Nationalist organisation, highly critical of the Parliamentary leadership both at national and Scottish levels and determined to follow a course of action which would lead to making Scotland ungovernable . . . there is a great deal of frustration around and it may be that they are working a rich seam. (Elder 1988b)

Speaking in 2018, Jack (now Lord) McConnell, remembered a feeling that the SLA were 'crypto-nationalists' intent upon 'undermining the party'. 'There was more kickback from Glasgow rather than London', he recalled. 'We were basically modernisers, Kinnock supporters who wanted a more radical stance in Scotland. Although they were hostile to our constitutional position, Kinnockites liked our energy and openness to new ideas' (interview with Lord McConnell, 9 July 2018). McConnell also pointed out that Labour included a small group of 'very Scottish' people such as Sam Galbraith, Janey and Norman Buchan, whose cultural nationalism was not matched by support for legislative devolution.

As McConnell suggested, UK Labour figures were uncomfortable with the Scottish party's tactics, not least Kinnock, a high-profile opponent of Welsh devolution in the 1970s. At the 1988 Scottish conference, Kinnock had made scant reference to devolution in his speech, an omission which did not go unnoticed. But as Mitchell observed, 'Scottish Labour's more radical conference resolutions were indulgently put up with by the party leadership, and so long as the party was winning elections, it was allowed a fair degree of informal autonomy' (Mitchell 1998: 134). This informal autonomy even led to periodic talk of the Scottish party formally seceding from the UK organisation, something *The Times* claimed (in August 1987) fifteen Scottish Labour MPs were contemplating should the Conservatives secure a fourth term.

Some in the UK party, meanwhile, attempted to slot the Scottish party's devolution commitment into a more holistic decentralist agenda, à la the Scottish Unionists in the late 1940s and early 1950s. John Prescott's *Alternative Regional Strategy* (1982) tackled England, while Alistair Darling later pursued a quasi-federal agenda of devolution-all-round for the nations and regions of the UK. But Labour's third Home Rule phase experienced a crisis in November 1988 when Jim Sillars – who had finally defected to the SNP in the early 1980s – won a by-election in Govan. Geekie and Levy were scathing, observing that like Dr Frankenstein, 'Labour politicians in Scotland have created a monster which now threatens to run completely out of control' (Geekie and Levy 1989). Speaking in 2018, Lord McConnell agreed there was 'a danger' in Labour's deployment of the no-mandate argument: 'It was certainly a position that nationalists could easily build upon' (interview with Lord McConnell, 9 July 2018).

Writing in the wake of the Govan result, Geekie and Levy were guilty of exaggerating the dangers faced by Labour, including the prospect of reversion, SNP-like, to 'nationalist fundamentalism'. The 'tartanisation' thesis also virtually ignored the party's earlier Home Rule phases, their analysis predicated upon a devolutionary nationalism having appeared out of nowhere. They also attempted to crowbar their narrative into Hechter's problematic theory of 'internal colonialism', positing that Labour had become a 'repository of Scottish nationalism' after a long 'centralist' phase, bolstered by 'ethnic cleavages' represented by 'segmented' professions such as lawyers, journalists and teachers in Scotland (Geekie and Levy 1989).

Following Govan – after which Jim Sillars said he would seek common ground with the 'nationalist wing of the Labour Party' – Donald Dewar fully embraced the idea of a cross-party Scottish Constitutional Convention (SCC), joking about the 'people' having to 'live a little dangerously in order to achieve what they want' (*Scotsman*, 22 October 1988). Some continued to have reservations. The Scottish Labour MEP David Martin said the SCC had to be 'about increased democracy and not independence' (Martin 1989: 85), although George Foulkes believed there was 'a socialist case, a nationalist case, an efficiency argument and an historical claim' for devolution (Foulkes 1989: 68–9). This, however, implied the status quo was somehow undemocratic. An SLA publication entitled *Proposals for Scottish Democracy* spoke of 'winning democracy for Scotland', as if it was governed by a totalitarian regime (SLA 1989: 3). Whatever the argument, Labour benefited from its involvement in the SCC. 'The party was not now seen, as had been the case in the 1970s,' judged Hutchison, 'to be endorsing Home Rule merely as a response – made under pressure and with marked reluctance – to political exigencies' (Hutchison 2001: 151).

The political battle then moved on to the Poll Tax, which, as Lord McConnell recalled, was 'tactical and ideological rather than constitutional', although at the same time it 'highlighted the no-mandate argument, and the [UK Labour] leadership couldn't accept it on that basis' (interview with Lord McConnell, 9 July 2018). Dewar also attempted, rather clumsily, to co-opt the SNP's new 'independence in Europe' slogan, framing devolution as 'independence in the United Kingdom'. Visiting Scotland, the English Labour MP Gerald Kaufman was scathing of such language, unaware it had been sanctioned by Dewar: 'It seems to be an irrelevant fantasy.' Scottish Secretary Malcolm Rifkind quoted this remark during a Commons debate on 'Scotland in Europe', adding that the idea of 'independence in the United Kingdom' was even 'more absurd than independence in Europe' (HC Deb 28 June 1989 Vol 155 c999).

At the Scottish Constitutional Convention, meanwhile, Canon Kenyon Wright protested that what they were doing was 'no narrow nationalism'; they had 'no interest in a little Scotland' (*Scottish Review*, 17 January 2017). This was the age-old separation between good and bad nationalism, Wright clearly considering the strikingly nationalist language of the 'Claim of Right', with its reference to 'the sovereign right of the Scottish people to determine the form of Government best suited to their needs', to be the positive variety.[13] The SNP, however, continued to poll well ahead of the 1992 general election, with one survey even showing majority support for independence. Strathclyde councillor Charles Gray's gloomy prognosis was that if Labour lost another election then 'young people ... might spearhead a breakaway from the Labour movement. I believe the Scottish people would be galvanised into some kind of active resentment' (*The Economist*, 6 April 1991).

Similarly gloomy was Dewar, with whom Tom Harris (later a Scottish Labour MP) recalled discussing the idea that pressure for independence would increase now that the Conservatives had secured a fourth consecutive term. 'Perhaps they're right', was Dewar's response (interview with Tom Harris, 7 August 2017), hinting at a 'conditional' unionism shared by some Conservatives and especially Ulster Unionists (see Chapter 10). At the same time, McLean argues that Dewar subsequently insisted on proportional representation for any devolved parliament as his way of protecting the union by depriving the SNP of a majority: 'He was a cultural nationalist but a political unionist' (McLean and McMillan 2005: 242).

When the new UK Labour leader Tony Blair announced that a future government would hold a pre-legislative referendum before establishing a Scottish Parliament, some nationalists feared backsliding. Actually the goal was to fashion a mandate that could not be resisted by Parliament (specifically the House of Lords), although the broader strategic aim, naturally, was keeping the SNP under control. 'A Scottish Parliament inside and strengthening the United Kingdom would kill the SNP', declared Shadow Scottish Secretary George Robertson, 'because the majority of people in Scotland want control over their own lives, over domestic affairs, but they don't want to wrench Scotland out of the United Kingdom' (Marr 2016).

During the referendum itself, Dewar went out of his way to involve Alex Salmond, whose party had withdrawn from the SCC and formally opposed legislative devolution since the late 1970s (along with the Scottish Conservatives). In Brian Wilson's view:

> The huge mistake, driven by Brown, was to invite Salmond into the tent from which they had excluded themselves – driven by paranoia that without them, there was the risk of losing. The first I knew of this was when I woke up to a *Daily Record* front page picture of Brown (or maybe Dewar) posing with Salmond in front of the Forth Bridge. From that moment, it was impossible to draw a line between devolution and independence with any credibility. (Interview with Brian Wilson, 28 July 2018)

The day after the affirmative referendum result, Blair reflected that Labour 'must get the message out loud and clear that there must be no pandering to nationalism, and we must stress that it's good for the UK, not just for Scotland' (Campbell 2011a: 148). 'A Nation Again' was the *Scotsman's* headline on 12 September 1997, the implication being that Scotland had somehow lacked nationhood before the majority yes/yes vote, something that would have been rejected by any self-respecting nationalist unionist over the past century.

Scottish Politics vs Identity Politics

There followed a change of tack from Scottish Labour. In a pamphlet entitled *New Scotland, New Britain*, Gordon Brown and Douglas Alexander argued that the real battle at the first Scottish Parliament elections in 1999 would

> be between those who put the politics of social justice first, and those who practice the politics of national identity above and before anything else. There is and always has been more to Scottish politics than identity politics. Solidarity – and working together – offers Scotland more than separation – and splitting ourselves apart. That is why a politics based on the expansive vision of social justice will defeat the narrow divisiveness of Nationalism. (Brown and Alexander 1999: 47)

'The decision the Scottish people will make is whether this election will be remembered as Devolution Day or Divorce Day', declared Blair, adding that in Scotland, his party was 'confirming that New Labour's values are Scotland's values' (*Herald*, 6 February 1999). As Gerry Hassan later observed, for those like him who had 'grown up with Scottish Labour's championing of the Scottish dimension in the 1980s, this new bold strategy at the time came as a bit of a shock: a hard, abrasive, populist anti-Scottish Nationalist message' (Hassan and Shaw 2012: 96). The late Willie Ross would have been proud.

Although Labour won the election, the campaign itself was fraught, with Dewar reportedly calling the *Herald* 'an out and out nationalist newspaper' (Ritchie 2000: 91). But now that Scotland was, to quote the *Scotsman*, 'a nation again', what was the purpose of the Scottish Labour Party?[14] As Dewar remarked to Steven Purcell, a young Glasgow councillor, a few months after the first elections: 'Whoever gets to the flag first, it is their values that will dominate this new Scotland' (*Herald*, 30 December 2016). Thereafter, Scottish Labour was locked in a battle with the SNP over who was best placed to 'stand up for Scotland'. Alex Salmond *et al.* did not get to the flag first, but it was clearly within their sights.

Henry McLeish, briefly First Minister following the untimely death of Dewar in 2000, realised this, floating the idea of changing the Scottish Executive's name to 'Scottish Government' and diverging from UK Labour policy by backing free personal care for the elderly. His reward was a series of dismissive briefings from Westminster colleagues who, feeling the loss of status as a consequence of devolution, quickly turned against the 'Scottish dimension'. Although it had long been harder to promote nationalist unionism in government rather than opposition, McLeish had at least tried.

Jack McConnell, First Minister between 2001 and 2007, had solid nationalist-unionist credentials as a leading light in Scottish Labour Action. Indeed, Gordon Brown (Chancellor during the same period) worried that 'Jack would flirt with neo-nationalism' (Campbell 2011b: 430). He certainly pursued greater differentiation – a bespoke Scottish immigration policy and international aid for Malawi – but after 2004 proved unable to match Alex Salmond and Nicola Sturgeon's upbeat mood music about the need for a change of government and, ultimately, independence. Some came to view the UK Labour Party's role in the 2007 Holyrood election as unhelpful, an indication that 'London Labour', as they were branded by the SNP, would only allow John Smith House in Glasgow so much autonomy.

Another new Scottish Labour leader, fellow SLA veteran Wendy Alexander, also attempted to define lines between Labour and the SNP now the latter was in government:

> Scotland is a country I love to the core of my being. However, 'Scotland' is not a political philosophy. 'Scotland' can just as easily be Adam Smith as it can be John Smith. The world over, politics comes down to a choice: right versus left, conservatives versus progressives, nationalists versus internationalists. (Alexander 2008)

'For most of our history Scots felt they could be both patriotic and unionist', Alexander had observed the previous year. 'That need not change' (Alexander 2007). She then initiated and supported greater powers for the Scottish Parliament via the Calman Commission, a tried-and-tested nationalist-unionist approach, but the Overton window of acceptable constitutional discourse was gradually shifting, the SNP having successfully neutralised voter concerns over independence by committing to a referendum. Alexander also challenged the SNP to 'bring it on', suggesting that Westminster would sanction such a plebiscite. Although essentially the strategy later pursued by David Cameron, Gordon Brown – Prime Minister since 2007 – blinked and Alexander's kite came crashing down, as would Brown's later attempts to rekindle a sense of Britishness.

Polls had long shown substantial (though minority) support among Scottish Labour supporters for independence, although this had been 'hidden' by the party's devolutionary nationalism of the 1980s and 1990s. But during the 2012–14 referendum campaign, in which a central part of the Yes campaign's strategy was peeling these voters away with promises of 'social justice', they were pushed into choosing between that vision and their traditional party allegiance. Brian Wilson protested that this 'utilitarian nationalism' was a 'pose' to cover up what was actually 'existential nationalism' (*Scotsman*, 5 December 2012); asked by the *New Statesman* if the SNP's was 'blood-and-soil nationalism', Better Together's Alistair Darling replied: 'at heart' (BBC News online, 11 June 2014). Labour had long pushed its opponents' nationalism to the periphery.

Labour, ironically, began to appear hostile to the Scottish Parliament it had delivered only fifteen years earlier, neither 'comfortable unionists', in the words of MSP Anas Sarwar, nor 'comfortable nationalists' (*Sunday Politics Scotland*, 8 May 2016). Instead the party promised that Scotland could have the 'best of both worlds' if it remained part of the UK. Even so, Scottish Labour struggled to make a cogent, left-of-centre argument for the status quo, although Brown's *My Scotland, Our Britain: A Future Worth Sharing* (2014) did articulate a welfare unionism based upon 'pooling and sharing', something also expounded in a series of well-received eve-of-referendum speeches.

At the 2015 general election, meanwhile, the 'smouldering pile' Arthur Woodburn had identified in 1947 produced a remarkable fifty-six SNP MPs. Scottish Labour – since the 1960s the party perceived as best placed to 'stand up for Scotland' at Westminster – elected just one. UK Labour – led since 2015 by Jeremy Corbyn – tried to re-anchor its philosophy in class politics rather than the constitution but it too had become a victim of its own success and political framing.

Conclusion

Labour's first-phase nationalist unionism naturally took a different form from that of Scottish Unionists and Scottish Liberals, although it borrowed heavily from the latter: support for 'Home Rule' within the British Empire and a recalibrated United Kingdom, together with the idea that 'radical' or 'progressive' Scotland was being held back by 'Tory' England. Later, however, it came to resemble that of the Scottish Unionists, support for 'administrative devolution' with a helping hand from Burns, Wallace and Bruce.

Labour's second phase also owed something to Scottish Unionists in co-opting some of its attack lines from the late 1940s and early 1950s, i.e.

the idea that Labour 'neglected' the justifiable 'grievances' of Scotland. By the 1960s this had been infused with the 'welfare unionism' begun by the Liberals in the 1910s and completed by Attlee in the 1940s. And like the Conservatives, Labour came to conflate party and nation, claiming that only it truly 'stood up for Scotland'. Its reward in 1966 was the sort of electoral hegemony enjoyed by Unionists only a decade earlier.

The third phase combined the first and second in reviving support for legislative devolution while pitching it to voters with purposeful moral force and familiar mythology relating to Scotland's 'distinct' (and it was posited) superior political culture, not to mention its institutional autonomy, which needed defending from the 'anti-Scottish' actions of 'alien' Conservative governments at Westminster. But just as Scottish Unionists had created trouble for themselves by framing Scottish political discourse in such a way, so too did the Labour Party during the 1980s and 1990s. Geekie and Levy spoke of it having created a Frankenstein's Monster, which would one day turn on its creator. The inevitable corollary of 'standing up for Scotland' was the accusation of 'talking Scotland down', to which Labour fell prey.

Like other unionist parties, Labour's nationalist unionism drew heavily on the myths and symbols from the pre-modern era, while it consistently pushed the 'extreme' nationalism of its chief opponents (the SNP) to the periphery, most tribally after the 1960s. And like the UK Conservative Party, Labour had its own 'territorial code', although this was applied inconsistently: in 1958, the 'centre' informed the 'periphery' that its historic commitment to Home Rule had been abandoned; in 1974, Harold Wilson instructed the party's Scottish Council to reverse its position and support legislative devolution. In the 1980s, meanwhile, Transport House tolerated 'crypto-nationalism' in Scotland as long as it kept the SNP at bay.

EIGHT

The SNP and 'Five Continuing Unions'

In July 2013, the then SNP leader and First Minister Alex Salmond told workers at the Nigg Fabrication Yard that Scotland's 'political and economic union' with England had to be changed 'as a matter of urgency'. He continued:

> But this union is one of SIX UNIONS that govern our lives today in Scotland. *My contention is that we can choose to keep five of these six unions* – with some differences certainly but still basically intact. Indeed we can embrace them in that spirit of interdependence that Saltoun recognised all those years ago, while using the powers of independence to renew and improve them.

Salmond listed these 'five unions' as:

> The European Union
> The Defence Union through NATO
> The Currency Union
> The union of the crowns
> And finally the Social Union between the peoples of these islands.
>   (Salmond 2013)[1]

As the journalist Alf Young joked, Salmond's willingness to preserve five out of these six unions meant that, by his own admission, he was 'five-sixths a unionist' (*Scotsman*, 27 July 2013). Just as nationalism was not the exclusive preserve of those who advocated full independence for Scotland, nor was unionism restricted to opponents of that independence. 'Home Rule' had always been, as Kidd observed, 'an ambiguous formulation, capable of encompassing devolution, devo-max, federalism and independence' (Kidd 2019: 224).

Rudolph and Thompson identified a range of options for territorially motivated groups, with only the most radical seeking 'a new independent state'

(Rudolph and Thompson 1985: 224–5), while Brown Swan and McEwen identified two 'ideal types', 'independence as separation' and 'embedded independence', the latter being 'a form of self-government which aspires to statehood, but sees that state embedded in transnational economic, political and institutional networks, including with the state from which independence is sought' (Brown Swan and McEwen forthcoming).

Strikingly, as the SNP grew electorally, so too did its unionism. Just as supporters of the Union co-opted nationalist rhetoric in order to harness Scottish sentiment, the SNP borrowed from unionist discourse in order to win over those opposed to independence, embracing 'the language of union, partly as a form of reassurance against accusations of separatism, but also to place their project in a broader context' (Keating 2009: 99). This chapter is thematic rather than chronological, examining Salmond's 'five unions' following an initial discussion of the party's imperialist origins.

Independence in the Empire

As Finlay (1994) has shown, pre-1945 Scottish nationalism was divided between pro- and anti-imperialist positions. In fact, he identified three groups, those who rejected the British Empire as hostile to Scottish interests (i.e. the Scots National League); those who saw Scotland taking its place alongside other self-governing Dominions in the commonwealth; and those who 'advocated Scottish nationalism primarily as a complementary factor to a wider and more all-embracing British nationalism' (Finlay 1992: 185).

Indeed, the newly formed Scottish National Party in 1934 included a large grouping of what Kidd called 'frustrated, reforming imperialists who wanted a properly British, or Anglo-Scottish empire' (Kidd 2019: 225). In this respect, the early SNP could be viewed as reforming unionists rather than the 'extreme' nationalists depicted by its Unionist and Labour opponents. This conception of 'Home Rule' had its origins in the Scottish Home Rule Association, which envisaged 'self-government' within the British Empire. Scotland, it was posited, would take its place alongside Canada, Australia and the Irish Free State at the League of Nations, while also attending Imperial Conferences.

This continuing connection to 'the Crown' was important to early Home Rulers and some nascent SNPers for it enabled them to refute their opponents' charge of 'separatism' (the European Union would later fulfil a similar role). A related argument was also familiar, a desire to ease the 'burden' of business at Westminster, rendering the 'Imperial Parliament' more 'efficient' in the process. As noted in Chapter 3, this argument enjoyed particular traction among a group of Scottish Unionists who found themselves increasingly frustrated with their party's stance vis-à-vis legislative devolution.

Particularly prominent in this respect was the Scots lawyer and occasional Unionist candidate Andrew Dewar Gibb. During the mid- to late 1920s, he came to believe that Scotland had been ill-served by the Union of 1707. He envisaged 'a close alliance – a *Bund* of two sovereign states [Scotland and England], each with a Parliament; each with an Executive', separate consular and diplomatic representation and 'full control of the national purse'. Above that, however, there would continue to be joint relationships for foreign affairs, colonial matters, defence and customs. Even an 'ultimately independent Scotland', concluded Dewar Gibb, had to be 'preserved' as 'a Mother-nation of the Empire' at 'all costs' (Dewar Gibb 1930c: 184–7).

The two parties which merged to form the SNP in 1934 captured different visions of what might be termed 'independence in the empire'. The National Party of Scotland (formed in 1928) said its policy was 'independence' within the British Empire; Sir Compton Mackenzie wrote of a 'Celtic federation of independent but interdependent states', with national rejuvenation only possible 'when we have a Scottish Free State under the Crown' (Mackenzie 1967: 139). The Scottish (Self-Government) Party (formed in 1930), meanwhile, objected to the National Party's socialism, pan-Celticism and cultural nationalism; Scottish nationalism and a Scottish Parliament were seen as a means to an end, the end being a stronger British Empire administered by a true Anglo-Scottish partnership. The Duke of Montrose spoke of Scotland playing 'her part with pride as an Empire builder enveloped in the robe of nationality', which to Finlay illustrated 'how clearly their Scottish nationalism was a subsection of a wider, and more dominating, British nationalism' (Finlay 1994: 132–3).

Ironically, therefore, the early SNP – later viewed as an unequivocal advocate of full independence – generally eschewed language like 'national sovereignty' and 'independence'. Rather it was more in line with previous Home Rule movements 'in that self-government was firmly placed within the context of the continuation of some form of overall British government' (Finlay 1994: 154). There was to be no 'separatism' here. As Mitchell observed, the party's goal was 'deliberately kept vague in order to bridge the divide between the moderate aspirations of those who wanted a Scottish Parliament with[in] the United Kingdom and those who sought to sever all political links with England' (Mitchell 1996: 183).

Speaking at the SNP's inaugural meeting at Glasgow's St Andrew's Halls, the former Liberal Home Ruler Sir Alexander MacEwen explained the new party's objective of 'self-government for Scotland on a basis which will enable Scotland, as a partner in the British Empire with the same status as

England, to develop its national life to the fullest advantage' (*Scotsman*, 8 April 1934). The following year, the Duke of Montrose instigated a visit to the Irish Free State, Northern Ireland and the Isle of Man in order to study their forms of self-government and further neutralise the separatist charge. The publication arising from this trip stated that

> (2) Scotland shall share with England the rights and responsibility they as Mother Nations have jointly created and incurred within the British Empire. (3) Machinery shall be set up whereby Scotland with the other British Nations shall deal jointly with such responsibilities and in particular with such matters as Defence, Foreign Policy and Customs. (SNP 1935: 30–1)

The SNP's imperial unionism, however, proved short-lived, for at its annual conference in May 1936 the party's objective was amended to 'Self-government for Scotland', with all subsidiary clauses concerning the empire and Commonwealth removed (Finlay 1994: 188). Ironically, this change occurred just as Andrew Dewar Gibb succeeded Sir Alexander MacEwen as leader of the party. His 1937 book, *Scottish Empire*, acknowledged that the 1931 Statute of Westminster meant 'nothing remains to be done' in terms of empire building, although it added presciently that with Scotland's

> imperial task ended, she will seek to form and to justify a new conception of her function in the framework of European civilization. If so, she will embark upon her undertaking with the knowledge that in every corner of the world her sons have shewn themselves no less fit to rule than any of the imperial peoples since time began. (Dewar Gibb 1937: 314–15)

Even beyond the SNP's increasing 'separatism', Dewar Gibb found his party's anti-Toryism distasteful. He resigned as chairman in 1940, although even at the 1945 general election he considered standing as an 'Independent Conservative or Scottish Independent or Scottish Conservative' (Dewar Gibb 1945).

In 1942, meanwhile, the SNP split over the question of independence, with John MacCormick leaving to form the devolutionist Scottish Convention. At this point, the party abandoned any talk of devolution, federalism or cross-party conventions, although it did not quite relinquish the idea of Dominion status. The SNP leader Douglas Young (whom MacCormick regarded as a dangerous radical) spoke warmly of federalism, Dominion status and, prior to leaving the party (he had remained a member of the Labour Party), 'a freely associated community of self-governing states' with 'equal sovereign status' for Scotland and Wales within the metropole (Young 1947: 16).

A neglected publication from 1956, *Our Three Nations*, jointly sponsored by Plaid Cymru, the SNP and the (English) Common Wealth Party, returned to this theme, advocating what it called 'Confraternity' of 'free and equal nations within the wider Commonwealth'. It examined how the 'nations of the British Isles' could 'dissolve into self-governing units' without disturbing the 'economic integration' from which they had all benefited. It also asserted that Scotland would

> be prepared to go as far as the other nations [England, Wales and Northern Ireland] in giving up some of her powers of national sovereignty for the common weal but she will not agree to any arrangement by which she is required to give up more than the other nations and accept a less sovereign status than any other nation in the confraternity. (SNP 1956: 46)

Robert McIntyre, the SNP's first MP following a 1945 by-election, told Sir John Boyd Orr, who he hoped would contribute a foreword, that it constituted a 'plea for decentralisation in the United Kingdom, and for Scottish and Welsh Parliaments', stressing 'the federal solution to the problem' (McIntyre 1955).

A forum through which different parts of the British Isles could deal with common interests was another running theme of SNP thinking. The old National Party of Scotland had spoken of a 'British Council' (Black c. 1933: 32), an idea revived by the SNP as an 'Association of States of the British Isles' in the 1970s. This perhaps explains why the later British–Irish Council – a product of the 1998 Good Friday Agreement – was enthusiastically embraced by the SNP in government after 2007, despite having been contrived by the Ulster Unionist leader David Trimble as a unionist counterweight to the North–South Ministerial Council.

SNP figures also continued to reject the 'separatist' charge. Writing in 1976, party veteran Arthur Donaldson argued that devolution was 'itself separation', while Scots Law and education had long been 'separate'. 'We are thus all separatists in large or small degree in Scotland', he added, offering the term 'equalist' as an alternative (Donaldson 1976). Billy Wolfe, the SNP's leader during its electoral breakthrough in the late 1960s and mid-1970s, even argued that the SNP 'need not be so obviously nationalist' on the basis that 'about 90% of the people of Scotland were already nationalist and did not require to be made particularly conscious of the fact' (Wolfe 1973: 83).

Much of the SNP's unionism – and indeed Alex Salmond's 'five continuing unions' – can be understood in terms of the gradualist/fundamentalist divide in the party before 1999. Gradualists were content to pursue their constitutional goals from within the unionist status quo, viewing devolution as a unionist means to a nationalist end, a stepping stone, as some put it, to independence. This gradualism therefore informed approaches to the monarchy, NATO and the European Union, all of which could constitute a prophylactic against charges of 'separatism'. Fundamentalists generally disagreed, seeing devolution as a unionist 'trap', particularly following SNP support for Labour's proposed Scottish Assembly in the 1970s. They desired full sovereignty in the nineteenth-century sense, what the 79 Group (of which Salmond had been a member) termed a 'Scottish Socialist Republic'.

But gradualism was not a wholly reliable guide in this respect. Throughout the 1980s and 1990s, the SNP's formal position was 'independence, nothing less', despite the support of prominent figures like Alex Salmond for devolution (members of the 79 Group were usually gradualist). In the late 1980s, the party also refrained from signing the strikingly nationalistic Claim of Right, which asserted the 'self-determination' of the 'Scottish people', or joining the Scottish Constitutional Convention on the grounds that it would not consider independence as an option.

In 1997, however, Salmond joined two unionist parties (Labour and the Liberal Democrats) under the 'Scotland Forward' banner in order to campaign for a devolved Scottish Parliament within the UK – the very aim that had taken John MacCormick out of the SNP back in 1942. While Donald Dewar and Jim Wallace argued that devolution would strengthen the union, Salmond believed it would gradually weaken it.[2] And even once the gradualist/fundamentalist split was largely removed by the existence of a primary law-making parliament in Edinburgh, Salmond retained something of his earlier caution, arguing (even as he negotiated the terms of an independence referendum with the UK government) that Scots might be asked about 'devo-max' in a multi-option plebiscite, a unionist 'third way' which would have retained the 'political union' most in the SNP wanted to end (Torrance 2015).[3]

Independence in Europe?

As Dewar Gibb had predicted in 1937, the evolution of the British Empire would lead Scotland and the SNP to consider a European rather than imperial supranational framework. What one academic called the 'Europeanisation' of the SNP, however, was a gradual process. There had been some enthusiasm for European co-operation in the late 1940s and early 1950s (see Pittock 2001: 126), but the party turned against the idea of a centralised Common Market in the 1960s. In his memoirs, Wolfe noted that the SNP had become 'identified in Scotland as the leading anti-E.E.C. organisation' Wolfe 1973: 97–8).

In 1972, the party opposed the UK's accession to the European Economic Community and urged a 'no' vote to continuing membership at the 1975 referendum. The party's Westminster leader said the EEC represented 'everything that our party has fought against: centralisation, undemocratic procedures, power politics and a fetish for abolishing cultural differences' (Lynch 1996: 35). The St Andrews speeches of a young Alex Salmond were similarly hyperbolic (Torrance 2015), while Winnie Ewing warned that a 'yes' vote in the referendum would clear the way for 'the further takeover of Scottish land by foreigners . . . and for Brussels to dictate the final ruin of fishing and agriculture' (*Scotsman*, 7 February 1979).

But when a majority of Scots voted in favour of continuing membership, the SNP gradually shifted to a more pro-European position. Usefully, those in favour of the EEC bridged the gradualist–fundamentalist divide on the independence question, thus it became viewed as a means of building internal unity while simultaneously combatting Labour's charges of 'separatism' or 'little Scotlandism'. After some debate in 1986, the SNP's National Council agreed that the Single European Act was compatible with Scottish independence (Lynch 2013: 198).

Important in this respect was the former Labour unionist Jim Sillars, who had joined the SNP in the early 1980s. A 1988 pamphlet entitled *No Turning Back* promoted what he called 'internal independence', arguing that 'Like it or not, we are in the European Community'. And on the 'separatist' charge from political opponents:

> It is the label which Unionist parties stuck upon the SNP as it rose to prominence in the 1960s and 1970s. The SNP was never able to overcome the problem. It was forced into ever more sophisticated rebuttals of the separatist charge, but in a sense the more it explained, the more convincing the label appeared.

Sillars went on to warn of a 'double separatist' charge if the SNP remained opposed to membership of a necessarily 'decentralised' EEC, urging it to reject the 'narrow nationalism' of British political Eurosceptics in favour of 'Scottish internationalism', an interesting attempt to reverse the long-standing unionist distinction between 'good' and 'bad' nationalism (Sillars 1988: 1–9).

During a Commons debate on 'Scotland in Europe' in 1989, the then Scottish Secretary Malcolm Rifkind asked whether this change of heart on EEC membership had been 'brought about by conviction or by opportunism':

> If, as a matter of principle, the hon. Gentleman [Sillars] believes that Scotland's membership of the United Kingdom after 250 years is fundamentally against Scotland's interests and that it is right and proper, as a matter of principle, to

campaign for the dissolution of the United Kingdom, why is he so willing to accept that after a mere 16 years, his position of principle has ceased to be relevant and that he must accept, however reluctantly, that Scotland should be in the Community? (HC Debs 28 Jun 1989 Vol 155 cc995–6)

The SNP's tilt towards Europe was not without contradictions, but in 1988 the 'independence in Europe' policy and slogan was formally adopted by the SNP a year after, as Pittock observed, 'a General Election fought [by the SNP] on a vigorously anti-EEC ticket' (Pittock 2001: 126). But by the early 1990s, as Dardanelli has written, the SNP mainstream 'perceived the European Union as a political system facilitating the achievement of the party's goal of Scottish independence whereas in the 1970s the EU was seen as placing additional constraints' (Dardanelli 2003).

Nationalist discourse began to portray what was now the European Union as a confederal union of independent member states in contrast with the unitary, centralised UK state. The SNP also made much of the fact that the institutional structure of the EU was favourable to small countries via the rotating council presidency, commissioners and in terms of voting rights, while Jacques Delors' vision of 'subsidiarity' within a 'Social Europe' was perceived as sympathetic to the SNP's goals, ideologically as well as constitutionally.

All this necessitated a revision of the SNP's understanding of national sovereignty, which 'ceased to be conceptualised as a monolithic, zero-sum entity' and was instead seen as something which 'could be pooled or vertically segmented without relinquishing it'. As Dardanelli also observed, the SNP ignored the contradictions that flowed from this, not least 'that the process of integration itself had the potential to run counter to nationalist aspirations' (Dardanelli 2003). The EU, after all, was committed to 'ever closer union'. Unwillingness to accept these contradictions led some anti-Europeans in the SNP to form the short-lived 'Scottish Sovereignty Movement' shortly after the policy shift.

Over the next decade or so, the SNP advanced a 'rigorously critical view of excessive Euro-enthusiasm, and creeping integrationism', adding that it had 'a robust view of the need to set clear limits to what can properly be done at the all-Europe level and what must be retained by the states and their regions in accordance with subsidiarity' (SNP 2001: 1–2). Most notably it opposed the Common Fisheries Policy, while in 2004 Kenny MacAskill observed that while still 'valid', the 'independence in Europe' aim had 'to be updated to take account of the new EU that has evolved. Opposition to a super state must be made clear but co-operation for a social and economic union must be championed' (MacAskill 2004: 67). But as Lynch (1996) and Mitchell pointed out, the party 'failed to take account of momentous changes taking place in the European Union' (Mitchell 2019). These contradictions never really went away, surfacing during the 2014 independence referendum and following the 2016 European vote.[4]

Defence Unionism

What of Alex Salmond's second union, the 'Defence Union through NATO'? On this, the 1992 SNP manifesto asserted that an independent Scotland would

> inherit the Treaty obligations of NATO membership but membership of a nuclear weapons-based system is inconsistent with the SNP non-nuclear defence policy. As long as NATO strategy remains based on nuclear deterrence the SNP will negotiate to disengage from the NATO command structure in a manner which does not destabilise the defence interests either of Scotland or of Europe. (SNP 1992: 9–10)

As the manifesto suggested, membership of NATO had long been viewed in the context of the SNP's opposition to nuclear weapons. Until the 1940s, the party had advocated sharing defence responsibilities with 'England', but this stance had been forced to evolve when the UK became a founding member of NATO in 1949, thus relinquishing a degree of sovereignty over defence policy.

The 1961 SNP conference expressed opposition to Polaris but reaffirmed support for membership of NATO, while three years later it envisaged 'Joint Defence Forces within the UK, to maintain NATO cover, while Scottish services are established' (SNP 1964). By the early 1980s, however, the party had hardened its position against both Trident and NATO. Although Gordon Wilson, SNP leader after 1979, attempted to reverse this position, he failed, while his successors basically 'left the issue alone', delaying discussion of the 'external support system in which an independent Scotland should operate'. Later, Mitchell et al.'s membership study found that more than half the SNP's members regarded NATO membership as in Scotland's interests. Few, however, felt very strongly about it (Mitchell et al. 2012: 30, 117, 130). There was some modest movement in the 1990s, when the party supported the 'Partnership for Peace' programme, which allowed non-NATO countries to develop a bespoke bilateral relationship with the organisation.

Only in 2012 did Alex Salmond move to change his party's stance on NATO, largely in order to close down a likely line of opposition attack ahead of the independence referendum. A lengthy debate at that year's party conference considered the issue purely in tactical terms; no one argued for the merits of NATO membership in and of itself, while Salmond squared the circle vis-à-vis remaining SNP opposition to nuclear weapons. 'Twenty-six out of the 29 countries in NATO are non-nuclear countries,' he argued, 'it is perfectly feasible for Scotland to be one of these but still engage in collective defence for friends and allies' (BBC News online, 19 October 2012). Delegates narrowly backed the leadership, although two of the SNP's MSPs later resigned, unable to reconcile membership of a nuclear-backed alliance with their opposition to Trident (Lynch 2013: 279).

Even beyond the question of NATO, on several occasions the SNP aligned itself with UK foreign and defence policy, a product of what Pittock called a 'strain of patriot unionism' present since the party's creation (Pittock 2001: 95). In the early 1980s it supported military action to retake the Falkland Islands (SNP MP Donald Stewart's Western Isles constituency had strong links with the British Overseas Territory), and also military engagement in the Gulf, Afghanistan and Libya, although not, famously, in Kosovo or Iraq. In the 1990s, the SNP also supported the 'save our Scottish Regiments' campaign (Pittock 2001: 12), an echo of Conservative George Younger's campaign in the late 1960s, later hinting that Scottish troops could continue to form part of the 'British' Army even after independence (*Herald*, 16 January 2008).

'It's Scotland's Pound Too'

Mitchell *et al.* also found 'no support for a separate Scottish currency' in their survey of SNP members (Mitchell *et al.* 2012: 122). The precise evolution of the SNP's currency policy is difficult to chart, largely because it has changed so often. In the 1970s, the party was clear that an independent Scotland would require an independent central bank in order to manage a 'Scottish pound', which was expected to gain strength against the English pound because of North Sea oil (SNP 1977). This remained its position for some time, Alex Salmond telling George Robertson in 1995 that Scotland should have 'a first-class currency like everyone else and not a second-class sterling as we have just now' (Salmond 1995).

A change appears to have occurred in 2005, when a policy paper stated that an independent Scotland's currency would 'continue to be sterling until such time as Parliament decides to change that position' (SNP 2005). Confusingly, however, Salmond continued to criticise sterling and talk up Euro membership. In 2009 he told a Catalan journalist that sterling was 'sinking like a stone' (Press Association, 7 January 2009). The Scottish Government's *Your Scotland, Your Voice* paper, meanwhile, said Scotland would continue to 'operate within the sterling system' until 'a decision to join the euro by the people of Scotland in a referendum when the economic conditions were right' (Scottish Government 2009: 31). After the eurozone crisis, however, sterling came to the fore (Keating 2017: 70–1).

As with the party's stance on NATO, the SNP's currency unionism was only fully articulated prior to the 2014 independence referendum. The 2013 independence white paper proclaimed that the pound was 'Scotland's currency just as much as it is the rest of the UK's' (Scottish Government 2013), while Salmond stressed that the Bank of England had been founded by a Scot and, despite its name, was a nationalised shared asset.

The Scottish Government's Fiscal Commission examined four currency options – sterling (pegged), sterling (flexible), a Scottish currency and membership of the Euro – but recommended 'retaining Sterling as part of a formal monetary union'. The white paper went on to highlight why this would be in 'both Scotland and the UK's interests':

1. the UK is Scotland's principal trading partner accounting for 2/3 of exports in 2011 . . .
2. there is clear evidence of companies operating in Scotland and the UK with complex cross-border supply chains
3. a high degree of labour mobility – helped by transport links, culture and language
4. on key measurements of an optimal currency area, the Scottish and UK economies score well – for example, similar levels of productivity
5. evidence of economic cycles shows that while there have been periods of temporary divergence, there is a relatively high degree of synchronicity in short-term economic trends. (Scottish Government 2013)

This was detailed currency unionism, the principles of which, ironically, reflected standard unionist critiques of Scottish independence, although that did not stop the pro-union UK government rejecting the pro-independence SNP's proposed monetary union (the Governor of the Bank of England was more positive, but warned of significant constraints on an independent Scotland's freedom of action). Ironically, the SNP found itself arguing in favour of a currency belonging to a union it wanted to leave (the UK), while rejecting the currency of another union it wanted to remain part of (the EU).

Elizabeth, Queen of Scots

More consistent was the SNP's position on Alex Salmond's fourth union, the 1603 'union of the crowns'. At no point in the party's existence had it formally advocated republicanism, the closest being a 1997 conference resolution in favour of a post-independence referendum on an elected head of state (see below). The old National Party of Scotland was clear that it was by 'virtue of his Scottish descent, as well as his English' that King George V was 'seated on his throne'. 'The only change we might welcome would be to see him crowned at Scone as well as Westminster' (Black c. 1933: 31). Even as the SNP moved away from imperial unionism, it retained its monarchism, the Declaration of Arbroath having 'infused nationalists . . . with a pride in Scotland as an historic kingdom' (Kidd 2013b).

John MacCormick's objections to pillar boxes bearing 'EIIR' in the early 1950s is often mischaracterised as republican, when in fact it was a robust defence of the correct numerical designation (there had been a similar row upon the 1910 accession of Edward VII). As the journalist Albert Mackie noted in a 1955 article on Scottish nationalism,

> most Nationalists . . . are loyal in their feelings towards the Queen. They disagree with the numeral 'the Second' in the Queen's title for historic reasons . . . and their main criticism of the Union is that it has been continually 'broken' by London. (*Picture Post*, 1955)

SNP policy was unchanged a decade later, a 1960s election leaflet stating that it stood for 'a free Scotland loyal to the Crown within the British Commonwealth' or a 'Constitutional Monarchy with the Queen as Head of State' (SNP 1964).

At an 'Arthur Donaldson Testimonial Ball' held in Montrose on 10 October 1975, an event attended by then SNP leader Billy Wolfe and several SNP MPs, the first toast was to Her Majesty, an official programme adding the words: 'Long may she reign' (SNP 1975). Two years later, however, this loyalty was tested when the queen, speaking in her Silver Jubilee year, told Parliament that she could never 'forget' having been crowned 'Queen of the United Kingdom of Great Britain and Northern Ireland', a remark taken by many Nationalists as a constitutionally inappropriate dig at the SNP. Gordon Wilson, an MP but not yet party leader, said the queen was 'intervening in domestic politics on behalf of the unionist cause' (Wilson 2009: 133).

According to *The Times*, the queen remarked to a 'prominent member' of the SNP that she had 'not realized it [the SNP] was a monarchist party' but was subsequently 'assured that the movement [was] not on the road to republicanism'. The queen's Westminster Hall speech had dominated the SNP's 1977 conference, at which the party's national executive moved to kill an amendment advocating a post-independence referendum on the monarchy. Speaking against it, Neil MacCormick, professor of public law at Edinburgh University and one of the SNP's main constitutional advisers, said: 'How grand it will be in the twenty-fifth year of the reign of Queen Elizabeth to say to her, "We will be with you if you will be with us"' (*The Times*, 28 May 1977).

During the subsequent 1979 general election, a supplementary manifesto statement went to great lengths to play down independence, asserting that the SNP did not stand for the break-up of the UK, 'as some of our opponents emotionally and wildly claim', but rather for the establishment of a 'new relationship under the crown . . . in an association of British states operating like the Nordic Union' (Levy 1990: 96). Indeed, Scandinavian unionism later became another prominent theme in SNP discourse, Westminster leader Angus Robertson arguing in 2014 that Scotland should join the Nordic Council upon leaving the UK (*Guardian*, 26 January 2014).

The party's stance on the monarchy, meanwhile, was later finessed. The SNP's 1992 manifesto added the caveat that the queen would remain head of state 'until such time as the people of Scotland decide otherwise' (SNP 1992: 4), although when, at the 1997 SNP conference, Roseanna Cunningham revived the 1977 idea of a post-independence referendum on the monarchy, Salmond expressed his opposition. Cunningham even suggested that few SNP activists would support the monarchist status quo. 'There are gey few of you who would be out there', she told delegates to rousing applause. 'I know that, you know that, the press know that and the public know that too and most of them think we're already a Republican party and are not bothered about it' (Torrance 2015: 129). An amendment calling on the SNP to campaign openly *against* the monarchy, however, was defeated by 208 votes to 153.

This reflected an internal division which had most likely existed since the 1960s, when the SNP began to move more to the left. Indeed, Mitchell *et al.*'s 2009 membership study found the monarchy to be an issue on which the party's official policy was 'at variance with the membership', with almost 60 per cent of the membership believing a hereditary head of state to have no place in a modern democracy. Only one in five disagreed, while there was 'little evidence of principled support' even among elected MPs and MSPs. The leadership view, concluded Mitchell, was that even were it desirable, an independent Scottish republic was not a priority (Mitchell *et al.* 2012: 133), not least because the connotations of 'republicanism' in a British Isles context were largely negative (and indeed violent) given events in Northern Ireland.

That was certainly Alex Salmond's view. As First Minister after 2007, he rarely missed an opportunity to enthuse about the head of state, whom he usually styled 'Queen of Scots'. In opposition, he had cultivated the

Prince of Wales, providing him with the same assurances given to his mother in 1977, and even attended the wedding of Prince William and Kate Middleton during the 2011 Scottish Parliament election ('I should have had this entire city [Edinburgh] covered in royal standards', he told one interviewer). 'There is a better case for an English republic than a Scottish one', he declared. 'I'm not saying Scotland is a classless society, but I still think inequalities in Scotland are not generally linked to the monarchy' (*Prospect*, June 2011).

This regal unionism enjoyed its fullest expression when the queen opened the fourth session of the Scottish Parliament in July 2011. Salmond quoted words she had used on her recent state visit to Ireland, 'firm friends and equal partners', saying the same would be true of Scotland whatever 'constitutional path' it chose. The First Minister also noted that before the 1707 Union, the queen's predecessors had 'reigned over two sovereign nations' and that 'there was nothing particularly unusual in that arrangement' (BBC News online, 1 July 2011).

Ahead of the 2014 referendum, however, there was a modest row when it emerged that the 1997 referendum policy had been quietly ditched. The SNP protested that 'the policy to retain the monarchy dates back to the founding of the SNP in 1934', but as the journalist Kenny Farquharson speculated, Alex Salmond might simply have 'decided that SNP party policy is inconvenient to his chosen strategy. So he has simply chosen to ignore it' (*Scotland on Sunday*, 17 January 2012). In retrospect, the change had actually taken place in 2002 when Article II of the SNP's draft 'Constitution for a Free Scotland' had stated that the queen would be head of state in an independent Scotland and, when not physically present, represented by the Presiding Officer of the Scottish Parliament (SNP 2002).

The monarchy was not debated at either of the SNP's conferences during 2012, while the pro-monarchy stance was formalised upon publication of the independence white paper the following year. This unequivocally stated that

> On independence Scotland will be a constitutional monarchy, continuing the Union of the Crowns that dates back to 1603, pre-dating the Union of the Parliaments by over one hundred years. On independence in 2016, Her Majesty The Queen will be head of state. (Scottish Government 2013: 22)

The white paper, however, left open the possibility that a future Scottish Government might wish to abolish the monarchy, though it made clear the current SNP administration did 'not support such a change'. 'We want to be part of the monarchical union,' Salmond declared elsewhere, and 'have the Queen as head of state' (Torrance 2013: 67).

The Social Union

This brings us to Alex Salmond's fifth and final union, 'the Social Union between the peoples of these islands', the cornerstone of which was support for a continuing constitutional monarchy. To Kidd, the social union appeared to involve 'an incongruous marriage of the loose, decentralized arrangements of the seventeenth-century Union of the Crowns with the values of the post-1945 Attlee Welfare State' (Kidd 2013b). It first featured prominently in the Scottish Government's 2007 paper, *Choosing Scotland's Future: A National Conversation*, which stated that

> On independence, Her Majesty The Queen would remain the Head of State in Scotland. The current parliamentary and political Union of Great Britain and Northern Ireland would become a monarchical and social Union – United Kingdoms rather than a United Kingdom – maintaining a relationship first forged in 1603 by the Union of the Crowns. (Scottish Government 2007: 24)

Mitchell *et al.* identified three different social unions, monarchical, 'friends and family' and welfare (Kidd 2013b), while the 2013 white paper – which reiterated talk of 'five continuing unions' – defined the 'social union' as 'made up of connections of family, history, culture and language'. This also included the three Crown Dependencies (Guernsey, Jersey and the Isle of Man) and thus the Common Travel Area, which it called an 'expression of the close economic, social and cultural ties across the nations of these islands' (Scottish Government 2013). Alistair Darling, who chaired the No campaign during the independence referendum, countered that the historical, social and cultural ties binding UK citizens together were not 'just something that is a nice bonus, a warm feeling around royal occasions and sporting triumphs – they underpin our economic union' (Torrance 2013: 182).

The social union was perhaps a conveniently ambiguous way of framing a redefinition of 'independence' which dated back several years. The SNP had embraced 'fiscal autonomy' under John Swinney's troubled leadership of the party, while in 2004 Mike Russell promoted the idea of a 'New Union', under which 'all matters reserved to Westminster' would be devolved to Holyrood except foreign affairs and 'military command' (Russell and MacLeod 2004: 126). In another publication, Kenny MacAskill (like Russell, a future Scottish Government minister) asked if there was

> a need for a separate DVLA or even Ordnance Survey? . . . Does a bureaucracy need to be created in Saltcoats as well as Swansea? Can we not simply pay our share as well as our respects? Do we need to reinvent the Civil Aviation Authority or other such Institutions as opposed to exercising control from

north of the border even if the Institution remains located in the south of it . . . There are numerous other organisations and Departments where separation is not necessary but the right to direct and instruct is.

'That is not the abandonment of Nationhood,' argued MacAskill, but 'an acceptance of the more complex world in which we live' (MacAskill 2004: 29–30). The same year, the SNP abandoned its long-standing goal of 'self-government in favour of independence', just as Russell and MacAskill were rethinking nationalism (Mitchell 2019). Paradoxically, it chose formally to adopt the language of full 'independence' just as its constitutional thinking grew more nuanced.

Writing in 2005, Professor Neil MacCormick was much more explicit, saying that unlike many of his 'political friends' in the SNP, he contended

in a quite unembarrassed way that there ought to remain some form of union between Scotland and England in the time to come as in the past four hundred years. We share an island, a huge amount of trade and of personal and familial interpenetration. This merits some political recognition and even celebration . . . A union through shared membership of the great confederation of the European Union, with a shared head of state but not of government seems to me a good version of 'new unions for old'. (MacCormick 2005: 250)

MacCormick had already explored what he called 'post-sovereignty' arising from internal and external constraints on state agency (MacCormick 1999), and indeed in this respect he was very much his father's son, 'King John' having consistently advocated greater autonomy short of independence. By 2011/2012, SNP strategists were calling this sort of thinking 'independence-lite', the idea that even post-independence Scotland and the UK would continue to share certain services, even welfare and pension payments (Scottish Government 2013). Mitchell reckoned the 'fingerprints' of MacCormick, who had been a special adviser to Alex Salmond between 2007 and his death in 2009, 'were all over' the 2013 white paper on independence (Mitchell 2019).

Interviewing Nationalists for their membership study, Mitchell *et al.* found a few senior members suggesting that there was 'no such thing as independence', although they were quick to insert a caveat along the lines of 'as sometimes/usually understood' (Mitchell *et al.* 2012: 122). Speaking on St George's Day in Carlisle in 2014, Alex Salmond wielded the Ireland Act 1949 as proof that Scotland would 'not be a foreign country after independence, any more than Ireland, Northern Ireland, England or Wales could ever be "foreign countries" to Scotland' (Salmond 2014). He neglected to mention that the Act also confirmed Northern Ireland's status as part of the UK and recognised that Eire had 'ceased . . . to be part of His Majesty's dominions' (Ireland Act 1949).

Similarly bold was the SNP embracing 'Britishness' as part of modern Scottish identity. In 1999, MSP Andrew Wilson's suggestion that this would survive independence provoked a backlash, while as leader John Swinney gave out mixed messages. In 2002 he spoke of Scotland continuing to invest in 'a shared cultural commonwealth of the British Isles' (BBC, 23 April 2002), but the following year told 'the Brits' to 'get off' during his conference address. Between 2007 and 2011, however, there was a definite shift. The SNP MP Pete Wishart moved from claiming that 'all vestiges of Britishness' would go (2008), to arguing that it would 'exist in Scotland long after we become independent'. In fact, he added, 'it could well be enhanced with independence' (2011) (Torrance 2013: 182–3).

Similarly, Alex Salmond – who in 1999 said Britishness had been claimed by thugs and racists (Torrance 2011) – now told the *New States-man* he had a 'multi-layered identity . . . Scottishness is my primary identity but I've got Britishness and a European identity'. Alex Neil said Scots could 'still call themselves British' after independence, while one SNP strategist even went so far as to claim that Scotland would remain a 'British nation' by virtue of its geographical location (Torrance 2013: 182–3). By 'acknowledging Britishness while retaining an emphasis on Scottishness in the SNP's language,' judged Mitchell and Johns, 'the SNP made it easier for those who retained at least some British identity – that is, the clear majority of Scots – to support the party' (Mitchell and Johns 2016: 59). One survey had found that nearly half the SNP's voters retained some element of British identity and pride in British history (Bechhofer and McCrone 2007).

This also dovetailed with the SNP's concept of 'civic nationalism', something that had 'become part of the lexicon of SNP politics amongst the party's elite and active membership' (Mitchell *et al.* 2012: 143). The phrase – and its implicit distinction – were likely borrowed from the Canadian public intellectual Michael Ignatieff, whose 1993 book *Blood & Belonging: Journeys into the New Nationalism* had drawn a clear separation between 'ethnic' and 'civic' nationalism (see Chapter 2).

Thereafter, Ignatieff's terminology found its way into SNP discourse just as the rise of Balkan nationalism gave rise to the same sort of terminological trouble as Continental nationalism in the 1930s. The party, therefore, willingly embraced this means of differentiating its 'good' nationalism from 'bad'. At the same time, some journalists – who along with academics helped popularise the dichotomy – were prone to exaggeration, Iain Macwhirter claiming that 'any trace of ethnic nationalism, and anti-English sentiment' had been 'expunged from the party in the 1970s' (*Herald*, 18 June 2015). Only a few years before, the writer Alasdair Gray – widely quoted by SNP politicians – had divided Scotland's English population into two groups, 'settlers' (good) and 'colonists' (bad) (Gray 2012).

Even Mitchell, strongly associated with the 'civic' nationalist interpretation, conceded that the findings of his SNP membership study might 'be interpreted as challenging the value of the civic-ethnic dichotomy', with the survey evidence showing SNP members willing to embrace 'many ways of being Scottish', including 'civic and ethnic definitions of belonging' (Mitchell *et al.* 2012: 143). Most nationalisms, meanwhile, required an 'other', although in the SNP's case this was not articulated as 'England' or 'the English' but represented by the word 'Westminster', 'a faceless institution firmly located in the territory of the Other' (Mycock 2012: 60). As Breeze concluded in her analysis of the SNP's 2010 and 2015 manifestos, this identified the enemy 'without using terminology that might prove offensive', part of a moderate 'populist' framing which depicted a unitary Scottish 'people' within a strong 'heartland' (Breeze 2019: 53).

Alex Salmond, a medieval historian by background, also lost few opportunities to stress Scotland's 'ancient' provenance. He urged 'Blood Scots' or 'ancestral Scots' to visit the motherland during the 2014 'homecoming' and, on a visit to Northern Ireland as First Minister, quoted a Scottish poet in observing that its inhabitants were 'the blood of our blood and the bone of our bone' (*Irish Times*, 18 June 2007).[5] 'Scotland is an ancient nation', was the opening line of Kenny MacAskill's book on nationalism. 'Forged on the anvil of wars of Independence and inveigled into the British State against the wishes of its people' (MacAskill 2004: 13).

The SNP and Yes movement also made much of inherent 'Scottish values' during the referendum campaign, a 'social nationalism' it shared with the unionist Labour and the Liberal Democrat parties (Scothorne *et al.* 2016). Nevertheless, sensitivity to charges of ethnic nationalism 'fuelled a determination to emphasise the party's civic side' (Mitchell and Johns 2016: 32), leading to talk of a name change and even denials of any sort of nationalism. Joining the SNP in September 2014, for example, the former Scottish Labour official Tommy Sheppard said he was 'not a nationalist' but a social democrat (*Edinburgh Evening News*, 25 September 2014).

At points this line of argument stretched credulity. In a 2012 speech, Nicola Sturgeon referenced Neil MacCormick's distinction between the 'existentialist' and 'utilitarian' strands of Scottish nationalism, suggesting that 'most' SNP members were an 'amalgam' of both. For her, the *fact of nationhood* or *Scottish identity* is not the motive force for independence. Nor do I believe that independence, however desirable, is essential for the preservation of our distinctive Scottish identity. And I don't agree at all that feeling British – with all of the shared social, family and cultural heritage that makes up such an identity – is in any way inconsistent with a pragmatic, utilitarian support for political independence. *My conviction that Scotland should be independent stems from the principles, not of identity or nationality, but of democracy and social justice.* (Sturgeon 2012, italics added)

Much was made in the referendum year of it being the seven-hundredth anniversary of the Battle of Bannockburn, although Salmond denied any deliberate linkage. Back in 1996 the SNP had wrestled control of the Wallace myth from unionists following the release of Mel Gibson's *Braveheart*, although as Pittock observed, many Nationalists were 'puzzled as to why public interest and support in and for the heroes of fourteenth-century Scottish independence failed to translate into twentieth-century nationalist votes' (Pittock 2001: 110). By 2014, Salmond was reinterpreting the Wallace and Bruce myths along 'civic' lines, highlighting the fact, as historian Tom Devine put it, that both 'Scottish heroes Robert de Brus and William Wallace came from immigrant families', French and Welsh respectively (*Herald*, 3 June 2014).

The SNP was more consistent when it came to defining who constituted 'a Scot', which in its view was anyone resident in Scotland regardless of origin. In this regard, the SNP's nationalism remained 'resolutely civic', even when analysis suggested a decisive majority of English-born voters had contributed to the defeat of the independence proposition in September 2014 (Mitchell and Johns 2016: 46). Although Alex Salmond mentioned the age profile of No voters, there was no repeat of Jacques Parizeau's famous invocation of 'money and ethnic votes' following defeat in the Quebec sovereignty referendum of 1995.

Conclusion

By that point, the SNP had set out a 'detailed vision of independent statehood embedded within a series of transnational frameworks' (Brown Swan and McEwen forthcoming). As Nicola Sturgeon had put it in 2013, 'far from marking a separation from our friends and relations across these islands, independence opens the door to a renewed partnership between us' (Sturgeon 2013). Alex Salmond even drew on Fletcher of Saltoun to legitimise this approach, specifically his observation on the eve of the 1707 union that 'all nations are dependent, the one on the many'. Saltoun, he added, was emphasising a truth which is especially relevant in the modern world. All nations are interdependent. And an independent Scotland will achieve its goals through partnership. But as an independent nation, we would be able to choose our aims, our partnerships and our priorities. (Salmond 2013)

So just as unionist parties in Scotland had long co-opted nationalist rhetoric, the SNP – Scotland's main nationalist party after 1934 – borrowed certain aspects of unionism from the Scottish political lexicon.

Partly this was tactical, an attempt to win over sceptical voters ahead of the 2014 independence referendum, but it also had deeper roots in the party's understanding of Scottish 'sovereignty', its historic status as an independent kingdom and especially Scotland's broader European and imperial bonds. Empire, monarchy and later Europe were all co-opted in order to rebut the 'separatist' charge of unionist opponents. The SNP was not unusual in this respect. At referendums in 1980 and 1995, the Parti Québécois had promised to keep the queen, the Canadian dollar and a common banking system in order to win over those opposed to sovereignty for the province.

But just as the unionist parties' nationalism contained contradictions, so too did the SNP's unionism. If, for example, it was desirable for an independent Scotland to 'keep' the queen, pound and membership of NATO and the European Union, then why was political union with England, Wales and Northern Ireland considered so intolerable? The unionists parties were not, like the EU, committed to a policy of 'ever closer union'; indeed quite the opposite, after 1999 all supported greater decentralisation, greater devolution and in some cases even federalism.

Ironically, as the unionist parties became more nationalist after 1999, in certain respects the SNP became more unionist, displeasing some within the party, not least when it came to the monarchy and defence policy. Even its 'Europeanisation' was not complete, a sizeable minority of SNP members and voters wanting to 'take back control' from Brussels as well as London. Nevertheless, the 'independence in Europe' policy allowed the party to depict British 'nationalism' (or Euroscepticism) as reactionary and the Scottish variety as 'internationalist', while the civic–ethnic dichotomy fulfilled a similar role in differentiating the SNP's 'good' nationalism from 'bad'.

Alex Salmond's support for 'five continuing unions' did not mean, of course, he wanted the United Kingdom to survive; rather he was recapturing something of his party's early reforming unionism, comfortable with the idea of constitutional interdependence and a view of national sovereignty which was both flexible and pooled. The SNP's unionist nationalism, much like the nationalist unionism of the Conservative, Labour and Liberal parties, contained multitudes.

NINE

'The Fair Claims of Wales'

This chapter answers Pocock's plea to break out of historical and politi-cal science 'silos' and consider our main theme – nationalist unionism – more 'holistically' (Pocock 1975: 16). Given the multi-national nature of the United Kingdom, it was not just in Scotland that parties of the union borrowed from nationalist discourse and promoted autonomous 'imagined communities'; arguably it occurred to an even greater degree in Wales and even, in a different form, in Northern Ireland (see Chapter 10).

Bulpitt's theory of 'territorial management' is relevant here, with Liberal, Conservative and Labour governments 'showing a proper respect for Wales and its cultural traditions' as one way of 'shoring up the United Kingdom' (Morgan 1981: 418). So too is Billig's 'banal nationalism', which in Wales pushed secessionist nationalism (in as much as it existed) to the periph-ery while promoting institutional, administrative and, later, legislative autonomy within the UK, an 'official' Welsh nationalism which, as in Scot-land, drew upon myths, symbols and historical motifs, most notably the 'invented tradition' of investiture ceremonies in 1911 and 1969.

But Wales was – and is – not Scotland, thus its nationalism operated in a different historical context and expressed itself in different ways. The mid-sixteenth-century Anglo-Welsh Acts of Union were not analogous to the Anglo-Scottish Treaty of 1707, for they did not preserve a panoply of distinct institutions which might have preserved Welsh national identity. The latter union flattered Scotland as an 'equal' partner, whereas the former refused even to view Wales as a distinct entity. To Morgan, the 'supreme object' of Welsh national leaders was essentially 'equality within the United Kingdom and an expanding empire, not severance from it' (Morgan 1995: 206–7).[1]

Until the 1920s, therefore, political nationalism – that is, the campaign for administrative or legislative devolution – was stronger in Scotland than in Wales, where it took a more cultural and religious form. Indeed, the cam-paign to disestablish the Anglican Church in Wales was 'an issue that raised passions difficult to comprehend in a more secular age' (Wyn Jones *et al.* 2002: 233), non-conformism having taken on a distinctly Welsh persona in the mid nineteenth century (Morgan 1995: 201).

During the existence of Bulpitt's 'Dual Polity', however, all Wales's major parties competed on nationalist-unionist territory, over who could best 'stand up for Wales' within the UK. Paterson and Wyn Jones identified a 'two-pronged strategy' followed by successive nationalists in all parties and none: securing political recognition of Welsh distinctiveness through some measure of devolution or Westminster parliamentary reform, while creating – and subsequently strengthening – civil society institutions (Paterson and Wyn Jones 1999: 174).

Nationalist Unionism in Wales

As in Scotland, however, Welsh party politics became more 'nationalistically inclined' during the 1880s, a result of cultural changes (the Eisteddfod was reorganised in 1880–1), agitation for disestablishment, franchise reform and boundary changes (1884–5), as well as the changing balance of forces at Westminster flowing from Gladstone's support for Irish Home Rule (Griffith 2006: 92; Morgan 1981: 94).

Based in Wales (Hawarden) and married to a Welshwoman, Gladstone was aware of the role 'sentiment plays in politics' and proved adept at 'playing on chords', such as his attendance – controversial at the time – at the 1888 Eisteddfod in Wrexham (Morgan 1995: 338). Speaking in Swansea the year before, the Grand Old Man had even offered what Coupland called 'a direct encouragement of Welsh nationalism', declaring that 'Wales has not told her own tale . . . It is time your representatives [in Parliament] . . . subject to the claims of imperial patriotism, laid their Welsh heads together and considered what are the fair claims of Wales' (Coupland 1954: 225–6).

These 'claims' were both cultural and educational, priorities which reflected the Victorian revival of interest in Welsh history, mythology and language. Cymru Fydd (Young Wales) was founded in 1886 at around the same time as the Scottish Home Rule Association (SHRA), its aim being the promotion of Welsh interests within the Liberal Party and beyond. Not only did it believe union with England to be 'inevitable', but something that provided

> the best opportunity that Wales could have to deliver her mission – if mission she has – to the world. The one condition that is insisted upon is that the connection shall not be made closer at the expense of Welsh nationality. (Quoted in Osmond 1977: 99)

Like the SHRA, Cymru Fydd was also strongly imperialist, imagining Wales as one part of a federated British Empire. These quasi-nationalist tendencies were reflected at Westminster with the formation of a 'Welsh Parliamentary Party' in 1888, naturally dominated by Liberal MPs.

Perhaps the pre-eminent exponent of Liberal nationalist unionism was Thomas Edward Ellis, the son of a tenant farmer who 'formulated a new concept of nationhood, in which the history, traditions, social culture, literature, and political institutions of his people would be organically linked' (Morgan 1981: 113). In 1885, he declared himself a 'Radical Nationalist' (Masterman 1976: 68) and, in the general election of 1886, used his election address to solicit 'suffrages as a WELSH NATIONALIST' (Coupland 1954: 227).

At a meeting of the Welsh Liberal Council in October 1888, Ellis called for a 'national programme' and a national assembly for Wales, self-government being 'at once the inspirer and goal of nationhood'. Yet he concluded his remarks with a declaration of allegiance to Gladstone and to Liberalism: 'I cannot share the nervousness of those who fear that firm insistence on the Welsh national programme implies separation from the Liberal party.' Such a statement, observed Masterman, indicated that Ellis's 'conception of Welsh nationalism in no way inhibited him from playing the role of a British Liberal politician since it could find its home within the Gladstonian Liberal party' (Masterman 1976: 114). And like Lord Rosebery in Scotland, Ellis was imperialist, envisaging an empire 'in which Wales was to take its full place with a total immersion in what had become Welsh tradition, its poetry and its Methodism' (Williams 1991: 227).

Ellis's decision to accept office as a junior whip in the 1892 Liberal government, meanwhile, demonstrated the tensions many nationalist unionists faced: in opposition, there was scope to pursue constitutional schemes and promote Welsh interests; in government, one had to toe the line. By then, the party's Newcastle Programme included Welsh disestablishment, robbing Welsh nationalism of its main impetus, while Bills to create a Secretary for Wales and National Council had both failed. 'These proposals offered Wales more national autonomy than Scotland possessed but far less than Gladstone wanted to give Ireland', judged Coupland. 'They were nothing like Home Rule. Nor were they an essay in federalism' (Coupland 1954: 230).

Ellis's appointment was regarded by many Welsh nationalists as a great betrayal, in that it removed the prospect of a separate Welsh nationalist party along Irish lines, as well as momentum towards Home Rule. Instead, Ellis used his position to promote administrative reforms, particularly when it came to education, and new institutions, chiefly a 'national' library and museum. He also proposed public monuments to Welsh 'heroes' and regularly invoked the patriot Owain Glyndŵr, who represented to Welsh

nationalist unionists what Wallace and Bruce did to their Scottish counterparts. Predictably for a nationalist unionist, Ellis also drew a distinction
between 'strong' Welsh nationalism and what he called 'narrow patriotism'
(Masterman 1976: 196).

In keeping with its territorial code, the UK Liberal Party took care
to meet some Welsh claims. Not only did Gladstone establish a Royal
Commission on Land in Wales and Monmouthshire, but in 1895 Lord
Rosebery travelled to Cardiff to promise that Welsh disestablishment
would be the first government measure of the new parliamentary session. In 1896, meanwhile, the Prince of Wales (the future King Edward
VII) was installed as Chancellor of 'the Welsh University' at Aberystwyth
(*Illustrated London News*, 4 July 1896), thereafter bestowing an honorary
degree on Gladstone. Belatedly, therefore, education in Wales acquired
the 'national overtones' which had long existed in Scotland (Morgan
1981: 105), the first distinctly Welsh statute – the Welsh Intermediate
Education Act – having been passed by the UK parliament in 1889.

T. E. Ellis died suddenly in 1899, a loss commemorated on plates, med-
als and jugs. Thereafter, most Welsh Liberals pursued administrative rather
than legislative devolution, while those of a more radical constitutional
bent drifted to the Labour Party, including E. T. John, who had promoted
several Home Rule Bills before the First World War. Administrative devolution took a different form than that in Scotland, with a 'Welsh Department'
being established within UK government departments. The first, at the
Board of Education, was established in 1907, while another at the Ministry
of Agriculture followed in 1919. A Welsh Board of Health was also created
to take account of the Welsh Insurance Commission provided for under the
1911 National Insurance Act.[2]

As Morgan observed, cultural nationalism in Wales had ended up having a 'constitutional and administrative impact', something that also owed
much to the 'benevolence and growing enlightenment of politicians and
civil servants in England who saw the recognition of Welsh culture as a
way of shoring up the United Kingdom' (Morgan 1981: 112, 122). The UK
Liberal governments of 1906–18 also appreciated the value of symbolism.
Wales got its own war memorial in Cardiff's Cathays Park, while in 1909
the same city – not yet a capital – hosted the 'National Pageant of Wales',
something a contemporary postcard summarised as 'Rhwysg Hanes Cymru.
Thrilling Episodes. Historic Costumes. Great National Spectacle' (author's
collection).

The 1911 investiture of the Prince of Wales at Caernarfon, meanwhile,
presented the new King George V and his heir as 'a symbol of an explicitly multinational Britishness' (Ellis 2008).[3] There was also a clear political

dimension, the Chancellor David Lloyd George believing the investiture would serve both to 'gratify Welsh national pride and, at the same time, to reassure traditionalists in every part of the Kingdom' (Grigg 1978: 303). The national press played along, with the *Daily Telegraph* observing that the investiture was 'essentially a festival symbolizing the combination of the spirit of racial patriotism with that of a larger union' (*Daily Telegraph*, 8 July 1911), and the *Morning Advertiser* arguing that the

> revival of Liberalism has definitely substituted for those ideals the concep-tion of nationalisms and a great commonwealth of free peoples. The visits [of George V] to Ireland, Wales and Scotland show the same idea at work nearer home. More and more the Crown becoming the symbol of unity in diversity. (*Morning Advertiser*, 13 July 1911)

Promotional material for the investiture stressed the Welsh origins of the Tudor monarchs, the ceremony itself – accompanied by a bilingual guide-book – being attended by the Prime Minister (Asquith), the Chief Secretary of Ireland and the Secretary of State for the Colonies. Wales's status within the UK and British Empire was everywhere flagged, as was the iconography of Welsh nationality.

Lloyd George, who had assumed the 'leadership of Welsh nationalism' after Tom Ellis joined the government in 1892,[4] spoke of 'Liberal enthu-siasm worked up to a glowing red by the blasts of patriotism' (Coupland 1954: 233). But, unlike Parnell, Lloyd George 'quite definitely *did* set a limit to the march of the *Welsh* nation'. According to his biographer John Grigg:

> He never intended that Wales's demands should be carried to the length of breaking the link with England or withdrawing from the United King-dom. His Welsh patriotism, though fervent, was part of his larger British and Imperial patriotism. To him there was no contradiction, but rather a necessary connection, between the two. As he said in a speech soon after he was first elected to Parliament: 'We are Imperialists because we are national-ists . . . we know that by the sum of the success, prosperity and happiness attained by little Wales, the great Empire of which she is a part will be the more glorious.' (Grigg 1988: 5–6)

This Scottish Unionist-like blend of Welsh, British and imperial identities clearly landed well. An issue of *Wales: THE National Magazine for the Welsh People* from January 1912, edited by the Liberal MP J. Hugh Edwards, an early biographer of Lloyd George and a Cymru Fydd veteran, included arti-cles on 'race and nationality', Welsh disestablishment, 'what the world owes to Welshmen', 'A Department of Agriculture for Wales', 'Welsh Nationalism as a Social Religion' and 'the influence of the Welsh on the Formation of the British Constitution' (*Wales*, January 1912). In 1914, another publication called *The Welsh Outlook* was launched, initially edited by the secretary to the Welsh Insurance Commissioners, Thomas Jones, although its first edition took a different line, arguing that 'local patriotism' was 'incompatible with imperial loyalty' (Williams 2006: 146).

Wales and Welshness, meanwhile, were still considered to be under threat, though few advocated legislative devolution by way of a response. Lewis suggested that what he called 'liberal-Cambrianists' articulated 'a rather soft, sentimental, type of nationalism which displayed little or no interest in political autonomy for Wales', instead championing union, Crown and empire. Others, such as Williams, disagreed, believing them to have a strong commitment to what they understood as 'Welsh autonomy', although this included a 'regressive, even reactionary' emphasis on Welsh birth and bloodlines, which naturally excluded lots of 'others' from notions of the 'true Wales' (Williams 2006: 153–6).

The Welsh Department of the Board of Education churned out guidelines (some published by the Welsh Outlook Press) encouraging the teaching of Welsh history, language and the celebration of St David's Day, indicating that this 'official' nationalist unionism was sanctioned by the Liberal government. One publication from 1915 – richly illustrated with dragons and Celtic motifs – linked the centenary of the death of the Welsh General Picton ('Wellington's right-hand man in his greatest battles against Napoleon') with the half-millennium since the death of Owain Glyndŵr. Its intended readership were the children of Wales, who were instructed to do their duty by

> loving Wales and, when the time comes, being willing to serve and defend her and the great Empire of which she forms the oldest part; by never bringing disgrace on her by mean of wrongful acts; by respecting our country's laws, and by upholding her institutions.

The Welsh language was to be spoken, read and written whenever possible ('we should never – under any circumstances – be ashamed of it or of our Nationality'), while Asquith and Lloyd George – who had, like Gladstone, attended Eisteddfods – were quoted by way of official validation. The then premier (Asquith) had spoken of Wales as 'a single and indivisible entity, with a life of its own, drawing vitality from the ancient past', while the Chancellor (Lloyd George) had alluded – in a speech to the London Welsh – to the Great War and the fight 'to vindicate the principle that small nationalities are not to be crushed by the arbitrary will of a strong and overmastering power' (WDBE 1915). In 1915, Lloyd George also created the Welsh Guards, 'a consequence of his demand for Welsh distinctiveness in the British Army', believing that nothing brought out the 'most soldier-like qualities' of men 'like an appeal to their enthusiasm for the honour and the fame of their country' (Grigg 1988: 11).

Further 'patriotic publications of the Welsh Department' included 'suggestions to local education authorities & teachers in Wales regarding the teaching of patriotism', in which permanent secretary Alfred T. Davies cautioned that to

> teach Patriotism, even in connection with a National Anniversary, is not easy ... [if children] are not to grow up with crude, and perhaps false, ideas regarding themselves, their country, and the great Empire to which they belong ... Wales may fitly take a leading share in inculcating in her children right conceptions of Patriotism, using the term in its widest sense.

This was the standard differentiation between 'good' and 'bad' nationalism, or what the publication called 'True Patriotism and False Patriotism':

> 'Our country, right or wrong' [is] a bad motto ... No nation is really great whose Patriotism takes the form of hating other nations ... Imagine Welshmen celebrating their national anniversary of St David's Day by singing songs full of jealousy and hatred of the English, Irish, or Scots! How horrible even the thought of such a thing. (WDBE 1916: 4, 16)

Grigg concluded that this official nationalism was 'largely politically motivated and emanated from the Welsh Department's desire to exert further influence in Welsh education' (Grigg 2018: 99), although that assumes that the children (and teachers) of Wales were somehow blank slates on to which 'true patriotism' could be etched.

By the end of the Great War, Morgan believed Welsh nationalism lacked a strongly political dimension because the 'battle' fought since the 1880s had essentially 'been won': 'Welsh schools and colleges, a Welsh university, a Welsh Land Commission, Welsh-speaking bishops, Welsh legislation and administrative departments and a commitment to Welsh disestablishment. Monmouthshire was restored as part of Wales. This became the new orthodoxy' (Morgan 1995: 378). After 1918, therefore, nationalist unionism in Wales – hitherto largely associated with the Liberal Party – began to articulate new 'claims' while entering the discourse and ideology of other political parties.

'The Champion of Local Patriotism'

Although a specifically Tory Welsh nationalism had gained some traction through the writings of John Arthur Price in the late nineteenth century, the party's opposition to disestablishment minimised its electoral support in Wales, as did its perceived identification with 'Englishness' and 'English interests', a factor 'undoubtedly accentuated by the anglicized nature of its leadership' (Aubel 1996: 105–6).

By the 1940s, however, Conservatives proved themselves more willing to make Gladstone-like appeals to Welsh sentiment, identifying themselves more closely with Welsh nationality and developing a distinct policy for Wales. In 1944 the party conceded a 'Welsh Day' in the House of Commons, something R. A. Butler later used to advocate an 'Ambassador for Wales' while atoning for past Conservative government sins in relation to the Welsh language.

At around the same time Unionists were developing their 'Scottish Control of Scottish Affairs' agenda in Scotland, Enoch Powell (who understood medieval Welsh) embarked upon two fact-finding tours of Wales, the product of which was a statement of policy published on St David's Day in 1949. This opened with praise for 'those living in Wales' having 'kept alive the consciousness that they are a separate and distinct nation'. 'Above all,' it continued, 'the possession of Welsh as a spoken tongue and of Welsh literature as a live and growing heritage has helped to preserve the national consciousness and has in turn been fostered by it.'

But the fully bilingual pamphlet (with a red dragon on the cover) asserted that there existed no 'economic separateness' of Wales which corresponded 'with its national separateness'. The arguments that followed were familiar:

> We believe therefore that the identity of Wales with England as an economic unit and its separateness as a national identity must alike be recognised . . . The traditional policy of Conservatism has always been to acknowledge, and indeed to foster, variety wherever found, in individuals or in nationalities . . . It is this conception which has made the Conservative Party the champion of local patriotism and the enemy of centralization. Only by a policy framed in this spirit can the true needs of Wales be satisfied.

The 'establishment of a Welsh Office as a separate department of state' would not meet those criteria, although Powell did not acknowledge the obvious inconsistency vis-à-vis Scotland. Rather he suggested 'that one member of the Cabinet should be given special responsibility for Wales', that minister keeping in 'direct contact with Welsh local feeling and opinion' (CUCO 1949b: 1–3). Blaxland thus views Powell 'as one of the key – but forgotten – architects of modern Welsh politics' in that his recommendations led to Conservatives using 'a new kind of language' in relation to Wales (Blaxland 2016). Even so, in 1952 he turned down junior ministerial responsibility for Welsh affairs, (rightly) considering 'a Welsh post difficult for an English MP to handle' (Melding 2009: 145).

As in Scotland, this Welsh nationalist unionism conveniently dovetailed with an attack on socialist centralisation. UK party chairman Lord Woolton declared Conservatism to be 'the enemy of centralisation, and the champion of local patriotism' (Cragoe 2007), although this approach did not convince every Conservative. At the 1949 UK Conservative Party conference, John Grigg (later Lloyd George's biographer) attacked the policy for not going far enough, i.e. not establishing an elected Parliament of Wales, while Lord Merthyr condemned it as 'simply a further instalment of Welsh nationalism, which has been fostered for years by the *Western Mail* in an ill-judged effort to increase circulation' (*Western Mail*, 5 March 1949).

But the point was that at the 1951 general election, the Conservatives entered the campaign 'with a policy on devolution that was more advanced than that of their Labour opponents' (Philip 1975: 297). Speaking in Merthyr, Anthony Eden echoed his Scottish speeches in arguing that 'unity is not uniformity. Wales is a nation. She has her own way of life', while Churchill promised to be 'very mindful of the national aspirations and special problems of Wales' (Melding 2009: 144). The party in Wales also produced a film called *Land of My Fathers*, portraying Conservatives as protecting 'the interests of all Wales' while promoting its pledge to create a Minister for Welsh Affairs (Blaxland 2016).

After the election, Sir David Maxwell-Fyfe, a Scot, was appointed to the post, although it hardly helped the party resist arguments for a full Secretary of State. The Scottish Covenant movement had also sparked a similar, if less high-profile, campaign in Wales, demanding 'self-government within the framework of the United Kingdom', which eventually attracted around 240,000 signatures. Megan Lloyd George (daughter of David and a Welsh Liberal MP) was the campaign's president. 'I am not ashamed to be called a nationalist', she once declared (Ward 2005: 96), having described Wales in the 1944 Welsh Day debate 'as a nation with a living language of its own, with hundreds of years of history behind it, and with its own culture' (HC Debs 17 Oct 1944 Vol 403 c2237).

In 1955, meanwhile, the Welsh Labour MP S. O. Davies introduced his *Government of Wales Bill* to Parliament, which sought to deliver the Parliament for Wales demanded by Megan Lloyd George. Responding for the government as Minister for Welsh Affairs, her brother Gwilym Lloyd George (a Conservative MP) was respectful but unsupportive. He quoted from Sir

Reginald Coupland's recent study of Welsh and Scottish nationalism, 'Does the spirit of a nation require a political body in order to maintain its life and vigour?', adding:

> It is on that fundamental point that the Government and the sponsors of the Bill disagree. We believe – I certainly do – that the vitality of the Welsh nation can be better preserved if the Welsh people remain within the framework of Great Britain, and that the proposals in the Bill would in the long run be advantageous neither to Wales nor to Great Britain. (HC Debs 04 Mar 1955 Vol 537 cc2469–70)

Parnell's 'boundary', as far as the UK Conservatives were concerned, remained fixed, although there was persistent – if usually unsuccessful – pressure from Welsh Conservatives for further concessions. Ahead of the 1953 coronation, the party's Welsh Advisory Committee urged incorporation of 'the Welsh emblem' in the Royal Standard, the formation of a regiment of Welsh-speaking soldiers and a 'Royal Harpist for Wales'. Two years later it proposed upgrading the Minister for Welsh Affairs to Cabinet rank, while others in the party supported creating a full Secretary of State. The UK party consulted on this but fudged it by going for 'Minister of State' rank instead (Melding 2009: 148).

In 1960, however, the Conservative government did bow to Labour pressure in establishing a Welsh Grand Committee – more than six decades after a similar move for Scotland – while in 1963, Sir Keith Joseph, the last Minister for Welsh Affairs, established a 'Welsh Office' to advise him on Welsh economic planning. There was also symbolism. Having designated Cardiff Wales's 'first city' in 1905, the Conservatives upgraded it to a national 'capital' half-a-century later, in order to 'gain some of the soft nationalist support for themselves' (Deacon *et al.* 2018: 7). At the British Empire and Commonwealth Games in 1958, meanwhile, the queen (in a recorded message) announced that Charles would be invested as Prince of Wales at Caernarfon.

Philip identified the 'high noon' for Welsh Conservatives as 1959 (rather than 1955 in Scotland), with Tom Hooson, the party's candidate in Montgomeryshire (and later the MP for Brecon and Radnorshire between 1979 and 1985), working hard to dispel the party's image as 'alien to Welsh cultural values'. He and the future Chancellor Geoffrey Howe[5] produced a weighty Bow Group tome called *Work for Wales* (which proposed creating 'The Conservative Party of Wales'[6]), while Peter Thomas's Eisteddfod Act passed in 1959, allowing local councils to support the cultural gathering from rates revenue. A few years later, Raymond Gower's Elections (Welsh Forms) Act 1964 also made valid Welsh-language versions of official election forms.

The flooding of the Tryweryn Valley in Meirionydd for the benefit of Liverpool, however, did much harm to the Conservative Party, reviving its Anglocentric and therefore 'anti-Welsh' reputation of a few decades earlier. At the 1964 general election the Conservatives polled less than a third of the vote in Wales and gained only one additional MP, having contested every Welsh constituency for the first time. Thereafter the party experienced a Scotland-like decline. At its 1968 conference, Young Conservatives in Wales narrowly supported an elected council, but the party proper found it increasingly 'hard to reconcile their sympathy for the Welsh cultural tradition with their strong belief in the constitutional status quo' (Philip 1975: 299, 302).

'Y ddraig goch a'r faner goch'

Nationalism was more obvious within the Labour Party in Wales. As MP for Merthyr Tydfil in the early twentieth century, Keir Hardie preached 'True Nationalism' rather than what he called the Liberals' 'spurious imitation' of Welsh patriotism (Ellis 2008: 245). Hardie was a Home Ruler, but by the early 1940s Welsh Labour nationalism usually took the form of calls for a Secretary of State and government department akin to that in Scotland, although this was far from a unanimous view.

Morgan characterised the resulting divide as 'Y ddraig goch a'r faner goch' ('the red dragon and the red flag'), the former represented by James Griffiths, a fluent Welsh speaker and consistent advocate of some sort of devolution, and the latter by Nye Bevan, a product of the South Wales coalfields and 'a strong critic of Welsh separateness' (Morgan 1995: 452). While Griffiths promoted an advisory 'Council for Wales and Monmouthshire' (whose logo featured a dragon and Welsh language banner beneath a crown), Bevan dismissed it as 'nothing but a messenger boy' (Philip 1975: 282).[7]

Morgan also believed Bevan's antipathy to Welshness (and particularly Welsh speakers) could be 'overdone', citing a 'remarkable' speech to the 1958 Eisteddfod which showed 'how important his vision of Welshness was to him' (Morgan 1995: 452). Bevan's contribution to the 1944 Welsh Day debate also highlighted these ambiguities. While he believed Wales had 'a special place, a special individuality, a special culture and special claims' and that there was an argument for 'considerable devolution of government', Bevan felt the debate itself was 'humbug':

> We heard to-day of a Welsh agricultural problem ... There are sheep on the Welsh mountains, and there are sheep on the mountains of Westmoreland and in Scotland, but I do not know the difference between a Welsh sheep, a Westmoreland sheep and a Scottish sheep. (HC Debs 17 Oct 1944 Vol 403 c2312)

As Wyn Jones put it, Welsh Labour had 'often tortuously complex attitudes' towards the 'national question' (Wyn Jones and Scully 2012: 28), but the fact that Wales's 'minority party' (the Conservatives) appeared to 'have become more Welsh than the majority party' in the early 1950s spurred some of Bevan's colleagues into action (Deacon *et al.* 2018: 7).

The 'red dragon' contingent were given a helping hand by the Council for Wales's third memorandum in 1957, which recommended that Wales should have, like Scotland, a department and secretary of state of its own. The government – now led by Harold Macmillan – rejected this out of hand, prompting Huw T. Edwards, the Council's Labour-supporting chairman, to resign in protest. In 1959 Edwards joined Plaid Cymru, although this 'journey to nationalism was more a rejection of [Hugh] Gaitskell than of the Union' (Ward 2005: 118–19).

As a result, James Griffiths and others renewed their calls for a Secretary of State, which to their surprise Hugh Gaitskell conceded ahead of the 1959 general election. This enabled Labour to outbid the Conservatives for the first time in more than a decade, and by the early 1960s the party could plausibly 'present itself as the national party of Wales', sympathetic to both steel workers and miners, hill farmers and Welsh speakers (Osmond 1977: 123).

Labour's pre-election statement of policy in 1964, *Signposts to the New Wales* (there were companion publications covering Wales and 'Ulster', but not England), built upon a Welsh egalitarian mythology once promoted by the Liberals:

> The people of Wales are amongst the most progressive and radical in the world. We have produced leaders whose influence within the Labour movement and beyond has been notable. For nearly thirty years now we have returned a majority of Labour Members to Westminster.

Not for the first time, 'progressive' Wales was depicted as being held back by 'Tory' England, which had naturally 'neglected' Welsh interests. Labour also moved to take possession of Welsh language issues from the Conservatives, promising to do 'everything possible to enrich the distinctive culture of our country and to preserve and strengthen the traditions and the language which are our heritage' (Labour Party 1964: 5). At the 1966 general election, eleven of Labour's new MPs in Wales were Welsh speakers.

Signposts to the New Wales also reiterated Labour's support for a senior minister in Cabinet so that 'the status of the people of Wales as a national community will be specifically recognised' (Labour Party 1964: 22). A

Secretary of State for Wales was created later that year, with the Welsh Office following in 1965, but just as this long-running internal debate was resolved, the party's nationalist unionism came under challenge by a competing variety, that of Plaid Cymru, the self-declared 'party of Wales'. Shortly after the 1966 election, Gwynfor Evans seized the Carmarthen constituency in a by-election caused by the death of Megan Lloyd George, giving Welsh Labour the kind of shock its Scottish colleagues would soon experience in Hamilton.

How the party responded depended upon who was Secretary of State for Wales. James Griffiths and Cledwyn Hughes, the first two holders of that new office, were more sympathetic to calls for devolution than George Thomas, the anti-devolution 'representative of English-speaking south-east Wales' (Morgan 1981: 381, 384) who battled 'nationalists within and without his party' (Ward 2005: 77). Indeed, Hughes and Thomas succeeded Griffiths and Bevan as representatives of the 'red dragon' and 'red flag' factions in Welsh Labour.

In 1968, Hughes (who had started life as a Liberal) proposed extending the Secretary of State's powers and creating a party-elected 'Welsh Council'.[8] 'Red flag' Labour MPs were hostile, as was Scottish Secretary Willie Ross given the likely knock-on effect in Scotland. This new internal battle reached a head in 1969, with Thomas – now Secretary of State – heading off demands for full legislative devolution by conceding Hughes' 'partly advisory and party executive' scheme, ironically rendering acceptable something he had previously rejected (Wyn Jones and Scully 2012: 30–1).[9]

Thomas was also willing to mobilise 'official' Welsh nationalism if necessary, not least in choosing to revive the 1911 investiture ceremony in 1969, perhaps in response to another strong challenge from Plaid in the Rhondda West by-election. Thus it became a high-profile event which Thomas hoped, à la Lloyd George nearly half-a-century before, would combine the right sort of Welsh nationalism with an updated British traditionalism. In the official souvenir programme, the new Prince of Wales himself hoped the occasion would 'serve to strengthen the bonds between Welsh people everywhere, remind many of the long history and the present continuity of Welsh culture and traditions, and produce a determination to work together for the future of Wales' (Investiture 1969: 5). In its evidence to the Royal Commission on the Constitution, meanwhile, the Welsh Council of the Labour Party insisted it had 'been in the forefront of the movement to accord Wales a greater influence and say in the political affairs of the U.K.' (Labour Party in Wales 1970: 18–19).

'Inheritors of Tradition'

Plaid Cymru's relatively strong showing at the two general elections of 1974 once again compelled Wales's three unionist parties to compete on soft-nationalist territory. Labour finally promised an elected Welsh Assembly, though the 'red flag' faction argued that even executive devolution would 'inevitably lead to separatism', undermine central planning and lead to domination by Welsh-speaking 'crypto-nationalists' (Morgan 1981: 399). Passions often ran high. When Plaid's Gwynfor Evans accused Neil Kinnock of being anti-Welsh on this basis, the future UK Labour leader threatened to sue him 'to the point of bankruptcy' (Westlake 2001: 127).

Plaid's success also meant the Welsh Liberals were no longer able to 'pose as the radical-nationalist alternative to Labour', the party's 'cultural-nationalist' stance having proved necessary but not sufficient to maintain its historic Home Rule mantle (Philip 1975: 311).[10] Thus Liberals wove Welsh devolution into their new argument for a federal UK, while the Conservatives promised more administrative devolution. But as Philip rightly pointed out, it would

> be a mistake to credit much of the new nationalism of Conservatives, Labour supporters, and Liberals solely to the competition offered by [Plaid] to their parties. The same intensification of Welsh-consciousness that allowed [Plaid] to make a political impact in the 1960s had also been slowly making its mark on the other parties since the 1940s. (Philip 1975: 315)

Following the Welsh electorate's overwhelming rejection of an assembly at the St David's Day referendum in 1979, the 1979 Conservative manifesto promised a fourth television channel for Welsh speakers, a pledge delivered (as S4C) under pressure from Gwynfor Evans' threatened hunger strike.

Nationalist politics in Wales had long rooted itself in the defence of language, something to which even the governments of Margaret Thatcher responded.[11] The Welsh-speaking North Walian Wyn Roberts was installed at the Welsh Office, while Thatcher's first Secretary of State, Nicholas Edwards, spoke of having 'a near total free hand' (Blaxland 2016), something echoed by his successor Peter Walker, whose tenure even gave rise to (hyperbolic) talk of a Welsh Conservative ideology known as 'Walkerism' (Walker 1991). This was Thatcher's 'composite' territorial code in action (Bulpitt 1983).

By the late 1990s, Ron Davies, Tony Blair's first Secretary of State for Wales, was casting Welsh Labour as 'Inheritors of Tradition', the natural successors of Keir Hardie's support for a Welsh parliament in 1895 (he 'saw no conflict between national identity and socialism') and the pro-devolu-tionists who had secured both a Council and Secretary of State for Wales, a 'strand' that for much of the twentieth century had 'been a minority' but was 'now once again in the ascendancy'. Davies acknowledged his own journey, having coming to accept that Welsh Labour needed ways of 'more forcefully expressing our identity politically', for example by establishing unequivocal support for the Welsh language. For this he was accused of 'having gone native', although, interestingly, Davies acknowledged that in 'securing one advance' his predecessors had 'nurtured the logic for the next' (Davies 1999: 3–4).

Although the animosity between Welsh Labour and Plaid Cymru was not as intense as that between Scottish Labour and the SNP, in 1992 the Welsh party's general secretary had dismissed any cross-party co-operation on the basis that Plaid 'do not agree with anything we say or do, and we do not agree with them' (Wyn Jones and Scully 2012: 41). During the devolution referendum campaign of 1997, however, the two parties worked together more closely, partly a consequence of Davies's nationalist unionism. The outcome of the referendum was tight, but then feelings of Britishness were stronger in Wales.[12]

Davies did not make it to Cardiff Bay as 'First Secretary' (he later joined Plaid Cymru), though his unenthusiastic replacement, Alun Michael, went through the nationalist-unionist motions by unveiling a plaque in Machynl-leth to commemorate Owain Glyndŵr's 1406 Parliament (Shipton 2011). Rhodri Morgan, who succeeded Michael in February 2000, was more of a true believer, realising that

> for Wales to embrace devolution, the leader would not just have to be from Wales but would need to be seen to have been made in Wales; and for Labour to succeed in the devolution era, the party would have to be unambiguously Welsh in its identity. (Brennan and Drakeford 2017: xiv)

Giving this a greater impetus had been Plaid's surprisingly good performance at the 1999 Assembly election, at which it made inroads into Labour's val-leys heartlands. Morgan pursued what he called a 'clear red water' strategy of differentiation from the Blairite consensus, while after the 2007 election Morgan and Carwyn Jones (his eventual successor) agreed to make Welsh Labour 'the natural home of those who saw themselves as patriotically Welsh', largely to avoid the fate of the Scottish party in apparently having ceded 'Scottishness' to the SNP (Jones 2019). As with Ron Davies, this led to 'facile accusations of crypto-nationalism' from Westminster colleagues (Brennan and Drakeford 2017: xv).

The fact that Labour in Wales – consistently in devolved government after 1999 – was able to frame this in opposition to at first a Conservative–Labour coalition and, after 2015, a majority Conservative administration at Westminster, was a nationalist-unionist gift, while both Morgan and Jones made a point of sustaining a specifically 'devolutionist' narrative. Interviewed shortly before his death in 2017, Morgan said he

> would never describe myself as a unionist because unionists were the people who were against devolution in the first place, whereas if you're a nationalist obviously you don't believe in devolution 'cause you don't think it goes far enough and you want to become a completely different country. It's trying to define this space of being passionate about devolution and not seeing it as a half-way house to independence or anything that's been conceded to the nationalists because otherwise there'd be problems; it's . . . a belief that the British constitution is much healthier for having devolution since 1999. (ITV Wales, 19 June 2017)

One commentator dubbed this the 'Welshminster consensus', something that embodied 'soft-nationalist cultural politics and political rhetoric; devo-maximising constitutional reform; and a social democratic policy agenda', a consensus within which all Welsh political parties after 1999 operated to varying degrees (Deacon *et al.* 2018).

The Welsh Conservatives were the exception that proved the rule, the soft-nationalist approach instigated by Enoch Powell in the late 1940s having disappeared by the mid-1960s. As Morgan observed, it was 'historically an anglicized party; its candidates seldom spoke Welsh, were frequently Anglicans, and viewed Welsh nationalism with a hostile eye' (Morgan 1981: 379). It even refused to give evidence to the Royal Commission on the Constitution, and while Chris Butler, a special adviser at the Welsh Office during the 1980s, claimed the Conservative Party was 'increasingly speaking for Wales' and even upholding the 'Welsh radical tradition', by 2001 anti-Conservatism had 'become part of the constellation of Welsh national identity . . . part of the "Other" against which Welshness is defined' (Wyn Jones *et al.* 2002: 235, 243).

Always more closely aligned to 'English' politics than Scotland's, the Welsh political system meant the Welsh Conservatives could rely on support from non-Welsh Wales; Rod Richards, the party's first leader in the National Assembly, even called for the Welsh party to be 'wrapped in the Union Jack' (Blaxland 2016). Later, however, another Assembly Member (AM) called David Melding convinced his colleagues to champion the Welsh language and, strikingly, campaign for more advanced devolution –

perhaps even federalism – something acknowledged as aiding a revival of the Welsh party between 2003 and 2011 (Convery 2016).

One Welsh Conservative AM referred to the party's 'Welshification' after 1999. 'Despite our pride in Welsh culture and heritage, and our Unionist credentials,' acknowledged Nick Bourne, who succeeded Richards as leader, 'Welsh Conservatives have been hindered by the notion that we are in some way an "English party".' Another AM told Convery the party had 'parked' its 'tanks on the nationalists' lawn', aiming to attract soft Plaid voters and even offer itself as a potential coalition partner with them and the Liberal Democrats (Convery 2016: 95, 102–3).

A later Melding essay viewed unionism and nationalism in Wales as 'closely related political phenomena' with each containing 'seeds of the other'.

> It is in the nature of a union of nations that nationalist and unionist sentiments mingle, separate and then combine in a constantly changing political kaleidoscope. If the Union really is a bargain between nations seeking to secure common values and interests, then nationalism is an entirely inherent force necessary for the health of the body politic. (Melding 2019)

Conclusion

During the twentieth century Wales was more culturally distinct yet at the same time more politically integrated with the rest of the United Kingdom than was Scotland. Nationalist unionism, therefore, was simultaneously stronger – certainly in rhetorical terms – and weaker – in terms of 'administrative devolution' – than that explored in Chapters 3–7. Nevertheless, the nature of nationalist unionism in Wales and Scotland was recognisable, ethno-symbolist in complexion, 'banal' in self-perception and part of a broader attempt to territorially manage the multi-national UK.

Like Scottish Unionists, their Welsh counterparts – whether Conservative, Labour or Liberal – believed that Welsh identity and autonomy could find adequate expression within the Union, ranging from modest cultural concessions, administrative devolution and ultimately a Welsh Assembly or Parliament (something captured by the differing views of Megan and Gwilym Lloyd George). The aim, as in Scotland, was to concede whatever was considered necessary to maintain the existing, and later evolving, 'state of unions'.

In 1911 and 1969, for example, Wales was offered state-sanctioned 'official' nationalism in the form of investiture ceremonies for the Prince of Wales, while in the late 1940s the Conservatives promised a Minister for Welsh Affairs which sparked a lengthy constitutional bidding war with the Labour Party, the logic of which led to the appointment of a Welsh Secretary in 1964, something long resisted by both parties. Each party in government ultimately retained its predecessor's concessions, thus producing a ratchet-like effect which also existed in Scotland.

This gave rise to similar contradictions, with the unionist parties attempting to fix the boundary to the march of the Welsh nation, only to alter that boundary when the acceptable parameters of constitutional discourse shifted. Why was their nationalist unionism acceptable but, at different points, legislative devolution or independence a step too far? Where, as in Scotland, did 'patriotism' end and 'nationalism' begin? And why was a Secretary of State and dedicated department acceptable in Scotland but not in Wales? As William Hague asked of Tony Blair in 1997: 'If you really believe that a Scottish parliament would work, why would Wales get a second-class version?' (Convery 2016: 175).

TEN

Northern Ireland and 'Ulster Nationalism'

Following the successful Ulster Workers Council (UWC) strike of 1974, which brought down a well-intentioned but ill-fated attempt to restore devolution in the province, the then Secretary of State Merlyn Rees called it an 'outbreak of Ulster nationalism'. During a subsequent debate in the House of Commons on 4 June, the term was thoroughly examined. Former Prime Minister Edward Heath considered it 'a misnomer, and a dangerous one', not conforming to any understanding of nationalism in 'any common, modern form'. It could only be Ulster nationalism 'if there were a genuine desire by both communities or by a majority of the majority community to go it alone for independence'; Heath preferred to call it 'a Protestant backlash' (HC Deb 04 Jun 1974 vol 874 c1064).

This might have been a 'modern' definition of nationalism but also a very narrow one; the minority position of the SNP and Plaid in February's election hardly meant it did not constitute nationalism. In the same debate, Mark Hughes (Durham) saw the UWC strike as a new 'expression' of a long-standing phenomenon (c1115), while Gerry Fitt of the SDLP believed 'Ulster nationalism' actually meant a 'Protestant ascendancy' that wanted Northern Ireland to revert to Stormont majority rule (c1135). Finally, Robert Redmond (Bolton West) resented the term 'loyalist':

> [To] whom are these so-called Loyalists loyal? Are they loyal to the Queen? Are they loyal to the constitution of this country? Are they loyal to the law of this country? I believe that they are loyal only to what they see as the Protestant faith and to what they see to be the Province of Ulster. In my view, that is what the Secretary of State meant by 'the new Ulster nationalism'. These people are not loyal to Britain. (c1156)

This came closest to capturing a more convincing definition of 'nationalist unionism' as it existed in Northern Ireland, a nationalism that claimed 'loyalty' to the Crown (if not the 1801 Act of Union) while viewing its ethnic 'community' as the true embodiment of what was usually called 'Ulster'. On this, however, the literature is more divided than that in Scotland and Wales.

Gibbon's view was that following the Ulster Unionist Convention of 1892, at which thousands of Unionist association delegates gathered in Belfast to express their opposition to Home Rule, Unionists 'were creating a form of nationalism' in so far as their emergence 'created a new set of political structures', and laid claim to an 'identity which was territorially based' (not to mention self-determined) and cultural distinctiveness embodied in the honest, loyal 'Ulsterman' (Gibbon 1975: 136). Similarly, in his later history of the Ulster Unionist Party, Walker felt the party's political project was 'arguably best described as either an ethnoreligious or an ethno-national entity'. He deployed Smith's definition of nationalism, in that Ulster Unionism oscillated between 'the civic and the ethnic' and drew upon a rich array of myths and symbols. Walker also detected a familiar contradiction within this nationalism:

> Ulster Unionism's ideological repertoire in many respects took on the complexion of contemporaneous nationalism in Ireland and elsewhere [yet] Ulster Unionists appeared to see no inconsistency in dabbling in the ethno-nationalism of 'Ulsterness' while denying the validity of Irish Nationalist claims and invoking notions of the 'higher wisdom' of Britishness. (Walker 2004: viii, 7–8)

Aughey, however, reckoned Ulster Unionism should not be assessed on the same conceptual ground as nationalism (Aughey 1989), while Miller saw it as more 'contrarian' than nationalist, a phenomenon he called 'conditional loyalty', nation-building having bypassed Ulster Protestants in the early nineteenth century.

At the same time, Miller's seminal work, *Queen's Rebels: Ulster Loyalism in Historical Perspective* (2007), supported most aspects of the Ulster nationalist thesis. He accepted that Ulster provoked loyalty, just not as a 'nation', with the claim to self-determination, which he also accepted, therefore not resting upon 'nationality'. Rather the clear difference in the situation of Unionists in Ulster and those in the rest of Ireland meant the former would 'develop its own character, identity, organisation and, ultimately, goals'. He quotes Buckland saying that the creation of Northern Ireland was 'not the product of the demand of a local Ulster nationalism *a la Basque*', but while that was undeniably true, it ignored the fact that its creation nevertheless gave Ulster Unionists something to defend after 1921, further strengthening a political 'nationalism' that had already emerged in the 1890s, its right to self-determination having been acknowledged by Asquith's suggestion that Ulster be excluded from any Home Rule settlement. As Miller himself argues, after 1932 Ulster Protestants made the 'Parliament Buildings' at Stormont 'the centre of their political life and a potential focus for allegiance' (Miller 2007: 91–130 *passim*), the mere existence of the 'state', as Beckett had suggested in 1971, producing a sort of 'Ulster patriotism', a 'kind of embryonic nationalism; or, at least, a state of mind out of which a sense of national, rather than merely regional, distinctiveness might, in certain circumstances, emerge' (Beckett 1971: 147).

In other words, it was Ulster 'nationalist unionism' rather than the secessionist variety defined by Heath *et al*. Miller also acknowledged the symbolic and mythical basis of Ulster Unionism, its 'modest' literature between 1913 and 1923 bearing a 'superficial resemblance to the rhapsodies on national heritage and character which characteristically accompany a nationalist movement', and that its 'spokesmen' had adopted 'the language of nationality when it was necessary to achieve their political goal', just as unionists in Scotland and Wales had done, and not just for expediency, but because it clearly resonated. As O'Leary put it, these

> narratives, myths, and symbols resonated, and made sense of each community's respective pasts – they were not mere fictions or myths, to be dispelled by therapy from a liberal educator . . . Their narratives, myths, and symbols have had significant historical truth content; without that, politicians and activists would have been less successful in their manipulative endeavors. (O'Leary 2019b: 6)

In another passage that came close to contradicting his own thesis, Miller acknowledged that between 1885 and 1920 overlapping groups of Ulster Protestants had 'the appearance of nationalities', thinking of themselves as Irish and Ulstermen. They had 'quasi-national feelings of attachment to Ireland, to "Ulster" and to a Britain which was less the real Great Britain than a vague concept of a Greater Britain which somehow the Empire might come to embody' (Miller 2007: 119–21). So not only is Smith's ethno-symbolism relevant here, but so too is Billig's 'banal nationalism', in which an 'imagined community' of loyal Protestants pushed the nationalism of their 'disloyal' Catholic opponents to the periphery as extreme and exclusive. Finally, although taking the Conservative whip at Westminster and ostensibly under the watchful eye of the Home Office, successive UK governments were content, until the late 1960s, with Ulster control of Ulster affairs.

As Özkırımlı has argued, while nationalism speaks the collectivist language of 'community', it often advances one such 'imagined community' over another. 'It thus includes in Northern Ireland the "unionist" version as well as the "nationalist" version, however much these are conventionally counterposed' (Özkırımlı 2005: 89, 102). Even writing in 1962, Heslinga was quite clear that 'Ulsterism' was a form of nationalism which, as in Scotland and Wales at that time, could not be fulfilled by political independence but rather the maintenance of a constitutional link with the British Crown (Heslinga 1962).

Ulster Unionist Identity

The creation of Northern Ireland in 1921 – engineered by the Welsh nationalist unionist David Lloyd George – had a profound impact upon the identity of Ulster Unionists. Unionism in Ireland had developed in response to the Home Rule movement,[1] but initially included a strong Irish dimension. At the 1892 Ulster Unionist Convention in Belfast, the Duke of Abercorn told delegates that they were 'descendants of English puritans' and of Scottish Presbyterians, members of a great empire, and also 'Irishmen' whom England must not desert. Another delegate suggested the British Empire comprised the union of English pluck, Scottish prudence and Irish enthusiasm (George Boyce 2006: 56).

As Miller observed, the Convention was decorated with Celtic designs, banners in Irish Gaelic and when Ulstermen spoke of 'our country' or 'our native land' they 'almost invariably meant *Ireland*' (Miller 2007: 110). Later, however, the creation of a devolved Northern Ireland Parliament narrowed this multi-layered sense of identity. 'Devolution hemmed its patriotism in', judged George Boyce (George Boyce 2006: 61), with Ulster Unionists no longer proclaiming their Irishness but instead becoming a 'pan-Protestant British nationalism, one that expressed Ulster Protestants' political, economic, and religious self-images and interests' (O'Leary 2019a: 359). Irish Unionism morphed into Ulster Unionism, accompanied by a process of 'othering' the Irish Free State and drawing on pre-modern raw material, largely from Scotland.

Official publications marking the opening of the 'Northern Parliament' at Belfast City Hall on 22 June 1921, the Prince of Wales's visit in November 1932 (including to open Stormont) and the opening of the Royal Courts of Justice Ulster on 31 May 1933 illustrate this declining sense of Irishness. The cover of the first features the obligatory red hand of Ulster but also the Irish harp and a shamrock (both adorned with crowns), as well as the St Patrick's cross (Opening of Parliament 1921). The cover of the 1932 document, however, eschews any Irish imagery, instead featuring the Northern Ireland coat of arms, the red hand and Welsh feathers and a dragon, references to another part of the United Kingdom. The Moderator of the General Assembly referred in his speech to 'all who hold high office in this State of Northern Ireland', while blessing 'the Empire of which we form a part'. The programme also notes that the carved statuary in Stormont's pediment represents 'Ulster carrying the golden flame of loyalty to Great Britain and the Empire' (Visit of HRH Prince of Wales 1932: 12, 17). Finally, the official programme for the opening of the Royal Courts features only the king's coat of arms, although it does note the use of Irish granite 'for external steps, curbs and pavings' (Opening of Royal Courts 1933). As the architectural historian Charles Brett later observed, Stormont constituted 'the corporate expression of embattled Unionism, and an effort (perhaps largely unconscious) to convert a brash and sprawling industrial centre into a politico-religious capital city' (Brett 1985: 65).

As Buckland noted, Ulster Unionists often had 'a very hazy sense of nationality':

> They neither felt themselves truly British, which is why they identified so strongly with the Empire instead of Britain the nation state, nor could they reject their Irishness. As one Ulster Unionist remarked in 1914, 'If in one sense, Ulstermen are Irishmen first and Britishers afterwards, in another sense they are Ulstermen first and Irishmen afterwards'. (Buckland 1980: 19)

The only certainty was what they were not, i.e. Catholic, thus the need, after 1921, to downgrade the more Irish aspects of their identity. Analysts of Northern Ireland's system of devolved government also tried to square the circle of defending institutions that had been imposed upon the province against the wishes of its majority community. Tom Wilson argued that it was 'precisely when national sentiment demands Home Rule that Home Rule may do serious harm' (Wilson 1955: xxiii), a point also made by Mansergh, who warned that 'should national feeling be aroused not for good, but for national, government then the day for Devolution has passed and that of national and independent institutions has dawned' (Mansergh 1936: 21–2).

As already noted, several Northern Irish writers worked hard to fashion an imagined community of strong, brave and honest Ulstermen (women rarely featured), with which those on the mainland appeared to concur, with certain modifications. 'They are a pugnacious people with a touch of the Scotch about them which is a very stubborn race', was Lloyd George's view; 'we are only behind them to the extent that we cannot allow civil war to take place at our doors which will embroil our own people' (quoted in Ferritter 2019: 13).

Others, such as the Scottish Unionist John Buchan, were more sympathetic, referring to Ulstermen as 'one blood and one creed' with 'as much history behind them as any nation might be proud of'. Furthermore, the

Ulster Covenant of 1912 had framed them as a 'sovereign people', as in Scotland. This was then turbo-charged on Belgian battlefields during the First World War, with the 'Nationalist martyrs of Easter 1916' joined by their 'Unionist counterparts on the Somme' (Walker 2004: 34, 40). Later, the 'Ulster Tower' was constructed to commemorate the specifically 'Ulster' sacrifice, another illustration of the importance of symbolism to nationalist unionism.

Walker has argued that there was something of a 'Presbyterianisation' or Ulster-Scots makeover of the Ulster Unionist identity, particularly around the time of the third Irish Home Rule Bill (1912–14). Books such as the Rev J. B. Woodburn's *The Ulster Scot* (1914) was an 'intervention designed to explain the stubbornness of the Ulster people to those in Britain who could not fathom the depths of their resolve and the intensity of their objections to Home Rule'. Later, *Ulster's Stand for Union* (1922) by the Unionist MP Ronald McNeill deployed the language of democratic rights as well as 'kith and kin' appeals to Ulster's Scots heritage. Presbyterianism 'provided the most usable narrative for the Ulster cause' and contained 'the vital ingredient of victimhood' (Walker 2016). This Presbyterianisation of Ulster identity endured. Even Terence O'Neill, who had been born and raised in England, promoted the idea of an 'Ulster-Scots people' as Prime Minister in the 1960s, mainly with a US audience in mind. McLean and McMillan identified 'Ulster-Scots intellectuals' as one of three 'intertwined strands of primordial unionism' in modern Northern Ireland, the others being 'the Gunmen' and 'the Evangelicals', all of them sharing a 'worldview in which they are a special people who struggle grimly against huge odds but with Divine assistance' (McLean and McMillan 2005: 137, 143).[2]

In the early 1920s, therefore, 'Ulster Unionism took shape as a form of nationalism, notwithstanding its preference to maintain the Union rather than pursue independence'.

> An Ulster national identity developed, ironically, out of the distinctly Irish experience of the Union ... Ulster Unionists wished for Union on the same terms as those understood by Scotland: as a joint venture rather than a takeover by the largest (English) part. (Walker 2004: 284)

Sir James Craig, Northern Ireland's first Prime Minister, assumed the role of 'tribal chief', feted by the Ulster Unionist Council as 'a great Ulsterman, a great Irishman, a great Imperialist' in whom 'Ulster saw an epitome of itself'. There was no mention, strikingly, of Craig's Britishness (Walker 2004: 87).[3]

Edward Carson, who had done so much to resist devolution, was given a 'state' funeral at Stormont in 1935, and indeed politicians and academics had a tendency to talk up the Northern Ireland Parliament's status and powers. Newark called it 'truly a sovereign body except in so far as its powers are expressly limited' (Newark 1955: 27). This helped fuel talk, at various points between the 1940s and 1970s, of Northern Ireland adopting 'Dominion status'. Craig had raised this possibility with Lloyd George during negotiations in 1921, while it arose thereafter defensively, proposed as a means of 'protecting' Northern Ireland either from 'socialist' Labour governments or Conservative administrations keen on involving Dublin in the province's affairs.

After the 1945 general election, an Ulster Unionist backbencher at Stormont, William F. McCoy, began a concerted campaign – backed by certain members of the Northern Irish cabinet – for greater autonomy and Dominion status along the lines of Canada, Australia and New Zealand.[4] This was fuelled by the twin fears of left-wing legislation being 'foisted' upon Northern Ireland by Clement Attlee's government and the potential hostility of Labour (with its history of pro-Irish nationalism) to Ulster Unionist interests. Thus McCoy made points not unlike those of later SNP politicians in relation to Westminster, that Stormont was 'controlled and trammelled' by the UK Parliament, which could override it as it wished. Therefore, the only way to safeguard Northern Ireland's position in the empire was for it to become legislatively independent (Walker 2004: 112).

The Labour government's actual conduct of constitutional affairs contradicts McCoy's fears, instead supporting Bulpitt's theory of 'territorial management' as applied to the Conservative Party. This meant Attlee was content to focus on 'high politics', welfare unionism and decolonisation, and leave Northern Ireland to its own devices. Indeed, the Ireland Act 1949, with its confirmation of the six counties' self-determination and status as part of the UK, was widely welcomed among Unionists and quickly neutralised the 'Dominion status' lobby. This did not stop John Miller Andrews, briefly Prime Minister during the Second World War, from denouncing McCoy et al. as 'separatist', a standard attack line for dissenters from the constitutional status quo.

The very existence of Stormont, meanwhile, furnished Scottish and Welsh nationalists (and some nationalist unionists) 'with a new and powerful argument for the adoption of a similar system in Scotland and Wales' (Coupland 1954: 123). Indeed, the Kirriemuir Plebiscite of 1949 had asked voters to choose between an independent Scottish Parliament, a Parliament like that of Northern Ireland, and the status quo (Walker 2010). Sir Basil Brooke, Prime Minister since 1943, even met representatives of the Scottish Covenant movement, 'who are studying the set up here with a view to a similar set up in Scotland. I told them that in my view it worked well' (Brooke 1950). Newark, however, was disdainful of what he called 'the façade of semi-independence as represented by flags, Parliamentary institutions [and] the creation of public offices' and sceptical of Dominion status in spite of its 'attractions':

> In order to sustain the role of a dominion a country needs not only the desire for independence but the capacity for maintaining that independence, and six counties with one modern city does not, to my eyes, possess the makings of a dominion – at least not a first-class dominion . . . the exit of Northern Ireland from the United Kingdom would knock the bottom out of every argument that the Unionist Party ever thought of. (Newark 1953: 15–16)

By the time Brooke (by now Lord Brookeborough) stood down as Prime Minister in 1963, his Unionist government had been deeply discredited by its failure to wring concessions from London, in other words its failure to adequately 'stand up for Northern Ireland' within the UK. At the same time, Ulster Unionists were fond of contrasting their more progressive health and welfare systems (which generally followed those on the mainland under the 'parity principle') with those in the Irish Republic, just as the SNP would (vis-à-vis England) in devolved government after 2007.

Indeed, Terence O'Neill, Brooke's successor as Prime Minister, was the first Northern Ireland premier to both evangelise about the merits of devolution while advocating its extension to other parts of the United Kingdom, thus avoiding the inconsistency of Scottish Unionists in defending devolution in one part of the UK while opposing it in another. O'Neill was relaxed about highlighting points of legislative divergence between Belfast and London while, more broadly, his goal was a sort of 'regional patriotism' that he hoped would transcend sectarian divisions.

Naturally, he pushed what he called 'the unrealistic theories of extreme nationalism' to the periphery, stressing that he did not endorse 'local' nationalism.

> As the nations form wider political and economic groupings, I believe a narrow separatist approach becomes increasingly inappropriate. I approve of a measure of regional devolution not as a step to weaken the nation, but as a step to strengthen it. It would allow the great assembly of the whole nation to devote more of its time to the weighty issues which confront Britain in a European and international setting. (O'Neill 1969: 97)

Even O'Neill's more progressive nationalist unionism retained traces of ethno-symbolism. In speeches he would refer approvingly to 'men of Ulster stock', 'our ancient link with Britain', as well as a table upon which the 1801 Act of Union was signed and a bible used by those sworn in to the

Privy Council of Ireland (and after 1921, Northern Ireland) since the early nineteenth century: 'These things are history, but they are also symbolism. They demonstrate that the Union is not a thing of any decade or generation, but an enduring part of British history' (O'Neill 1969: 83, 47, 50). In 1962, the Belfast Municipal Museum and Art Gallery had also been renamed the 'Ulster Museum' and recognised as a 'national' museum, an Ulster identity subsequently reinforced by (muted) celebrations of Northern Ireland's half-centenary in 1971. As Anderson (1991) had observed, the 'census, map and museums' of a territory could be important source material for its 'imagined community'.

Ulster Nationalism Redux

Identity and Ulster Unionism would evolve once more during the Troubles, often defensively. Rose had been the first to explore the connection between national identity in Northern Ireland and religion, finding, unsurprisingly, that most Protestants thought of themselves as British or 'Ulster' and most, but not all, Catholics identifying as 'Irish'. At the same time, 20 per cent of Protestants also claimed an Irish identity. By 1978, however, there had occurred a significant swing towards 'British' among Protestants, although 20 per cent still said 'Ulster', as did 14 per cent in a 1986 survey, along with 11 per cent who identified as 'Northern Irish' (Whyte 1991: 67–9).

For Rose, a 'substantial proportion' of Ulster Unionists could therefore be termed 'proto-nationalist' in that they felt allegiance to a perceived Northern Ireland state rather than the 'sovereign' Westminster parliament. And as sectarian violence increased after the late 1960s, this even meant a majority of Protestants in Northern Ireland 'would endorse violence to defend the Protestant state', with figures like William Craig exploiting this 'embryonic Protestant nationalism by advocating independence for the Province and the severance of the British link' (Madgwick and Rose 1982: 203). Neal Ascherson wrote in 1977 of Craig 'clinging to his dream of fitting a Protestant Ulster with inviolable and entrenched rights into a federal Britain' (*Edinburgh Review* 100, 1999). Craig's Ulster-centric thinking was later taken up by Glen Barr and John McMichael in the late 1970s, when the paramilitary Ulster Defence Association publicly backed an independent Ulster.

The same surveys cited above, however, generally found low support for an 'independent' Northern Ireland, although this tended to rise if presented as the only alternative to a united Ireland. The Troubles era spawned a plethora of such proposals, including some from the Nationalist community (for example, Eddie McAteer's 1972 pamphlet, *Won't You Please Sit Down?*). It was also the Troubles that prompted Nairn to predict a move towards 'more than a nominal "Ulster nationalism"', later adding that in place of a 'normal' nationalism there instead existed 'a lunatic, compensatory emphasis of the two ideologies already strongly present in its community, militant Protestantism and imperialism' (Nairn 1981: 236, 240–1).

Although this variety of Ulster nationalism falls outwith the scope of this book, it is worth analysing some of the discourse that flowed from Nairn's argument that only by embracing this 'normal' nationalism could Protestants cease 'to be backward, religion-ridden, lunatic reactionaries'. Ulstermen, he added provocatively, 'are not British'. This and Merlyn Rees's aforementioned reference to the 'new Ulster nationalism' prompted a counterblast from the British and Irish Communist Organisation (BICO), which called for the full integration of Northern Ireland into the UK in the 1970s and 1980s, as well as for the Labour Party to organise in the six counties. BICO believed the fledgling Northern Ireland Office and sections of the media to be 'surreptitiously' promoting Rees's concept, concluding that not only would Protestant nationalism 'be reactionary, but it would do nothing whatever to solve the national problem in Ulster' (BICO 1975: 81).

Kenneth Lindsay's 1972 pamphlet, *Dominion of Ulster* (which followed *Ulster – A Nation*) had revived the late 1940s' 'dominion status lobby' in response to another perceived threat from Westminster, that of a Conservative government which most likely wanted to wash its hands of a troublesome (and expensive) province. This set out three constitutional choices, integration (à la BICO), a federation or 'an independent Ulster linked to Great Britain and the other member states of the Commonwealth by a common allegiance to the Crown'. This was spun as a 'well-tried constitutional development' with room for an 'Ulster' which was 'independent, democratic, flexible, imaginative and deeply British' (Lindsay 1972: 5, 19).

Bourke referred to the 'meticulously crafted ambiguities' (Bourke 2003: 227) of 'Ulster Vanguard', the new unionist organisation to which Lindsay, William Craig and others (such as the future Ulster Unionist leader David Trimble) attached themselves, a 'post-Unionist' ideology extensively charted by Watson in his journal article of the same name (Watson 2013). Beginning in the late 1960s, Craig (no relation to Sir James) had echoed W. F. McCoy in framing Stormont as the ultimate source of political and constitutional authority in Northern Ireland, an interpretation dismissed by Terence O'Neill as akin to Southern Rhodesian UDI. 'We cannot', declared O'Neill, 'be a part of the United Kingdom merely when it suits us' (O'Neill 1972: 145–9).

This was ironic, for Craig's views could be seen as the logical extension of O'Neill's desire for a more expansive form of Northern Irish devolution. As Gordon (a biographer of O'Neill) put it, Craig was simply an 'O'Neillite who took O'Neillism in earnest' (Gordon 1989: 134). In another irony,

Craig – as vice-chairman of the Queen's University Unionist Association – had once criticised McCoy for promoting a philosophy predicated on the 'un-Unionist' principles of 'Ulster nationalism' (*Londonderry Sentinel*, 31 January 1952). By the 1960s, however, Craig was himself criticising aspects of Northern Ireland's constitutional settlement, including the imperial contribution and the 'parity principle'.

Vanguard's early 1970s publications, therefore, took this journey to its natural conclusion. One of them, *Community of the British Isles*, also extended O'Neillism by envisaging an independent Ulster nation along non-sectarian lines:

> Both communities love Ulster, their small but dearest land. Mr Craig [in a 1972 speech] touched a reconciling emotion that all Ulstermen share, an emotion that may be correctly called patriotic. Community differences arise over the political structure within which Ulster is to be set. Ulster people have not, as has been shown, been asked to choose for Ulster alone, but rather between two structural alternatives, each of which divides them.

The pamphlet then sketched out an ecumenical ethno-symbolism which 'Ulstermen of whatever political affiliations' could 'explore together', symbols of Ulster's 'mighty past', 'the Ulster Cycle of heroic legends, the sagas of Fionn and Ossian, Ulster's heraldic Red Hand, St Patrick – [which] enrich the heritage of Western civilisation'. The 'visible monuments' of Northern Ireland's pre-history were 'scattered over Ulster to excite and enthral all men' (Ulster Vanguard 1972). This was not completely off the wall, given Rose's finding that Northern Ireland's two communities perhaps had more in common with one another than they did with either of their alleged 'imagined communities' in Great Britain or the Irish Republic (Rose 1971: 214).

Vanguard also drew upon an anti-Englishness which also found expression on the Ulster Unionist right, in the later Democratic Unionist Party and even some Nationalists. Vanguard quoted Eddie McAteer saying on the fall of Stormont that he would rather be ruled by fellow Ulstermen than from the smoke-filled rooms of Westminster, just as the UUP MP and minister John Taylor had lambasted, with prorogation looming, English politicians for not understanding 'how the Ulsterman thinks' (*Belfast Telegraph*, 26 January 1972). Miller noted how both Vanguard and the Rev. Ian Paisley spoke of Westminster as a distant and out-of-touch body, disparaging terms not unlike those used by the SNP several decades later, but, keen not to subscribe to any idea of 'Ulster nationalism', argued that such expressions in the 1970s amounted to 'a reluctant matter-of-fact nationalism, perhaps a nationalism of despair, a nationalism arising out of immediate events and circumstances, not out of long-term social processes'; the nationalism contained in another Vanguard publication, *Ulster – A Nation*, constituted 'only a thin veneer over the old contractarian modes of thought' (Miller 2007: 154).

Brian Faulkner, Northern Ireland's last Prime Minister and its only 'Chief Executive',[5] disparaged Vanguard in the same way O'Neill and Andrews had earlier advocates of Dominion status, referring to William Craig's journey from conventional Ulster Unionist to Protestant 'Sinn Féiner', with the added implication that independence (like unification) would be politically and economically catastrophic. In his memoirs, he speculated that these hitherto 'unspoken separatist tendencies' had arisen as a result of an insular Stormont system producing 'illusions of self-sufficiency' (Faulkner 1978: 26). To Craig, this was 'scare-mongering' which fuelled the bogus contention that Northern Ireland could survive 'only if it was in receipt of subsidies and special payments from the UK treasury' (Watson 2013). Again, Craig's arguments resembled those of the SNP during the Scottish independence referendum campaign of 2012–14.

Enoch Powell, who had made the curious transition from mainland Conservative to Ulster Unionist MP in 1974, dismissed Vanguard's arguments on the basis that he believed Northern Ireland ought to be fully integrated into the UK (not only politically, but also party politically). He also rejected the idea of an Ulster 'identity' or nationalism, accepting only an Ulster 'dimension', which he viewed as akin to 'other regional dimensions in Britain, profound, historic and self-conscious'. This put him at odds with not only his new party but the emerging Democratic Unionists, both of which supporting restoring different forms of devolution. Powell even branded Ian Paisley 'anti-Unionist' and 'Protestant Sinn Féin' on this basis.

Yet at the same time Powell took an expansive view of nationhood, concluding in his short history of Britain (co-authored with Angus Maude) that 'they are a nation who think they are a nation: there is no other definition'. On that basis, if Scotland and Wales clearly wished 'no longer to be part of this nation, that wish ought not to be resisted'. Generally, Powell believed pro-Stormont Ulster Unionists were guilty of inconsistency, in that their 'assertion of oneness' with the rest of the UK was 'at odds with their assertion of . . . parliamentary independence' (Corthorn 2019: 11–12, 135–7, 147). This was not an isolated view. Writing in 1976, the Conservative MP John Biffen observed that the existence of Stormont had created 'a feeling of separateness as far as the remainder of the United Kingdom was concerned' (Biffen 1976: 7).

Under Miller's thesis, each new 'threat' to Ulster thereafter provoked a similar response from 'conditional' Unionists: for example, the UK government's pursuit of the Anglo-Irish Agreement in 1985, with its acceptance of an 'Irish' dimension in the future of Northern Ireland, i.e. consultation with Dublin. In response, the Orange Order threatened to establish a 'Scottish Unionist Party' to run against supportive Conservative MPs in the north of the mainland (Gallagher 1988), while the DUP's Peter Robinson once again canvassed the independence option 'with some gravity', although as Aughey pointed out, the Robinson who 'talked of Northern Ireland being on the "window-ledge" of the union was the same Peter Robinson who argued that unionists should not jump off that window-ledge' (Wilson Foster 1995: 17).

Ulster Unionist paranoia was not completely misplaced. In 1990, Northern Ireland Secretary Peter Brooke declared that the UK government 'had no selfish strategic or economic interest in Northern Ireland', opposing not reunification but its violent expression. In other words, 'Ulster' could be detached from 'Britain'. 'It was not part of Britain's totality,' observed Billig, 'as imagined by the British and Irish governments; both governments could imagine Ulster becoming part of Eire's totality' (Billig 1995: 76).

Evolving Ulster Unionism

In his analysis of Protestant political ideology, Wright drew a distinction between 'liberal' and 'extreme' varieties of Ulster Unionism (Wright 1973). More broadly, this might be seen as 'civic' versus 'ethnic' unionism, a distinction applied to Scottish nationalism from the early 1990s (see Chapter 8). As Richard English put it, rather than representing an alternative 'ethnic or religious nationalism', Ulster Unionism was essentially civic in that it 'argued for the reasonableness (indeed, the necessity) of maintaining Northern Ireland's place within the multi-national, multi-faith, multi-ethnic United Kingdom state' (Wilson Foster 1995: 135).

Indeed, as the Troubles era approached its end in the mid- to late 1990s, it was generally accepted that the Ulster Unionist Party had evolved from cultural in nature to a predominantly civic configuration, with the vacated ethnic territory filled by Ian Paisley's DUP. This culminated in David Trimble's reference to a 'pluralist parliament for a pluralist people', which deliberately drew on a famous, if misquoted, phrase from his predecessor Sir James Craig. Two core Unionist arguments reflected this dichotomy: the first, more ethnic aim was the preservation of Protestantism, and the second, more civic aim was the belief that the Union brought benefits to both Ireland and Great Britain (and, previously, to the British Empire).

Porter's typology viewed contemporary unionism as gravitating towards the three major poles of cultural, liberal and civic unionism. Todd also distinguished between those who identified as 'British Unionist' (their primary empathy being with Britain) and those who regarded themselves as 'Ulster Loyalist' (who took the six counties as their predominant imagined community). Porter's 'cultural' unionism was more exclusive than the 'liberal' and 'civic' varieties, regarding Protestantism as superior and drawing upon a range of strong identifiers: religious, British and historic. 'Liberal' unionism and Todd's 'British Unionist' tradition, however, were generally secular and promoted Northern Ireland as one part of a multi-national UK with equal citizenship, a welfare state, etc. Finally, 'civic' unionism takes this one step further by stressing inter-community bonds, with Aughey arguing that it 'has little to do with the idea of the nation and everything to do with the idea of the state', a rational political choice rather than an emotional one (Hennessey *et al.* 2019: 122–4).

Under David Trimble's leadership of the Ulster Unionist Party this was termed 'new unionism', something aided by a formal break with the Orange Order and reconstitution of the Royal Ulster Constabulary, both of which had once strongly been linked with the UUP. Into this mix Trimble threw the Vanguard-era idea of a 'Council of the Isles', which became a reality (as the British–Irish Council) via the Good Friday Agreement and was enthusiastically taken up by the SNP after 2007.[6] Trimble conceived of the UK not as a centralised but a 'union state', into which a restored Northern Ireland Assembly and a civic nationalist unionism could easily fit, particularly when accompanied with devolution, as O'Neill had envisaged, for Scotland and Wales.

In a 1999 lecture on 'Devolution and the Union', Trimble made some prescient observations about the likely impact of the new Scottish Parliament and National Assembly for Wales on the mainland 'unionist' parties. Labour, he predicted, would continue to marginalise its 'crypto-nationalist element', its inevitable electoral battles with the SNP turning it into a 'unionist' party, albeit with a small 'u', the same being true, to a lesser degree, with the Liberal Democrats. 'Either they will compete with the nationalists or they will follow them', concluded Trimble. 'If they compete with the nationalists then they will necessarily be moving to a unionist position' (Trimble 2001: 161).

This was a little simplistic, truer of Scottish Labour and the Scottish Conservatives (at least initially) than Welsh Labour and the Welsh Conservatives, who both managed to compete with Plaid Cymru on soft-nationalist terms. Trimble also skirted over the likely impact on the UUP of its support for the Good Friday Agreement and power-sharing with the nationalist Sinn Féin and SDLP in the new Northern Ireland Assembly, where Ulster Unionists left themselves vulnerable to accusations of backsliding, of not being Unionist enough, rather like Scottish Labour after the Scottish independence referendum. In Northern Ireland, the DUP proved to be the beneficiaries of this altered dynamic.

Thus the 'meaning and consequence' of Northern Irish identity 'developed over the post-conflict period', growing more expansive but also becoming harder to pin down. According to Hennessey *et al.*'s membership study, by the early twenty-first century it included 'commonplace discourses and everyday storytelling which convey a recognizable narrative, reproduced alongside habitual symbolism, commemoration, and memorials', which together 'provide the tools to interpret experience, thought, and imagination in terms, not just of the past, but also the present and possibilities in the future' (Hennessey *et al.* 2019: 135–6, 144).

Those possibilities did not include a full merger, ironically, with the mainland Conservative and Unionist Party, apparently proposed by its leader David Cameron in 2008. The leader of the 'Northern Ireland Conservative and Unionist Party' would have been the Anglo-Scottish Cameron, with a five-strong executive comprising three Conservatives and two representatives from the UUP. Ulster Unionists, however, baulked at the prospect of abandoning their distinctive organisation, autonomy and history (BBC News online, 30 March 2009). Besides, by then it had been displaced by the Democratic Unionist Party as Northern Ireland's main unionist party, in part because the UUP was no longer seen as a credible guardian of Ulster Unionist identity.

Conclusion

Many analysts of Northern Ireland have argued that there exists some form of 'Ulster nationalism', Sir James Craig's much-quoted 'boast' that 'we are a Protestant Parliament and Protestant State' having articulated a standard nationalist requirement for congruence between people and state. As an 'imagined nation' Northern Ireland or 'Ulster' clearly emerged in the modern period, a response to the Irish Home Rule movement of the late nineteenth century. Yet it also drew, as per Smith, on a rich plethora of symbolism and mythology from an earlier era, which was augmented and extended following the creation of the devolved Parliament of Northern Ireland in 1921.

Ulster Unionists oscillated between 'civic' and 'ethnic' arguments for the benefits they believed Northern Ireland derived from the Union, though the often 'conditional' nature of this proclaimed 'loyalty' to the British Crown was heavily predicated on a belief in self-determination, meaning that their view of the UK was very much as a 'state of unions'. Until the late 1960s the Westminster 'centre' generally left the Stormont 'periphery' alone, although

thereafter Northern Ireland became the most difficult part of British territory to be 'managed' by Labour and the Conservatives. As in Scotland and
Wales, most 'nationalist' debate occupied the large space in between those
proposing outright assimilation (Enoch Powell) or 'independence' (the two
Williams, McCoy and Craig), and, predictably, Ulster Unionists – as the
main 'carriers' of non-secessionist Ulster nationalism – pushed what they
regarded as the 'extreme' variety to the periphery of political debate.

ELEVEN

Conclusion

palimpsest
'palim(p)sɛst/
noun
1. a manuscript or piece of writing material on which later writing has been superimposed on effaced earlier writing.
2. something reused or altered but still bearing visible traces of its earlier form.

The modern era, to quote the nationalist theorist Anthony D. Smith, is 'not a blank slate', but rather resembles 'a palimpsest on which are recorded experiences and identities of different epochs and a variety of ethnic formations'. Earlier epochs influence – and are in turn modified by – later eras, 'to produce the composite type of collective cultural unit which we call "the nation"' (Smith 1995: 59–60).

From the moment the 1707 political union between Scotland and England was agreed, a palimpsest union was born, incorporating the earlier Anglo-Welsh union and which was later overlaid with the 1801 union of 'Great Britain' and Ireland. The resulting nation, or nation-state, was viewed differently from Edinburgh, Cardiff and Dublin (later Belfast). For Scotland, the foundational document was the Treaty of Union; for Dublin/Belfast, it was an Act of Union agreed in 1800 and enacted the following year.

During the seventeenth and eighteenth centuries this palimpsest union was imagined as 'Britain' or 'Great Britain' and its 'official' nationalism became known as 'unionism'. But within that nationalism there existed other, competing stories, memories of former epochs in which Ireland, Scotland and Wales had possessed their own degree of sovereignty. The unions of 1707 or 1801, for example, had not erased two of those alternative narratives; as Dicey and Rait wrote of the former, 'the sacrifice of Scottish independence' did not mean the 'loss of Scottish Nationalism'.

Thereafter this 'official' nationalism in Scotland, Wales and later Northern Ireland (or 'Ulster') took a number of forms, operating in concert – rather than in conflict – with a broader British nationalism and imperial 'patriotism'. In Scotland it was both defensive (epitomised by Sir Walter Scott and his defence of banknotes) and proactive (demanding administrative reform); in Wales it was initially more cultural and religious than political; and in Northern Ireland it took the form of a localised defence of Britishness. The aim of these 'nationalist unionists' was both the preservation of autonomous traces from earlier epochs and the creation of new civic institutions.

In 1886 all of these were turbo-charged by Gladstone's pursuit of Home Rule for Ireland, although, importantly, movements in Scotland and Wales preceded that critical constitutional juncture. Crucially, none challenged the primary nation-state in the manner of other nineteenth-century nationalist movements – that was not in question. Rather, these nationalists desired greater autonomy, attention and 'equality' *within* the union. Smith defined nationalism as 'an ideological movement for attaining and maintaining the autonomy, unity and identity of a nation', and despite their lack of interest in statehood, nationalist unionism in Scotland, Wales and Northern Ireland all conformed to what Smith had earlier called the 'basic pattern of nationalism'.

This 'autonomy' took a number of forms: devolution (either administrative or legislative), special committees or parliamentary time at Westminster, policy concessions and, perhaps most strikingly, symbolism. Nationalist unionists viewed Scotland and Wales as 'nations' (Northern Ireland was more complicated) and sought to defend that nationhood, railing against 'amalgamation', 'assimilation' or 'uniformity' imposed from the centre. Claiming to 'stand up' for their respective nations, unionists therefore operated within – and sustained – a nationalist framework, a product of their own discursive strategies. After all, and as Smith also observed, nationalism had a 'chameleon-like ability to transmute itself according to the perceptions and needs of different communities' (Smith 1995: 3).

All three UK political parties – Conservative, Labour and Liberal – helped fashion Scottish, Welsh and Ulster identities which were simultaneously Celtic, British and imperial (and later, European), a dual or triple identity articulated by Scottish unionists such as Arthur Balfour and Walter Elliot, Welsh Liberals like David Lloyd George and Tom Ellis, and the Ulster Unionist Terence O'Neill. Within a nationalist-unionist framework, this presented no contradiction.

Indeed, by 2014 even the Scottish National Party was championing Britishness alongside the Scottish and European strands of Scotland's national identity. Keating spoke of 'neo-nationalists' who viewed the UK as a framework for managing common issues between self-governing nations, competing with 'neo-unionists', who still took the UK to be the primary unit but asked 'how power might be reordered within it' (Keating 2009: 130–1). Thus nationalism and unionism overlapped and complimented one another, much like socialism, liberalism and conservatism, an 'orthographic battle' – as Nairn put it – between 'the upper and the lower cases'.

Territorial management

As Kidd has written in a seminal analysis of this phenomenon, nationalist-unionist inflections were 'neither English nor metropolitan' but rather those of 'an embattled Presbyterian provincialism somewhat distrustful of the motives of the English core of the United Kingdom' (Kidd 2008: 13–14), something also true of Northern Ireland and Wales (though nonconformism was to the fore in the latter). But while the union was not in question, nationalist unionists usually took care to fix the 'boundary' of the march of the Scottish and Welsh nations, a constitutional 'line' that could not be crossed, at least until events required it to be.

For Sir George Younger in 1914 this was everything short of legislative devolution, a line that held (with exceptions in 1918–21 and 1968–76) until 1999, while for Liberal and Labour politicians it was usually any measure short of actual independence. By the 2000s, Scottish and Welsh nationalist unionists drew the line at common taxes and welfare, similar to that which had held in Northern Ireland between 1921 and 1972 (via the 'parity principle'). In 2011, Ruth Davidson called it a 'line in the sand', though that too was quickly washed away. The SNP's 'line', meanwhile, was the resumption of sovereignty which, once secured, might facilitate all sorts of unionism. Where the 'line' fell generally depended upon the 'Overton window', the range of acceptable constitutional discourse at any given time.

This necessitated a 'delicate' balancing act 'between the forces of unity and the forces of separation' (Kellas 1980: 11–12), something Bulpitt later identified as a system of 'territorial management' common to all parties. From the 1880s, Conservatives, Liberals and Labour politicians at the 'centre' were content to govern Scotland, Ireland and Wales indirectly and informally, a 'code' which reached its zenith between the secession of Ireland in 1922 and the turbulent 1960s. All three parties often made sympathetic noises about Home Rule in opposition but failed to deliver in government, though after 1999 an updated unionist 'code' incorporated legislative devolution, morphing into a complex and imperfect system of inter-governmental relations.

Concessions were key to the centre's management of this constitutional real estate. Salisbury spoke of 'redress' for the 'wounded dignities of the Scotch people', but those – along with those of the Welsh and Northern Irish – often proved difficult to satisfy. Administrative devolution was the first concession (1885 in Scotland, 1965 in Wales), followed by the legislative variety in 1999. The centre continued to make concessions to the 'periphery' even after the twentieth century had given way to the twenty-first, thus Calman (2011), Silk (2012) and Smith (2014) were latter-day Gilmours (1937) or Balfours (1954) in seeking to alter the balance between Scottish or Welsh nationhood and the union. While usually driven by nationalist unionists on the periphery, this territorial code was also reinforced by figures at the centre, Gladstone, Baldwin, Churchill and David Cameron all championing 'local patriotism'. This was vividly put in the 1950s when the Anglo-Scottish Harold Macmillan said the union of 'our two great Kingdoms and the Principality of Wales' must be that 'of the wedding ring not of the handcuff'.

This constitutional bidding war manifested itself not just in policy but also in rhetoric and party organisation. The centre – whether Liberal or Conservative – generally found itself dealing with the Scottish and Ulster Unionist parties and the Welsh and Scottish Liberal federations on the periphery, or the Welsh Parliamentary Party and Scottish Unionist Members Committee at Westminster. Some parties zealously wielded their 'independence' as proof they did not always do London's bidding. Even the Labour Party, more centralised than its opponents, possessed Welsh and Scottish 'Councils'. Sometimes, territorial tensions led to talk of these semi-autonomous organisations 'seceding' from their respective UK party frameworks.

Most parties on the periphery possessed nationalist or devolutionary wings, this red dragon/red flag split being most pronounced within the Welsh Labour Party. Members of the same family ended up occupying different positions: Gwilym Lloyd George (a Conservative) believed Welsh nationhood was best protected without legislative or even administrative devolution, while his sister Megan (a Liberal) believed it could only flourish with a parliament to call its own. Labour in particular struggled to reconcile its nationalism in Scotland and Wales with the socialism of its centre. As Bulpitt said of Labour and the Liberals, both posed 'as a party of peripheral defence whilst at the same time pursuing a fundamentally centrist strategy'.

If their parties were electorally strong on the periphery, then Labour, Liberals and Conservatives were usually inclined to let local nationalist unionists do their own thing, i.e. Churchill and the Scottish Unionist Association in the late 1940s, Harold Wilson with Willie Ross in the 1960s, and Neil Kinnock with Scottish Labour in the 1980s, though they

(Kinnock as well as Gordon Brown) often worried that 'crypto-national-ism' might get out of hand. If things were not going well, then the centre was more interventionist, i.e. Heath in 1968 and Wilson with his Scottish Council in 1974. Unionists also had to balance their peripheral national-ism with ambitions at the centre; Lord Rosebery in Scotland and Tom Ellis in Wales epitomising a general trend to give preference to the latter.

The territorial code, meanwhile, did not treat Scotland, Wales and Northern Ireland equally. After 1921, the last of that trio had quasi-dominion status *within* the UK, while Scotland was usually prioritised on the basis of its distinct legal system. Wales's claims were of a different nature in that its nationhood was not necessarily a given. While the three main unionist parties were comfortable with acknowledging a distinctly Scottish national economic interest, for example, they were not in Wales. Territorial management, it could also be said, worked best when conces-sions to Scotland and Wales dovetailed with a broader strategy, i.e. Home Rule all round or 'decentralisation' in the 1950s (Conservative) and 1990s (Labour).

But this constitutional bidding war was subject, particularly in the sec-ond half of the twentieth century, to the law of unintended consequences, a ratchet-like effect between not only parties but different parts of the UK. Once Ireland enjoyed administrative devolution, Scotland agitated for the same; once Scotland had its own government minister and department, Wales demanded equal treatment; if 'disloyal' Ireland was to be granted a Home Rule assembly then why not 'loyal' Scotland?; if legislative devolu-tion was good enough for Northern Ireland after 1921, then why not also Scotland?; and, in the early twenty-first century, if the Scottish Parliament was to be granted more autonomy over income tax and welfare, why not the National Assembly for Wales? Occasionally, there were warnings of a 'slippery slope' leading to the wrong sort of nationalism, although union-ists rarely ceased to provide further lubrication.

Welsh Secretary Ron Davies, for example, acknowledged that in 'securing one advance', his predecessors had 'nurtured the logic for the next', while hav-ing revelled in the argument that distinct Scottish problems merited distinct solutions in the late 1940s, Scottish Unionists could hardly complain when Labour directed the same argument at them a decade later. Ironically, the most unionist of the three parties tasked with territorial management – the Conservatives – repeatedly contributed to rising expectations among voters, as did Labour with its Royal Commission on the Constitution and utopian framing of legislative devolution in the 1980s and 1990s. 'Who speaks for Scotland?' asked the *Daily Record* in 1950, and the question was posed con-sistently thereafter.

With each crank of the ratchet it became easier for voters to 'imagine' Scotland and Wales as even more autonomous, perhaps even independent, nations. But much of the territorial code was tactical in nature, a calculation by the centre that concessions to the periphery would deliver votes and thus preserve the union. In 1947, for example, the Anglo-Scottish Conservative Iain Macleod thought it 'good tactics' for Scottish Unionists 'to concede a little of the ground' when it came to devolution, affecting, as Hutchison put it, an 'anti-Whitehall posture to counter the threat of Scottish nationalism and pull back Liberals into the fold'. This often worked in the short term, but contributed to longer-term problems.

Ethno-symbolism

But it is not enough, as Paterson concluded, to 'explain this as the state's having to adopt the language of nationalism in order to placate national-ist critics'. The discourse and practice of politicians and civil servants in Scotland (but also in Wales) demonstrated 'a conception of the Scottish national interest in their minds as they governed' (Paterson 1994: 24). This raises the question of what animated nationalist unionism – was it 'civic' or 'ethnic'?

Writing in 1996, MacCormick understood 'civic nationalism' to mean its members' shared allegiance 'to certain civic institutions . . . political rep-resentative organs, branches of public and local administration, the orga-nization of education, churches and religious communities in their secular aspect, and other like institutions having an understood territorial location with which they are connected'. Furthermore, this 'civic nation' was, in principle, open 'to anyone who chooses to dwell in the territory and give allegiance to the institutions' (MacCormick 1996: 562–3). This, with occa-sional lapses (Scottish Unionists, for example, in the 1920s and 1930s), was true throughout the period under examination, something informed by the ostentatiously 'civic' nature of Britishness and its multi-national empire.

It seems inadequate, however, to gauge the ethnic or cultural content of Scottish nationalism by citizenship or immigration policy alone. By that measurement, it was undeniably open and non-exclusive, but what Mac-Cormick also called 'existential' nationalism (as opposed to the 'utilitarian' variety), something based purely upon the 'fact' of nationhood, can be mea-sured in other ways, not only in the treatment of Scotland as a primordial given, but rhetorically and, perhaps most importantly, in the promotion of myths, symbols and historical events associated with that nationhood. Although anyone, of course, is able to co-opt these existential aspects upon joining 'the nation', they are unlikely to resonate beyond their (arguably) intended audience: Scots with a deeper provenance, through ancestry and birth as well as residency.

First of all, the framing of Scotland's nationalism as predominantly 'civic' is a relatively recent phenomenon that has been subsequently back-dated to cover the whole modern period (i.e. the last two centuries). It was rarely considered in those terms before the 1970s; indeed, journalists and academics beginning in the late nineteenth century openly acknowledged that nationalism was motivated by a range of concerns, civic as well as cultural, administrative as well as sentimental. Nationalist unionists constantly referenced 'national sentiment', 'feeling' and even the 'psychological appeal of Scottish nationalism'. It was obvious, in other words, to those contesting elections that politics was more than just an appeal to material concerns, or to 'civic' institutions.

So while modernism captured one side of this nationalism, it has not adequately dealt with its emotional or 'romantic' component, either ignoring it or considering it to be 'invented'. Hearn spoke perceptively of the broad 'network of intellectuals, academics, artists, writers, journalists and media figures' through whom the ideas of the self-government movement were constantly 'articulated and re-articulated' (Hearn 2000: 39). One of this network's most prominent ideas was the strongly 'civic' nature of nationalism in Scotland, something that by the late 1990s had become such conventional wisdom that it was rarely questioned.

Yet it was the *fact* of nationhood that underpinned nationalism (and therefore nationalist unionism), for its institutions were rarely constant and often unloved (think Westminster and the Scottish Office) and, more to the point, had all been formulated on a 'national' basis, that basis being the 'ancient' Scottish nation first 'imagined' almost a millennium ago and discussed ever since. In that sense, the civic–ethnic dichotomy was not fit for purpose, for the two could not be fully separated; rather one (civic) rested upon the other (ethnic). Strikingly, the modernist thesis took hold just as its basis went in steep decline; as McCrone observed, it was hard (in 1992) to claim that the 'holy trinity' of Scots Law, the Kirk and education were 'as powerful determinants of social life as they were even a century ago' (McCrone 1992: 211).

As Keitner observed, even the most ostentatiously civic nationalism involved 'allegiance to a nation', and while that nation 'may coincide with state institutions, the focus of loyalty is the people conceived as internally cohesive and separate from state structures' (Keitner 1999: 347). It therefore follows that the corresponding 'flagging' of that nation has to draw upon a pre-political basis for communal solidarity. No 'intellectual adhesion to abstract principles' can credibly replace what Schnapper called the 'emotional mobilization aroused by the internalization of the national tradition', meaning the necessary myths and symbols will reference nationhood 'as a concrete social and political form' and not a set of governing arrangements (Schnapper 1998: 60).

So while Scottish nationalism and a sense of Scottish national identity were clearly products of the modern era, strongly fashioned by Sir Walter Scott in the early nineteenth century, it had not magically flowed, fully formed, from his Abbotsford pen: rather it had deeper roots, drawing sustenance from what Nairn called cultural 'raw material' dating back centuries. Thereafter, unionist nationalists or nationalist unionists were endlessly willing to borrow from the past not only names but battle slogans and costumes in order to present 'independence' in what Marx called 'time-honoured disguise and borrowed language' (Marx 1972: 1).

Central to this were the myths of Bruce and Wallace, revered for having enabled Scotland to join England on 'equal' terms in 1707. Blackie, a Liberal, had invoked them in the late nineteenth century, while Labour 'Clydesiders' patronised Bannockburn and Wallace rallies in the early 1920s. Thereafter, the two 'heroes' were taken up by Scottish Unionists like Walter Elliot, who even arranged a permanent memorial at the scene of Wallace's execution in London. Other Conservatives sponsored a statue near Stirling, while by 1999 both Bruce and Wallace were back in Scottish Labour hands, referenced by Donald Dewar in a rousing speech at the opening of the Scottish Parliament. The independence referendum found Alex Salmond updating them along 'civic' lines, stressing their French and Welsh ancestry. Owain Glyndŵr fulfilled a similar role in Wales, as did William of Orange in Ulster.

Modernists could hardly argue this obviously pre-modern material was 'invented', but even if it had been, Hobsbawm and Ranger themselves acknowledged that only those 'traditions' broadcast 'on a wavelength to which the public was ready to tune in' generally succeeded (Hobsbawm and Ranger 1983: 263). And while Smith conceded the existence of nineteenth-century invention in the context of nationalism, he rightly believed calling them 'invented' did 'scant justice to the complex ways in which these, and other ceremonies, were reconstructed and reinterpreted' (Smith 1998: 131).

Take the Stone of Destiny, little discussed before its removal (by a Scottish Liberal as well as other nationalists) from Westminster Abbey in the early 1950s but thereafter something Scottish Conservatives and Unionists felt compelled to handle with care. In an act of symbolic desperation it was 'returned' to Scotland in 1996, although its failure to generate support for the Scottish Conservative Party rather missed the point: it was certainly viewed as a cynical political stunt, but not one that anyone suggested should be reversed. Indeed, in 2019 Murdo Fraser, another Scottish Conservative, called for it to be repatriated *within* Scotland, from Edinburgh to Perth.

The symbolism upon which nationalist unionists drew often had royal associations, a nod to Scotland's pre-modern status as a kingdom in its own right. Monarchy was, however, most ostentatiously utilised in Wales, when investitures of the Prince of Wales were contrived (in 1911 and 1969) to appease rising nationalism with the 'official' variety while simultaneously updating British traditions, presenting George V as head of a multi-national union which championed local nationalisms (provided they did not go too far). In Scotland, meanwhile, the queen made a 'state' visit to Edinburgh in 1953, while the 1989 'Claim of Right' reached back to the original 1689 statement of 'contractual' monarchy, as did the Scottish Constitutional Convention in referencing the 1320 Declaration of Arbroath.

Would any of this have resonated with those resident, but not born or raised, in Scotland, either in the 1980s or in the preceding century? It seemed unlikely, while, in any case, the genuinely non-Scottish population, certainly before the 1950s, would have been very small. As O'Leary remarked of this use of narratives, myths and symbols in the context of Northern Ireland, these helped make 'sense of each community's respective pasts' and were not in any sense 'mere fictions or myths, to be dispelled by therapy from a liberal educator'. Without 'historical truth content', he added, politicians and activists 'would have been less successful in their manipulative endeavours' (O'Leary 2019b: 6). The same was arguably true in Scotland and Wales, whose respective communities were less divided than those in the north of Ireland.

As Leith and Soule have written, an ethno-symbolic approach 'accepts that myths and symbols are subjectively interpreted, but not that they are "constructed" in the pejorative sense of the term. Instead, a national mythology is drawn from the past and the history of the peoples in question' (Leith and Soule 2012: 9). The idea of 'the nation', therefore, occupies the core of nationalist ideology. 'One of the founding myths of all nations is the idea of some historic roots', observed Mitchell and Johns, and thus 'the appeal to past glories or defeats is a feature of nations' (Mitchell and Johns 2016: 33).

The self-appointed task of nationalist unionists, therefore, was to 'rediscover' the Scottish nation, 'and to sift and reinterpret its traditions, so as to mobilize the people and regenerate the community' (Smith 2004: 23). Even Keating accepted that Scottish nationalism was based on 'historical memories, symbols, myths', although he separated these from Smith's 'ethnic core' (Keating 2009: 41). But, as Kearton perceptively concluded, no matter how hard intellectuals and political actors attempted to ringfence ethnicity, it invariably ended up coming in 'through the back door of history'.

As Keating observed of independence supporters during the 2012–14 referendum campaign, they 'drew on longstanding myths of Scottish egalitarianism' (Keating 2017: 17), something else that highlights the difficulty of separating civic and ethnic nationalism. For the idea that Scotland is more 'progressive' than its southern neighbour and is there-fore 'held back' by 'Tory' England – as articulated by Liberal, Labour and SNP politicians over the past century and more – is predicated upon the belief in a 'distinct' and *inherent* Scottish character, which could not be anything other than a belief based upon ethnicity.

This was not just an argument made by nationalist unionists of the left, but also those of the right. To Walter Elliot the 'special qualities' of Scottish-ness were 'industry, fury, romance', while the Church of Scotland constituted a 'characteristic gathering' of 'our people . . . a Covenant sealed in blood'. A later statement of Scottish Unionist policy added a belief in 'sound educa-tion', 'traditions of loyalty and service' or, more generally, the 'distinctive national traditions and characteristics of Scotland'. But while right and left might have disagreed on an exact definition, both promised, as the Labour MP Hector McNeil once did, to 'protect these Scottish characteristics'.

By the mid-1990s, all Scotland's political parties were engaged in an attempt to claim what had become known as 'Scottish values', which, much like 'British values', were notoriously difficult to define. In 1993, the Conservative education minister James Douglas-Hamilton said allowing schools to 'opt out' of state control was 'in tune with the Scottish values of self-reliance, community involvement, and thrift' (*Herald*, 27 September 1993), while Alex Salmond accused Labour of moving 'further and further away from [the] mainstream Scottish values' he claimed the SNP better rep-resented (Press Association, 3 October 1994). In selling the repeal of Clause 4 to the Scottish Labour Party, meanwhile, Tony Blair protested that these were 'Scottish values and they are Labour values' (*Irish Times*, 11 March 1995). Another feature of nationalist unionism was this attempt to conflate party with a nation's 'values', which held as much in Wales as in Scotland, Labour having claimed in 1964 that the Welsh were 'amongst the most pro-gressive and radical in the world'.

By 2014 this belief in Scottish egalitarianism (as Scottish 'values' were generally taken to mean) was as much of a 'given' as the fact of Scottish nationhood, together with talk – usually from the SNP but inherited from Labour – of a different 'ethos' surrounding the Scottish political system, its more positive attitude to immigration, commitment to social justice, and so on. The pollster Andrew Cooper identified two main groups of definite 'Yes' voters, 'Scottish exceptionalists', those who would support independence even if it impoverished the country, and 'blue-collar Bravehearts', working-class, largely male voters who identified themselves as Scottish *not* British (*Guardian*, 15 December 2014).

This highlighted a gap between elite concepts of 'civic' nationalism and mass attitudes, which were also nothing new. Survey evidence had long suggested that Scottish (and Welsh) identity was based on both,[1] while political scientists also identified the detrimental electoral effect to political parties, particularly Conservatives in Scotland and Wales, of being perceived as 'too English', a curious phenomenon if Scottish nationalism was predominantly civic and free of anti-Englishness. Nationalist unionists also took great care to promote policies more familiar to non-civic nationalists, i.e. promotion of the Welsh and Gaelic languages, something always justified on a cultural basis.

Lines were constantly drawn between the Scottish and Welsh present and both nations' pre-modern past. History was not only deployed to legitimize the unions of 1536, 1603, 1707 and 1801, but wielded when a major U-turn on constitutional policy was required. In 1968 the Scottish Conservatives scoured the archives to justify their belated conversion to legislative devolution, as did Scottish Labour in 1974. Alex Salmond also channelled Fletcher of Saltoun in order to legitimise his support for 'five continuing unions' once the political variety had been broken.

At various points between 1884 and 2014, meanwhile, nationalist unionists fretted about the possible disappearance of the Scottish nation and its distinctive characteristics. Local government reorganisation in the late 1920s was deemed by Labour to 'denationalise' Scotland by sweeping away its autonomous boards, a charge which resurfaced 20 years later, only this time as a Unionist description of Labour's plans for the post-war nationalisation of industry. Parties also accused each other (and colleagues) of 'neglecting' the Scottish nation: Rosebery of Gladstone in the 1880s, Unionists of Labour in the 1950s, then Labour of Conservatives in the 1960s and again, in the most sustained assault, during the 1980s, when an ostensibly unionist party depicted Thatcher's government of being 'anti-Scottish' and imposing an 'alien' ideology – battle cries requisitioned by the SNP prior to 2014, only applied to Labour and the Liberal Democrats as well as Conservatives.

Thus concessions to the periphery were offered on the basis of – and in recognition of enhanced – 'nationhood', i.e. the construction of St Andrew's House in 1939, which fulfilled a similar architectural and symbolic purpose as Stormont in Northern Ireland, nationalist unionism in bricks and mortar. As Paterson observed, it was also for 'essentially nationalist reasons' that there was no transfer of administrative powers *away* from the Scottish Office after 1945. For if the 'devolution' of responsibilities from Whitehall to Edinburgh (and Cardiff from 1965) had been purely 'rational', then one might have expected this process to be reversed 'whenever the nature of the economy and society changed' (Paterson 1994: 114).

Powers and responsibilities were not transferred to sectors of the economy or particular professions but to 'Scotland'. In this way nationalist unionists all helped construct a narrative of a unified Scottish 'people' anchored in the Scottish 'nation' and defending themselves and their way of life from common enemies or an 'other', usually 'Whitehall' (Unionists in the early 1950s) and later 'Westminster' (Labour in the 1980s; the SNP in the 2010s), 'civic' institutions (ironically) depicted as distant, uncaring and out-of-touch. In 1949, Unionists warned that Labour members of a hypothetical Scottish Parliament would be compelled to follow orders from 'London headquarters', a cry taken up by the SNP fifty years later when that parliament became a reality. Ideology also played a part: just as 'socialism' was considered to pose a threat to the Scottish nation in the 1920s and 1940s, so too was Conservatism between the 1980s and 2010s.

To have denied – as certain nationalist unionists and the SNP did from the 1990s – any cultural or emotional aspect to this nationalism therefore lacks credibility. Modernists ended up focusing too much on the ends (a Scottish Parliament) rather than the means (the rhetoric and arguments deployed) in their framing and analysis of nationalism in Scotland, missing (or ignoring) much that animated it in the process. In a 2012 speech, the SNP politician Nicola Sturgeon took this to its logical conclusion by arguing – to much media and political acclaim – that her nationalism was based on neither 'the fact of Scottish nationhood' nor 'Scottish identity', although if that were true then there would not have been much left, either in the early twenty-first century or the late nineteenth. As Brown observed, while nationalism certainly had 'two ideological faces, civic and cultural', its political character was 'surely protean rather than Janus-faced' (Brown 1999: 300).

Banal nationalism

Much of the ethno-symbolic content of Scottish nationalism, however, was so commonplace that it warranted little attention, contributing to the 'hidden' nature of most nationalist unionism. As Billig observed, this 'reminding' was 'so familiar, so continual, that it is not consciously registered as reminding', the 'metonymic image' of this 'banal nationalism' being the flag 'hanging unnoticed on the public building' (Billig 1995: 8).

And although some protagonists self-identified as 'nationalists', i.e. Walter Elliot ('an unrepentant Scottish Nationalist'), John Buchan ('every Scotsman should be a Scottish Nationalist') and Tom Ellis in Wales, others quite deliberately sought to separate their nationalism from that of others with different constitutional aims, either legislative devolution or independence depending on where the Overton window was situated. A. J. Balfour, for example, saw his Scottish nationalism as a 'sentiment of nationality' or 'patriotism' nestled within the 'larger patriotism' of Britishness and imperialism.

This 'patriotism', therefore, was elevated above a variety of pejorative terms for what was deemed the wrong or 'bad' sort of nationalism, for the banal variety took great care to push competing nationalisms to the periphery of acceptable political discourse, depicting them as quite unnecessary for the preservation of Welsh or Scottish identity. In the late nineteenth century, Conservatives and Liberal Unionists attacked those seeking Home Rule for Ireland as 'separatists' rather than devolutionists, while during the Great War the Welsh Department of the Board of Education issued official guidance on 'true' patriotism while disparaging the 'false' variety. Even in the 1980s, the Liberal leader David Steel was contrasting his 'positive patriotism' with the SNP's 'narrow' or 'negative' nationalism.

Such distinctions could even operate *within* parties. In Northern Ireland, Terence O'Neill attacked colleagues advocating dominion status as 'separatists' despite promoting his own 'regional patriotism', while Enoch Powell branded Ian Paisley 'anti-Unionist' or 'Protestant Sinn Féin' for supporting the restoration of Stormont. Nationalist-unionist Cabinet ministers, meanwhile, would predict 'bad' or 'extreme' nationalism to extract further concessions (usually financial or industrial) from the centre: Lord Lothian in the 1880s, Tom Johnston during the Second World War, Willie Ross in the late 1960s and successive Conservative Secretaries of State for Scotland and Wales during the 1980s.

But where did moderate patriotism end and 'extreme' nationalism begin? The terminology was highly subjective and politically loaded. As Home Rulers protested in the 1890s, they wanted to reform the union through legislative devolution, not 'separate' Ireland from Britain or Scotland from England, while the SNP's Arthur Donaldson pointed out that most Scots were already 'separatist' to some degree, educationally, legally or spiritually. It was as if a 'really secure nationalism, already in possession of its own nation-state, can fail to see itself as "nationalist" at all' (Williams 1983: 183).

After 1999, meanwhile, 'home rulers started calling themselves – or were called by the SNP – unionists' (Keating 2017: 8), a means by which once 'extreme' nationalists could turn the tables by depicting their nationalist-unionist opponents as somehow anti-devolution even as they were increasingly drawn towards 'the SNP's turf' (Jeffrey 2009: 155). The Labour MP, peer and MSP George Foulkes illustrated this phenomenon. Considered a 'crypto-nationalist' in the 1980s given his talk of a Scottish 'mandate', by 2014 he was depicted by SNP critics as an 'arch' unionist, or 'British Nationalist' in social media parlance, for his spirited support of the unionist status quo. The SNP's 'Europeanisation' after 1988 also allowed it to contrast the 'reactionary' or 'xenophobic' British 'nationalism' of its Conservative opponents to its own 'progressive' internationalism. Later, meanwhile, there was a general refutation of any sort of nationalism. In her maiden speech, the SNP MP Mhairi Black claimed that 'nationalism [had] nothing to do with what's happened in Scotland' (HC Debs 14 July 2015 Vol 598 c776); the *Washington Post* even called it 'post-national nationalism' (*Washington Post*, 29 August 2016).

Similarly, in 1999 the Scottish Labour Party suddenly repudiated its recent 'tartanisation' and attempted to shift political debate back to left–right territory. But it was too late, for Labour (not to mention the Liberal Democrats) had become trapped by their own discourse and framing. When, between 2012 and 2014, Liberal Democrats such as Michael Moore and Labour figures like Jim Murphy denied being 'Unionists' they invited ridicule, for the term 'unionist', even to describe those (which was most) who supported devolution and more of it, had become a pejorative term, much like 'separatist' had been for much of the twentieth century. With supreme historical irony, the muddled typology of the early twenty-first century would have categorised Isaac Butt or Charles Stewart Parnell as 'unionists'.

Contradictions in nationalist unionism

As Orwell observed in a 1945 essay, all nationalists had 'the power of not seeing resemblances between similar sets of facts'. 'A British Tory', he wrote, 'will defend self-determination in Europe and oppose it in India with no feeling of inconsistency' (Orwell 1945). Similar paradoxes existed with nationalist unionism. In the 1920s, Baldwin saw no contradiction in elevating Scotland's minister to the status of 'Secretary of State' while insisting that even a junior minister for Wales was quite unnecessary. Thereafter, Westminster repeatedly shored up the Scottish Office while denying the need for a Welsh equivalent.

At Westminster too, 'Grand Committees' and other mechanisms increasingly isolated Scottish and Welsh matters from other parliamentary business. In the late 1960s, Richard Crossman observed the irony of his anti-independence colleague Willie Ross wanting to keep 'Scottish business absolutely privy from English business', and by the 1990s these Grand and 'Select' Committees even became physically removed from the UK Parliament, meeting in Cardiff, Belfast and Edinburgh. While this was intended as a prophylactic against legislative devolution, to some degree it had the opposite effect, as had 'administrative devolution' a century earlier.

The most glaring contradiction was that posed by the Stormont Question: if legislative devolution was good enough for Northern Ireland, then why not less contested parts of the union such as Scotland and Wales? Scottish Unionists were alive to this, attempting to square the circle by hinting that a Scottish Stormont would not enjoy the same generous financial settlement as that on the outskirts of Belfast, as if that constituted a fatal intellectual blow (more logically, some Ulster Unionists supported extending devolution to other parts of the UK). By the 1990s, the Stormont Question had evolved but posed the same dilemma for John Major as he worked hard on restoring (power-sharing) devolution while resisting it with equal vigour in Scotland and Wales.

Liberal and Labour politicians were more alive to this contradiction and generally promised 'Home Rule all round', even if they did not necessarily make good on such pledges once in office. Even beyond Stormont, if Scotland 'deserved so much administrative devolution, how could legislative devolution be denied, with a democratically-elected body in Scotland to hold the Scottish Office to account?' (Kellas 1994: 684–5). And, logically, if legislative devolution was necessary to make Scotland and Wales 'nations again', then what precisely was the argument against independence? As McLean and McMillan concluded, 'Unionism in the UK has always suffered from deep intellectual incoherence' (McLean and McMillan 2005: 239).

As with the ratchet-like effect of their wider 'territorial code', nationalist unionists' efforts to depict modest constitutional concessions as something greater created a discursive frame that required careful management. The language of taking back 'control', for example, was not new in 2014 and 2016. In 1949 the Scottish Unionists promoted 'Scottish Control of Scottish Affairs'; Liberals later spoke of giving Scotland 'control of her own affairs', while Labour's George Robertson promised a Scottish Parliament would facilitate 'control over their own lives'. Donald Dewar even toyed with selling legislative devolution as 'independence in the United Kingdom'.

Nationalist unionists, therefore, consistently created expectations they could not necessarily match, not least the Royal Commissions of 1954 and 1973. A draft pamphlet by the journalist Colm Brogan was rejected by Scottish Unionists on the basis that readers were unlikely to derive a 'clear impression' of 'why a separate Scottish Parliament' was 'undesirable', given its broader arguments about Scottish nationhood, its justifiable 'claims' and 'neglect' by Westminster. Later, the SNP fell into a similar trap, undermining its own belief in 'independence' by stressing the benefits to Scotland of several 'continuing' unions, often deploying 'unionist' arguments they explicitly rejected in other constitutional contexts.

'Standing up for Scotland'

Nevertheless, when nationalist unionists managed to adequately 'balance' Scottish or Welsh nationhood with the union, their claim to 'defend' those nations was often electorally advantageous. As Brown, McCrone and Paterson asserted, 'parties only succeed in Scotland when they address Scottish issues. When they are perceived no longer to do so, they suffer accordingly at the polls' (Brown *et al.* 1996: 120). At the same time, claiming to 'stand up for Scotland' or Wales was necessary but not sufficient – it also required credibility.

Consistent support for Home Rule or devolution saw Scottish and Welsh Liberals make little headway for most of the twentieth century, while Michael Forsyth's attempt to revive Tory nationalist unionism in the mid-1990s generated ridicule rather than votes. But when it worked, it worked. Miller (1981) believed there was clear evidence that the 'nationalist' component of Scottish Unionist strategy had contributed to their Scottish electoral success in 1950, 1951 and 1955, as did Brown *et al.* of Scottish Labour's vote shares during the 1980s and 1990s.

Similarly, in every election from 1935 the SNP claimed it was best placed to represent Scotland's interests at Westminster, but it only began to appear credible in 1974, and later benefited from a perfect storm in 2015. In Wales, it said something that Labour managed to retain control of devolved government consistently after 1999, a success rate which owed at least something to its carefully cultivated nationalist unionism (Awan-Scully 2018). A similar stance also brought a period of recovery for the Welsh Conservatives, while Plaid Cymru, despite representing the fullest expression of Welsh nationalism, was generally weak, its arguments – often similar to those of the SNP – failing to sufficiently resonate.

Until the early twenty-first century this 'everyday' nationalism often appeared weaker than it was due to its dispersal among several parties. In 1947, Labour's Arthur Woodburn had presciently described this as a 'smouldering pile', and indeed the fact that it caught fire (in Scotland) after 2011 was due in part to the contradictions of nationalist unionism over the past century. Brand wrote of 'a gradual restructuring' of the Scottish electorate's 'political consciousness', one that had led more and more voters to back a party which primarily 'stood for Scotland' rather than representing traditional class cleavages (Brand 1978: 297, 300).

There were ghosts of empire in all of this. As Anderson observed of the nineteenth-century British colonial metropole, its 'Census, Map, Museum' approach to overseas territories had 'dialectically engendered the grammar of the nationalism that eventually arose to combat it'. The centre had almost 'imagined' its peripheral 'adversaries' as if in an 'ominous prophetic dream, well before they came into historical existence' (Anderson 1991: xiv). Geekie and Levy accused Labour in Scotland of creating a Franken-stein's monster, 'nationalist rhetoric' the Conservative peer Lord Forsyth said later came back to 'bite' Labour, a consequence of its 1980s claims of Conservatives 'having no mandate in Scotland', or Scots getting 'a govern-ment they didn't vote for' (*Scotsman*, 29 April 2017).

Even beyond Labour's more ostentatious rhetoric, decades of nationalist unionism – whether 'official' or 'oppositionist' – had ended up creating 'a world of dense Scottishness' which created 'a feeling of natural allegiance in nearly everyone who has been brought up here, or who has lived here for an appreciable length of time' (Paterson 1994: 181). Not only that, but successive concessions had persistently strengthened the periphery while neglecting the centre. Reflecting on his own party's approach in 2016, Tony Blair acknowledged the 'mistake' of trying to 'out nationalist or go with the nationalists in the belief that . . . Westminster or London was something sort of bad and everything had to be centred in Scotland' (Blair 2016). As he had concluded in his memoirs, you 'can never be sure where nationalist sentiment ends and separatist sentiment begins' (Blair 2010: 251).

An unintended consequence of 'standing up' for Scotland or Wales after 1884 was, therefore, dialectically engendering the grammar of the nation-alism that eventually rose to combat it, chiefly a 'grievance politics' based upon accusations of 'neglect' from London and an assertion of Scottish superiority, be it legal, moral or educational, something the historian Tony Judt called that curious 'admix of superiority and *ressentiment*' (Judt 2010: 706). The idea, for example, that Scotland was 'fixed upon for experiments', reached back to Sir Walter Scott and forward to the Community Charge, all of which was combined with a quixotic belief in constitutional change (initially administrative) as a panacea for Scotland's ills.

Even so, the continuing 'integrity of the Union' had seemed to all nationalist unionists, in the end, 'to provide the best means for the main-tenance of their distinctive Scottish, Welsh and Northern Irish identities' (Ward 2005: 186). But the consequence of this approach was, as Paterson put it, a series of radical challenges to the centre followed by 'pragmatic adjustment' as the state ceded just enough power 'to keep the Union intact for the time being, a compromise which sows the seeds of the next phase of radical rebellion'. Thus the 'Scottish question' had never really been settled (Paterson 2015), and nor, most likely, would it be even were Scotland to become independent (Mitchell 2014).

So nationalist unionists opted for short-term solutions rather than holis-tic and longer-lasting reform (federalism or economic decentralisation); to paraphrase Oscar Wilde, they helped kill the very thing they professed to love, delegitimising the central 'civic' institutions of the British state, chiefly Westminster (only the monarchy emerged relatively unscathed, thanks to SNP support), so that by the 2014 referendum, independence was imaginable, even 'banal', well within the ever-shifting Overton window. Alex Salmond even presented it as the natural culmination of Scotland's '100-year home rule journey', one that had been fuelled by nationalist-unionist arguments.

Perhaps it would be an exaggeration, or too much of a Whig indulgence, to argue that the logical culmination of 1884's 'national meeting' was the independence referendum of 2014, yet at the same time there was a striking continuity between the concerns of the late nineteenth century and those of the early twenty-first. The result in 2014 was, in that respect, unimportant, for its rhetorical palette produced a palimpsest of nationalist arguments, with the SNP co-opting aspects of unionism as deftly as unionists had nationalism: those arguing for independence did not question the validity of certain unions, while those championing the Anglo-Scottish 'political' union promised greater autonomy on the basis of Scottish nationhood.

As Smith observed, different sorts of nationalism 'frequently overlap', with nations often displaying 'ethnic as well as civic components', moving 'from one type to another and back' (Smith 1995: 232). In 1884 as in 2014, nationalism and unionism were not absolutes but existed on a spectrum and, as per Walt Whitman's 'Song of Myself', often appeared to contradict themselves. For nationalist unionism was large and contained multitudes, endlessly redrawing the boundary between union and Scottish, Welsh or Northern Irish nationhood, summoning historical heroes to its cause and running the risk, however slim it had at first appeared, of falling victim to its own success.

ENDNOTES

Chapter 1

1. The Convention viewed itself as the 'third estate' of the old Scots Parliament, something specifically preserved by the Treaty of Union. Sitting for two days each year in Edinburgh, according to a contemporary commentator it did 'its best . . . to recall the departed glories of the Scottish Parliament' (*Scottish Review*, April 1890). Similarly, a historian of the Convention viewed it as a body 'which has always taken a singular interest in maintaining Scottish rights' (W. O. 1899: 6–7). In 1914 it published a report arguing for 'Local Self-Government for Scotland', but by the 1950s the Convention had set itself against legislative devolution for Scotland. It was abolished upon the reorganisation of Scottish local government in 1975.
2. Scotland's provosts (the equivalent of mayors in England) were particularly well represented at the 1884 national meeting as it was they who suffered the frustrations of doing business with Whitehall departments.
3. Keating was a notable dissenter. Calling this nationalism seemed to him to 'be stretching the term too far', for the 'mainspring' of the 1884 national meeting 'was a mundane concern by businessmen about the inefficiency of the ramshackle system of boards which ran most Scottish administration' (Keating 1988: 87).
4. The thirteenth Earl of Eglinton, the driving force behind the NAVSR, had twice acted as viceroy of Ireland.

Chapter 2

1. One could also include Cromwell's 'Commonwealth' during the seventeenth century, although that was both short-lived and involuntary.
2. In the United States, the term 'unionist' has a different but similar provenance, originating from the American Civil War. When another 'union' was challenged

by the secession of the southern 'independent and sovereign' states, their opponents were known as 'unionists'.

3. Writing of Northern Ireland in 1955, Newark claimed the terms 'Nationalist' and 'Unionist' had 'almost gone out [of use] in favour of the terms "Anti-Partitionist" and "Partitionist"' (Newark 1955: 26).

4. Kidd noted the sizeable gap between a 'huge literature on the nationalist movement' but only 'a couple of books' attempting 'to grapple with the appeal of the Union' (Kidd 2008).

5. The term 'periphery' is not disrespectful to Scotland, Wales or Northern Ireland, but is a social science term well used in the literature on which this book draws.

6. Coupland added: 'Nationalism in this sense is virtually identical with patriotism.'

7. I am indebted to the historian Catriona MacDonald for first suggesting this formulation to me.

8. Ignatieff's book and later documentary were widely covered in the Scottish media during 1993 and 1994, with many commentators adopting the same 'ethnic' and 'civic' dichotomy. As in the 1940s, European wars in the early 1990s had tainted the term 'nationalism', and it could be that the SNP welcomed the opportunity to differentiate its 'civic' nationalism from the ethnic variety then playing out (on television screens) in the Balkans.

9. Hanham believed Scottish nationalism to be 'as old as the Scottish nation' (Hanham 1969: 64).

10. Nairn later became more sympathetic to primordialism (or 'neo-primordialism'), arguing that the key to understanding nationalism lay in 'human nature' (Nairn 1997: 13).

11. Perennialism rejects the idea of nations as 'natural' but points to cultural continuities and identities over long time spans, linking medieval or ancient nations to their modern counterparts.

12. Arguably key in terms of journalists and commentators were Neal Ascherson, Ian Bell, Joyce Macmillan and William McIlvanney (also a novelist). McIlvanney's 1987 lecture at the SNP conference, 'Stands Scotland Where It Did?', is a classic statement of Scottish distinctiveness and moral superiority.

13. One could have said the same of academics and Marxism.

14. Chapters 3–7 make the most use of archival material; Chapters 8–10 are largely derived from secondary sources.

Chapter 3

1. Mitchell attributes the phrase 'administrative devolution' to the civil servant Patrick Laird in 1928 (Mitchell 1989).

2. The Duke of Sutherland lobbied for junior ministerial office on the basis that his family had 'such a long connection with Scottish Affairs'. 'You would not find me lacking in keenness and enthusiasm in the Cause of Scotland', he wrote to Sir John (Sutherland 1926).

3. At around this time, Sir John Gilmour was also involved in a 'scheme to prepare the history of Scotland in Parliament, both before and after the Union', as were John Buchan, Lord Clyde, Sir Robert Rait and the former Labour Prime Minister Ramsay MacDonald. The planned volumes never appeared (Gilmour 1937).

Chapter 4

1. The Unionist-turned-Nationalist James Porteous had written to Lord Selkirk on 23 March 1947 to praise his 'fine speech' at the recent Scottish 'National Assembly' and invite him to join the Scottish Convention. Selkirk replied on 4 April, referring to a 'remarkably representative gathering which agreed very substantially in expressing their desire for something which they found difficult to bring out in concrete practical words' (Selkirk 1947b).
2. The SNP leader Douglas Young had used the phrase 'Scottish Control of Scottish Affairs' in a 1948 speech and pamphlet, a year before the Unionist Party's statement of policy appeared.

Chapter 5

1. Cooper's observations on parliamentary sovereignty were later taken as proof that the 'Scottish people' (rather than parliament) were 'sovereign', although the qualification 'unlimited' was rarely quoted.
2. On 1 March 1980, exactly a year after the referendum, some SNP members travelled to the Hirsel (Lord Home's Borders home) 'to offer Sir Alex thirty pieces of silver' (*Bulletin of Scottish Politics*, Autumn 1980).
3. All references from the excellent website, www.margaretthatcher.org.
4. In memoirs published the same year, Thatcher said the Scots had 'an undoubted right to national self-determination . . . Should they determine on independence no English party or politician would stand in their way' (Thatcher 1993: 624).
5. Two former Scottish Conservatives, the historian Michael Fry and financier Peter de Vink, dissented, campaigning *for* independence from a libertarian perspective (Torrance 2013).

Chapter 6

1. During this campaign, Gladstone had made the first of several apparently supportive comments regarding devolution for Scotland: 'We have got an over-weighted Parliament, and, if we can make arrangements under which Ireland, Scotland, Wales and portions of England can deal with questions of local and special interest to themselves more efficiently than Parliament now can, that, I say, will be the attainment of great national good' (Keating and Bleiman 1979: 30–1).
2. Welsh nationalist-unionists would later adopt this approach, at first arguing for a Welsh university, library and museum, and later for a Welsh minister.

3. The 1885 election addressed another long-standing Scottish grievance – representation – with Scotland's number of MPs increasing from 58 to 70.

4. During the campaign, the Liberal Unionist Joseph Chamberlain declared: 'We also have to recognize and to satisfy national sentiment, which is in itself a praiseworthy and patriotic and inspiring feeling, and which both in Scotland and Ireland had led to a demand for a local control in purely domestic affairs' (Mansergh 1936: 48).

5. Parnell was making his first public visit to Edinburgh. He had previously irritated Scots with his apparent claim that 'Scotland was no longer a nation' (*Scottish Review*, July 1888).

6. A few years earlier, there had been similar frustration among Scottish Liberals at Gladstone's failure to commit to disestablishment of the 'national' Church of Scotland.

7. In February 1887, the *Scotsman* had run editorials supportive of Home Rule, but then turned against it (Mitchell 1996).

8. Gladstone had made a similar point in 1880, arguing that what really 'endangered' the union with Ireland was sustaining an 'alien' church and an 'unjust' land law, while the 'true supporters of the union' were those who upheld the supremacy of parliament but believed in exercising that authority 'to bind the three nations by the indissoluble tie of liberal and equal laws' (Ward 2005: 4).

9. McKinnon Wood's pledge was still being quoted in Scottish Liberal Party literature in the late 1940s, in order to demonstrate its Home Rule credentials.

10. Before the beginning of the Second World War, MacCormick had been in talks with Sir Thomas and Lady Glen-Coats regarding a cross-party Scottish National Convention at Glasgow's City Hall, for which resolutions were drawn up (Hanham 1969: 166).

11. For a full account of the Paisley by-election, see Chapter 4.

12. In 1930, Bannerman had been appointed a farm manager on land owned by the Duke of Montrose, a prominent nationalist unionist who had a complicated relationship with the Scottish Liberals.

13. One of the Stone's captors had been Bill Craig, a member of the Scottish Liberal Party.

14. Hutchison disagrees, arguing (unconvincingly) that the 1960s found Liberals 'back-pedalling on devolution for Scotland', more interested in Europe than 'pushing for Scottish Home Rule' (Hutchison 2001: 119). This is at odds with party literature from that decade.

15. At the 1967 Scottish Assembly, Kennedy had tabled a resolution calling for Home Rule to be the 'principal aim and object of our policy'. This was carried unanimously but thereafter ignored. Michael Starforth, meanwhile, did later defect to the SNP (Mitchell 1996: 212).

16. Of Jo Grimond, Mackie observed cryptically that it 'was very difficult to get Jo to talk about a Scottish Parliament, although he would talk happily about devolution' (Mackie 2004: 164).

17. The SDP memo continued: 'As the only political party in Scotland without an organizer we would be regarded as an alien intruder . . . the <u>SDP</u> would become what the SNP has always claimed it was, an English party' (SDP 1988).

Chapter 7

1. See Ferguson (1978: 375) for a discussion of Maxton's Scottish nationalism.
2. Lord Cooper had been the Scottish Unionist MP for Edinburgh West between 1935 and 1941 and, later, as Lord President of the Court of Session, would make his famous observation about parliamentary sovereignty (see Chapter 5).
3. This might have been a 1948 J. Arthur Rank film entitled *Future of Scotland*, which featured Johnston advocating the 'middle course' of devolution for Scotland.
4. In forewords to the 2018 updated edition of Russell Galbraith's biography, SNP leader Nicola Sturgeon and former UK Labour leader and Prime Minister Gordon Brown both laid claim to Tom Johnston's nationalist legacy.
5. At the October 1974 election, the Labour Party published its first specifically 'Scottish manifesto'.
6. Gordon Brown had been a student of Mackintosh's at Edinburgh University.
7. Neil recalled a 'key' meeting in 1974 as having taken place at the House of Commons between him, Ted Short and a couple of others. 'I clinched it by saying that in normal circumstances, when another election was several years away, we could get away without committing to devolution, but we couldn't as the October 1974 election was so near; the SNP were in second place in dozens of Labour constituencies. After that, Short told Harold Wilson he had to U-turn on devolution' (interview with Alex Neil, 25 May 2016).
8. The once-unionist *Scotsman* warned in a somewhat hyperbolic front-page editorial that a No vote would 'complete the process of assimilation, of reducing Scotland to a mere geographical expression'. 'Scotland's survival as a nation, as a worthy partner in the UK', it added, 'depends upon an emphatic and decisive Yes' (*Scotsman*, 1 March 1979).
9. Iain McLean speculated that devolution was supported by a clear majority but lacked salience, making it vulnerable to No campaign arguments about the likely cost of an assembly. He also believed the Labour Movement Yes Campaign 'never really succeeded in establishing the distinct Labour, as opposed to nationalist, argument for devolution' (McLean 1991b: 36–7).
10. There was a lot of talk in the early 1980s of these Labour figures forming some sort of alliance with the left of the SNP, i.e. the 79 Group, which comprised individuals like Alex Salmond and Kenny MacAskill (Torrance 2015).
11. Dennis Canavan left the Labour Party on not being selected as a candidate for the first Scottish Parliament elections in 1999. He later chaired the 'Yes' campaign during the independence referendum campaign.
12. 'I've never been an extravagant supporter of the Scottish dimension', Cook had said after the 1983 election. 'But I have changed my mind. I don't give a bugger

if Thatcher has a mandate or not, I will simply do all I can to stop her' (*Radical Scotland*, June/July 1984).

13. Jim Ross, who helped draft those words, had worked on the ill-fated devolution legislation of the 1970s, as well as Scottish Labour policy following the 1983 general election.

14. The Scottish Council of the Labour Party had finally been rebranded in 1994, in anticipation of devolution.

Chapter 8

1. Salmond made a series of speeches on each 'union' during 2013.
2. At the launch of the 1997 'yes/yes' campaign, the independence-supporting actor Sean Connery quoted from the Declaration of Arbroath (Kearton 2012: 35).
3. The SNP preferred to forget its imperialist origins, and indeed Scotland's role in the empire. Salmond said that with independence, Scotland 'would carry none of the baggage of the imperial past' (Mycock 2012: 63).
4. During a Charles Kennedy memorial debate at Glasgow University in September 2015, the SNP minister Fiona Hyslop committed a memorable slip of tongue after explaining why Scotland should remain part of the European Union, concluding: 'You have to stay in the UK, er, Europe' to ensure the EU remains a global force (author's recollection).
5. In 1886 the Fife-born Irish politician Sir T. W. Russell had implored a Scottish audience to consider Ulster Protestants as 'bone of your bone, flesh of your flesh' (Macdonald 1998: 5).

Chapter 9

1. Some of Morgan's work, however, tends to equate the desire for 'Home Rule' with 'separatism', as did late-nineteenth-century Liberal Unionists (Morgan 1995).
2. This meant 'Home Rule all round' was implemented in at least one respect. Once the 'demands' of Ireland for a separate insurance commission had been conceded, those of Scotland and Wales followed, especially as the responsible minister (Lloyd George) hailed from the latter (McLean and McMillan 2005: 157). The separate 'national' commissions were later abolished by the Attlee government.
3. According to John Grigg, the idea for the investiture came from Bishop Edwards of St Asaph, who had picked it up from Queen Victoria's eldest daughter, the Empress Frederick, while at Windsor (Grigg 1988: 10).
4. 'Ellis's nationalism was based on the inheritances of the folk,' judged Morgan, 'Lloyd George's on the imperatives of the state' (Morgan 1995: 378).
5. Howe was part of a prominent generation of Welsh born or raised Conservative MPs with a national/UK profile, others being Michael Heseltine and Michael Howard.

6. In Welsh, this would have translated as 'Plaid Ceidwadol Cymru' (Melding 2009: 152).

7. Significantly, the Council for Wales was sanctioned by Herbert Morrison, a Labour Cabinet minister who generally resisted similar concessions to Scottish nationalism.

8. Hughes' command paper, *Wales: The Way Ahead* (Cmnd 3334, July 1967, Cardiff: HMSO) opened with a quotation in Welsh by T. Gwynn Jones (1902): 'Here still our ancient hopes we cherish,/Here too, high aspirations flourish', as well as a bilingual introduction. He piloted through a Welsh Language Act the same year.

9. Out of government in the 1970s, George Thomas set himself against any sort of devolution for Wales.

10. In 1959, the secretary of the Liberal Party of Wales said his party had to 'recognise the Nationalist challenge' by declaring itself an 'autonomous and quite independent organisation' similar to the Scottish Liberal Party (Philip 1975: 307).

11. Later, in 1993, John Major's government passed a second Welsh Language Act, recognising it as an official language.

12. The Welsh Referendum Study also suggested that feelings of 'Welshness' contained civic as well as ethnic characteristics (Paterson and Wyn Jones 1999: 184).

Chapter 10

1. Isaac Butt's Home Government Association, founded in 1870, was nationalist-unionist in tenor, calling for 'full control over our domestic affairs'. Butt also promoted the idea of a Hapsburg-style 'dual monarchy', with the British monarch separately head of state in Ireland.

2. 'I speak as a unionist but also as an Ulster Scot,' said the then DUP leader and First Minister Peter Robinson before the 2014 Scottish independence vote. 'We cherish the relationship that we have. Nowhere else in the UK would the bonds be more tightly drawn between any other part of the UK from Northern Ireland's point of view than with Scotland' (*Guardian*, 13 January 2012).

3. Ulster Unionists also defended their identity, with several senators protesting against the use in schools of D. C. Somervell's *History of Great Britain* 'on the ground that the book contained disparaging references to the achievements and policy of the Ulster Unionists' (Mansergh 1936: 279).

4. The Ulster Unionists had turned the same year's Stormont election into 'a referendum on the autonomy of Northern Ireland from the British Labour government' (Ward 2005: 156).

5. Shortly after resigning, Faulkner told a massive rally at Stormont that the Government of Northern Ireland felt they had 'been betrayed from London'. John Taylor, who was present on the balcony, said the 'display of Unionism' was 'rejecting British rule' (*The Troubles: A Secret History*, BBC4, 10 September 2019).

6. In his contribution to the 1975 publication, *Your Future: Can Ulster Survive Unfettered?* Trimble first mooted the possibility of 'some community of the British Isles'.

Chapter 11

1. In a 2016 YouGov survey, a majority of those surveyed believed that only those born and raised in Scotland were 'really' Scottish (https://yougov.co.uk/topics/politics/articles-reports/2016/09/07/what-makes-person-scottish).

BIBLIOGRAPHY

Alexander, W. (2007), Speech entitled 'A New Agenda for Scotland', University of Edinburgh, 30 November 2007.

Alexander, W. (2008), Speech to Scottish Labour annual conference, 28 March 2008.

Anderson, B. (1991), *Imagined Communities* (second edition), London: Verso.

Anderson, D. (1963), Dumfries by-election address, SCUA Papers Acc 10424/133, Edinburgh: NLS.

Anderson, P. J. (1902), *Rectorial Addresses Delivered in the Universities of Aberdeen 1835–1900*, Aberdeen: Aberdeen University Studies.

Armstrong, A. (2018), '"Britishness", the UK State, Unionism, Scotland and the "National Outsider"', in Davidson, N. *et al.* (eds), *No Problem Here: Understanding Racism in Scotland*, Edinburgh: Luath, 32–52.

Arnott, M. and Macdonald, C. M. M. (2012), 'More Than a Name: The Union and the Un-doing of Scottish Conservatism in the 20th Century', in Torrance, D. (ed.), *Whatever Happened to Tory Scotland?*, Edinburgh: Edinburgh University Press, 43–61.

Ascherson, N. (1980), 'After Devolution', *Bulletin of Scottish Politics* 1, 1–6.

Atholl, Duke of (ed.) (1932), *A Scotsman's Heritage*, London: Alexander Maclehose & Co.

Aubel, F. (1996), 'The Conservatives in Wales, 1880–1935', in Francis, M. and Zweiniger-Bargielowska, I. (eds), *The Conservatives and British Society 1880–1990*, Cardiff: University of Wales Press, 96–110.

Aughey, A. (1989), *Under Siege: Ulster Unionism and the Anglo-Irish Agreement*, Belfast: Blackstaff.

Awan-Scully, R. (2018), *The End of British Party Politics?* London: Biteback.

Balfour, A. (1913), *Nationality and Home Rule*, London: Longmans, Green & Co.

Balfour, Lord (1954), *Report of the Royal Commission on Scottish Affairs, 1952–1954*, Edinburgh: HMSO.

Bechhofer, F. and McCrone, D. (2007), 'Being British: A Crisis of Identity?', *Political Quarterly* 78:2, 251–60.

Beckett, J. C. (1971), 'Northern Ireland', *Journal of Contemporary History* 6:1, 121–34.

Benn, T. (1989), *Against the Tide: Diaries 1973–76*, London: Arrow.

Biagini, E. F. (ed.) (1996), *Citizenship and Community: Liberals, Radicals and Collective Identities in the British Isles, 1865–1931*, Cambridge: Cambridge University Press.

BICO (1975), *Against Ulster Nationalism*, Belfast: British and Irish Communist Organisation.

Biffen, J. (1976), *A Nation in Doubt*, London: Conservative Political Centre.

Billig, M. (1995), *Banal Nationalism*, London: Sage.

Black, C. S. (*c.*1933), *Scottish Nationalism: Its Inspiration and Its Aims*, Glasgow: National Party of Scotland.

Blair, P. J. (1945a), Letter dated 9 February 1945, SUMC Papers 1/47, Oxford: Bodleian Library.

Blair, P. J. (1945b), Letter dated 28 May 1945, SUMC Papers 1/47, Oxford: Bodleian Library.

Blair, P. J. (1947a), Letter dated 28 March 1947, SUMC Papers 1/51, Oxford: Bodleian Library.

Blair, P. J. (1947b), 'The Unionist Party's Policy Regarding Scottish Affairs', SUMC Papers 1/51.

Blair, P. J. (1947c), Letter dated 16 July 1947, SUMC Papers 1/51.

Blair, P. J. (1947d), Letter dated 29 November 1947, SCUA Papers Acc.11368/80(iii), Edinburgh: NLS.

Blair, P. J. (1948a), *Scotland and the United Kingdom*, Edinburgh: Scottish Unionist Association.

Blair, P. J. (1948b), Letter dated 26 June 1948, SCUA Papers Acc.11368/80(iii), Edinburgh: NLS.

Blair, P. J. (1949), Memo dated 3 March 1949, SCUA Papers Acc.11368/80(iv), Edinburgh: NLS.

Blair, T. (2010), *A Journey*, London: Hutchinson.

Blair, T. (2016), Transcript of interview for *Scotland and the Battle for Britain*, BBC.

Blake, R. (1968), 'Scottish Nationalism', 5 June 1968, Conservative Party Archive LCC(68)187, Oxford: Bodleian Library.

Blaxland, S. (2016), 'The Conservative Party in Wales, 1945–1997', PhD thesis: Swansea University.

Bochel, J. *et al.* (eds) (1981), *The Referendum Experience: Scotland 1979*, Aberdeen: Aberdeen University Press.

Bogdanor, V. (1980), 'Devolution', in Layton-Henry, Z. (ed.), *Conservative Party Politics*, London: Macmillan, 75–94.

Bond, R. (2000), 'Squaring the Circles: Demonstrating and Explaining the Political "Non-Alignment" of Scottish National Identity', *Scottish Affairs* 32:1, 15–35.

Boothby, R. (1940), Robert Boothby to Winston Churchill, 14 May 1940, Churchill Papers CHAR 20/4a, Cambridge: Churchill College.

Boothby, R. (1947), *I Fight to Live: Autobiography*, London: Victor Gollancz.

Bourke, R. (2003), *Peace in Ireland: The War of Ideas*, London: Random House.

Bradbury, J. (2006), 'Territory and Power Revisited: Theorising Territorial Politics in the United Kingdom after Devolution', *Political Studies* 54, 559–82.

Bradbury, J. and John, P. (2010), 'Territory and Power: Critiques and Reassessments of a Classic Work', *Government and Opposition* 45:3, 295–317.

Brand, J. A. (1978), *The National Movement in Scotland*, London and Henley: Routledge & Kegan Paul.

Breeze, R. (2019), 'Representing the People: Claiming the Heartland in Scottish Election Manifestos', in Macaulay, M. (ed.), *Populist Discourse: International Perspectives*, Basingstoke: Palgrave Macmillan, 27–58.

Brennan, K. and Drakeford, M. (2017), 'Foreword', in Morgan, R., *Rhodri: A Political Life in Wales and Westminster*, Cardiff: University of Wales Press, vii–xv.

Brett, C. E. B. (1985), *Buildings of Belfast*, Belfast: Friar's Bush Press.

Brogan, C. (1947), Draft of pamphlet entitled 'SCOTLAND and the UNION', SUMC Papers 1/51, Oxford: Bodleian Library.

Brooke, B. (1950), Diary of Sir Basil Brooke, Wednesday, 20 December 1950, D3004/D/41, Belfast: Public Record Office.

Brown, A., McCrone, D. and Paterson, L. (1996), *Politics and Society in Scotland*, London: Macmillan.

Brown, D. (1999), 'Are There Good and Bad Nationalisms?', *Nations and Nationalisms* 5:2, 281–302.

Brown, G. (1982), 'The Labour Party and Political Change in Scotland, 1918–1928: The Politics of Five Elections', PhD thesis: Edinburgh University.

Brown, G. (2014), *My Scotland, Our Britain: A Future Worth Sharing*, London: Simon & Schuster.

Brown, G. and Alexander, D. (1999), *New Scotland, New Britain*, London: The Smith Institute.

Brown Swan, C. and McEwen, N. (forthcoming), 'Embedded Independence: Self-Government and Interdependence in the Scottish National Movement', in Lecours, A. (ed.), *Constitutional Politics in Multinational Democracies*.

Browne, J. N. (1950), Note on the Scottish National Covenant, 16 June 1950, SUMC Papers 2/5, Oxford: Bodleian Library.

Buckland, P. (1980), *James Craig, Gill's Irish Lives*, Dublin: Gill and Macmillan.

Budge, I. and Urwin, D. W. (1966), *Scottish Political Behaviour: A Case Study in British Homogeneity*, London: Longmans.

Bulpitt, J. (1983), *Territory and Power in the United Kingdom: An Interpretation*, Manchester: Manchester University Press.

Burness, C. (2003), *Strange Associations: The Irish Question and the Making of Scottish Unionism, 1886–1918*, East Linton: Tuckwell Press.

Burns, T. (1938), *Plan for Scotland*, Perth: London Scots Self-Government Committee.

Cairncross, A. K. (ed.) (1954), *The Scottish Economy*, Cambridge: Cambridge University Press.

Calhoun, C. (1997), *Nationalism*, Buckingham: Open University Press.

Cameron, D. (2012), Speech at Scottish Conservative Party conference, 23 March 2012.

Cameron, E. A. (2010), *Impaled upon a Thistle: Scotland since 1880*, Edinburgh: Edinburgh University Press.

Cameron, E. A. (2016), 'Unionism and Nationalism: The Historical Context of Scottish Politics', in McTavish, D. (ed.), *Politics in Scotland*, Abingdon: Routledge, 6–23.

Campbell, A. (2011a), *The Alastair Campbell Diaries 2: Power and the People 1997–1999*, London: Hutchinson.

Campbell, A. (2011b), *The Alastair Campbell Diaries 3: Power and Responsibility 1999–2001*, London: Hutchinson.

Campbell, M. (2012), *The Home Rule and Community Commission of the Scottish Liberal Democrats*, Edinburgh: Scottish Liberal Democrats.

Castle, B. (1980), *The Castle Diaries, 1974–76*, London: Weidenfeld & Nicolson.

Chamberlain, A. (1936), *Politics from the Inside: An Epistolary Chronicle 1906–1914*, London: Cassell.

Chiao, W. H. (1969), *Devolution in Great Britain*, New York: AMS Press.

Churchill, W. S. C. (1949), 'Mr. Churchill's Speech at Ibrox Stadium, Glasgow, 20th May, 1949', SCUA Papers Acc.11368/80(iii), Edinburgh: NLS.

Churchill, W. S. C. (1950), 'Election Address, 14 February 1950', in Rhodes James, R. (ed.) (1974), *Winston S. Churchill: His Complete Speeches, 1897–1963 8*, 1950–63, New York: Chelsea House.

Churchill, W. S. C. (1952), Cabinet minutes and associated correspondence, PREM 11/252, London: The National Archives.

Clark-Hutchison, G. I. (1946), Letter dated 15 May 1946, SUMC Papers 1/46, Oxford: Bodleian Library.

Clark-Hutchison, G. I. (1947), Letter dated 29 October 1947, SUMC Papers 1/51, Oxford: Bodleian Library.

Clyde, J. L. (1947), 'The Importance of Scottish Nationalism', SUMC Papers 1/51, Oxford: Bodleian Library.

Colley, L. (2003), *Britons: Forging the Nation 1707–1837*, London: Pimlico.

Consultative Committee (1947), minutes dated 5 May 1947, SUMC Papers 1/51, Oxford: Bodleian Library.

Convery, A. (2014), 'Devolution and the Limits of Tory Statecraft: The Conservative Party in Coalition and Scotland and Wales', *Parliamentary Affairs* 67, 25–44.

Convery, A. (2016), *The Territorial Conservative Party: Devolution and Party Change in Scotland and Wales*, Manchester: Manchester University Press.

Cooper, Lord, Meston, M. C. and Sellar, W. D. (1949), *The Scottish Legal Tradition*, Edinburgh: The Saltire Society.

Coote, C. (1965), *A Companion of Honour: The Story of Walter Elliot*, Glasgow: Collins.

Corthorn, P. (2019), *Enoch Powell: Politics and Ideas in Modern Britain*, Oxford: Oxford University Press.

Coupland, R. (1954), *Welsh and Scottish Nationalism*, London: William Collins.

CPA (1966), 'Nationalism and Regionalism', 26 July 1966, SUMC Papers SUMC(66)8, Oxford: Bodleian Library.

CPA (1968), 'The Motivations behind Scottish Nationalism', March 1968, Conservative Party Papers CCO500/50/1, Oxford: Bodleian Library.

CPS (1946), *Notes on Conservative Policy*, London: Conservative Parliamentary Secretariat.

Cragoe, M. (2006), 'Conservatives, "Englishness" and "civic nationalism" between the Wars', in Tanner, D. *et al.* (eds), *Debating Nationhood and Governance in Britain, 1885–1945*, Manchester: Manchester University Press, 192–210.

Cragoe, M. (2007), '"We Like Local Patriotism": The Conservative Party and the Discourse of Decentralisation, 1947–51', *English Historical Review*, 122:498, 965–85.

Cragoe, M. (2015), 'Defending the Constitution: The Conservative Party and the Idea of Devolution, 1945–1974', in Williams, C. and Edwards, A. (eds), *The Art of the Possible: Politics and Governance in Modern British History: Essays in Memory of Duncan Tanner*, Manchester: Manchester University Press, 162–87.

CRBS (1884), *The National Meeting in Favour of the Creation of a Separate Department of State for Scotland*, Edinburgh: Convention of Royal Burghs of Scotland.

Crewe, Marquess of (1931), *Lord Rosebery I*, London: John Murray.

Crossman, R. (1977), *Diaries of a Cabinet Minister 3*, London: Hamish Hamilton.

CUCO (1949a), *General Election 1950: The Campaign Guide*, London: Conservative and Unionist Central Office.

CUCO (1949b), *The Conservative Policy for Wales and Monmouthshire*, London: Conservative and Unionist Central Office.

CUCO (1955a), *United for Peace and Progress*, London: Conservative and Unionist Party.

CUCO (1955b), *The Campaign Guide, 1955: The New Political Encyclopaedia*, London: Conservative and Unionist Central Office.

CUP (1949), *The Right Road for Britain: The Conservative Party's Statement of Policy*, London: Conservative and Unionist Party.

CUP (1950), *This Is the Road: The Conservative and Unionist Party's Policy*, London: Conservative and Unionist Party.

CUP (1951), *Britain Strong and Free*, London: Conservative and Unionist Party.

CUP (1964), *The Campaign Guide, 1964: The Unique Political Reference Book*, London: Conservative and Unionist Central Office.

Dalgleish, S. W. (1883), 'Scotland's Version of Home Rule', *Nineteenth Century* 71: January 1883, 14–26.

Dalyell, T. (2016), *The Question of Scotland*, Edinburgh: Birlinn.

Dardanelli, P. (2003), 'Ideology and Rationality: The Europeanisation of the Scottish National Party', 8th EUSA International Conference, 27–29 March 2003.

Davidson, N. (1999), 'In Perspective: Tom Nairn', *International Socialism* 2:82, 97–136.

Davidson, N. (2000), *The Origins of Scottish Nationhood*, London: Pluto Press.

Davidson, R. (2011), Speech entitled 'Winning for Scotland', Edinburgh, 9 September 2011.

Davidson, R. (2013a), Speech entitled 'Strengthening Scotland, Taking Scotland Forward', 26 March 2013.

Davidson, R. (2013b), Speech entitled 'A Scotland That Succeeds', Stirling, 8 June 2013.

Davidson, R. (2015), Speech at Dover House, London, 22 June 2015.

Davidson, R. (2017), Speech entitled 'Nationalism Should Not Be Confused with Patriotism', Edinburgh, 15 May 2017.

Davies, R. (1999), *Devolution: A Process Not an Event*, The Gregynog Papers 2:2, Cardiff: Institute of Welsh Affairs.

Day, G. and Thompson, A. (2004), *Theorizing Nationalism*, Basingstoke and New York: Palgrave Macmillan.

Deacon, R., Denton, A. and Southall, R. (2018), *The Government and Politics of Wales*, Edinburgh: Edinburgh University Press.

Dewar, D. (1999), Speech at the opening of the Scottish Parliament, 1 July 1999.

Dewar Gibb, A. (1928), Memo to SUA and letter from John Buchan, Dewar Gibb Papers, Dep 217, Box 5 (1), Edinburgh: NLS.

Dewar Gibb, A. (1930a), Letter to Stanley Baldwin dated 23 June 1930, Dewar Gibb Papers, Dep 217, Box 5 (1), Edinburgh: NLS.

Dewar Gibb, A. (1930b), Newspaper articles on *Scotland in Eclipse*, Dewar Gibb Papers, Dep 217, Box 7/7, Edinburgh: NLS.

Dewar Gibb, A. (1930c), *Scotland in Eclipse*, Edinburgh: Humphey Toulmin.

Dewar Gibb, A. (1937), *Scottish Empire*, Glasgow: A. Maclehose & Co.

Dewar Gibb, A. (1945), Diary, 1939–47, 22 May 1945, Dewar Gibb Papers Dep 217/19, Edinburgh: NLS.

Dewar Gibb, A. (1950), *Scotland Resurgent*, Stirling: Eneas Mackay.

Dicey, A. V. and Rait, R. S. (1920), *Thoughts on the Union between England & Scotland*, London: Macmillan.

Donaldson, A. (1976), *Whys of Scottish Nationalism: First of Many? The Breakthrough Seven*, Edinburgh: SNP.

Drucker, H. M. and Brown, G. (1980), *Politics of Nationalism and Devolution*, London: Longman.

Dyer, M. (2003), '"A Nationalist in the Churchillian Sense": John MacCormick, the Paisley By-election of 18 February 1948, Home Rule and the Crisis in Scottish Liberalism', *Parliamentary History* 22:3, 285–307.

EDC (1948), SCUA Papers Acc 10424/44, Edinburgh: NLS.

EDC (1949), Minute dated 8 April 1949, SCUA Papers Acc 10424/44, Edinburgh: NLS.

Elder, M. (1988a), Murray Elder to Charles Clarke, 4 March 1988, Jack McConnell Papers SPA/JMC/SN/SLA/7, Stirling: Scottish Political Archive.

Elder, M. (1988b), Murray Elder to Larry Whitty, 4 March 1988, Jack McConnell Papers SPA/JMC/SN/SLA/8.

Elgin, Lord (1889), Letter to Charles Stewart Parnell on behalf of SLA executive, Scottish Liberal Party Papers, Edinburgh: NLS.

Elibank, V. (1948), Letter dated 24 June 1948, SCUA Papers Acc.11368/80(iii), Edinburgh: NLS.

Elliot, W. (1946), Election address for the November 1946 Scottish Universities by-election, SUMC Papers 1/51, Oxford: Bodleian Library.

Elliot, W. (1949), Submission entitled 'Scottish Administration', Walter Elliot Papers Acc 6721/9/5, Edinburgh: NLS.

Elliot, W. (1956), Correspondence and newspaper coverage relating to the Wallace Memorial, Walter Elliot Papers Acc 6721 Box 2 F5, Edinburgh: NLS.

Ellis, J. S. (2008), *Investiture: Royal Ceremony and National Identity in Wales, 1911–1969*, Cardiff: University of Wales Press.

Farmer, L. (2001), 'Under the Shadow over Parliament House: The Strange Case of legal Nationalism', in Farmer, L. and Veitch, S. (eds), *The State of Scots Law*, London: Butterworths, 151–64.

Faulkner, B. (1978), *Memoirs of a Statesman*, London: Littlehampton.

Ferguson, W. (1978), *Scotland: 1689 to the Present*, Edinburgh: Oliver & Boyd.

Ferguson, W. (1998), *The Identity of the Scottish Nation: An Historic Quest*, Edinburgh: Edinburgh University Press.

Ferritter, D. (2019), *The Border: The Legacy of a Century of Anglo-Irish Politics*, London: Profile.

Finlay, R. (1992), '"For or Against?": Scottish Nationalists and the British Empire, 1919–39', *Scottish Historical Review* 71:191/2, 184–206.

Finlay, R. J. (1994), *Independent and Free: Scottish Politics and the Origins of the Scottish National Party, 1918–45*, Edinburgh: John Donald.

Finlay, R. (1996), 'Scottish Conservatism since 1918', in Francis, M. and Zweiniger-Bargielowska, I. (eds), *The Conservatives and British Society 1880–1990*, Cardiff: University of Wales Press, 111–26.

Finlay, R. J. (1997), *A Partnership for Good? Scottish Politics and the Union since 1880*, Edinburgh: John Donald.

Finlay, R. J. (2004), *Modern Scotland 1914–2000*, London: Profile.

Forrester, Duncan B. (1999), 'Ecclesia Scoticana: Established, Free, or National?', *Theology* March/April 1999, 80–9.

Foulkes, G. (1989), 'The Claim', in Dudley Edwards, O. (ed.), *A Claim of Right for Scotland*, Edinburgh: Polygon, 62–9.

Fraser, M. (2011), Speech entitled 'A new party for Scotland', Edinburgh, 5 September 2011.

Fry, M. (1991), *Patronage and Principle: A Political History of Modern Scotland* (second edition), Aberdeen: Aberdeen University Press.

Fry, M. (2013), *A New Race of Men: Scotland 1815–1914*, Edinburgh: Birlinn.

Galbraith, J. K. (1958), *The Affluent Society*, London: Houghton Mifflin.

Galbraith, R. (2018), *Without Quarter: A Biography of Tom Johnston*, Edinburgh: Birlinn.

Galbraith, T. (1949), Letter dated 13 October 1949, SUMC Papers 2/4, Oxford: Bodleian Library.

Gallagher, T. (1988), 'Scotland and the Anglo-Irish Agreement: The Reaction of the Orange Order', *Irish Political Studies* 3:1, 19–31.

Geekie, J. and Levy, R. (1989), 'Devolution and the Tartanisation of the Labour Party', *Parliamentary Affairs* 42:3, 399–411.

Gellner, E. (1983), *Nations and Nationalisms*, Oxford: Blackwell.

George Boyce, D. (2006), 'A Place Apart? Ulster, Britain and Devolution, 1886–1939', in Tanner, D. *et al.* (eds), *Debating Nationhood and Governance in Britain, 1885–1939*, Manchester: Manchester University Press, 45–63.

Gibbon, P. (1975), *The Origins of Ulster Unionism*, Manchester: Manchester University Press.

Gibbs, E. (forthcoming), *Coal Country: The Meaning and Memory of Deindustrialization in Postwar Scotland*, London: IHR.

Gilmour, J. (1937), Secretary of Fife Unionist Association to Sir John Gilmour, 2 May 1937, Gilmour Papers GD383/52, Edinburgh: National Archives of Scotland.

Glass, B. S. (2014), *The Scottish Nation at Empire's End*, Basingstoke: Palgrave Macmillan.

Glendinning, M (2004), *The Architecture of Scottish Government*, Dundee: Dundee University Press.

Gordon, D. (1989), *The O'Neill Years: Unionist Politics 1963–69*, Belfast: Athol Books.

Grant, J. P. (ed.) (1976), *Independence and Devolution: The Legal Implications for Scotland*, Edinburgh: W. Green & Son.

Gray, A. (2012), 'Settlers and Colonists', in Hames, S. (ed.), *Unstated: Writers on Scottish Independence*, Edinburgh: Word Power.

Griffith, W. (2006), 'Devolutionist Tendencies in Wales, 1885–1914', in Tanner, D. *et al.* (eds), *Debating Nationhood and Governance in Britain, 1885–1939*, Manchester: Manchester University Press, 89–117.

Griffiths, J. (1978), *James Griffiths and His Times*, Cardiff: Labour Party Wales.

Grigg, J. (1978), *Lloyd George: The People's Champion 1902–1911*, London: Eyre Methuen.

Grigg, J. (1988), *Lloyd George and Wales: The Welsh Political Archive Lecture 1987*, Aberystwyth: National Library of Wales.

Grigg, R. (2018), '"You Should Love Your Country and Should Ever Strive to be Worthy of Your Fatherland": Identity, British Values and St David's Day in Elementary Schools in Wales, c.1885–1920', *Welsh History Review* 29:1, 99–125.

Hanham, H. J. (1967), 'Mid-Century Scottish Nationalism: Romantic and Radical', in Robson, R. (ed.), *Ideas and Institutions of Victorian Britain: Essays in Honour of George Kitson Clark*, London: G. Bell & Sons, 143–79.

Hanham, H. J. (1969), *Scottish Nationalism*, London: Faber & Faber.

Harvie, C. (1981), 'Labour and Scottish Government: The Age of Tom Johnston', *Bulletin of Scottish Politics* 2, 1–20.

Harvie, C. (1992), 'Scottish Politics', in Dickson, A. and Treble, J. H. (eds), *People and Society in Scotland Volume III 1914–1990*, Edinburgh: John Donald, 241–60.

Harvie, C. (1998), *No Gods and Precious Few Heroes: Twentieth-Century Scotland* (third edition), Edinburgh: Edinburgh University Press.

Harvie, C. (2004), *Scotland and Nationalism: Scottish Society and Politics 1707 to the Present* (fourth edition), London: Routledge.

Hassan, G. and Shaw, E. (2012), *The Strange Death of Labour Scotland*, Edinburgh: Edinburgh University Press.

Hastings, A. (1997), *The Construction of Nationhood: Ethnicity, Religion and Nationalism*, Cambridge: Cambridge University Press.

Hearn, J. (2000), *Claiming Scotland: National Identity and Liberal Culture*, Edinburgh: Polygon.

Hechter, M. (1985), *Internal Colonialism: The Celtic Fringe in British National Development, 1536–1966*, London and Henley: Routledge & Kegan Paul.

Hechter, M. (2000), *Containing Nationalism*, Oxford: Oxford University Press.

Henderson, A. (2007), *Hierarchies of Belonging: National Identity and Political Culture in Scotland and Quebec*, Montreal and Kingston: McGill-Queen's University Press.

Hennessey, T. *et al.* (2019), *The Ulster Unionist Party: Country before Party?*, Oxford: Oxford University Press.

Heslinga, M. (1962), *The Irish Border as a Cultural Divide*, New York: Humanities Press.

Hobsbawm, E. (1990), *Nations and Nationalism since 1780: Programme, Myth, Reality*, Cambridge: Cambridge University Press.

Hobsbawm, E. J. and Ranger, T. (eds) (1983), *The Invention of Tradition*, Cambridge: Cambridge University Press.

Hogg, Q. (1948), *The Case for Conservatism*, London: Penguin.

Hogge, J. M. (1910), December 1910 election address for Camlachie Division of Glasgow, Scottish Liberal Party Papers Acc 11765/77, Edinburgh: NLS.

Hogge, J. M. (1912), Edinburgh East by-election address, Scottish Liberal Party Papers Acc 11765/78, Edinburgh: NLS.

Hogge, J. M. (1918), 1918 election address for Edinburgh East, Scottish Liberal Party Papers Acc 11765/80, Edinburgh: NLS.

Horne, R. (1933), Letter from Sir Robert Horne, SCUA Papers Acc 10424/7(i), Edinburgh: NLS.

Hroch, M. (2000), *Social Preconditions of National Revival in Europe*, New York: Columbia University Press.

Hutchison, I. G. C. (1998), 'Scottish Unionism between the Two World Wars', in Macdonald, C. M. M. (ed.), *Unionist Scotland 1800–1997*, Edinburgh: John Donald, 73–99.

Hutchison, I. G. C. (2001), *Scottish Politics in the Twentieth Century*, Basingstoke: Palgrave.

Hutchison, I. G. C. (2005), 'Anglo-Scottish Political Relations in the Nineteenth Century, c.1815–1914', in Smout, T. C. (ed.), *Anglo-Scottish Relations from 1603 to 1900*, Oxford: Oxford University Press, 247–66.

Ichijo, A. (2004), *Scottish Nationalism and the Idea of Europe*, Abingdon: Routledge.

Ichijo, A. (2012), 'Entrenchment of Unionist Nationalism: Devolution and the Discourse of National Identity in Scotland', *National Identities* 14:1, 23–37.

ICUAC (1932), *Manifesto*, Glasgow: Imperial Committee of the Unionist Association of Cathcart.

Ignatieff, M. (1993), *Blood & Belonging: Journeys into the New Nationalism*, London: Chatto & Windus.

Ignatieff, M. (1994), *A Different Country*, Glasgow: BBC Scotland.

Investiture of His Royal Highness The Prince of Wales KG as Prince of Wales and Earl of Chester by Her Majesty The Queen (1969), Caernarvon Castle 1 July 1969.

Jackson, A. (2003), *Home Rule: An Irish History 1800–2000*, London: Weidenfeld & Nicolson.

Jackson, A. (2012), *The Two Unions: Ireland, Scotland, and the Survival of the United Kingdom, 1707–2007*, Oxford: Oxford University Press.

Jeffrey, C. (2009), *The Scottish Parliament 1999–2009: The First Decade*, Edinburgh: Luath.

Johnston, R. (1979), *Scottish Liberal Party Conference Speeches 1971–1978*, Unknown: Bookmag.

Johnston, T. (1952), *Memories*, Glasgow: Collins.

Jones, C. (2019), Speech to Study of Parliament Group, Oxford, 4 January 2019.

Judt, T. (2010), *Postwar: A History of Europe since 1945*, London: Vintage.

Kearton, A. (2012), 'Imagining the "Mongrel Nation": Political Uses of History in the Recent Scottish Nationalist Movement', *National Identities* 7:1, 23–50.

Keating, M. (1988), *State and Regional Nationalism: Territorial Politics and the European State*, Hemel Hempstead: Prentice Hall.

Keating, M. (2001), *Plurinational Democracy: Stateless Nations in a Post-Sovereignty Era*, Oxford: Oxford University Press.

Keating, M. (2009), *The Independence of Scotland: Self-government and the Shifting Politics of Union*, Oxford: Oxford University Press.

Keating, M. (2017), *Debating Scotland: Issues of Independence and Union in the 2014 Referendum*, Oxford: Oxford University Press.

Keating, M. and Bleiman, D. (1979), *Labour and Scottish Nationalism*, London: Macmillan.

Keitner, C. I. (1999), 'The "False Promise" of Civic Nationalism', *Millennium: Journal of International Studies* 28:2, 341–51.

Kellas, J. G. (1968), *Modern Scotland: The Nation since 1870*, London: Pall Mall Press.

Kellas, J. (1980), *Modern Scotland* (second edition), London: George Allen & Unwin.

Kellas, J. G. (1989), *The Scottish Political System* (fourth edition), Cambridge: Cambridge University Press.

Kellas, J. (1994), 'The Party in Scotland', in Seldon, A. and Ball, S. (eds), *Conservative Century: The Conservative Party since 1900*, Oxford: Oxford University Press, 671–93.

Kellas, J. G. (1998), *The Politics of Nationalism and Ethnicity*, London: Palgrave Macmillan.

Kennedy, J. (2015), *Liberal Nationalisms: Empire, State, and Civil Society in Scotland and Quebec*, Montreal and Kingston: McGill-Queen's University Press.

Kidd, C. (1993), *Subverting Scotland's Past: Scottish Whig Historians and the Creation of an Anglo-British Identity, 1689-c.1830*, Cambridge: Cambridge University Press.

Kidd, C. (2008), *Union and Unionisms: Political Thought in Scotland, 1500–2000*, Cambridge: Cambridge University Press.

Kidd, C. (2013a), 'Unionism – a very Scottish idea' [accessed: 30 April 2017].

Kidd, C. (2013b), 'From Jacobitism to the SNP: The Crown, the Union and the Scottish Question', The Stenton Lecture 2013.

Kidd, C. (2019), 'Independence and Union Revisited', in Hassan, G. (ed.), *The Story of the Scottish Parliament: The First Two Decades Explained*, Edinburgh: Edinburgh University Press, 219–28.

Kinnaird Rose, W. and Macaulay Smith, R. (1895), *The Liberal Platform: A Hand-Book of Political Reference*, Edinburgh, Glasgow and London: Scottish Liberal Association.

Labour Party (1962), *Signposts for Scotland*, London: Labour Party.

Labour Party (1964), *Signposts to the New Wales*, London: Labour Party.

Labour Party in Wales (1970), *Evidence of the Labour Party in Wales to the Commission on the Constitution, into the Seventies*, Cardiff: Labour Party in Wales.

Leith, M. S. and Soule, D. P. J. (2012), *Political Discourse and National Identity in Scotland*, Edinburgh: Edinburgh University Press.

Levitt, I. (ed.) (1992), *The Scottish Office: Depression and Reconstruction 1919–1959*, Edinburgh: Scottish History Society.

Levy, R. (1990), *Scottish Nationalism at the Crossroads*, Edinburgh: Scottish Academic Press.

Levy, R. (1994), 'Nationalist Parties in Scotland and Wales', in Roberts, L. *et al.* (eds), *Britain's Changing Party System*, London: Leicester University Press, 147–65.

Liinpää, M. (2018), 'Nationalism and Scotland's Imperial Past', in Davidson, N. *et al.* (eds), *No Problem Here: Understanding Racism in Scotland*, Edinburgh: Luath, 14–31.

Lindsay, K. (1972), *Dominion of Ulster*, Belfast: Ulster Vanguard Publication.

Lloyd George, D. (1911), Speech opening Young Scots Club in Edinburgh, Scottish Liberal Party Papers Acc 11765/77, Edinburgh: NLS.

Lloyd-Jones, N. (2014), 'Liberalism, Scottish Nationalism and the Home Rule Crisis, c.1886–93', *English Historical Review* 129, 862–87.

Lukacs, J. (2005), *Democracy and Populism*, New Haven, CT: Yale University Press.

Lynch, P. (1996), *Minority Nationalism and European Integration*, Cardiff: University of Wales Press.

Lynch, P. (1999), *The Politics of Nationhood: Sovereignty, Britishness and Conservative Politics*, Basingstoke: Macmillan.

Lynch, P. (2013), *SNP: The History of the Scottish National Party* (second edition), Cardiff: Welsh Academic Press.

McAdam, D., McCarthy, J. D. and Zald, M. N. (1996), *Comparative Perspectives in Social Movements*, Cambridge: Cambridge University Press.

MacAskill, K. (2004), *Building a Nation: Post Devolution Nationalism in Scotland*, Edinburgh: Luath.

McCallum, D. (1943), Letter dated 20 September 1943, SUMC Papers 1/12, Oxford: Bodleian Library.

McCallum, D. (1945), Letter dated 6 February 1945, SUMC Papers 1/47, Oxford: Bodleian Library.

MacCormick, J. M. (1955), *The Flag in the Wind: The Story of the National Movement in Scotland*, London: Victor Gollancz.

MacCormick, N. (1996), 'Liberalism, Nationalism and the Post-sovereign State', *Political Studies* 44, 553–67.

MacCormick, N. (1999), *Questioning Sovereignty: Law, State, and Nation in the European Commonwealth*, Oxford: Oxford University Press.

MacCormick, N. (2005), 'New Unions for Old', in Miller, W. L. (ed.), *Anglo-Scottish Relations from 1900 to Devolution*, Oxford: Oxford University Press.

McCrone, D. (1989), 'Representing Scotland: Culture and Nationalism', in McCrone, D., Kendrick, S. and Straw, P. (eds) (1989), *The Making of Scotland: Nation, Culture and Social Change*, Edinburgh: Edinburgh University Press, 161–74.

McCrone, D. (1992), *Understanding Scotland: The Sociology of a Stateless Nation*, London: Routledge.

McCrone, D. (2001), *Understanding Scotland: The Sociology of a Nation* (second edition), London: Routledge.

MacDiarmid, H. (1968), 'Scotland', in Dudley Edwards, O., Evans, G., Rhys, I., and MacDiarmid, H. (eds), *Celtic Nationalism*, London: Routledge, 299–358.

Macdonald, C. M. M. (ed.) (1998), *Unionist Scotland 1800–1997*, Edinburgh: John Donald.

Macdonald, C. M. M. and McFarland, E. W. (eds) (1999), *Scotland and the Great War*, East Linton: Tuckwell Press.

MacEwen, A. M. (1932), *The Thistle and the Rose: Scotland's Problem To-day*, London: Oliver & Boyd.

McFarland, E. (2014), *'A Slashing Man of Action': The Life of Lieutenant-General Sir Aylmer Hunter-Weston MP*, Oxford: Peter Lang.

McIntyre, R. D. (1955), Robert D. McIntyre to Sir John Boyd Orr, 16 December 1955, McIntyre Papers Acc 10090/62, Edinburgh: NLS.

Mackenzie, A. M. (1947), *Scotland in Modern Times 1720–1939*, London: Chambers.

Mackenzie, C. (1967), *My Life and Times: Octave Six, 1923–1930*, London: Chatto & Windus.

MacKenzie, M. (1988), *Scottish Toryism, Identity and Consciousness: A Personal Essay*, London: Tory Reform Group.

Mackie, G. (2004), *Flying, Farming and Politics: A Liberal Life*, Stanhope: Memoir Club.

McLean, R. (1991a), *Labour and Scottish Home Rule Part 1: Mid-Lanark to Majority Government 1888–1945*, West Lothian: Scottish Labour Action.

McLean, R. (1991b), *Labour and Scottish Home Rule Part 2: Unionist Complacency to Crisis Management 1945–1988*, West Lothian: Scottish Labour Action.

McLean, R. (2001), 'Gallant Crusader or Cautious Persuader? Donald Dewar's Role in Securing Scotland's Parliament', *Scottish Affairs* 34, 1–10.

McLean, I. and McMillan, A. (2005), *State of the Union: Unionism and the Alternatives in the United Kingdom since 1707*, Oxford: Oxford University Press.

Macleod, I. (1947), Letter dated 6 May 1947, SUMC Papers 1/51, Oxford: Bodleian Library.

McNair, B. (2008), 'The Printed Media', in Blain, N. and Hutchison, D. (eds), *The Media in Scotland*, Edinburgh: Edinburgh University Press, 227–42.

Madgwick, P. and Rose, R. (eds) (1982), *The Territorial Dimension in United Kingdom Politics*, London: Palgrave Macmillan.

Mansergh, N. (1936), *The Government of Northern Ireland: A Study in Devolution*, London: Allen & Unwin.

Mar and Kellie, Earl of (1926), Earl of Mar and Kellie to Sir John Gilmour, 28 May 1926, Gilmour Papers GD383/23, Edinburgh: National Archives of Scotland.

Marr, A. (1995), *The Battle for Scotland*, London: Penguin.

Marr, A. (2016), *Scotland and the Battle for Britain*, Glasgow: BBC Scotland.

Martin, D. (1989), 'The Democratic Deficit', in Dudley Edwards, O. (ed.), *A Claim of Right for Scotland*, Edinburgh: Polygon, 80–5.

Marx, K. (1972), *The Eighteenth Brumaire of Louis Bonaparte*, London: Progress.

Masterman, N. (1976), *The Forerunner: The Dilemmas of Tom Ellis 1859–1899*, Swansea and Llandybie: Christopher Davies.

Melding, D. (2009), *Will Britain Survive beyond 2020?*, Cardiff: Institute of Welsh Affairs.

Melding, D. (2019), Speech entitled 'Unionism and Nationalism in Welsh Political Life', Hay-on-Wye, 27 May 2019.

Miller, D. (1995), *On Nationality*, Oxford: Oxford University Press.

Miller, D. W. (2007), *Queen's Rebels: Ulster Loyalism in Historical Perspective*, Dublin: University College Dublin Press.

Miller, W. L. (1981), *The End of British Politics? Scots and English Political Behaviour in the Seventies*, Oxford: Clarendon Press.

Mitchell, J. (1989), 'The Gilmour Report on Scottish Central Administration', *The Juridical Review* 34, 173–88.

Mitchell, J. (1990), *Conservatives and the Union*, Edinburgh: Edinburgh University Press.

Mitchell, J. (1996), *Strategies for Self-government: The Campaigns for a Scottish Parliament*, Edinburgh: Polygon.

Mitchell, J. (1998), 'Contemporary Scotland', in Macdonald, C. M. M. (ed.), *Unionist Scotland 1800–1997*, Edinburgh: John Donald, 117–39.

Mitchell, J. (2000), 'From National Identity to Nationalism, 1945–99', in Dickinson, H. T. and Lynch, M. (eds), *The Challenge to Westminster: Sovereignty, Devolution and Independence*, East Linton: Tuckwell Press, 154–64.

Mitchell, J. (2003), *Governing Scotland: The Invention of Administrative Devolution*, Basingstoke: Palgrave Macmillan.

Mitchell, J. (2009), *Devolution in the UK*, Manchester: Manchester University Press.

Mitchell, J. (2014), *The Scottish Question*, Oxford: Oxford University Press.

Mitchell, J. (2018), 'Devolution', in Brown, D. *et al.* (eds), *The Oxford Handbook of Modern British Political History, 1800–2000*, Oxford: Oxford University Press, 173–88.

Mitchell, J. (2019), 'Looking Back Five Years On . . .', http://sceptical.scot/2019/09/looking-back-five-years-on/ [accessed 21 September 2019].

Mitchell, J. and Johns, R. (2016), *Takeover: Explaining the Extraordinary Rise of the SNP*, London: Biteback.

Mitchell, J., Bennie, L. and Johns, R. (2012), *The Scottish National Party: Transition to Power*, Oxford: Oxford University Press.

Montrose, Duke of (1933), *Self-Government for Scotland*, London and Tonbridge: Whitefriars Press.

Montrose, Duke of (1952), *My Ditty Box*, London: Jonathan Cape.

Moran, M. (2017), *The End of British Politics?*, London: Palgrave Macmillan.

Morgan, K. O. (1981), *Rebirth of a Nation: Wales 1880–1980*, Oxford: Oxford University Press.

Morgan, K. O. (1995), *Modern Wales: Politics, Places and People*, Cardiff: University of Wales Press.

Morton, G. (1999), *Unionist Nationalism: Governing Urban Scotland, 1830–1860*, East Linton: Tuckwell Press.

Morton, G. (2008), 'Scotland Is Britain: The Union and Unionist-Nationalism, 1807–1907', *Journal of Irish Scottish Studies* 1:2, 127–41.

Muir, E. (1935), *Scottish Journey*, London: Heinemann.

Murray, C. de B. (1938), *How Scotland Is Governed*, Edinburgh and London: Moray Press.

Mycock, A. (2012), 'SNP, Identity and Citizenship: Re-imagining State and Nation', *National Identities* 14:1, 53–69.

Nairn, T. (1981), *The Break-up of Britain: Crisis and Neo-Nationalism* (second edition), London: Verso.

Nairn, T. (1997), *Faces of Nationalism: Janus Revisited*, London: Verso.

Naughtie, J. (1989), 'Labour, 1979–1988', in Donnachie, I. *et al.* (eds), *Forward! Labour Politics in Scotland 1888–1988*, Edinburgh: Polygon, 130–55.

Newark, F. H. (ed.) (1953), *Devolution of Government: The Experiment in Northern Ireland*, Institute of Public Administration, London: Allen & Unwin.

Newark, F. H. (1955), 'The Law and the Constitution', in Wilson, T. (ed.), *Ulster under Home Rule: A Study of the Political and Economic Problems of Northern Ireland*, Oxford: Oxford University Press, 14–54.

NLFS (1886), Address to members of the Liberal Associations of Scotland, 1 October 1886, Glasgow: National Liberal Federation of Scotland.

Noble, M. (1958), 'Noble for Argyll', Argyll by-election address, SCUA Papers Acc 10424/132, Edinburgh: NLS.

Norton, P. (1994), 'The Parliamentary Party and Party Committees', in Seldon, A. and Ball, S. (eds), *Conservative Century: The Conservative Party since 1900*, Oxford: Oxford University Press, 97–144.

NUA (1922), *The Campaign Guide 1922, Fourteenth Edition*, London: National Unionist Association.

OCUPS (1959), *Scotland and the Government*, Edinburgh: Office of the Chairman of the Unionist Party in Scotland.

O'Leary, B. (2019a), *A Treatise on Northern Ireland, Volume I: Colonialism*, Oxford: Oxford University Press.

O'Leary, B. (2019b), *A Treatise on Northern Ireland, Volume III: Consociation and Confederation*, Oxford: Oxford University Press.

O'Neill, T. (1969), *Ulster at the Crossroads*, London: Faber & Faber.

O'Neill, T. (1972), *The Autobiography of Terence O'Neill: Prime Minister of Northern Ireland 1963–1969*, London: Rupert Hart-Davis.

Opening of the Parliament of Northern Ireland by His Most Gracious Majesty King George V June 22nd 1921, Belfast: HMSO.

Opening of the Royal Courts of Justice Ulster by His Grace the Duke of Abercorn, K.G., K.P. Governor of Northern Ireland, 31st May 1933, Belfast: HMSO.

Orwell, G. (1945), 'Notes on Nationalism', *Polemic* 1, October 1945.

Osborne, C. (1950), Letter dated 9 May 1950, SUMC Papers 1/47, Oxford: Bodleian Library.

Osmond, J. (1977), *Creative Conflict: The Politics of Welsh Devolution*, Llandysul: Gomer Press.

Overton, J. (2017), 'The Overton Window: A Model of Policy Change' [accessed: 2 June 2017].

Özkırımlı, U. (2005), *Contemporary Debates on Nationalism: A Critical Engagement*, Basingstoke: Palgrave.

Paterson, L. (1994), *The Autonomy of Modern Scotland*, Edinburgh: Edinburgh University Press.

Paterson, L. (2015), 'Utopian Pragmatism: Scotland's Choice', *Scottish Affairs* 24:1, 22–46.

Paterson, L. and Wyn Jones, R. (1999), 'Does Civil Society Drive Constitutional Change? The Case of Wales and Scotland', in Taylor, B. and Thomson, K. (eds), *Scotland and Wales: Nations Again?*, Cardiff: University of Wales Press, 169–97.

Paton, H. J. (1968), *The Claim of Scotland*, London: Allen & Unwin.

Pentland, G. (2015), 'Edward Heath, the Declaration of Perth and the Scottish Conservative and Unionist Party, 1966–70', *Twentieth Century British History* 26:2, 249–73.

Philip, A. B. (1975), *The Welsh Question: Nationalism in Welsh Politics 1945–1970*, Cardiff: University of Wales Press.

Phillips, J. (2008), *The Industrial Politics of Devolution: Scotland in the 1960s and 1970s*, Manchester: Manchester University Press.

Pickard, W. (2011), *The Member for Scotland: A Life of Duncan McLaren*, Edinburgh: Birlinn.

Pittock, M. (2001), *Scottish Nationality*, Basingstoke: Palgrave.

Pittock, M. (2008), *The Road to Independence? Scotland since the Sixties*, London: Reaktion.

Pocock, J. G. A. (1975), 'British History: A Plea for a New Subject', *Journal of Modern History* 47:4, 601–21.

Pollok, J. (1997), *Restless Nation*, Glasgow: BBC Scotland.

Porteous, J. A. A. (1935), *The New Unionism*, London, George Allen & Unwin.

Porteous, J. A. A. (1948), *Unionist Policy for Scotland: A Criticism*, Glasgow: Scottish Convention.

Pryde, G. S. and Rait, R. S. (1954), *Nations of the Modern World: Scotland* (second edition), London: Ernest Benn.

Rait, R. S. (1914), *History of Scotland*, London: Thornton Butterworth.

Ramsden, J. (1995), *A History of the Conservative Party: The Age of Churchill and Eden 1940–1957*, London: Longman.

Ramsden, J. (1996), *A History of the Conservative Party: The Winds of Change – Macmillan to Heath, 1957–1975*, London: Longman.

Reid, J. M. (1959), *Scotland Past and Present*, London: Oxford University Press.

Reid, J. M. (1971), *Scotland's Progress: The Survival of a Nation*, London: Eyre & Spottiswoode.

Reith, Lord (1975), *The Reith Diaries*, London: HarperCollins.

Renan, E. (1882), *Qu'est-ce qu'une Nation?*, Whitefish: Kessinger.

Ritchie, M. (2000), *Scotland Reclaimed*, Edinburgh: Saltire Society.

Rokkan, S. and Urwin, D. (eds) (1982), *The Politics of Territorial Identity: Studies in European Regionalism*, London: Sage.

Rose, R. (1971), *Governing without Consensus: An Irish Perspective*, London: Faber & Faber.

Rose, R. (1982), *Understanding the United Kingdom: The Territorial Dimension in Government*, London: Longman.

Ross, E. (1983), 'Devolution', in Lansman, J. and Meale, A. (eds), *Beyond Thatcher: The Real Alternative*, London: Junction Books, 190–6.

Rudolph, J. and Thompson, R. (1985), 'Ethnoterritorial Movements and the Policy Process: Accommodating Nationalist Demands in the Developed World', *Comparative Politics* 17, 291–311.

Russell, M. and MacLeod, D. (2004), *Grasping the Thistle: How Scotland Must React to the Three Key Challenges of the Twenty First Century*, Edinburgh: Argyll.

Salisbury, Lord (1885), Lord Salisbury to the Duke of Richmond, 13 August 1885, Goodwood MS 871, Chichester: West Sussex Record Office.

Salmond, A. (1995), *The Great Debate*, Glasgow: BBC Scotland.

Salmond, A. (2013), 'The Six Unions', speech at Nigg Fabrication Yard, 12 July 2013.

Salmond, A. (2014), St George's Day 2014 speech, 23 April 2014.

Salmond, A. (2018), *Conversations: Alex Salmond*, London: BBC Parliament.

Sanderson, Lord (2010), *Building for Scotland: Strengthening the Scottish Conservatives*, Edinburgh: Scottish Conservative Party.

SCA (1953), *The Unionist Party and Scotland*, Glasgow: Scottish Covenant Association.

Schnapper, D. (1998), *Community of Citizens: On the Modern Idea of Nationality*, London: Transaction.

SCLP (1971), Evidence to the Royal Commission, Glasgow: Scottish Council of the Labour Party.

Scothorne, R., Gallagher, C. and Westwell, A. (2016), *Roch Winds: A Treacherous Guide to the State of Scotland*, Edinburgh: Luath.

Scottish Conservative Party (1970s), Tory leaflet from the 1970s, Stirling: Scottish Political Archive.

Scottish Convention (1946), *Scottish Convention: Questions We Are Asked*, Glasgow: Scottish Convention.

Scottish Government (2007), *Choosing Scotland's Future: A National Conversation*, Edinburgh: HMSO.

Scottish Government (2009), *Your Scotland, Your Voice*, Edinburgh: HMSO.

Scottish Government (2013), *Scotland's Future*, Edinburgh: HMSO.

Scottish Office (1993), *Scotland in the Union: A Partnership for Good*, Edinburgh: HMSO.

SCUA (1926), Scottish Unionist Association Annual Report 1926, Scottish Conservative and Unionist Association Papers Acc 11368/77(iv), Edinburgh: NLS.

SCUA (1934), Scottish Unionist Association Annual Report 1926, Scottish Conservative and Unionist Association Papers Acc 11368/77(iv), Edinburgh: NLS.

SCUA (1936), Scottish Unionist Association Annual Report 1926, Scottish Conservative and Unionist Association Papers Acc 11368/77(iv), Edinburgh: NLS.

SCUA (1937), Papers concerning jubilee presentation to Sir Lewis Shedden, SCUA Papers Acc 10424/10(viii), Edinburgh: NLS.

SCUA (1938), Scottish Unionist Association Annual Report 1926, Scottish Conservative and Unionist Association Papers Acc 11368/77(iv), Edinburgh: NLS.

SDP (1983), 'First Consultative Assembly in St Andrews on 26/27 February 1983', SDP (Scotland) Papers GB 1847 SDP, Glasgow: Glasgow Caledonian University.

SDP (1988), SDP (Scotland) Papers, SDPAR 3/1, Glasgow: Glasgow Caledonian University.

Seawright, D. (1996), 'The Scottish Unionist Party: What's in a Name?', *Scottish Affairs* 14, 90–102.

Seawright, D. (1998), 'Scottish Unionism: An East West Divide?', *Scottish Affairs* 23, 54–72.

Selkirk, Earl of (1947a), Letter dated 26 March 1947, SUMC Papers 1/51, Oxford: Bodleian Library.

Selkirk, Earl of (1947b), Exchange of letters with James Porteous dated 23 March and 4 April 1947, Porteous Papers Acc 7505 No 1, Edinburgh: NLS.

Seton-Watson, H. (1977), *An Enquiry into the Origins of Nations and the Politics of Nationalism*, London: Methuen.

Shipton, M. (2011), *Poor Man's Parliament: Ten Years of the Welsh Assembly*, Cardiff: Poetry Wales Press.

Sillars, J. (1988), *No Turning Back*, Edinburgh: SNP.

Sillars, J. and Eadie, A. (1968), *Don't Butcher Scotland's Future*, Ayr: Labour Party.

SLA (1887), 'Report of Deputies Commissioned to Visit Ireland by the Executive of the Scottish Liberal Association', Scottish Liberal Party Papers Acc 11765/35, Edinburgh: NLS.

SLA (1890), Executive letter to Gladstone, Scottish Liberal Party Papers Acc 11765/3, Edinburgh: NLS.

SLA (1900), *Current Politics from a Liberal Standpoint: A Handbook for the Use of Liberals*, Edinburgh and Glasgow: Scottish Liberal Association.

SLA (1989), *Proposals for Scottish Democracy: A Scottish Labour Action Discussion Document*, Edinburgh: Scottish Labour Action.

SLF (1925), *Liberal Principles and Aims Adopted by the Scottish Convention of Liberals*, Edinburgh and Glasgow: Scottish Liberal Federation.

SLF (1937), *A Policy for Scotland: Interim Report of the Industrial Policy Committee*, Edinburgh and Glasgow: Scottish Liberal Federation.

SLF (1941), Annual conference at Edinburgh, 12 September 1941, Edinburgh: Scottish Liberal Federation.

SLP (1947), Minutes of executive meeting on 4 October 1947, Scottish Liberal Party Papers Acc 11765/53, Edinburgh: NLS.

SLP (1948), Minutes of executive meeting on 14 January 1948, Scottish Liberal Party Papers Acc 11765/56, Edinburgh: NLS.

SLP (1949a), Annual Report of the Executive Committee, 1948–49, Scottish Liberal Party Papers Acc 11765/45, Edinburgh: NLS.

SLP (1949b), Minutes of an executive meeting on 5 March 1949, Scottish Liberal Party Papers Acc 11765/53, Edinburgh: NLS.

SLP (1949c), *Scottish Self Government*, Edinburgh: Scottish Liberal Party.

SLP (1950), *Manifesto of the Scottish Liberal Party: The Scottish Party of Progress*, Edinburgh: Scottish Liberal Party.

SLP (1951), Minutes of an executive meeting on 8 December 1951, Scottish Liberal Party Papers Acc 11765/54, Edinburgh: NLS.

SLP (1952), Minute of executive meeting on 1 March 1952, Scottish Liberal Party Papers Acc 11765/54, Edinburgh: NLS.

SLP (1953), Minute of executive meeting on 30 May 1953, Scottish Liberal Party Papers Acc 11765/54, Edinburgh: NLS.

SLP (1966), Minute of Council meeting dated 3 September 1966, Scottish Liberal Party Papers Acc 11765/57, Edinburgh: NLS.

SLP (1967a), *The Liberal Crusade: People Count – The Liberal Plan for Power*, Edinburgh: Scottish Liberal Party.

SLP (1967b), SLP annual conference, 18–20 May 1967, Scottish Liberal Party Papers Acc 11765/58, Edinburgh: NLS.

SLP (1971–4), Conference '71, '72 and '74 Agendas, Scottish Liberal Party Acc 11765/58, Edinburgh: NLS.

SLP (1987), Scottish Liberal Party 1987 Conference Agenda, Scottish Liberal Party Papers Acc 11765/60, Edinburgh: NLS.

Smith, A. D. (1979), *Nationalism in the Twentieth Century*, Oxford: Martin Robertson.

Smith, A. D. (1986), *The Ethnic Origins of Nations*, Oxford: Blackwell.

Smith, A. D. (1991), *National Identity*, London: Penguin.

Smith, A. D. (1995), *Nations and Nationalism in a Global Era*, Cambridge: Polity Press.

Smith, A. D. (1996), 'History and Modernity: Reflections on the Theory of Nationalism', in Hall, J. A. and Jarvie, I. (eds), *The Social Philosophy of Ernest Gellner*, Atlanta and Amsterdam: Rodopi, 129–46.

Smith, A. D. (1998), *Nationalism and Modernism: A Critical Survey of Recent Theories of Nations and Nationalism*, London: Routledge.

Smith, A. D. (2004), *The Antiquity of Nations*, Cambridge: Polity Press.

Smith, A. D. (2009), *Ethno-symbolism and Nationalism: A Cultural Approach*, Oxford: Routledge.

SNP (1935), *Self-Government in* Practice, Glasgow: Scottish National Party.

SNP (1956), *Our Three Nations: Wales, Scotland, England,* Unknown: unknown.

SNP (1964), Election leaflets entitled 'Independent Self Government? Yes! Separatism? No!', SPA/GW/EM/2/12, Stirling: Scottish Political Archive.

SNP (1975), Arthur Donaldson testimonial dinner programme, Stirling: Scottish Political Archive.

SNP (1977), *SNP & You: Aims & policy of the Scottish National Party,* Edinburgh: SNP.

SNP (1992), *Independence in Europe: Make it Happen Now! The 1992 Manifesto of the Scottish National Party,* Edinburgh: SNP.

SNP (2001), *Heart of the Manifesto,* Edinburgh: SNP.

SNP (2002), *A Constitution for a Free Scotland,* Edinburgh: SNP.

SNP (2005), *Raising the Standard,* Edinburgh: SNP.

Somerville, P. (2013), *Through the Maelstrom: A History of the Scottish National Party 1945–1967,* Stirling: Scots Independent.

Sproat, I. (1964), Rutherglen by-election address, SCUA Papers Acc 10424/133, Edinburgh: NLS.

State Visit to Scotland Her Majesty the Queen and His Royal Highness The Duke of Edinburgh June 1953, Edinburgh: Pillans and Wilson Ltd.

Stewart, W. (1925), *J. Keir Hardie: A Biography,* London: Independent Labour Party.

Stuart, J. (1954), 'Note for Record' dated 6 July 1954, T222/686, London: The National Archives.

Sturgeon, N. (2012), Speech entitled 'Bringing the Powers Home to Build a Better Nation', University of Strathclyde, 3 December 2012.

Sturgeon, N. (2013), Speech entitled 'Independence: A Renewed Partnership of the Isles', University of Edinburgh, 6 June 2013.

SUA (1914a), Memo entitled 'Scottish Home Rule', Bonar Law Papers BL/32/3/30, London: Parliamentary Archives.

SUA (1914b), *Campaign Guide, Thirteenth Edition,* Edinburgh: Scottish Unionist Association.

SUA (1948), *Scotland and the United Kingdom,* Edinburgh: Scottish Unionist Association.

SUA (1949), *Scottish Control of Scottish Affairs: Unionist Policy,* Edinburgh: Scottish Unionist Association.

SUA (1950), Loose flyer, SCUA Papers Acc 11368/80(iv), Edinburgh: NLS.

SUA (1954), *Scotland under the Unionist Government,* Edinburgh: Scottish Unionist Association.

SUA (1955), *East of Scotland Year Book and Scottish Parliamentary Election Manual,* Edinburgh and Glasgow: Scottish Unionist Association.

SUA (1957), *The Year Book for Scotland and Scottish Parliamentary Election Manual,* Edinburgh and Glasgow: Scottish Unionist Association.

SUA (1958), *The Year Book for Scotland and Scottish Parliamentary Election Manual,* Edinburgh and Glasgow: Scottish Unionist Association.

SUA (1961), *The Year Book for Scotland and Scottish Parliamentary Election Manual*, Edinburgh and Glasgow: Scottish Unionist Association.

SUMC (1945), Minute dated 20 February 1945, SUMC Papers 1/47, Oxford: Bodleian Library.

SUMC (1946), Minute dated 5 November 1946, SUMC Papers 1/51, Oxford: Bodleian Library.

SUMC (1947a), Letter dated 24 March 1947, SUMC Papers 1/51, Oxford: Bodleian Library.

SUMC (1947b), Minute dated 10 July 1947, SUMC Papers 1/51, Oxford: Bodleian Library.

SUMC (1949a), Minute dated 15 February 1949, SUMC Papers 2/4, Oxford: Bodleian Library.

SUMC (1949b), Minute dated 29 March 1949, SUMC Papers 2/4, Oxford: Bodleian Library.

SUMC (1950a), Meeting dated 19 May 1950, SUMC Papers 2/5, Oxford: Bodleian Library.

SUMC (1950b), Minute dated 25 July 1950, SUMC Papers 2/5, Oxford: Bodleian Library.

SUMC (1950c), Minute dated 21 November 1950, SUMC Papers 2/5, Oxford: Bodleian Library.

SUMC (1952), Minute dated 26 February 1952, SUMC Papers 2/6, Oxford: Bodleian Library.

SUMC (1954), 23 November 1954, SUMC Papers 2/16, Oxford: Bodleian Library.

SUMC (1955), Speech dated 10 November 1955, SUMC Papers 1/25/1, Oxford: Bodleian Library.

SUMC (1956a), Note dated 27 February 1956, SUMC Papers 2/16, Oxford: Bodleian Library.

SUMC (1956b), Minute dated 24 April 1956, SUMC Papers 2/16, Oxford: Bodleian Library.

SUMC (1957), Notes dated 1 March 1957 and 22 January 1958, SUMC Papers 1/54, Oxford: Bodleian Library.

SUMC (1958), Letter dated 11 November 1958, SUMC Papers 1/57, Oxford: Bodleian Library.

SUMC (1959), Note dated 11 September 1959, SUMC Papers 1/54, Oxford: Bodleian Library.

SUMC (1959b), 'The Scottish Nationalists', 27 July 1959, SUMC Papers 1/54, Oxford: Bodleian Library.

SUMC (1960), Notes dated 6 January 1960, SUMC Papers 1/54, Oxford: Bodleian Library.

Sutherland, Duke of (1926), Duke of Sutherland to Sir John Gilmour, 26 October 1926, Gilmour Papers GD383/23, Edinburgh: National Archives of Scotland.

SUWO (1928), *Questions of the Day in Scotland*, Edinburgh: Scottish Unionist Whips Office.

SUWO (1932), *Scottish Nationalism*, Edinburgh: Scottish Unionist Whip's Office.

SUWO (1935), *The National Government: What Has It Done? What Is It Doing?*, Edinburgh: Scottish Unionist Whip's Office.

SUWO (1945), *The Answer to the Scottish Nationalists*, Edinburgh: Scottish Unionist Whip's Office.

Thatcher, M. (1993), *The Downing Street Years*, London: HarperCollins.

Thomson, R. C. (2010), *Nationalism in Stateless Nations: Selves and Others in Scotland and Newfoundland*, Edinburgh: John Donald.

Thornton-Kemsley, C. (1949), Minute dated 29 March 1949, SUMC Papers 2/4, Oxford: Bodleian Library.

Tomlinson, J. and Gibbs, E. (2016), 'Planning the New Industrial Nation: Scotland 1931 to 1979', *Contemporary British History* 30:4, 584–606.

Torrance, D. (2006), *The Scottish Secretaries*, Edinburgh: Birlinn.

Torrance, D. (2008), *George Younger: A Life Well Lived*, Edinburgh: Birlinn.

Torrance, D. (2009), *'We in Scotland': Thatcherism in a Cold Climate*, Edinburgh: Birlinn.

Torrance, D. (ed.) (2011), *Great Scottish Speeches*, Edinburgh: Luath.

Torrance, D. (ed.) (2012), *Whatever Happened to Tory Scotland?*, Edinburgh: Edinburgh University Press.

Torrance, D. (2013), *The Battle for Britain: Scotland and the Independence Referendum*, London: Biteback.

Torrance, D. (2015), *Salmond: Against the Odds* (third edition), Edinburgh: Luath.

Trimble, D. (2001), *To Raise up a New Northern Ireland: Articles and Speeches 1998–2000*, Belfast: The Belfast Press.

Tyrell, A. (2010), 'The Earl of Eglinton, Scottish Conservatism, and the National Association for the Vindication of Scottish Rights', *The Historical Journal* 53:1, 87–107.

Ulster Vanguard (1972), *Community of the British Isles*, Belfast: Ulster Vanguard.

Urwin, D. W. (1966), 'Scottish Conservatism: A Party Organization in Transition', *Political Studies* 14:2, 145–62.

Visit of His Royal Highness the Prince of Wales K.G. K.P. to Northern Ireland, Wednesday to Friday 16–18 November 1932, Belfast: HMSO.

Walker, D. M. (1989), *St. Andrew's House: An Edinburgh Controversy 1912–1939*, Edinburgh: Historic Scotland.

Walker, G. (2004), *A History of the Ulster Unionist Party: Protest, Pragmatism and Pessimism*, Manchester: Manchester University Press.

Walker, G. (2010), 'Scotland, Northern Ireland, and Devolution, 1945–1979', *Journal of British Studies* 49, 117–42.

Walker, G. (2016), 'The Ulster Covenant and the Pulse of Protestant Ulster', *National Identities*, 18:3, 313–25.

Walker, P. (1991), *Staying Power: An Autobiography*, London: Bloomsbury.

Wallace, S. (2006), *John Stuart Blackie: Scottish Scholar and Patriot*, Edinburgh: Edinburgh University Press.

Ward, P. (2005), *Unionism in the United Kingdom, 1918–1974*, Basingstoke: Palgrave Macmillan.

Ward-Smith, G. (2001), 'Baldwin and Scotland: More than Englishness', *Contemporary British History* 15:1, 61–82.

Watson, G. (2013), '"Meticulously Crafted Ambiguities": The Confused Political Vision of Ulster Vanguard', *Irish Political Studies* 28:4, 536–62.

WDBE (1915), *St David's Day*, Cardiff: Welsh Outlook Press/Welsh Department Board of Education.

WDBE (1916), *Patriotism: Suggestions to Local Education Authorities & Teachers in Wales Regarding the Teaching of Patriotism*, London: HMSO/Welsh Department Board of Education.

WDC (1950), Undated paper from Western Divisional Council, SCUA Papers Acc 10424/7(viii), Edinburgh: NLS.

WDC (1959), Western Divisional Council annual report, SCUA Papers Acc 10424/27(ix), Edinburgh: NLS.

Webb, K. (1978), *The Growth of Nationalism in Scotland*, London: Pelican.

Westlake, M. (2001), *Kinnock: The Biography*, London: Little, Brown.

Whyte, A. G. (1926), *Stanley Baldwin*, London: Chapman & Hall.

Whyte, J. (1991), *Interpreting Northern Ireland*, Oxford: Clarendon.

Williams, C. (2006), 'The Dilemmas of Nation and Class in Wales, 1914–45', in Tanner, D. *et al.* (eds), *Debating Nationhood and Governance in Britain, 1885–1939*, Manchester: Manchester University Press, 146–68.

Williams, G. A. (1991), *When Was Wales?*, London: Penguin.

Williams, R. (1983), *Towards 2000*, London: Harmondsworth.

Williamson, P. (1999), *Stanley Baldwin: Conservative Leadership and National Values*, Cambridge: Cambridge University Press.

Wilson, G. (2009), *SNP: The Turbulent Years 1960–1990*, Stirling: Scots Independent.

Wilson, T. (ed.) (1955), *Ulster under Home Rule*, Oxford: Oxford University Press.

Wilson Foster, J. (ed.) (1995), *The Idea of Union*, Vancouver: Belcouver Press.

W. O. (1899), *The Third Estate of Scotland*, Edinburgh: Convention of Royal Burghs.

Wolfe, B. (1973), *Scotland Lives*, Edinburgh: Reprographia.

Woodburn, A. (1947), Cabinet paper entitled 'Scottish Demands for Home Rule or Devolution', 6 December 1947, HH36/92, Edinburgh: National Archives of Scotland.

Wright, F. (1973), 'Protestant Ideology and Politics in Ulster', *European Journal of Sociology* 14, 212–80.

Wyn Jones, R. and Scully, R. (2012), *Wales Says Yes: Devolution and the 2011 Welsh Referendum*, Cardiff: University of Wales.

Wyn Jones, R., Scully, R. and Trystan, D. (2002), 'Why Do the Conservatives Always Do (Even) Worse in Wales?', *British Elections & Parties Review* 12:1, 229–45.

Young, A. S. L. (1947), Letter dated 29 March 1947, SUMC Papers 1/51, Oxford: Bodleian Library.

Young, A. S. L. (1949), Letters dated 7 and 8 February 1949, SCUA Papers Acc.11368/80(iv), Edinburgh: NLS.

Young, D. (1947), *The International Importance of Scottish Nationalism*, Glasgow: Scottish Secretariat.

Younger, G. (1914), Letter to Bonar Law dated 15 May 1914, Bonar Law Papers BL/32/3/30, London: Parliamentary Archives.

YSS (1911), *Manifesto and Appeal to the Scottish People on Scottish Home Rule*, Glasgow: Young Scots Society.

YSS (1914), *The Bannockburn Sexcentenary and Home Rule for Scotland*, Glasgow: Young Scots Society.

INDEX

A Scotsman's Heritage, 41
Abercorn, Duke of, 189
Aberdeen, Earl of, 1
Adamson, William, 35
Airlie, Earl of, 57, 61–2
Airlie, Lady, 73
Alexander, Douglas, 144
Alexander, Wendy, 145
Anderson, Benedict, 16, 18, 20, 29, 41, 194, 217–18
Anderson, David, 83
Andrews, John Miller, 192, 197
Anglo-Irish Agreement, 197–8
The Answer to the Scottish Nationalists, 50
Armstrong, Alan, 8, 99
Arnott, Margaret, 86
Ascherson, Neal, 137, 194
Asquith, H. H., 114, 119, 172, 173, 188
Atholl, Duchess of, 43
Attlee, Clement, 66, 95, 126–7, 147, 162, 192, 225n
Aughey, Arthur, 187, 199

Baldwin, Oliver, 59
Baldwin, Stanley, 33–4, 37, 47, 59, 63, 205, 215
Balfour, A. J., 1, 2, 5, 28–9, 90, 203, 214
Balfour, Lord, 75, 76, 79, 90, 205
Balfour of Burleigh, Lord, 1
Bannerman, John, 110, 112, 114, 115, 223n
Barr, Glen, 194
Barr, Rev. James, 35, 108, 124
Beaverbrook, Lord, 39
Beckett, J. C., 188

Benn, Tony, 135
Better Together, 118, 146
Bevan, Nye, 178, 180
Biagini, E. F., 119
Biffen, John, 197
Billig, Michael, 15, 16, 21, 122, 168, 188, 213
Black, Mhairi, 215
Blackie, John Stuart, 102
Blair, Colonel P. J., 49–50, 53, 54–5, 56, 57, 60, 62
Blair, Tony, 117, 143–4, 181, 182, 185, 211, 218
Blake, Lord, 86
Blaxland, Sam, 175–6
Bleiman, David, 97, 124, 125, 134, 135
Blood & Belonging: Journeys into the New Nationalism, 164
Bogdanor, Vernon, 59, 70
Bonar Law, Andrew, 24, 26, 127
Bond, R., 14
Boothby, Sir Robert, 49, 57, 80
Bourke, R., 195
Bourne, Nick, 184
Boyd Orr, Sir John, 152
Bradbury, J., 10
Brand, Jack, 17, 41, 217
Braveheart, 90, 166
Breeze, R., 165
Brett, Charles, 190
Britain Strong and Free, 69
British and Irish Communist Organisation, 195
British–Irish Council, 199
Brogan, Colm, 56, 57, 216

Brooke, Sir Basil, 192–3
Brooke, Peter, 198
Brown, Alice, 217
Brown, D., 213
Brown, Ernest, 49
Brown, Gordon, 83, 134, 138, 143, 144, 145, 146, 206, 224n
Brown, James, 35–6
Brown Swan, Coree, 149
Browne, J. N., 68
Bruce, Malcolm, 116
Bruce, Robert the, 12, 19, 83, 102, 103, 121, 146, 166, 171, 209
Bruce-Gardyne, Jock, 86
Buchan, Janey, 141
Buchan, John, 32, 36–7, 40, 42, 45, 52, 87, 190, 222n
Buchan, Norman, 141
Buchanan, George, 123, 124
Buckland, Patrick, 190
Budge, I., 84
Bulpitt, Jim, 9–10, 11, 47, 99, 101, 122, 124, 133, 168, 169, 192, 204
Burke, Edmund, 80
Burns, Robert, 103, 121, 132, 146
Burns, Thomas, 126
Bute, Marquis of, 3, 27
Butler, Chris, 183
Butler, R. A. ('Rab'), 74–5, 175
Butt, Isaac, 226n

Cairncross, A. K., 81
Calhoun, C., 21
Callaghan, James, 136
Calman Commission, 92, 118, 145, 205
Cameron, David, 92, 93, 94, 145, 200, 205
Cameron, Ewen, 22, 32, 79, 94
Cameron, John, 65–6
Campbell, Alastair, 145
Campbell, Sir Menzies, 116–17, 118
Canavan, Dennis, 138, 140, 224n
Carlyle, Thomas, 103
Carnarvon, Lord, 86
Carson, Sir Edward, 191
Castle, Barbara, 134
Chamberlain, Joseph, 99, 223n
Charles, Prince, 177, 180
Chiao, W. H., 30
Choosing Scotland's Future: A National Conversation, 162
Christie, Campbell, 90
Christison, Philip, 80

Church of Scotland, 5, 17, 19, 30, 32, 41, 46, 47, 64, 79, 97, 211
Churchill, Winston, 49, 53, 55, 63, 66, 67, 68, 69, 71, 72, 73, 74, 77, 128, 133, 176, 205
Claim of Right for Scotland, 116, 142–3, 153, 210
Clark, G. B., 122
Clark-Hutchison, Sir George, 56–7
Clarke, Charles, 140
Clyde, James L., 53–4, 55, 56, 57, 76, 83, 222n
Clyde, Lord *see* James L. Clyde
Clydesmuir, Lord, 83
Cochrane, A. D., 32
Colley, Linda, 7
Common Wealth Party, 152
Community of the British Isles, 196
Connery, Sean, 225n
Convention of Royal Burghs of Scotland, 1, 64, 96, 98, 220n
Convery, Alan, 11, 184
Cook, Robin, 140, 224–5n
Cooper, Andrew, 211
Cooper, (Lord) Thomas, 36, 72, 128, 222n, 224n
Corbyn, Jeremy, 146
Council for Wales and Monmouthshire, 178, 179, 226n
Coupland, Sir Reginald, 3, 13, 98, 99, 104, 170, 176–7, 221n
Cowan, Sir Henry, 106–7
Cowan, Sir William, 25
Cragoe, M., 41, 42, 85–6
Craig, Bill, 223n
Craig, Sir James, 191, 192, 195, 198, 200
Craig, William, 194, 195–6, 197, 201
Craik, Sir Henry, 31
Cromwell, Oliver, 220n
Crossman, Richard, 133, 215
Crowther, Speaker, 28
Cunningham, Roseanna, 160
Cunningham Grahame, Robert, 33, 122
Cymru Fydd, 103, 169–70, 172

Dalgleish, Scott W., 98
Dalhousie, Earl of, 1, 4
Dalkeith, Earl of, 87
Dalyell, Tam, 116, 135–6
Dardanelli, P., 155
Darling, Alistair, 141, 146, 162
Darling, Sir William Y., 57, 62
Davidson, James, 112, 113

Davidson, Neil, 15, 20
Davidson, Ruth, 15, 92, 93, 95, 204
Davies, Alfred T., 174
Davies, Ron, 181–2, 206
Davies, S. O., 176
Day, G., 15
Day, Sir Robin, 136
de Vink, Peter, 222n
Declaration of Arbroath, 42, 116, 159, 210, 225n
Declaration of Perth, 113, 134
Deerin, Chris, 94
Delors, Jacques, 155
Democratic Unionist Party *see* DUP
Devine, Tom, 166
Devolution: The End of Britain?, 136
The Devolution of Power, 134
Dewar, Donald, 121–2, 132, 134, 139, 140, 142, 143, 144, 153, 209, 216
Dewar Gibb, Andrew, 36–7, 41, 42, 44, 51, 68, 150, 151, 153
Dicey, A. V., 29, 31, 100, 202
Disraeli, Benjamin, 43
Dominion of Ulster, 195
Donaldson, Arthur, 152, 159, 214
Don't Butcher Scotland's Future, 135
Douglas, Dick, 90
Douglas-Hamilton, James, 211
Douglas-Home, Sir Alec (Lord Home), 78, 83–4, 87, 88, 92–3, 222n
Drucker, Henry, 83
Dundas, Henry, 9
Dunnett, Alastair, 128
DUP, 197, 200
Dyer, Michael, 60

Eadie, Alex, 135
Eden, Anthony, 64, 69, 77, 80, 176
Edward VII, King, 159, 171
Edward VIII, King, 45
Edwards, Bishop, 225n
Edwards, J. Hugh, 172–3
Edwards, Huw T., 179
Edwards, Nicholas, 181
Eglinton, Earl of, 220n
Elder, Murray, 140
Elgin, Lord, 101
Elibank, Viscount, 60
Elizabeth II, Queen, 73, 159–61, 162
Elliot, Arthur, 100
Elliot, Walter, 28, 31, 34, 35, 41, 45, 46, 49, 52–3, 59, 64, 66, 67, 72, 78–9, 126, 203, 209, 211, 213

Ellis, Thomas Edward, 97, 170–1, 172, 203, 206, 213
England's Case Against Home Rule, 100
English, Richard, 198
Erskine-Hill, Alexander, 49
Evans, Gwynfor, 180, 181
Ewing, Harry, 134
Ewing, Winnie, 85, 154

Farquharson, Kenny, 22, 161
Faulkner, Brian, 197, 226n
Ferguson, William, 20, 224n
Finlay, Richard, 41, 124, 149, 150
Finnie, Ross, 118
Fitt, Gerry, 186
Fletcher of Saltoun, 166–7, 212
Ford, Sir Patrick, 39
Forsyth, Lord (Michael), 90–1, 95, 217, 218
Foulkes, George, 138, 142, 214
Fraser, Murdo, 92, 209
Fraser, Tom, 132
Frederick, Empress, 225n
Fry, Michael, 222n

Gaitskell, Hugh, 131, 132, 179
Galbraith, John Kenneth, 17
Galbraith, Russell, 224n
Galbraith, Sam, 141
Galbraith, Tom, 64, 82
Galloway, George, 137, 139, 140
Geekie, J., 122, 140, 141–2, 147, 218
Gellner, Ernest, 18
George V, King, 45, 159, 172, 210
George VI, King, 45, 73
George Boyce, D., 189
Gibbon, P., 187
Gibbs, Ewan, 12, 126
Gibson, Mel, 90, 166
Gilmour, Sir John, 32, 34, 35, 36, 44, 54, 205, 221n, 222n
Gladstone, W. E., 98, 99, 100, 101–2, 103, 114, 119, 169, 170, 171, 173, 175, 203, 205, 212, 222n, 223n
Glass, B. S., 12
Glen-Coats, Lady, 109, 111, 223n
Glen-Coats, Sir Thomas, 223n
Gloucester, Duke of, 45
Glyndŵr, Owain, 170–1, 173, 182, 209
Gomme-Duncan, Colonel, 53, 62, 63
Good Friday Agreement, 152, 199
Gower, Raymond, 177
Graham, James *see* Montrose, Duke of
Graham Kerr, Professor John, 41

Grant, Lady, 59
Gray, Alasdair, 165
Gray, Charles, 143
Greenwood, Arthur, 128
Griffiths, James, 178, 179, 180
Grigg, John, 172, 174, 176, 225n
Grimond, Jo, 110, 113, 223n
Gulland, J. W., 103

Hague, William, 185
Halifax, Lord, 43
Hanham, H. J., 12, 35, 100, 112, 221
Hardie, Keir, 122, 123, 135, 178, 181–2
Harris, Tom, 143
Harvie, Christopher, 28, 34
Hassan, Gerry, 144
Hearn, Jonathan, 14, 208
Heath, Edward, 85, 86, 87, 94, 95, 113, 134, 186, 188, 206
Hechter, Michael, 15, 16, 141–2
Henderson, Ailsa, 14
Hennessey, T., 200
Heseltine, Michael, 225n
Heslinga, M., 189
Hobsbawm, Eric, 16, 20, 209
Hogg, Norman, 139
Hogg, Quintin, 64
Hogge, James Myles, 104, 106, 107
Home, Lord see Sir Alec Douglas-Home
Home Robertson, John, 138
Hooson, Tom, 177
Horne, Sir Robert, 27, 31, 37, 39–40, 43, 50, 58
How Scotland Should Be Governed, 113
Howard, Michael, 225n
Howe, Geoffrey, 177, 225n
Hughes, Cledwyn, 180, 226n
Hughes, Mark, 186
Hunter-Weston, Sir Aylmer, 27–8
Hutchison, I. G. C., 55, 99, 109, 134, 142, 207, 223n
Hyslop, Fiona, 225n

Ichijo, A., 19, 20–1
Ignatieff, Michael, 17–18, 164, 221n

Jackson, Alvin, 30–1, 32, 65, 73
John, E. T., 171
Johns, Rob, 164, 210
Johnston, Douglas, 59
Johnston, Russell, 111–12, 114, 115
Johnston, Tom, 34, 49, 70, 75, 124, 126, 127–8, 129, 133, 214

Jones, Carwyn, 182, 183
Jones, T. Gwynn, 226n
Jones, Thomas, 173
Joseph, Sir Keith, 177

Kaufman, Gerald, 142
Kearton, A., 20, 33, 210
Keating, Michael, 15, 17, 97, 124, 125, 134, 135, 204, 210–11, 220n
Keitner, C. I., 208
Kellas, James, 3, 13, 14, 27, 32, 34, 83
Kennedy, Charles, 225n
Kennedy, James, 14–15, 103, 106
Kennedy, Ludovic, 112, 223n
Kidd, Colin, 7, 12, 16, 37, 148, 149, 162, 204, 221n
Kidd, James, 28
Kilbrandon Commission see Royal Commission on the Constitution
Kinnock, Neil, 140, 141, 181, 205–6
Kirkwood, David, 124, 126

Labour and the Nation, 125
Laird, Patrick, 221n
Lambie, David, 135
Lang, Ian, 89
Laski, Harold, 128
Leith, Murray, 21, 210
Let Scotland Prosper, 131
Levy, Roger, 14, 122, 140, 141–2, 147, 218
Lexden, Lord, 85
The Liberal Crusade: People Count – The Liberal Plan for Power, 111
Liberal Unionists, 6
Liddell, Helen, 136
Liinpää, Minna, 20
Lindsay, Kenneth, 195
Lloyd George, David, 99, 102, 104, 125, 172, 173–4, 176, 180, 189, 190, 192, 203, 225n
Lloyd George, Gwilym, 176–7, 184, 205
Lloyd George, Megan, 176, 180, 184, 205
Lothian, Marquis of, 1, 214
Lukacs, J., 15
Lynch, Peter, 155

McAskill, Kenny, 155, 162–3, 165, 224n
McAteer, Eddie, 194, 196
McCallum, Duncan, 49
McConnell, Jack, 140, 141, 142, 145
MacCormick, John, 13, 53, 59, 60, 61, 64, 68, 72, 73, 74, 109–10, 114, 128, 131, 151, 153, 159, 163, 223n

MacCormick, Neil, 13, 18, 159–60, 163, 165, 207
McCoy, William F., 192, 195, 201
McCreadie, Bob, 116
McCrone, David, 17, 19, 208, 217
Macdonald, C. M. M., 86, 221n
MacDonald, Ramsay, 102, 122, 123, 125, 222n
McDowall, Kevan, 38
MacEwen, Sir Alexander, 108, 150–1
McEwen, J. H. F., 66
McEwen, Nicola, 149
McFadyean, Andrew, 110
McGahey, Mick, 136
McGregor, Rev. Dr, 1
McIlvanney, William, 221n
McIntyre, Robert D., 50, 73, 152
Mackenzie, A. M., 40, 43, 45
Mackenzie, Sir Compton, 37, 39, 44, 80, 150
Mackie, Albert, 159
Mackie, George, 112, 223n
McKinnon Wood, Thomas, 106, 223n
Mackintosh, John P., 134–5
McLaren, Duncan, 4, 100
McLean, Bob, 121–2, 123, 128
McLean, Iain, 8, 82, 123, 133, 143, 191, 216, 224n
Maclean, John, 123
McLeish, Henry, 145
Macleod, Iain, 55, 207
McLetchie, David, 92
McMichael, John, 194
McMillan, A., 8, 82, 123, 133, 143, 191, 216
Macmillan, Harold, 51, 77, 80–1, 82, 83, 179, 205
Macmillan, Joyce, 221n
Macmillan, Lord, 41
McNair, B., 42
McNeil, Hector, 131, 211
McNeill, Ronald, 191
Macpherson, Niall, 60
Macquisten, Fred, 35
Macwhirter, Iain, 165
Madgwick, P., 10
Mair, John, 7
Major, John, 89, 90, 95, 117, 216, 226n
Malcolm Thomson, George, 37
Mansergh, Nichola, 190
Mansfield, Earl of, 60
Mar and Kellie, Earl of, 34
Marshall, David, 138
Martin, David, 142

Marx, Karl, 209
Mary, Queen, 45
Mary Queen of Scots, 46
Masterman, Neville, 170
Maxton, James, 124, 126, 224n
Maxwell-Fyfe, Sir David, 61, 68, 176
Mazzini, Giuseppe, 103
Meek, Brian, 88
Melding, David, 90, 183–4
Merthyr, Lord, 176
Michael, Alun, 182
Michie, Ray, 115
Middleton, Kate, 161
Miller, David, 23
Miller, David W., 187–8, 189, 196, 197
Miller, William L., 46, 67, 70, 75, 82, 217
Milligan, W. R., 76
Mitchell, James, 8, 14, 36, 46, 75, 78, 141, 156, 157, 160, 162, 163, 164, 165, 210, 221n
Montrose, Duke of, 27, 42–3, 44, 51, 54, 150, 151, 223n
Moore, Michael, 215
Moore, Sir Thomas, 39, 62, 130
Moran, Michael, 129
Morgan, Kenneth, 168, 171, 174, 178, 183, 225n
Morgan, Rhodri, 182, 183
Morrison, Herbert, 127, 129, 226n
Morton, Graeme, 11, 12, 18–19, 23
Moving to Federalism: A New Settlement for Scotland, 117
Muirhead, Roland, 123
Munro Ferguson, R. C., 108
Murphy, Jim, 215
Murray Macdonald, John, 28
My Scotland, Our Britain: A Future Worth Sharing, 146
Mycock, Andrew, 19

Nairn, Tom, 16, 19, 20, 91, 134, 137, 194–5, 204, 209, 221n
National Association for the Vindication of Scottish Rights (NAVSR), 3, 97, 100
National Party of Scotland, 42, 125, 150, 152, 159
NATO, 148, 153, 156–7, 158
Naughtie, James, 138–40
Neil, Alex, 134, 164, 224n
New Scotland, New Britain, 144
The New Unionism, 42
Newark, F. H., 192–3, 221
No Turning Back, 154–5

Noble, Michael, 80
Norton, Philip, 26

O'Leary, Brendan, 188, 210
O'Neill, Sir Hugh, 68
O'Neill, Terence, 191, 193–4, 195–6, 197, 199, 203, 214
Orange, William of, 209
Orange Order, 198, 199
Orwell, George, 15, 18, 215
Osborne, Cyril, 67
Our Three Nations, 152
Overton window, 4, 25, 88, 95, 145, 204, 214, 219
Özkırımlı, U., 188–9

Paisley, Rev. Ian, 196, 197, 198, 214
Parizeau, Jacques, 166
Parnell, Charles Stewart, 46, 101, 172, 177, 215, 223n
Paterson, Lindsay, 3–4, 11–12, 21, 169, 207, 217, 218
Paton, H. J., 71–2
Pentland, Gordon, 86, 87
Philip, A. B., 181
Phillips, Jim, 9, 82
Picton, General, 173
Pittock, Murray, 15, 20, 155, 157, 166
Plaid Cymru, 152, 179, 180, 181, 182, 186, 199, 217
Plan for Scotland, 126
Pocock, J. G. A., 168
Pollok, John, 134
Polwarth, Lord, 53, 57, 83
Porter, Norman, 198
Pourteous, James A. A., 42, 43, 51, 58–9, 68, 222n
Powell, Enoch, 175–6, 183, 197, 201, 214
Prescott, John, 141
Price, John Arthur, 175
Proposals for Scottish Democracy, 142
Prudhomme, Georges, 108
Pryde, G. S., 78
Purcell, Steven, 144

Queen's Rebels: Ulster Loyalism in Historical Perspective, 187–8

Rait, Sir Robert, 29–30, 31, 37, 50, 58, 202, 222n
Ramsden, John, 81
Ranger, T., 16, 209

Redmond, Robert, 186
Rees, Merlyn, 186, 195
Reid, J. M., 76, 87, 127
Reid, J. S. C., 60, 79
Reith, Lord, 128
Renan, Ernst, 29
Rennie, Willie, 118
Richards, Rod, 183
Richmond, Duke of, 4
Rifkind, Malcolm, 87, 88, 142, 154–5
The Right Road for Britain, 64
Roberts, Wyn, 181
Robertson, Angus, 160
Robertson, George, 117, 143, 157, 216
Robertson Sullivan, Denis, 116
Robinson, Peter, 198, 226n
Rokkan, S., 7
Rose, Richard, 8, 10, 194, 196
Rosebery, Lord, 19, 97–8, 99, 101, 102, 106, 170, 206, 212
Ross, Ernie, 137
Ross, Jim, 225n
Ross, Sir Ronald, 68
Ross, Willie, 132, 133, 134, 135, 144, 180, 205, 214, 215
Royal Commission on the Constitution, 114, 133–4, 180, 183, 206, 216
Royal Commission on Scottish Affairs, 110, 131, 205, 216
Rudolph, J., 148–9
Russell, Mike, 162, 163
Russell, Sir T. W., 225n

Salisbury, Lord, 4, 9, 90, 98, 205
Salmond, Alex, 19, 92, 93, 116–17, 118, 121, 139, 143, 144, 145, 148, 149, 152, 153, 154, 156–7, 158, 160–1, 162, 163–4, 165, 166–7, 209, 211, 212, 219, 224n, 225n
Saltire Society, 42
Sanderson, Lord, 92
Sarwar, Anas, 146
Schnapper, D., 208–9
Scotland and the United Kingdom, 58
Scotland in the Union: A Partnership for Good, 89–90
Scots National League, 149
Scott, Tavish, 118
Scott, Sir Walter, 33, 56, 66, 72, 121, 203, 209, 218
Scottish Conservative (and Unionist) Party, 15, 22, 26, 63, 84–95, 96, 98, 133, 143, 199, 209, 212

Scottish Constitutional Convention, 116, 119, 142, 210
'Scottish Control of Scottish Affairs', 21, 48, 64–5, 66, 69, 71, 72, 73, 76, 132, 175, 216, 222n
Scottish Convention, 51, 59, 62, 70, 129
Scottish Covenant Association, 51, 53, 73, 74, 130, 131, 132, 176
Scottish Empire, 151
Scottish Home Rule Association, 100, 102, 104, 107, 122, 123, 124–5, 149, 169–70
Scottish Labour Action, 140–1, 142, 145
Scottish Labour Party, 17, 115–16, 117, 118, 119, 121–47, 165, 182, 199, 205, 209, 211, 212, 215, 217, 225n
Scottish Liberal Association, 97, 99, 100, 103, 106–7
Scottish Liberal Democrats, 17, 116–18, 119, 121
Scottish Liberal Federation, 108, 205
Scottish Liberal Party, 96–116, 122, 226n
Scottish National Assembly, 60, 61, 64, 68, 109
Scottish National Development Council, 126
Scottish National Party see SNP
Scottish Self-Government, 113
Scottish (Self-Government) Party, 42, 108, 150
Scottish Unionist Association, 24, 26, 31, 34, 38, 49, 61, 64–5, 68, 80, 203, 205
Scottish Unionist Members Committee, 49, 51, 52, 53, 55, 56, 61, 62, 63, 68, 73, 74, 75, 79, 205
Scottish Unionist Party, 21, 24–47, 48–70, 71–85, 89, 94, 96, 97, 102, 105, 119, 122, 123, 130, 132, 138, 141, 146, 147, 149, 175, 184, 193, 206, 207, 211, 216, 217
Scottish Young Unionists, 55
SDP, 115–16, 224n
Seawright, David, 32, 84–5
Self-Government for Scotland, 42–3
Selkirk, Earl of, 53, 54, 222n
Seton-Watson, H., 8
Shedden, Sir Lewis, 32
Sheppard, Tommy, 165
Short, Ted, 224n
Signposts for Scotland, 132
Signposts to the New Wales, 179
Silk Commission, 205
Sillars, Jim, 90, 134, 135, 141, 142, 154

Sinclair, Sir Archibald, 114
Sinn Féin, 128, 197, 214
Smith, Adam, 145
Smith, Anthony D., 13, 18, 19, 69, 71, 187, 188, 200, 202, 203, 209, 210, 219
Smith, John, 137–8, 145
Smith, Dr Walter C., 2
Smith Commission, 119, 205
SNP, 13, 17, 21, 42, 44, 50, 85, 116, 127–8, 132, 133, 134, 137, 143, 145, 147, 148–67, 186, 199, 204, 212, 213, 214–15, 216, 217, 219, 221n, 224n, 225n
Social Democratic Party see SDP
Social Democratic and Labour Party (SDLP), 186
Somervell, D. C., 226n
Somerville, P., 60
Soule, Daniel, 21, 210
Speirs, Bill, 139
Sproat, Iain, 83
Stair Society, 42
Starforth, David, 112, 223n
Steel, David, 112, 115, 116, 117, 214
Steel, Judy, 118
Stewart, Donald, 157
Stone, Jamie, 118
Stone of Destiny, 12, 90–1, 110, 117, 209, 223n
Stormont (Parliament of Northern Ireland), 44, 52, 56, 65, 68, 82, 90, 188, 190, 192, 195, 197, 200, 214, 216
Stuart, James, 61, 66, 68, 72, 73, 76
Sturgeon, Nicola, 121, 145, 165–6, 213, 224n
Sutherland, Duke of, 221n
Swinney, John, 162

Tait, Thomas S., 45
Taylor, John, 196, 226n
Templeton, William Paterson, 45
Thatcher, Margaret, 10, 88, 89, 90, 94, 95, 138, 140, 181, 212, 222n, 225n
This Is the Road, 66
The Thistle and the Rose: Scotland's Problem To-day, 108
Thistle Group, 86–7
Thomas, George, 180, 226n
Thomas, Peter, 177
Thompson, A., 15
Thompson, R., 148–9
Thomson, Frederick, 28
Thomson, G. M., 127

Thomson, R. C., 14
Thorneycroft, Peter, 59
Thornton-Kemsley, Colin, 62–3
Thorpe, Jeremy, 113
Todd, Jennifer, 198–9
Tomlinson, J., 12, 126
Tory Reform Group, 89
Trevelyan, Sir George Otto, 103–4
Trimble, David, 152, 195, 198, 199, 227n
Tweedsmuir, Lady, 87
Tweedsmuir, Lord, 52

Ulster – A Nation, 195, 197
Ulster Covenant, 191
Ulster Defence Association, 194
The Ulster Scot, 191
Ulster's Stand for Union, 191
Ulster Unionist Convention, 187, 189
Ulster Unionists, 143, 152,
    186–201, 216, 226n
Ulster Workers Council, 186
The Union of 1707 and Its Results: A Plea for
    Scottish Home Rule, 102
United for Peace and Progress, 77
United Kingdom Independence Party
    (UKIP), 8
Urwin, D. W., 7, 84, 85

Vanguard, 196–7, 199
Victoria, Queen, 102, 225n

Waddell, Ronald, 116
Wales, Prince of, 161, 171–2, 177, 180, 184,
    189, 210
Wales: The Way Ahead, 226n
Walker, Graham, 187, 191
Walker, Peter, 10, 88, 181
Wallace, Jim, 117, 153
Wallace, Robert, 99–100
Wallace, Sir William, 12, 19, 28, 76, 78,
    102, 103, 121, 124, 146, 166, 171, 209
Ward, P., 9, 34, 119
Ward-Smith, G., 33
Watson, G., 195
Watt, Harry, 105
Webb, Keith, 17
Wellington, Duke of, 173

Welsh Conservatives, 217
Welsh Labour, 178, 179, 180, 181, 182,
    199, 205
Welsh Liberals, 97, 103, 170, 171, 181,
    217
The Welsh Outlook, 173
Westwood, Joseph, 129
Wheatley, John, 124
Whitman, Walt, 219
Whitty, Larry, 140
Whyte, Adam, 33
Wilde, Oscar, 219
William, Prince, 161
Williams, G. A., 173
Wilson, Andrew, 164
Wilson, Brian, 135, 140, 143, 146
Wilson, Gordon, 156, 159
Wilson, Harold, 132, 133, 147, 205, 206,
    224n
Wilson, Provost, 1
Wilson, Tom, 190
Wishart, Pete, 164
Wolfe, Billy, 152, 153, 159
Won't You Please Sit Down?, 194
Woodburn, Arthur, 57, 59, 67, 129–30, 131,
    133, 146, 217
Woodburn, J. B., 191
Woolton, Lord, 60, 176
Work for Wales, 177
Wright, Canon Kenyon, 116, 142
Wright, Esmond, 133
Wright, F., 198
Wyn Jones, Richard, 169, 179

Young, Alf, 148
Young, Sir Arthur, 50, 52, 62
Young, Douglas, 63, 151, 222n
Young Scots Society, 103–6, 107, 108, 124,
    140
Young Wales Society see Cymru Fydd
Younger, George (4th Viscount), 10, 86, 88,
    157
Younger, Sir George (1st Viscount), 24, 25,
    26, 204
Your Future: Can Ulster Survive Unfettered?,
    227n
Your Scotland, Your Voice, 157–8